W9-ART-875

August Benziger
International Portrait Painter

August Benziger, Self-Portrait, 1923

August Benziger
International Portrait Painter

by Marieli Benziger

Edited by Janet Reberdy

Sheed & Ward

Sheed & Ward™ is a service of The National Catholic Reporter Publishing Company.

_____

Library of Congress Cataloguing in Publication Data

Benziger, Marieli G.
    August Benziger : international portrait painter / by Marieli Benziger ; edited by Janet Reberdy.
       p.   cm.
    ISBN: 1-55612-614-X (acid free)
    1. Benziger, August, 1867-1955. 2. Portrait painters--Switzerland --Biography. I. Reberdy, Janet. II. Title.
ND1329.B463B46   1993
759.9494--dc20
[B]   93-19230
                                        CIP

_____

Published by: Sheed & Ward
                 115 E. Armour Blvd.
                 P.O. Box 419492
                 Kansas City, MO 64141-6492

To order, call: (800) 333-7373

Contents

Illustrations

CHAPTER 1

Introduction

The most tactful maneuvering was required on August Benziger's part to avoid becoming hopelessly involved with the bevy of schemers who hemmed him in from all sides. It was constantly necessary to keep before himself his purpose in coming to Austria. The very wealthy and betitled, the simple country girl, the very young and even the old used every ruse to capture the handsome and gifted student's affections. One and all, including scheming parents, tried to force his hand in marriage.

Vienna was filled to overflowing with noblemen. Bachelors and married men with roving eyes had come from Hungary, Bohemia, Transylvania and Yugoslavia, all in search of mistresses. These glamorous if dissolute gentlemen sported grand titles, paraded in stunning uniforms and lived successfully off the laurels won by their famous ancestors, yet there was one thing they shared in common: they might be land-rich but few of them had as much as a pfennig!

But Benziger, the Swiss artist-to-be, had money. His father gave him a handsome monthly allowance which enabled him, after certain deductions were made for the cost of his studies, to live regally. Having fun in Vienna was inexpensive, but what he valued most of all was the priceless gift of Austrian warmheartedness. The spirit of laughter, the innate courtesy of these people was different from anything he had ever experienced. August would not have missed a moment of this frivolity for anything in the world. He was intelligent enough to realize that being in Vienna was a wonderful experience in itself. Here was a moment in his life in which to meet people and see a nation different from anything else in Europe, but he certainly had no intention of becoming sidetracked by strangling or possessive affairs of the heart.

The Swiss Minister in Vienna was a strict adherent to protocol, yet even he had to admit that the more he saw of this stunning

1

young man, the better he liked him. It was all too well known that there were few of his countrymen with aristocratic backgrounds. Here was one who was both attractive and popular. His social success was *un fait accompli*.

Since August was by now the talk of Viennese society, it seemed fitting that he should be presented at court. Admission to the regal pomp and splendor of the Imperial Palace was reserved solely for a few carefully-scrutinized members of the nobility and the higher echelons of the diplomatic corps. The gala functions within the Hapsburg Court were witnessed only by chosen outsiders.

August was scarcely one to pursue the favors of any human being, let alone royalty; he was far too much of a democrat. Yet, after considerable hesitation, he yielded to the entreaties of the Swiss Attaché; by the time he gave his consent, however, the period for formal presentation at court had ended.

The Hapsburg Court observed the liturgical calendar of the Catholic Church as rigidly as nuns in their convents or monks in their abbeys. For the Court of that era, the pre-Christmas season of Advent was a period of self-denial, prayer and preparation during which no marriages, dances or formal court functions took place. These austerities lasted until Midnight Mass on Christmas Eve when the birth of the Savior was celebrated with solemn festivities.

The Court presentation at Schönbrunn had to be very informal. This situation delighted August, since it was the Swiss Minister in person who proffered the name of August Benziger. Emperor Franz Josef sat on a small raised dais. He wore his regal white uniform, and smiled cordially as August bowed, then turned to his consort seated on a throne beside him and spoke a few words to her. Empress Elisabeth, who was one of the most beautiful women in Europe, looked up and nodded; there was a faint, sad smile on her lips. A keen observer, August noticed that the Empress fixed her sad eyes on his, then once again he made his formal bow.

The Empress's personal magnetism was such that August was captivated by the expression of tragic beauty. He no longer saw her perfect complexion, her "burnished chestnut hair," nor the magnificent gown she was wearing. He was completely intrigued by the ethereal appeal of this queen—so poetic, so romantic of soul, so very lonely in spite of all her great wealth, and so vilified by her enemies because of her frequent and long absences from court.

As August moved away, he felt too stunned to collect his thoughts or even attempt to sketch as he often did when he was deeply moved. Then, suddenly, the familiar voice of the Swiss Minister broke into his musings: "Quickly! Follow me, Benziger! Her Imperial Highness, the Empress, would like to speak to you." As if in a dream, August followed him with unaccustomed meekness. Young Benziger was led past the Emperor who, by now, was mingling with the palace guests. Empress Elisabeth, seated in a gilt armchair, was talking to a few of her ladies-in-waiting. At a given signal these slipped away, leaving August standing alone before the woman with the enigmatic expression. Instead of a sense of reality, he felt as though this meeting was taking place in the world of fantasy. After it, he could remember few of the details. He recalled only the gentle voice and the precariously welling tears. She looked up and asked if he really remembered her dear cousin, Ludwig, King of Bavaria, reputed by some to have been mad, by many as having been murdered.

At this question, August took from his breast pocket the chain that held his precious blue-enameled watch. Elisabeth spontaneously held out her hand to examine it closely, and into it August placed the diamond-studded timepiece given him as a child by Ludwig II. Silently, the empress studied the ornate letter "L" outlined in diamonds and surmounted by a crown of sparkling stones. Her perplexed eyes looked beyond August, taking no notice of his presence. She seemed lost in a reverie of past events. Then, slowly, she spoke words so fantastic that later all August could recall was the implication of what they meant.

She, too, had loved Ludwig. Like the Benzigers, she felt her cousin to have been a great genius, one pathetically misunderstood—a man born before his time. Yes, Ludwig had been happy, so very happy in Brunnen at the Benzigers' estate. During those last five years of his life, he had often spoken to her of his joyful time spent at lovely Villa Gutenberg which had been built by August's father, Adelrich Benziger. August's visit with Elisabeth was brought to a sudden end by the reentry of the ladies-in-waiting. In later years, he was often to return to this moment-out-of-time.

Days and events closed over this experience. From the time he had arrived in Vienna, he had faithfully kept a diary of his appointments, the people whom he met, the daily events of interest which had taken place.

Long evening hours were spent in the Brahms home in the Karlsgasse as guest of the great musician. Utterly spellbound, he would listen as the master played his own wonderful melodies. Many noted orchestra conductors visited Brahms; one of his closest friends was Johann Strauss, the "Father of the Waltz."

Vienna was a town of melody. Night after night, August, who loved music passionately, could attend the Imperial Opera. On gala nights the Emperor attended in state, decked in magnificent regalia. What pageantry! What music! Represented were men of a dozen nations wearing richly-embroidered uniforms, displaying dazzling native finery. A brilliant spectacle never to be forgotten were the Poles, Czechs, Ruthenians, Slovens, Latvians, Magyars, Romanians and Slovaks—all subject to the Emperor of the vast Austro-Hungarian Empire.

There were days when August was in the company of distinguished lawyers, bankers, architects. The mayor of Vienna, one of his father's clients, took such a liking to the young Swiss that he invited him to have dinner in his home. The *Bürgermeister's* eldest daughter, pretty Mitzi, promptly fell in love with their handsome guest. Mitzi decided then and there that this was the man she was going to marry.

It was Shrovetide in Vienna and the winter's most talked of event was the impending *Faschingsball*, for at this eagerly anticipated occasion the mayor's daughter would select the most eligible bachelor in Vienna to open the Mardi Gras ball.

Every unmarried man in Austria hoped to be the lucky one. Noblemen, of course, were favorites. Nothing could have been more unexpected by August than the secret notice advising him to prepare himself at once; he was the chosen one, and the *Bürgermeister's* coach would call for him in time for him to arrive for the opening of the Ball. This important news had to be kept secret. Gold-braided footmen escorted him stealthily to the *Bürgermeister's* four-in-hand. The coachman bowed low, and cracked the whip as the handsome gold coach raced through the cobbled streets of Vienna. The young Swiss wore a domino mask over his eyes as a disguise, and arrived at the Ball feeling disconcertingly like Cinderella's Prince Charming. Royalty, aristocracy and the plain citizens of Vienna awaited his mysterious entrance. Everyone was puzzled about who this man might be. A dramatic burst of fanfare announced the opening march. Proud Mitzi appeared with her dashing escort; together they danced the first waltz. Spectators began speculating: who might this tall, blond guest-of-honor be? He waltzed and whirled with such flawless grace that he must be a Viennese; only an Austrian could dance with such ease!

When the masks were removed, the astonishment of the assembly was great, greater still the gossip. Why, a foreigner! A Swiss, of all people! Yet, in spite of their amazement, all acquiesced; he had received the coveted honor, he had been named officially Vienna's most eligible bachelor.

Who was this man whose life seemed to have been fashioned of the stuff of fairy tales? He was, in fact, a flesh-and-blood human being indeed who can be portrayed with all his faults upon him (and they were many), and still emerge as an extraordinary man, one strong and gentle, tumultuous and often even-handed, gifted and, in some respects, limited. As Boswell said of Samuel Johnson, the greatest honor one can pay such a man is to paint him "with all his warts upon him." Such a man will emerge as extraordinary still.

After his death, his eldest daughter, Marieli, wrote of him:

> Mother, so it seemed to us, had always been in love with those delft-blue eyes of father . . . she had learned gracefully to submit to his caprices, to his charms, to his unique manner of doing all things. Strangely enough, mother just never got angry.
>
> August had a way with women, all women. He had a special way with mother. That she never rebelled, left us wondering. Yet to her, the August who could bellow like a kettledrum, who smoked murderously strong cigars, was also tender, gentle August who cloaked a great loving heart with a brusque exterior.
>
> August started running things almost from the moment he was born. In Europe, every male became a boss at birth; that was his prerogative. August, the irresistible Swiss lad, was definitely spoiled and coddled. At times, the pampered little August could only be tamed into submission with threats. His soft-spoken mother and kindly nurse soon learned that he was afraid of very little, but he *was* afraid of the many names given him when he was christened. When the calls of "August" failed to bring a response, his nurse shouted, loud and long: "August—Karl—Jacob—Nikolaus!"

> Then the small boy obeyed instantly. He had a great fear
> that his patron saints might get into a huddle with his Guard-
> ian Angel.

Marieli wrote a substantial book about her father of which
this present volume is a rewritten version, but its contents affirm
with her that the things that happened to her father happened to
few other men. Further, to her, to her mother and sisters, to all his
doting entourage, he was always the artistic genius. He "never acquired nicknames, he was seldom called Benziger." The man about
whom this book is written was always August Benziger *der
Künstler,* August Benziger, the Artist. In "An Appreciation," pref-
aced to Marieli Benziger's book, J. Daniel Woodward wrote, on
August 30, 1958;

> No man was more admirably suited to be the painter prince,
> portraying the grand finale of European royalty. He did not,
> however, treat his epoch as the twilight of the gods, but as a
> preamble to a new life in America with settings designed by
> himself.

The life of August Benziger was lived in two worlds, those of Europe and America; he had two worlds to conquer. He needed all of
his Benziger force and fortitude; he needed, perhaps even more, his
intelligent, gentle, compassionate American wife. He, himself, was
keenly alive to this fact. Toward the end of her life, Gertrude
Benziger annotated a missive she received: "A beautiful letter to
be kept and highly treasured from my dear August written from the
Arlington Hotel, Washington, D.C., sent to me by my daughter
Hélène." (February 13, 1960).

> Well my dear Gertrude I have only one desire, that you may
> always be very happy. I know that I shall be happy as long
> as you are around me.

> I see all the little and big attentions you pay to me and my
> comfort. The little you ask for yourself or nothing. I must
> say I often feel cheap that I am not nicer to you. I make
> often unkind remarks, but you must never think that I would
> hurt your feelings, and when I do hurt them you must for-
> give me right away just as you do it now always.

> God bless you as you deserve it. You are the dearest crea-
> ture on earth and I am sure He [God] will always protect
> you. Remain as good as you are and be sure I am the proud-
> est man on earth, because I have a wife that is full of quali-

ties and exactly my ideal in character and in almost everything.

I can assure you that I have no greater desire than to make you happy, very happy, the happiest wife if it were possible.

With a heart full of love and best kisses.

Your ever devoted husband
August.

Besides being blessed with wealth, artistic talent, strength and an extraordinary wife, what else went into the making of August Benziger, the accomplished portrait painter?

CHAPTER 2

"zum Adler" ("from the Eagle") (1867)

All the Benzigers for a period of six centuries stemmed from the tiny mountain hamlet of Einsiedeln which nestled on an elevated plateau close to a great Benedictine abbey. Throughout the centuries, the history of the monks and that of the Benziger forebears was closely interwoven. The hamlet was damp, desolate and inhospitable as far as climate was concerned. Arthritis and rheumatic fever eventually claimed most of its mountaineers. Proximity to two lakes kept the heavy snows away most of the year but sunshine was a rarity, known only in summer.

In 1826, a solitary monk, seeking a lonely, secluded hermitage, had chosen Einsiedeln which was then nothing but a cluster of pine trees; here he had built himself a hut and a shrine. Meinrad, the monk, and a son of the House of Hohenzollern, was, in time to become known as St. Meinrad. His Madonna in her tiny chapel and her reputed healing miracles brought Swiss pilgrims in great numbers, and news of the cures and spiritual favors spread across Europe. Brother Meinrad was eventually murdered by thieves covetous of the precious jewels that adorned the Madonna and her Child, which had been the tokens of grateful people for answered prayers. Eventually, followers of this saintly anchorite erected the Benedictine abbey which still dominates the town. Within a magnificent basilica was encased the tiny wooden chapel, just as it had appeared when Meinrad constructed it.

Such was the simple beginning of Einsiedeln, later to become a notable center of learning and pilgrimage. Gradually the abbey acquired more and more land and its boundaries spread into Alsace, the Black Forest and the Tyrol. In 965, its abbot, Gregory III, was made a Prince of the Holy Roman Empire. By 1274, Rudolph of Hapsburg decreed that, from then on, the abbey and its territories were to form an independent principality, and that its Prince Abbot was to exercise spiritual and temporal jurisdiction over 96 churches and chapels. He thus became a sovereign ruler in his own name.

For years the names of Einsiedeln and Benziger became inextricably interwoven. Clergy and laity worked side by side, devoting their lives and their energy to "the propagation of the faith." As early as 1411, an Albert Benziger, in 1483 a George Benziger and in 1597 a Konrad Benziger won theological scholarships—the first two to the University of Heidelberg, and the third to Paris.

In earlier times, persecution had driven this family from the Canton of Appenzell, their place of origin. All of Switzerland had been Catholic, as was the rest of Europe. However, during the course of years, because of its renown as a republic, reformers flocked to it, and soon thereafter discord and strife divided villages and even homes. The Benzigers, known for their granite tenacity and hot tempers, were easily roused to indignation and prompt to use the sword in defense of good. In the end, however, refusing to accept the role of what they considered renegade, they chose to abandon a home and area which had been theirs for generations rather than live in perpetual conflict and upheaval.

Many in central Europe flocked to Einsiedeln on pilgrimage during this troubled time, among them the Benzigers. The first of the family to be recorded in the village was Heinrich the *Kessler*, Heinrich Benziger the Pot-maker. The date is uncertain but apparently he and his family liked the area so much that they chose it as their new home, and here they put down new roots. By the 29th of May in 1584, Henry Benziger the Weaver had secured permission from the Prince Abbot to live there and so had paid his burgher rights of 25 gulden. Four years later, Henry entered his name in Schwyz, the capital of the Canton Schwyz in which Einsiedeln was located, three different times as property owner, burgher and weaver.

Those who had moved their residence to a Catholic Canton fared better than those who had remained in Appenzell, which became embroiled in a bitter religious struggle. The state was divided into the *Innerrhoden,* who remained Catholic, and the *Ausserrhoden,* who became Protestant. Hans Benziger was murdered during the time of this fratricidal strife sometime during the year 1597. The two heads of state, the Abbot of the Monastery of St. Gall and the Governor of the Canton who represented the Protestant faction, united in an effort to put an end to this senseless burgher war.

Since the murder of Hans Benziger could not be laid to any one individual, the entire village of Goldach was penalized. On the day of his funeral, 300 citizens were forced to march in procession to the church and attend the services, carrying two-penny candles. Further, as it was customary during the offertory period of the Requiem Mass for worshippers to proceed two-by-two to the altar to present gifts, each of the 300 villagers was required to place a penny on the offertory plate as symbolic alms!

No sooner was the funeral over than these same villagers, by the Governor's decree, were ordered to raise funds for a permanent memorial. On Hans Benziger's grave they were to erect a five-foot cross; then, after the funeral expenses were met, were also to make a pilgrimage of reparation to Einsiedeln where money was to be left for the reading of six Masses.

In 1670, another Benziger had married a niece of the Prince Abbot. In time, he began what would eventually develop into a long-enduring family business, the establishment of inns. By the year 1700, many apprentices had earned sufficient money to rent a number of them from the abbey for the housing of pilgrims (the Benzigers acquired eight), and also shops for the purchase of religious goods and memorials of the pilgrimage to Einsiedeln. In 1716, Karl Benziger became the first villager to rent one of these religious goods shops held by the monks. In 1760, he turned over to his son, Karl the Younger, four more buildings which he had remodeled for the same use. Thus, more and more was the life of the monastery and that of the burgher Benzigers interwoven. The senior Karl Benziger, who had leased the original store, was a strapping, burly mountaineer who had begun to earn money by peddling religious articles, rosaries and statues from place to place as an itinerant salesman. His son joined him in this enterprise. On one occasion, he and Karl the Younger, with their wares strapped on their backs, tramped through France, Germany, Austria and Italy. Their venture was so successful that Karl's wife and the rest of the children ran several other stores in the village during the Karl's very frequent absences.

On one memorable occasion, the elder Karl and his son were nearing home after a long and arduous trip. They were unshaven, disheveled and exhausted after struggling for weeks to climb the mountain passes. On reaching the last lap of their journey, both men breathed a sigh of relief. Looking over the valley leading to Einsiedeln, the father turned to his son and, in the gruff-sounding dialect of Canton Schwyz, said: *"Wemmer' ae?,"* meaning, "Shall we?" Karl the Younger nodded and both men reached for their pockets. This question, accompanied by the swift gestures, had been observed by several pilgrims resting by the roadside who had often been warned of the dangers of robbers. They were sure that these rough-looking men were bandits preparing to seize their money. Immediately falling to their knees, they began to plead to be spared!

With hearty laughter, both men pulled their hands from their pockets, and held their rosaries high for the frightened pilgrims to see. This was "Rosary Hour," when every member of the family joined their absent ones in asking the Mother of God to protect them.

Innumerable Benzigers had worked as apprentices at the monastery presses. By 1781, Sales Benziger was given the impressive title of *Imprimeur de son Altesse le Prince Abbé* (Printer to His Highness the Prince Abbot) and entered on the monastery payroll as such. He was also sent to foreign lands as an emissary of the abbot and to bring back the latest techniques essential for up-to-date publishing. That is how Sales became the man to introduce copper engraving into Switzerland. Some of Einsiedeln's finest etchings were done by him.

Sales' oldest son followed in his father's footsteps. As an apprentice, he was sent to the Benedictines at St. Blasien in the Black Forest. There he became manager, and also developed a lifelong friendship with another apprentice, Bartholomaeus Herder, scion of a family of publishers eventually to become known as Herder and Herder. These two young men were so studious and earnest about their work that they spent their nights poring over ancient manuscripts, studying by candlelight. When the anti-clericals forced the Benedictines to close their monastery, young Herder went to Freiburg, in Germany, where he became the founder of the publishing firm of Herder and Cie.

But Sales, his son and all of Europe were now in the tide leading to the French Revolution and its terror. The fateful year of 1789 had arrived and all of France was in turmoil: Louis XVI and Marie Antoinette, together with their children, had fled to the Swiss frontier for safety, but had been seized, returned to Paris, swiftly sentenced as traitors by their fanatical judges, and then guillotined. In 1783, when the ghastly Terror began, over 1400 homeless and hunted French priests had fled to the Swiss monastery at Einsiedeln. The Benedictine monks were forced to beg for charity, otherwise they and their guests would have starved. Among the destitute refugees were bishops, simple parish priests and religious from countless Orders and congregations. By April 1789, word reached Einsiedeln that there was war. The leaders of the rabid mobs of revolutionaries, the *sans-culottes* (so-called because while the nobles wore knee-britches, they wore pantaloons), formed a new type of army, breaking with the old established traditions—fighting without arms, without money or even food. They sacked, pillaged, raped and murdered. Still many were convinced that these terrorists were merely opportunists out to plunder, to massacre and to destroy whatever they could lay their hands on, and that then they would leave. The Benedictines of Einsiedeln hesitated to abandon their ancient and beautiful abbey, but Joseph Adelrich Benziger knew better. As a Swiss Guard who had served at the court of the king, Louis XVI in France, he had seen the seething mob at work. He knew they would stop at nothing during this first surge of class resentment and in the grip of hunger and hatred.

The monks had had no fear of the French; they had always respected and admired their neighbors. Yet, when the former Swiss Guard painted them a graphic picture of the blood flowing in the streets of Paris, they fled at once, as they were urged to do, carrying with them Meinrad's Madonna from their shrine. On May 3, 1789, General de Schauenberg and his thundering rabble stormed Einsiedeln. Terror and bloodshed stalked the one priest and several lay brothers who had remained and were hidden by courageous villagers. The revolutionaries plundered the basilica; the great church doors and those of the abbey were hacked into kindling wood, the altars were desecrated, the sacristy robbed, the sacred vessels smashed. Some of the mob then climbed to the twin belfries and, in their wild frenzy, hurled the bells into the courtyard below. Priceless books were burned, mutilated or sold for a song. The famous printing presses were turned over the Helvetian Republic which the revolutionaries had founded.

The Benzigers had sent their women and children to the Tyrol in the care of some of the men in the family chosen for that mission. From their places of hiding, they learned that those who had ignored the warnings of rape and murder had been killed, attacked on the streets, in their homes, even in their churches. Sales Benziger, fearful of losing everything by remaining in exile, risked his life by daring to return to his native village. He alone knew the value of the abbey presses. Managing to trace their whereabouts, he rushed to Bern, conferred with the Helvetian officials there, and bought two of the presses for a fabulous price. These he installed in one of the stores run by his brother. Karl Benziger of the *zur Taube*, the Taube branch of the family, became the owner of the first publishing business run by the laity. Prayer books, leaflets, spiritual writings, all had been destroyed. The Benziger family was soon united in this new venture of replacing and disseminating the religious texts which had been lost.

The French finally left. The monks returned, but all was in ruins. Sales Benziger now offered to return the presses to the monks, but the brothers and priests were far too busy beginning life anew to attempt any but essential projects then. Further, they saw their primary work was that of caring for the villagers left to their ministrations.

Their feudal principalities, their farms and the power that accompanied ownership of land had all vanished, but what remained was the loyalty and respect of the inhabitants of Einsiedeln. During the period of exile, the villagers had hidden many precious books, church vestments, vessels and fine works of art in the forest and other inaccessible places—in haylofts, barns, stables. These they now returned to the monastery, and so assisted in the rebuilding of their abbey.

The spiritual ties that bound the abbey and Sales Benziger continued to grow. As he had been educated in accordance with the traditions of the Benedictines, he now bent his efforts toward maintaining their meticulous standards. He felt that his printing enterprise must have an outstanding *cachet* of its own since he and his colleagues were aspiring to achieve papal approbation as a publishing establishment. To show his support in this project, and to express his gratitude and that of the abbey for the Benziger's innumerable proofs of fidelity, the Prince Abbot declared them to be free forevermore from all financial obligations to the monastery.

Nikolaus Benziger, who was to become the grandfather of August, was a born leader endowed with outstanding managerial capabilities. He launched his program of expansion by increasing the size of his printing establishment. In 1844, he replaced the old hand presses, and two years later, introduced stereotyping; by 1856, steel and copper printing were utilized in his establishment. To facilitate production, electrotyping was given a trial and proved a successful innovation. Nikolaus laid a solid foundation for his work. Stability having been achieved, he extended his vision beyond the confines of Switzerland and even the borders of Europe as he set his sights on the New World, which loomed large with untapped possibilities.

Nikolaus married Aloysia Benziger, a cousin who was a member of the *zum Schlüssel* branch of the family. Her forebears had, early on, gone into the business of housing pilgrims and had amassed a considerable fortune. With some of her dowry, he bought the mansion where she would live out her life and bear ten children, among them Adelrich, the future father of August. Aloysia Benziger was more renowned for her beauty than for her generosity. She was, reputedly, condescending to the poor and haughty in manner. To her immediate family she was sometimes seen to be dictatorial and even stingy. Exceptionally well-dressed and queenly in bearing, she bitterly resented the fact that, on her husband's death, she was no longer to be mistress of the *zum Adler* household. She moved to a top-floor apartment of the mansion and became a figure of happily-exciting fearsomeness to the grandchildren of the family, if not always to her son, Adelrich, and his gentle wife, Marie.

At the height of his power, Nikolaus Benziger had felt that he needed a trustworthy representative for his sortie into the business affairs of the New World. For this task, he chose Adelrich and arranged for him to leave aboard a sailing vessel with an old family friend, the Reverend Martin Marty, one of the Einsiedeln Benedictines, who had been chosen to preach Christianity to the Indians in North America and to found a monastery, St. Meinrad's, in Indiana. Father Marty and Adelrich, who was barely 18 at the time, struck up a close friendship which lasted many years, but soon after their separation, Adelrich set to work and opened, in 1853, the first Benziger store which he located at 311 Broadway in New York. He then branched out rapidly and started others in Cincinnati, St. Louis and Chicago.

Adelrich, the young man who had been raised in the introverted village of Einsiedeln, loved America. He liked its way of doing business, the tempo of its people, their hospitality. In writing home, he called it: "A land of vision, with a people who have no past but have a tremendous future ahead of them. We Europeans can learn much from the Americans . . . ."

During his New York sojourn, Adelrich met a beautiful young woman of considerable wealth and admirable character. They fell in love and he had dreams of remaining in America to run the firm and of marrying her; but his father, who had become ill, had other plans and, when Adelrich did not return home at once, notified him that if he had not packed up his belongings and returned to Einsiedeln by a given date, he, Nikolaus, would sell the family business and close the firm of Benziger Brothers!

This emphatic ultimatum made Adelrich realize that he had no alternative. Aware that his father had chosen him to become his successor as manager of the firm, he bade farewell to New York after four years of great happiness. As he felt that it would be sheer folly to ask any American woman to abandon the vitality of the New World for the provincialism of his tiny Swiss village, he left without ever proposing to his friend. In time, she married the head of the Grace Steamship Line. Years later, both Mr. and Mrs. Grace were to become the most generous benefactors of one of Adelrich's sons, a missionary bishop in India.

Adelrich now assumed the leadership of his father's firm. For nine years he directed it through a process of stabilization expansion and technical development and then went to check on the progress of the American stores. In Washington, the Swiss Minister was delighted to welcome so distinguished a visitor. He proudly presented Adelrich to the President of the United States, at the White House. President Abraham Lincoln had been told that "Benziger is not only a colonel in the cavalry, but commander of a battalion." The President was so pleased with the interview that, on parting, he presented Adelrich with a richly-ornamented sabre.

That was Adelrich's last visit to his loved America. He returned to Switzerland to survey the progress of Benziger Brothers—to see out of what it had come and where it should go.

At the beginning, he had had only a few dozen workers, and the factories were mediocre, but he was a human dynamo, and he brought back to Europe from the New World some of the American speed and zest for living. His tempo was such that the villagers were totally bewildered. Einsiedeln and the countryside were transformed into beehives of activity. Work for all, the best of pay, and an opportunity to talk things over with the directors and owners were radically new concepts in labor-management relationships.

He not only began to implement these ideals, but founded banks and established hostels so that his workers might have a decent start in life.

Anxious to maintain contact with the American public and provide them with the best in Catholic literature, he had his famous *Die Alte und Neue Welt* (*The Old and the New World*—later, *Benziger's Magazine*) publish the finest pictures and textural material he could assemble. At its peak, there were 70,000 readers of this publication; in those days, that was a vast reading public for this sort of offering. By 1867 he became "Printer to the Holy Apostolic See" and later headed "The Pontifical Institute of Christian Art."

All things were accomplished on a grand scale. Benziger Brothers needed light, so Adelrich brought lighting to his factories, letting the entire town benefit thereby at no added expense. New chemical procedures were introduced to accelerate various printing processes. He saw that though photography was still in its infancy, he should send his managers to Paris, London and Munich to learn the newest methods, as he was convinced that photography would revolutionize and simplify printing.

Chromolithography was prohibitive in terms of time and money. Twenty-seven heavy stones and tedious processing were required before a single color picture could be produced. In Paris, at the outbreak of the Franco-Prussian War, Adelrich learned of the contemplated sale to Americans of four of the newest color presses, which would greatly simplify the procedure. Risking bankruptcy, he staked all he had in the world on the venture and ordered the four presses shipped to Einsiedeln. His master engraver was given an impressively high salary equivalent to thousands of dollars, a fabulous sum for the times, as Adelrich was determined that his apprentices should learn from the most skilled teachers available.

The beginnings had been modest. At first, a mere 35 bookbinders had been employed, most of them working in their homes. This handful of workers swelled to 2500 during his lifetime. Adelrich constructed two new factories on the outskirts of the village for bookbinding, which alone required the services of 400 skilled tradesmen. Meanwhile, over 200 artists were placed under contract. They submitted their sketches in penciled outlines, which were carefully studied by Adelrich, then returned with corrections. As he firmly believed that "the right kind of picture speaks in every language," he sent his salesmen to North America, Latin America, North Africa and every country of Europe.

Late into the night, Adelrich labored. He leaned over a special elevated desk, even when almost overcome with sleep, signing countless letters. Though he usually kept five or six secretaries busily at work, he sought to have his sons with him as much as possible since he felt that it was an education in itself for them to observe what was being accomplished in the worlds of printing and of religious art. The boys loved to sneak into his office to watch him sign letters with a flourish of his long quill. The secretaries subsequently made the necessary copies. After Adelrich had dried the ink with a pinch of fine sand, they would first sponge the letter with water, then transfer it onto thin rice paper. The damp replica was then clamped under a heavy iron paper press.

Many of these letters underscored his view that expressions of saccharine sentimentality were to be firmly avoided by his agents, who were in search of fine examples of religious art. He drummed into them the concept that the saints were not mediocrities, that they were men and women of flesh and blood who had lived and died heroically; hence it was vital to reproduce representations of them which were in keeping with their dignity. Further, he was acutely aware of strange Jansenistic theories in existence concerning the use of the Bible. He held a strong conviction that this book should be found in every home, those of the rich and poor alike, so he produced a wonderful array of illustrated Bibles in 12 different languages.

Adelrich's products were unexcelled. Factories continued to be built, but also new dormitories and youth hostels for his foreign apprentices. The nuns at the Marienheim were reimbursed for caring for the sick and ailing among his workers, and he also lent support to the hospital, provided a fund for the aged and established a savings bank. He was, by far, the most forceful and forward-looking man of his area and his day, a man of compassion with a vigorous sense of justice, for he was deeply convinced that the working man was entitled to the same privileges, opportunities, security and comfort as his employers. Knowing these facts makes it easier to understand why he was doggedly insistent that his son, August, whatever August's tastes in the matter, should be trained to take on the future management of the business when the time came to pass it on to a new generation.

Adelrich and Marie Benziger had five children during these years of Papa's intense dedication to his work. There were two boys, Albert and Adelrich (later to take the Carmelite name Aloysius), two girls, Marie and Anna, and then a third son, August. Adelrich or, to use his Carmelite name, Aloysius, became Bishop of Quilon in India, while his sister, Anna, also entered a Carmelite convent, she in Bruges, Belgium. Like Aloysius, she was given a religious name, that of Sr. Marguerite Marie du Sacré Coeur.

Into this group of strongly individualized characters August was born. He entered it dramatically in the midst of one of the most severe winter snowstorms ever to hit the Central Swiss Cantons. Adelrich, like many strong and energetic men, was thus deeply disturbed by the sight of physical suffering, and he was aware that his wife was in the grip of mounting pain. Was it a false alarm or a sign of the baby's imminent arrival? Should he summon the doctor and the midwife? With all the snow and ice, how could he get them to his home? He turned to his formidable mother, the domineering Aloysia who lived on the top floor of the *zum Adler* after her husband's death. The village folk called her *Frau Statthalter*, for the women of Switzerland carried the same titles as did their husbands. Nikolaus, being the most respected and competent man in Einsiedeln, had, early on, been given the title of Statthalter (governor), but it was his strong-minded widow who carried the title beyond his death. As she disliked very much taking second place in what had been her own household, she had convinced herself that Marie, Adelrich's wife, was unsuited to assume the household duties of a man who had become Governor of the State and also one of the heads of the Swiss army.

Late that snowy New Year's evening of 1867, Adelrich had taken his new American thermometer to the sickroom. His mother followed him and shook her head; she had no use for these new-fangled instruments nor for the calling in of a physician for every minor ailment. Clearly she was irritated by the attention her son paid his wife. What a strange combination, she felt: so brilliant a son, and a woman of such simple background—yet both so compatible, so understanding of each other's needs.

Frau Statthalter assured her son that he should wait until morning. Knowing his will of iron, she was doubly emphatic, and even indulged in minor histrionics, dabbing at her eyes with her fine lace handkerchief. Adelrich knew that his mother had suffered much, as her husband's death at the age of 56 had been a blow she had not yet quite been able to interiorize. Her loss of position in the home rankled within her as she looked at Marie, who was her complete opposite in character. Marie was happy to efface herself and let her husband dominate. She fitted happily into second place and was a thorough *hausfrau*. All of these facts upset his mother; he realized the fact and made due allowances for her but, finally, this night, he refused to listen to her. His thermometer showed that his wife's temperature was 104 degrees. She was a very ill woman and a strange sixth sense warned him that death might be just around the corner. Child mortality was rampant in this part of the world. In one family alone, had he not seen that out of thirteen children, only four survived?

Adelrich went to his study and rang for Mr. Zingg, his secretary, who was, understandably, dubious about the possibility of fetching Dr. Gyr and the *Hebamme*, midwife, at this time of the night and in such a blizzard. However, in time, it was decided that Fritz and Sep, the devoted coachmen, would make a heroic effort as the situation seemed critical. In the distance, the sounds of New Year's merry-making could be heard. In homes and inns, old and young hugged the great porcelain stoves. There was plenty of cheer as the men played *Jass,* warming themselves with hearty swigs of Kirschwasser, the famous *Chrisi* brandy for which Canton Schwyz was renowned. They were munching what was left of the brittle *Tierkli* and peeling precious tangerines that made a yearly appearance only for the festive Yule season.

Meanwhile, the sturdy Fritz and Sep moved outside looking like grotesque highwaymen, with their faintly glowing lanterns in their hands. Their great *Loden* capes slapped like sails in the icy wind and sleeting snow. With great difficulty, they located the tiny hut of the midwife, Frau Anklin, and finally roused her. The disgruntled woman had been up all of the preceding night delivering a baby and had gone to bed exhausted, longing for a full night's rest. However, when she heard who needed her, she hurriedly stuffed an apron into her nurse's kit and joined Fritz and Sep. The sleigh proceeded to the home of the village doctor. Dr. Gyr was the best that Canton Schwyz could produce, and that was better than average. He was an expert on herbs and well acquainted with French and German medical books. In Einsiedeln, where everything was judged according to the Benedictine standards, he was a prominent man as he was the abbey physician who cared for the 300 students, plus an equal number of monks. The village folk, on the other hand, could not afford the luxury of a doctor.

Jovial Dr. Gyr was amused at being called by Governor Benziger at this late hour. He readied himself and joined the half-frozen procession that braved the hissing wind and pelting snow. They struggled on through biting cold until the seven-storied *zum Adler* mansion came into sight. There candles and kerosene lamps lit up the building while the house bell clanged fitfully, and the head of the house rushed to the great oak door to welcome them. Seeing the expression of his friend, Dr. Gry realized at once the seriousness of the situation.

From the bannister on the next floor leaned *Frau Statthalter* Benziger. In her thick Swiss dialect, she proclaimed: "Doctor, I fear you and Mrs. Anklin have come on a wild-goose chase. The baby is not due for another month. My daughter-in-law is imagining things. She is merely suffering from a bad case of *grippe*. You had better examine my son. He has lost his head, for once, and is needlessly worried and nervous." Dr. Gyr knew the elderly lady very well and liked to joke with her, but he was convinced that, this time, she was wrong.

Coming into the hall a few minutes later, he nodded cheerfully. "No need to worry any longer. We are just in time. Mrs. Anklin is getting everything ready. She will call me when I'm needed. I hope it will be another girl."

"Oh, no!" remonstrated the head of the house. "There are quite enough girls in our family. I need more sons. . . . Girls have to be protected; they need huge dowries. Boys count. God grant me another son who can help me carry on the business."

He added: "I have only a mere handful of children. Look at my poorer relatives—they have 15 or 16. We are living in dangerous times. Children mean security in old age. Children mean family continuity."

No one knew better than Dr. Gyr. Was not the village cemetery filled with the graves of children? The percentage of those who reached maturity was appallingly small. Epidemics of smallpox, typhoid, diphtheria, scarlet fever and cholera wiped out entire villages. No one knew how to combat rheumatic fever. Louis, the Governor's youngest son, was a semi-invalid as a result of that incurable disease; the child hovered between life and death. Gyr regarded the bearing of many children as being synonymous with reaping a successful harvest. A family that had few offspring risked much for, when epidemics came, overnight they might be stricken and become childless. A childless old age, he felt, was perhaps the most tragic of all fates.

While he teased Adelrich, deep in his heart Dr. Gyr hoped that his friend would have another son. No one in all of Switzerland worked harder, and Adelrich needed a whole regiment of sons to keep up with him, to aid him in his later years, and to carry on the vast enterprise he had founded.

Upstairs, in the room with the wild-rose wallpaper, lay a tiny woman. Now and again, a pitiful moan came from the depths of the great down-covered bed. Frau Anklin had taken things in hand. Brusquely, she called the maids, requested jugs of hot water and clean wash basins. Next, she looked to make sure that the pile of swaddling bands and diapers was inside the porcelain stove. They would need to be very warm on such a chilly night.

Just as the New Year's Day of 1867 was making an exit, a struggling little rascal came into the world with a howl. Then, deathly silence settled over the great mansion as doctor and midwife fought to save the mother. Due to her sudden turn for the worse, the exact hour of the infant's birth was never recorded. Later on, no one remembered whether August's birthday should be celebrated on New Year's day or whether he was merely a second-of-January child.

Rosalie, the faithful nurse, as she abhorred modern inventions, distrusted the kerosene lamp in her mistress's bedroom. Just when the doctor and midwife were busiest, out of it shot tongues of flame in the direction of the ceiling and then a shower of fine black soot settled over everything. It covered the baby, the mother, the fine lace pillows, the embroidered linen sheets, the white eiderdown feather bedding but there seems to have been no spreading blaze. Rosalie seized two candles and held them, one in each hand, right under the doctor's nose. It was at that inauspicious moment that August chose to be born—a dramatic entrance if there ever was one!

Upstairs, the world of the newborn was ruled by Rosalie. First, there was the problem of bottle-feeding the infant, as no respectable Swiss mother would nurse her baby. A cat, a dog or a cow suckled its young, but not a lady! Also, it would have been every bit as much a disgrace for the Governor's wife to go to a hospital for delivery. Only the poorest of the poor crossed the threshold of such places. It was the work of Rosalie to straighten the tiny arms and legs and then hold them firmly in place with the swaddling bands. As a last precaution, a heating pad was placed at the foot of the beautiful carved-wood cradle. This heating pad had been specially made by Rosalie for each succeeding member of the family. She had saved cherry pits, and carefully dried and cleaned them. These were then inserted into a felt bag. Whenever needed, the bag and its contents were placed in a coal oven and left to get pleasantly warm. Cherry pits retained the heat much longer than metal containers and were safer for babies than the earthenward brandy jugs which often leaked, wetting both bed and child.

By dawn the happy mother was resting. As she heard the great abbey bells booming, she united herself in spirit with the early Mass being said at the altar of the Madonna. Had little August not been in so much of a hurry she, too, would have been kneeling there. Snow muffled the sounds of footsteps outside. A tangible peace settled over the Benzigers as the lady of the house rang her bell. All seemed to be back to normal, but on this second morning of January, when she had rung that bell to assemble the domestics, she had done so, not so that she could give orders, but for the purpose of asking them to join her in a rosary of thanksgiving.

In a few days, she would be back to her routine of daily living. By five in the morning, she was generally to be found in the basilica, attending the first Mass being offered by her cousin, Father Albert Kuhn, a historian who spent much time with her husband as an advisor on historical matters. After Mass, she would post the order of day in the kitchen, then personally distribute food and wines, the *Most* (cider) and cheese consumed by the household staff, as well as the supplies needed to prepare the family meals. Her home was run much like a hotel, with its secretaries and a dozen or so domestics. While her husband was unpredictable, he liked to eat at home as often as he could and, no matter how many unexpected guests arrived, they were always invited to partake of the family meal. While this arrangement meant precise judgment on the part of Mrs. Benziger, she seemed prepared for most emergencies, just as she had been prepared for the unexpected early arrival of her son.

Immediately after the birth, the proud Governor canceled all previous engagements and postponed writing important letters. His chief preoccupation became the preparations for the baptism of his infant son. In Catholic countries at this time, parents believed it imperative for the christening to take place at once. Newborn infants were carried to church within the first 24 hours lest death hover over the cradle.

From her sickbed, the lady of the house delegated the duty of airing the parlors to the maids. Shutters were thrown open for such a festive occasion; otherwise, the best salon was kept locked. In this room, the bamboo furniture beater was used on red plush chairs with their silken fringes and the musty-smelling silk pillows were shaken, while the nobly-embroidered red felt tablecloth was dusted off and shaken. Souvenirs collected over the half a century were carefully wiped clean, and each had to be returned to its exact original place. Then came the artificial flowers, the family daguerreotypes, ostrich eggs from a Sahara expedition, the handsomely-decorated sword given to Adelrich by Abraham Lincoln, the gold and bronze medals presented by various popes. The center of the table held a large, black marble bowl in which lay a stack of visiting cards which had been left by prominent callers who came to the house to pay respects to the head of the house of Benziger.

The village folk loved nothing better than a christening. No invitations were issued; everyone took it for granted that he or she was expected to participate. A christening was just as exciting as a wedding or funeral, as much fun as Shrovetide, the carnival or the country fair! Church solemnities served to break the humdrum monotony of living; they helped bind the villagers together.

On this occasion, Alderich had hired the banquet hall of the Pfauen Hotel. His own goldenrod Hostel, where he usually lodged his foreign apprentices, was put into order for the party. The Benziger printing factory, right behind the *zum Adler* mansion, was so conveniently located that it would serve as a place to entertain the overflow guests. Here, the 2000 workers who manned his factories, ran his printing presses and supervised the bookbinding, as well as the draymen who hauled the heavy loads, were all entitled to a holiday. They would help him celebrate this momentous event.

No sooner had the twin belfry bells sounded their call to vespers than the whole village closed shop. The butchers, bakers, drapers, the religious articles shops were all suddenly deserted. Owners and customers hurried up the icy slope leading to the basilica. These, in turn, were joined by the Benziger workers and farm hands struggling up the steep steps, flanked by statues of German emperors and embankments of freshly piled snow. The great front court was packed with humanity—men, women and children in their Sunday best.

This was a strange setting, and a dismal one with a backdrop of snow as far as the eye could reach. From a distance, the villagers looked more like ravens than celebrants. Most wore black. Even the children had long black stockings and ankle-length black dresses. Women wore their somber raiment trailing in the snow while the men were decked out in black hats, black suits, black ties, for black was the traditional Sunday-go-to-meeting attire; color was seldom used, even for Christmas or Easter, except by a few of the very old families who treasured beautiful native costumes which had been passed on through successive generations. They were exquisite, very valuable, but seldom worn except, perhaps, for an occasional High Mass at Easter. Then the lacy headdresses, the bodices adorned with heavy gold or silver chains, the costly green, red, blue or pink brocades and silks made their rare appearances.

Adelrich was seen as the central lay figure in Einsiedeln, as the uniter of branches of the family which had, on occasion, been at odds. Behind lace curtains of tightly-closed windows during the long winters, friction did arise from time to time, usually rooted in petty matters and personality incompatibilities, but all of these complexities, when pieced together, were seen as merely opportunities for relieving one's boredom. While petty jealousies sometimes offset religious convictions and many villagers were no longer on speaking terms, whether they were friendly or not, all the Benzigers came to August's christening. To be absent meant the beginning or continuation of a family feud, with endless repercussions. Therefore, a united village population filed into the little chapel of St. Meinrad's Madonna, enclosed as it was in the vast basilica. the procession proceeded toward the baptismal font and, under the smile of the image given to Meinrad by his aunt, the Abbess Hildegarde, the ceremony began. Felicitas Benziger, August's godmother, placed August on the Lady altar, then his other godparent, Carl Benziger, read aloud an act of consecration of the child to the Mother of God. When the baptism had been completed, the Guest Master of the abbey whispered to Adelrich that the Abbot would like to bless the baby. He led the immediate family past the wrought-iron grating and through the sanctuary ablaze with candles. A large oak door was thrown open and the small group entered into the Hall of Princes, lined as it was with life-sized portraits of emperors and their consorts, of kings, queens, princes who had come, as had they, to pray at the Einsiedeln shrine. The Prince Abbot smiled and remarked that he was happy to welcome another Benziger, tiny as he was, who had come to the monastery to pay his respects. He hoped that the link that bound the Benzigers and the Benedictines would be like a great chain, enduring through the centuries.

Thus did August Benziger begin his life rooted in the rugged and realistic soil of Einsiedeln, of Switzerland, in the psychological strength, determination and organized ambience of the Benziger clan, loyal as they were to their faith and their convictions and in the company of princes, men of power and just plain folks who would surround him all his life. August Benziger was to become a man with an eye capable of seeing the subtle differences in members of the human race on both sides of the Atlantic and in all classes of society, and a man capable of depicting them in such a way that he could, in large measure, bridge the gap between human life as lived during the *Ancien Régime* and the modern industrialized era. His vision materialized on canvas.

CHAPTER 3

Childhood Days in Einsiedeln
(1867-1870)

Very early in his life, August was initiated into the religious and historical background of his village. As his nurse, Rosalie, came from a family of Einsiedeln who for generations had worked in the Benziger home, she was as steeped in the local lore and traditions as were the other members of the household. She surrounded her charge with tales of St. Meinrad, told in such a manner as to eclipse any fairy tale, and the young boy entered into the scene with riveted attention. After all, the huge basilica which had grown from Meinrad's tiny hermitage stood just in front of his home so it was not difficult for him, with his sensitive mind and alert imagination, to picture each detail of Meinrad's life and death at the hands of bandits, the long lines of pious pilgrims coming to the shrine of the Madonna throughout the centuries and the tiny and immense events which engulfed the village in the long-line course of its history.

From the beginning, she told him, miracles had been performed at the Madonna's shrine and they were still taking place, as was evidenced by the crutches, canes, wooden legs and arms that were deposited as tokens of gratitude for limbs restored to health. The first great recorded miracle to be commemorated yearly, she affirmed, was that of the "Angel's Consecration," (*die Engelweihe*). Conrad, Bishop of Constance, had been invited by the first abbot of the monastery to consecrate the newly-built basilica. As the bishop was about to start the lengthy ceremony, a voice was heard: "Keep your hands off this church. This church has been consecrated by God himself." Three times this command was repeated. The date was September 14, 1498. For centuries, when the "Angel's Consecration" was celebrated, pilgrims would come from all parts of Europe to pray for aid. The consecration which had been planned to take place never happened.

It is understandable that young August spent a good bit of his early childhood with his nose glued to the front windows of the *zum Adler*. From his balcony seat, he could watch the activities in the cobblestone courtyard below where both sides were flanked by long arcades, each lined with tiny shops in which village women carried on a brisk trade selling rosaries, medals and candles. These were the very shops which had originally belonged to the monastery but which had eventually been rented out to laymen, as had also been the inns and hospitals because, with the growing numbers of pilgrims, the monks could no longer shoulder by themselves the heavy duties of hospitality and hospital care, of spiritual counseling and the provision of religious goods. The local butchers, bakers, grocers, apothecaries and innkeepers were all carefully chosen and trustworthy citizens who related affectionately to the monastery but who also paid yearly taxes into its coffers. Before long there was a total of 90 inns, many of them under the aegis of the Benzigers.

Rosalie loved to tell her little charge all about the pilgrims—how, until a few years before he was born, they had worn special garb. They had dressed, she said, in long black cloaks and carried pilgrim staves to which were attached gourds filled with wine, brandy or water. Across each man's back was strapped a sturdy leather knapsack and on his head was a broad-brimmed hat bearing its unique identification of a cockleshell, the distinguishing sign of the pious wayfarer on pilgrimage.

A special Pilgrim's Mass was celebrated at the beginning of each expedition, a ceremony during which the devotee's staff, knapsack and rosary were placed at the foot of the altar to be blessed. Each pilgrim then received a passport signed by the bishop or pastor—a *laissez-passer*—which provided immunity from road taxation and protection from brigands and guaranteed him shelter in monasteries or churches. If there was insufficient accommodation in inns and other dwellings, the church was kept open to house the wanderers for the night. There was also an underside to this practice: while fulfilling the beneficent role of hospitality provision, the church also unavoidably served on occasion as a haven for criminals, men who had the right to seek sanctuary from the civil authorities and then demand "justice."

August knew pilgrims as the intrepid travelers of his and previous times. They often came vast distances. The Italians usually struggled over the dangerous and daunting St. Gotthard Pass and, when they reached the Lake of the Four Cantons, they found awaiting them huge rowboats manned by 16 oarsmen. In this type of craft they were rowed across to Brunnen where they set out to struggle by foot over the Pass of the Katzenstrick or the insidious Mythen Mountains. The French, the Belgians, the Dutch and Alsatians came through Lucerne or the Lake of Zurich. In 1455, the abbey chronicler listed 130,000 faithful as having arrived within a period of two weeks. In the years 1867, 1868 and 1869, the early years of August's childhood, 200,000 came to revere God and pay homage to the Madonna of St. Meinrad. From the start of his life, the young boy was in contact with travelers from many lands and his mind was opened to a world beyond national boundaries.

On festival days, the crowds outgrew even the enormous capacity of the basilica, and a huge altar was erected in the village square. Plainsong was chanted in the open air, candles shone from every window, garlands were festooned from eaves and lampposts. After the liturgical celebration, the strains of violins and the rumbling tones of the massive organ rode to the heights of the mountains, so even the Alps were engulfed in the celebration.

Next door to August's home was located the postilion terminal where mail arrived when weather permitted. At the *Hotel Pfauen,* owned by cousins, the small boy could hear the exciting sound of the bugle blown loudly and pompously by the coachman to announce arrivals from and departures to many lowland villages and towns. Horse and coaches were the only mode of conveyance. The Benziger brothers operated their own draying service and used the finest horses in the canton to cart paper, ink and machinery from the Thalwil railway depot, 15 kilometers below, up the steep mountain trail to Einsiedeln, for no train reached the village.

August, in later years, had many recollections of his childhood, some of the most vivid of which were connected with his eccentric grandmother, Frau Nikolaus Benziger. Although this beautiful, elderly and strong-minded woman who lived in retirement on the top floor of *zum Adler* (and whose domineering presence had firmly complicated the lives of his mother and father on the night of his premature birth) was often a presence at the backs of the minds of the rest of the family, rarely did the youthful members of the household or of the neighborhood attempt to visit her. She had come to live the life of a recluse, lost in her memories and armored by her routine. Her clear disapproval of the "modern" mode of living, as evidenced by the behavior of the younger generation, drove people from her. Proud, vain and luxury-loving, she donned the finest of lace ruffles and crowned her massive coils of black hair with exquisite and regal tortoise-shell combs. The first sunny day of spring always meant that all her hermetically-sealed windows were to be thrown wide open and out would come the bedding to be sunned and aired. Even the poorest Swiss, noted for their austerity of living and their spirit of frugality, enjoyed the luxury of comfortable beds.

While few cared to venture to the domain on the top floor of the *Adler*, August was a decided exception. A person so stately and mysteriously refined as was his grandmother aroused his curiosity. He loved to pay her impromptu visits for, even as a child, he was one to see for himself about people and things, and only then to form his own judgment. Thus it was that he would climb the stairs to his grandmother's realm, although at the same time summoning the courage to go unannounced. Quaking with a little slightly delicious fear, he would present himself before the stiff, elderly woman. She had no alternative to inviting him in to be seated next to her while she continued with her occupation of the moment. Clearly, as August often came while his grandmother was at luncheon, his untimely arrival was seen by her as no less than a brazen breach of etiquette and treated accordingly. The small boy observed with an incipient artist's sharp attention and unsatisfied hunger each morsel she consumed, even though he was never invited to partake of any of the tempting dishes on the table. As he always held a tiny hope that one day she might change, he swallowed both his pride and indignation as he watched this remarkable old woman. With the aromas of tripe soup, snail stew and a tantalizing broiler in his nostrils, August would return to his nurse and observe sadly, "Rosalie, grandmother is stingy and selfish. She wouldn't let me have a single bite."

Grandmother Benziger was feared quite as much as she was revered; nevertheless, once a year, during the Shrovetide holidays, she invited all the children to a late afternoon feast—a pale echo of the celebrations being prepared for their elders who were dressing for the masked ball at which all of the adult Einsiedeln ate and danced and sang. On one particular Shrove Tuesday, August and his cousins were presented with a huge bowl of whipped cream, a rare delicacy reserved for festive occasions. The children's exuberant reaction to it was so enthusiastic that their grandmother, dismayed by such an outburst of noise, excused herself from the party and left Uncle Marty in charge. The middle-aged, portly old man with a jovial sense of humor offered a prize to the child who could win the whipped cream contest. The rules were given out. In a matter of seconds, masses of fluffy cream crammed the mouths of each participant. Whoever could say "Puff" most loudly under these challenging circumstances would be awarded the prize, so "Puff" was shouted and sputtered until the cloud-like substance spattered nearly every inch of the low ceilinged room. The place was a sight to behold! Grandmother Benziger, wondering why the group had suddenly grown so silent, reappeared unexpectedly to compliment Uncle Marty on his skill in handling the boisterous little crowd. Each young guest remained glued to the floor, transfixed with horror as her scathing glance encompassed the damage and each one of them, leaving no doubt as to her condemnation of all present villains and their part in this heinous crime. Words were unnecessary. A shudder of apprehension swept through the youthful assembly. Each child was seized with but a single thought: "Get out! Get out as fast as you can!" Chairs were overturned as the panic-stricken guests scrambled for the kitchen door and fled down the stairs to safety below.

Not only on Shrove Tuesday, but also on New Year's Day, it was the custom for all Benziger relatives to visit each other. Grandmother Benziger preferred to deal with all the younger ones as a group; consequently, they were assembled by their parents and left standing at her door. These small well-wishers, all dressed in their Sunday best, were filled with apprehension that they might not say or do the right thing. The whipped cream party had been such a fiasco that grandmother felt it due her dignity that the children be kept waiting. Outside, the snow was crisp, the sun shining; the youngsters longed to romp and play. Instead, they dutifully waited, first on one foot and then the other, until, finally, the front door was held ajar. At a signal, the younger generation charged forward, eager to accomplish its unpleasant duty as speedily as possible but, alas, the stampede was so swift and thunderous that the large cuckoo clock in the hall was knocked violently to the floor. It fell with a terrifying clash of pendulum and bell, accompanied by the shrill and perfectly timed cry of the cuckoo!

Silence. Frozen terror yet again, and then pandemonium in the form of immediate retreat by 20 pairs of feet. No one ever quite knew what had happened, who really was responsible for the fateful deed, but the small catastrophe served to abolish forever any necessity for the continuance of the dreaded ceremony of "visiting grandmother." Peace reigned among the small folk.

August was left to seek out other worlds to conquer. He was a light sleeper and awoke every morning at the sound of monastery chimes—and it was only 4:30 when the Matins and Lauds bells pealed their call for prayer to monks and lay villagers as well. He heard his mother rise, for she went daily to the 5:00 Mass said by her cousin, Father Albert Kuhn. August hurried to be on time, and to carry his mother's little folding stool, her coiled taper of wax and her missal.

At that early hour, the basilica was dimly lit. The lighting was so poor, consisting of only a few scattered candles, that it was necessary for each worshipper to provide his or her own yellow taper in order to see well enough to read. The congregation knelt on the cold marble pavement in the unheated church, and August and his mother, well-padded with layers of warm woolen underclothes, only just avoided being turned to ice. As he grew a little older, August was put to learning Latin, and eventually became an acolyte assisting the presiding priest at the 5:00 morning Mass. Clothed in cassock and white surplice, he became an integral part of the basilica, on call to serve the innumerable celebrants who met the needs of pilgrims and villagers alike. In the sacristy where he donned his liturgical accoutrement, he was surrounded by priceless chalices and vestments which had been gifts of emperors and popes. "In 1500," he was told, "the abbot had invited the gold embroiderers of Regensburg to visit the monastery for six months. During that busy period, they made new vestments and repaired the old ones." This ambience left an indelible impression on August.

But, though he was clothed in a long cassock and stiffly-starched surplice, young August was by no means as angelic as he appeared! Once the serving of Mass was over, he wandered freely about the church semi-incognito. Since most of the altar boys looked more or less alike to the preoccupied monks, he was pretty sure to escape observation by them.

A section of the basilica which aroused his inordinate interest was the wing set aside for confessions. Some 30 priests were in the confessionals all day long during the time of pilgrimages and were able to speak to the penitents in 12 languages. Mystified by two enormous doors bearing the sign, "Confessions for the Deaf," August was puzzled as to how a priest could communicate with a deaf and mute person. Consumed with curiosity, he tried his best to peek in, but failed to learn anything.

On one occasion, a huge Alsatian peasant woman, dressed in her native costume, entered the clearly-marked door. Here was August's long-awaited opportunity. Knowing that the woman could not hear him and probably would not suspect his presence, he dodged behind her voluminous skirts and slipped into the room with her. The door was closed. Unaware of her eavesdropper's presence, the penitent knelt to begin her confession. From nowhere, a heavy hand suddenly fell on August's shoulder. He would have shrieked in terror had he not been afraid of instant recognition, exposure and inevitable punishment. He did not wait to learn the solution to the enigma of the secret room, but wriggled from the strong grasp and fled out the door, losing himself in the throng of worshippers.

August also joined other acolytes in playing pranks in the village square. The area was dominated by a huge black marble fountain equipped with 14 jets of icy mountain water, and at its center stood a statue of a smiling Madonna. In the year 800, Brother Meinrad had discovered this spring where, since his time, pilgrims had come to bathe their weary feet, their sick bodies and aching minds. Many proclaimed that here they had been healed. Ever since, the efficacy of this water had brought throngs who either made the rounds and drank from each of the 14 spigots in turn, or else carried some away for distribution to others. It was the usual practice of pilgrims to place handkerchiefs as markers at the first spigot from which they had sipped so that they would know where they had begun their water cure. At each succeeding jet, they would meditate on the passion briefly and then move on to the next font until all 14 had been sampled in this manner.

August and his plotting friends played a waiting game. They remained in the background, all innocence and light, until the devout women were on the opposite side of the fountain, then they stealthily crept forward to move the handkerchiefs. Their ruse was so successful that their victims often made the rounds more than once and, weary from all this walking and water-drinking, the women wondered how others had borne this strenuous penance. The game continued until some compassionate and observant monk whistled a stern warning and sent the pranksters scurrying back to the sacristy.

August had a mother who was both impartial and understanding, although there was, perhaps, a special place in her heart for her youngest son, the mischief-maker, who adored her and dreaded her punishments far more than those administered by his father. Mrs. Benziger was a deeply-spiritual and determined little woman, simplicity personified. Her hair was parted in the middle and braided in neat coils at the back of her head. Only on Sundays and holidays did this fragile woman ever change from one of her simple black dresses, substituting her high-collared black silk one for these special occasions. The moment she returned from Mass, she donned her black brocade apron. At her side hung the large bunch of keys which denoted that she was mistress of an important household. Her cellars, larders, linen rooms and storerooms were always kept locked, and in the autumn were especially full as it was necessary to secure provisions in advance for the long, cold winters. Wine had to have time to settle in the great wooden casks, cheese to mellow, fruit to ripen. Excursions into the icy cellars two stories underground were great adventures for August. As a small child, he loved to accompany and help his mother, even though, at his age, he might have been more of a nuisance than an aid. Still, his mother never showed annoyance and, until he was old enough to attend school, he followed her like a shadow wherever she went.

Maria Benziger's life had not been an easy one. She had been a sweet, unsophisticated country girl when she married one of the most renowned men in Switzerland, yet her innate refinement, her deep humility and gentle adaptability made her both a wonderful wife and mother. She was also an exceptional hostess. The *Adler* mansion was more like a huge hotel than a home. Guests arrived at all hours needing to be welcomed and, often, fed. Her husband, Adelrich Benziger, was host to statesmen, clergy and simple workers as well. "Governor" Benziger, as he was called, for he really was *Landammann* of the state, had an international reputation. His visitors came from many lands. Be that as it may, he was as thorough in his planning for his family as he was in all other areas of his life.

Already, when August was only four, his father had insisted that the boy take drawing lessons. The child was passionately fond of horses so as soon as he could hold a pencil properly, he began to sketch his equine friends with unqualified enthusiasm. His father, recognizing that there was, at least, a certain skill displayed in the drawings, soon made arrangements for his son to go regularly to the factory, located just behind the family house. There Professor Stucki, a well-established pen-and-ink artist of that time and place, supervised the printing and etching—and August's early efforts. Hour after hour, before he could either read or write, the boy had learned to draw in a professional way, had made models for woodcuts and even experimented with engravings of a simple kind.

One evening, shortly after his fifth birthday, he was missed. He had not appeared for luncheon nor for supper. Leni, the cook, had planned a nice egg soufflé to please the Governor, but the eggs, like the boy, had disappeared! Leni was certain that August had eaten them for, while other children sought treats like cakes and cookies, August craved eggs—and they were both expensive and rare in the wintertime. Leni was forced, at last, to look for Mrs. Benziger in order to request more eggs from the larder. Until that moment, no one had really worried about the missing child. He often paid visits to the farm or went sleighing with his favorite cousins. By nightfall, he was usually safely home. Finally, Governor Benziger was notified, and his son, Adelrich, three years older than August, decided to look in the attic because, he said to his father, "The last time I saw him was this morning. He was heading for the attic with an easel in his hand and some paint brushes. . . ."

The trail was quickly followed by the searching party. When the attic door was opened, there lay August, curled up, fast asleep. Near him stood the easel. A flickering candle, held closer, revealed several egg shells thrown about. Leni was beside herself with brimming indignation; the evidence of guilt seemed only too obvious.

Governor Benziger, not wishing to be rash in his judgment, took the candle and peered carefully about the room. He suddenly stopped short, catching his breath. On the easel lay a simple, naive picture of the Christ Child his son had painted. He shook the boy gently, rousing him from sleep. Suddenly alert, August's first thought was for the safety of his work. "Oh, don't touch my Christ Child. The painting's not dry. I wanted to surprise you . . . only there was no way of getting varnish. Professor Stucki told me that egg white could be used . . ."; then, noticing Leni's fury, he added cheerfully: "Don't worry, Leni. I saved the egg yolks for you!"

Adelrich Benziger walked away pensively. His prayer had been for an artist son. He knew that in order to really succeed, his firm needed an artist of the first rank, possessed of skill and imagination, to serve as art critic for the establishment. August had proved that he had talent. His Christ Child, seated on a rock, was filled with dignity. The face had expression, the colors were vivid and well chosen and the baskets of wheat and bright flowers lying at the feet of the Christ Child were clear and realistic.

After the picture episode, Governor Benziger decided that it was high time for his son to go to school. Although August could look angelic, all the while he was thinking up a new plan involving him in mischief. The Benzigers as a whole were a quiet, dignified, restrained lot, but this boy could even outsmart his older brothers in seeking adventure. Lately, the prankster had finally found a companion with leanings like his own, his cousin Franz, who was just his own age. The two of them were headed for stormy times.

August, who had the accurate eye of an incipient artist, had perfect aim with spitballs; leaning out of his window, he rarely missed a target, especially if it were a bald head. One of his father's advisors, a holy old priest known as Father Peter, often walked in the garden below, studying or reading his breviary. When he least expected, he would be stung sharply on the top of his pate by something that was neither a fly nor a bee. If one of the monks, engrossed in saying his beads, happened to have no enticing bald spot to serve as bull's eye, August would aim for the center of his page. Strangely enough, no one ever suspected that these disturbances emanated from the window of the cherubic-looking youngest son in the Benziger mansion. Success in these initial sorties urged him on to what seemed greener pastures.

For his new adventure, August called upon the assistance of Franz whose father owned a large bakery. Aided by a few coins which Mrs. Benziger had slipped into August's pocket as a token of her affection, the two boys could afford to buy such extravagances as *Schafböckli*, the wonderful cookies shaped like plump, wooly sheep. Unfortunately, the bakery also carried a goodly provision of brandy and other spirits. On this occasion, August sent Franz, as the owner's son, to bribe the salesgirls to sell them a bottle of cherry brandy. At the age of six, they marched off proudly with their contraband. People, they speculated, drank brandy, so it was apparently harmless; they would try its effects on the barnyard animals. They walked the three miles to the farm *zum Gross,* where August's father kept his stallions as well as the poultry for household use. First, the boys tied 30 pieces of bread to long strands of twine and dipped them into the brandy. Finally, they tossed the morsels into the pond. The effect of the alcohol on the waterfowl was both startling and instantaneous. The quacking, flapping, whirling in the air of 30 ducks and geese, all bound to each other, was an incredible sight to behold! The frantic farmhands rushed out, believing the devil in person to have bewitched the miserable feathered creatures. Hidden behind the hazelnut bushes, the small villains crept away, triumphant in the knowledge that, during the excitement, no one had discovered that they were the perpetrators of the mayhem.

Another of the boys' experiments involved *Kümmel*, a strong, white caraway *liqueur* which Franz again bought at his father's bakery. There was one worker in whom the two were especially interested, a German apprentice who had taken quite a fancy to these young villagers. This Ziegler was often so homesick for his fatherland that he occasionally got drunk. The boys were worried on his behalf for wasn't drinking "a sin of gluttony"? Ziegler would have to be reformed, and the sooner the better, or else he would surely lose his job and be shipped back to Germany in disgrace.

One noon hour, they passed the sweet, colorless drink to him. After each of the boys had first taken a sip, they asked Ziegler to sample it, too. Their German friend took first one swallow, then a second. In no time at all, he had emptied the extra-sized bottle to its last drop. The *Kümmel* soon took its toll, and Ziegler began to sway dangerously. His youthful benefactors steered him safely to the front door of the *Marienheim*, a conservative old ladies' home run by kindly nuns. As their friend slumped on the threshold, the boys rang the bell. Anxious of mien, they gravely informed the portress that this sick man needed urgent help. Naturally, the Superior, knowing the boys to be related to Adelrich Benziger, was solicitude itself. She sent a messenger to the monastery, and a priest hurried over to administer the last rites. The unconscious Ziegler was gently nursed and given every possible attention during the following 24 hours. Such a crowd had never prayed over him before!

When he recovered, after the proper lapse of time, he found the boys and vowed he would never again touch drink. He had been terrified by the excessive attention on the part of the nuns who insisted that he was dying. Once again Einsiedeln had failed to learn that it was Franz and August who had succeeded in their scheme, and had "made a man" of their *protégé*.

Now there was a different sort of escapade brewing in August's brain. It ripened slowly. He very much loved being invited to join his father on the long train rides down to the Lake of Zürich. At Thalwil, the Governor would catch a train, and then extend his journey to Zürich, Paris or London. Once, however, there was business to be attended to in Rapperswil, the old fortress city built on the Lake of Zürich some 15 kilometers away. August's father had not invited him to come along and, of his own accord, the boy would not have dared to voice his request a second time. The first hint having failed, and repetition being out of the question, he decided to try an experiment. Since the road was covered with ice, he put on his skates. Although only six years of age, he was perfectly at home on slippery, icy surfaces. He waited until his father had pulled his fur cap snugly over his ears and had been well tucked in with the warm bear rug. August then caught the strap at the back of the sleigh. The trip was long, fast, dangerous as the horses raced along the edge of a frozen torrent, down the valley, through dense forests. Not another human being was to be seen on this treacherous, bitterly cold day.

The coachman finally halted as they reached the toll bridge leading to Rapperswil. The guards on duty called his attention to the back of the sleigh. Sep, the coachman, got out . . . then gasped, as he found a tired, red-faced little lad still clinging determinedly to his strap. He gathered up the small, nearly-congealed heap of humanity and dropped him into his father's lap.

Governor Benziger roundly reprimanded August for so foolhardy an experiment. He might have tripped and fallen, injuring himself, nor would a soul have suspected his presence or been able to come to his aid. The wolves, numerous that winter, most certainly would have devoured him without leaving a trace behind.

August remained quiet for a time after his latest adventure and focused on his love of horses which seemed, at times, to exceed his love for humans. Every spare moment he could muster was spent in the stables where he was surrounded by excellent stock. Back in the year 1575, some of the monastery's most spirited steeds had been sold to the Counts of Mantua, the Counts of Gonzalez of Florence and to other Italian and French noblemen. August divided his time between the monks' horses, kept just a stone's throw from his home, and those on his father's farm three miles away.

Adelrich Benziger owned the second-finest stables in Switzerland. With him, to do so was a matter of necessity rather than of luxury. An outstanding equestrian, he commanded a cavalry regiment in his Canton. Furthermore, his horses were an indispensable part of his business as his factories were situated at the top of a remote mountain plateau; isolated as he was, his horses constituted his lifeline, his means of communication. On one occasion August was invited to join his father in visiting an aunt in the village of Unter-Ageri. Aunt Ursula also kept an excellent stable. While his father chatted with the family, August went to the box stalls to pay his respects to his favorite steeds. There he found "Negro," a wild stallion feared by everyone. Efforts to sell him had proven vain, for no one would risk buying such an ugly-dispositioned animal, yet the boy felt a particular sympathy for the outcast. With the aid of kind words and strategic lumps of sugar, he was able to loosen the halter of the nervous beast, throw open the stall door, leap into the feed rack in order to mount, and ride off clutching the stallion's mane. In a cloud of dust, the two thundered down the road. Villagers and coachmen alike were convinced that this dare-devil adventure spelled certain death for the child, for this horse was a vicious killer. He had been known to trample to death dogs that stood in his path. No one had ever mounted him before nor succeeded in breaking him. Fear ran high. Half an hour later, when the frantic searchers returned unsuccessful, August was seen riding calmly through the center of the village. The boy handled the unruly beast like a professional, still proudly holding on to the animal's mane.

With a switch, he called a halt as he returned to Aunt Ursula's stable. "Negro" came to a stop. Not a word of reproach was said about the incident; the drive home was achieved in silence. Then, as they reached the front door, the Governor said quietly: "August, you were most disobedient to ride a horse that could have killed you. Ask your mother to give you a sound spanking."

The culprit dreaded no punishment quite as much as a whipping at the hands of his mother. That wise and gentle lady understood child psychology. Her son's misdemeanor having been reported to her, she nodded her head but said nothing. August used to hope, on such occasions, that perhaps she had not heard him, that possibly she had even forgotten! Unfortunately for youthful daydreaming, she always did remember, even though the chastisement often was not meted out until two or three weeks later. She had the most disconcerting way of summoning him for this painful duty when least expected. Words were not needed. She merely pointed to a switch over the bedroom mirror. August climbed on a chair and slowly brought it down. Down, too, came his pants. Down on his backside came the switch with the deferred spanking. Somehow, punishments administered weeks later always hurt much, much more than promptly dispatched ones.

About this time, it became known that Governor Benziger was about to publish a collection of biographies of the saints. For this purpose, he needed accurate reference material about the life and times of each one, so he invited a well-known historian from Germany to take up residence at the *Adler* for two years. Whenever possible, the two men checked every detail pertaining to this publication, but every evening Father Wirt took his daily "constitutional" alone. Since he invariably set forth in the direction of the nearby village, August's curiosity was aroused. The boy had an instinctive feeling that the scholarly cleric might not be as innocent as he appeared to be; because the priest could not resist the enticement of a small inn on the outskirts of the neighboring village, surely some motive other than benefit to his health lay behind these evening walks.

In all probability he returned, comforted by a few glasses of good beer, too tired and happy to say night prayers, but August could not let his suspicions go and, more than once, hotly debated this point with Rosalie who was less than receptive to his ideas. Now, more than ever, he was determined to prove his point. He removed from his father's office a large bottle of purple indelible ink. One evening, while Father Wirt was taking his usual after-dinner exercise, August crept into the priest's bedroom and replaced the contents of the holy water font with ink. This trap should prove clearly whether Father Wirt did, or did not, use holy water, whether he said his evening prayers or omitted them!

Late that evening, on his return from his perambulations, the priest not only devoutly blessed himself, but also, as was his habit, blessed everything else that surrounded him. The floor, the rug, the walls, the bed, even the ceiling bore testimony to Father Wirt's energetic dealings with the shadows of night. The damage was irreparable. Every item in the room had been sprinkled with indelible ink. In spite of Rosalie's hard work to efface the marks, they remained as proof of a small boy's disbelief—and of a good priest's integrity.

The sacristan described Father Wirt's strange appearance the next morning. The chapel had been dark when he arrived to say Mass. As he turned to face the congregation at the words, *Dominus vobiscum,* his streaked face brought peals of laughter, and some discomfort to August. The sacristan, mirror in hand, demonstrated to the unsuspecting *padre* that something was radically wrong.

The would-be detective tried his best to avoid any future meetings with Father Wirt but, weeks later, when they collided unexpectedly in the corridor, the priest cornered the culprit. "Wait till I get my hands on you," he said, but he never did capture him, for August was too agile. As the boy later admitted, Father Wirt was a wonderful sport for he did not make any trouble for the lad by reporting him to the Governor as he easily could have done.

This incident was soon forgotten; it faded before the enormity of another near catastrophe, this time a potentially major one.

To the villagers of Einsiedeln, Meinrad's Madonna was a source of faith and protection, now as well as in earlier centuries. What happened on the night of November 13, 1879, appeared to them once again to be proof that she was guardian of their world. She saved the entire village from being consumed by flames.

Marie, August's oldest sister, was 22. She had gone to Montreux for a few weeks' holiday, and to visit her sister, Anna, who had been sent to school in Fribourg to learn French. Her father, his heart filled with worry and deep gratitude, wrote to Marie on the 18th of November, giving her firsthand news of the events that had transpired. He wrote:

> At three in the morning of November thirteenth, your dear mother awakened me. For a few terrifying moments, we believed that the upper floors of our dear *Adler* home were on fire. Across the square, mirrored in the monastery and basilica walls, were the hungry, fire-red tongues of flame. Was our home burning?

> Fortunately, the leaping fiery shadows proved to be just a reflection of the actual holocaust. Thousands of live sparks fell into the garden, in the churchyard and on the convent

roof. What had alerted us had been the stampede from the top floors of the maids and your brothers, August and Albert, breathlessly seeking refuge in our bedroom. This was the first we knew that our warehouse, the *St. Anton* just behind us, was totally enveloped in flames.

To make matters worse, a frightful blizzard was raging. An exceptionally powerful *Föhn* wind blew burning brands on to our roof and into the house. The fire was completely out of hand. Before anyone could get near enough with water to attempt to extinguish it, the roof of the *St. Anton* was a blazing inferno. Due to the strong winds borne by the blizzard, the smoldering flames had not been noticed.

There were countless delays in fighting the conflagration. Two of the fire hoses froze, then burst. In the end, after an interminable wait, there proved to be no water. It, too, had frozen.

As a last resort, the women of the village assembled the monastery students. Together they formed a bucket brigade. The only running water available was taken from the fountain of our dear Blessed Virgin, right in the center of the monastery square. Pail after pail was passed from person to person, till water reached the fire. In a desperate spurt of energy, the county fire department attempted to attach a hose to the monastery hydrant, quite some distance away. This belated effort finally met with success.

Your dear mother at once assembled a number of old men. These helped her carry water to the attic. A large hand pump was readied for emergency use. In the living room, your mother worked speedily, awaiting at any moment the order to abandon everything. She had laid out the precious tin box containing the Brunnen silver, as well as my brief case filled with my most vital business papers.

Just that very evening, a priceless manuscript had reached me. I was also preparing to read and edit a new geography. We rushed to the offices of the *Ochs* and *Wirt* to save these irreplaceable documents. There we hastily packed all the contents of those offices into sacks and crates. The manuscripts of H. Meister and H. Gerber, plus those of the *Alte Welt,* were immediately transported to the corridors of the *Adler.*

All the artists were notified of the imminent peril. They ran to their desks to rescue their originals. In my lower office, still more crates were filled. We attempted to save only original manuscripts and as many of the more expensive books as could hurriedly be salvaged. Orders were then given to remove nothing until the last possible moment. All our dray horses were harnessed to freight wagons and kept in readiness, behind the *Adler*. In the meantime, the contents of the *Schwert*, the *Schäfli* and other houses nearby were removed to safety.

Not until after six o'clock in the morning were we certain of escape. By seven o'clock, the fire was at last under control. The roof and top floor of the *St. Anton* were totally destroyed, the rest of the building flooded with water. We, thank God, escaped with only the horror of it all.

The results would have been far more disastrous had it not been for the zealous and united efforts of the villagers working as a team, and for the fact that all the roofs were weighted down with a heavy blanket of snow. Had this not been the case, the damage would, indeed, have reached the point of near catastrophe. The winds were so strong that burning shingles were blown all the way to the cemetery.

I have been writing this letter to you, dear Marie, since early morning. Now it is time for me to stop—to go to the office. The workers are already in the factories. Yet, before I end this letter, I would like to remind you and your sister Anna of the great lesson we can all learn from this misfortune.

Nothing . . . nothing on this poor earth is ours, or can be called our very own! All that is ours is our heart and our deeds. One day we will have to render an accounting of how we have used the powers of our mind, our body and our worldly possessions. Have we done so honestly and usefully for ourselves and for others?

I hoped against hope to rescue my vital papers. Yet, had all been destroyed by fire, I would again have started at the bottom to work my way up. For, my most earnest wish is to be able to earn a living for each of you in order to educate you properly and fit you for life.

Ask yourself, "Who are those with a good education? Who are those who possess the riches of the earth?" Those with a pure heart are rich beyond compare! Those with a good conscience own the wealth of this land. Likewise, those who have as few wants as possible, yet succeed in remaining independent of even these.

This does not imply that we should avoid striving for material gain. On the contrary, the wealthy man who is lazy, who accomplishes naught with his wealth instead of aiding others with his fortune, becomes a burden. Let us not be so bound to our fortune that, if we should lose it, we would despair.

Should that happen, we must thank God for leaving us our health, the mental and physical strength to strive anew to reacquire it. Even though denied money or earthly possessions, he who has health is by far richer than the sick or stupid, who may have great wealth yet become a burden by always being dependent on others.

Fortunately, during this moment of frightful calamity, I was able to be calm. From the bottom of my heart, I kept repeating to myself: "As God wills—as God wills!" I begged for health of soul and body. I knew I would never again be able to rebuild the business I had once helped to establish, for my strength has gradually diminished with the years. I am older now, soon will be—old! This caused me greater anxiety now than it would have in the past, when younger, because of you children.

Had the good Lord planned for me to lose my fortune, I am sure that you all would have helped me to begin again. We would have looked on this as a trial, coming to us from the Hand of God. Together, we would have started at the bottom rung—with resignation to God's Will.

Never forget, dear Marie, that he who expects little from life is the master of his destiny. That person is by far the happiest, the richest.

Do you remember the beautiful saying that my father Nikolaus once wrote me? "The only love that lives and lives eternally is sacrificial love. This sacrificial love alone ennobles us." On another occasion, he wrote: "He who lives for others and learns to serve mankind multiplies his life."

There, now, dear daughter. There's no need for me to explain the contents of these lines—though I want you, in the light of what has happened, to take these deep thoughts into yourself.

CHAPTER 4

Years of Transition
(1870-1886)

Adelrich's gestating plans to begin August's formal schooling in earnest were delayed for a time by world events which almost fully occupied the father's mind and time. Europe, on the eve of the War of 1870, sat on a volcano. There were rumors of war, of arming and rearming, as people spoke in hushed whispers of the Prussian army on the march. Suddenly came the outbreak of hostilities. Through it all, the cool-headed and clear-sighted businessman of Einsiedeln steered straight ahead.

Governor Benziger, as a linguist, was equally at home in French, German or English as well as in his native dialects, and bargaining with the French people had made him a lover, not only of their language but of them and their mentality. He was constantly in Paris, selecting new types of paper, buying inks or machinery. The publishers liked him and needed his trade. He, in turn, came to know intimately Charles and René Lorilleux and the famous Hachette and Didot families. They were closer to him than his own relatives, apart from his immediate family, and they admired and respected him. It was largely through them that he kept his hand on the pulse of national and international events.

On one visit to Paris, he was told that war was imminent. His friend Lorilleux, head of the vast Puteaux Factories outside of the city, advised him to take back to Switzerland great quantities of printing inks and paper. Though the French publishers had tried repeatedly, they had lacked the capital to buy four of the newest inventions in color lithography. These monstrous presses of tremendous value were the first to print two colors simultaneously. The inventor had been financed by American friends and so the machinery was packed and awaiting shipment to them, but when war was declared and France invaded, the presses could not be moved across the Atlantic.

On July 19th, all who were able fled Paris. Adelrich Benziger assisted the Lorilleux, the Didots and the Hackettes to evacuate their wives and families to their country estates. In gratitude for his services, they reminded him of the color presses which would revolutionize printing. The inventor, realizing that his life's work would now be unable to leave Paris and that no Frenchman had sufficient funds to pay his required price, was glad to turn them over to Benziger of Einsiedeln, but how was Adelrich to get the crated machinery out of the city, to say nothing of the country? The Didots, the Hackettes and the Lorilleux families pressed their own horses and carts into emergency service, hauling the valuable cargo to the station. There Adelrich caught the last train to leave Paris. He personally traveled in the wooden box-car in order to protect his valuable merchandise for these machines were to alter completely all existing printing processes—these presses would enable Switzerland to lead the world in color lithography.

When Governor Benziger told his six partners the amount of money he had spent on the new enterprise, they refused to back him. In fact, he was ridiculed for venturing into new fields at a time when Switzerland might be invaded at any moment. Adelrich accepted the challenge, assumed the full risk and responsibility; he would personally pay for the machinery to the very last cent. As had always been the case in the past, he would take courageous steps that led into new ventures, alone and unaided.

No sooner had the presses been installed in Einsiedeln than Adelrich found that, as head of the cavalry of his state, he was mobilized. The mere act of sounding the *tocsin*—its loud bells booming their call to arms—meant that every able-bodied male between the ages of 18 and 65 dropped whatever they were doing to report for duty fully-armed. Governor Benziger, as a colonel, held the highest rank awarded any man in time of peace. He and his troops, who called him Commander, were sent to the Alsatian frontier where the fighting was heaviest. Night and day these Swiss remained on duty, guarding the border, protecting, watching. These were trying days when bloodshed and suffering snuffed out the lives of hosts of young men. What hurt Adelrich most was seeing French and German soldiers dying a stone's throw away, and yet being unable to do anything to alleviate their last ordeal. Aware of the pain of his troops, he was sensitive and gentle, but he could also be a stern leader; he demanded unflinching obedience. When his best friend, a lawyer from Schwyz, disobeyed his orders, he sent the man home in disgrace.

During these grave times when the fate of nations hung in the balance, young August's mother shouldered all family responsibilities. Her eldest daughter, Marie, assisted as best she could with the care and discipline of the younger children. Restless and homesick for his soldier father, August had been up to his usual pranks. That Christmas, with the head of the household at the front, little time could be spared for the proper reprimanding of disobedient children. As August had been naughty, he had been promptly banished to the dismal, damp apple cellar to spend all of Christmas Eve there.

Mrs. Benziger had been so rushed, attending to the hundreds of details of daily living and of getting food parcels off to the front, that her youngest son was overlooked. He spent not only Christmas Eve in isolation, but also part of Christmas Day. True, he had been sent to the cellar in punishment, yet certainly no one would have exiled the small boy for such a lengthy period of time, especially on Christmas. During the rest of his life, August could never completely erase the bitterness of a lonely Christmas spent without his father, or anyone at all; never again would he feel quite the same toward that usually joyful feast.

Conditions in Switzerland and in all of Europe now reached a critical state. Switzerland was now running out of gold. As a result, Commander Benziger was recalled from his post at the front. Devoted to his regiment, he could ill afford to leave his men at this decisive moment of heightened fighting, but orders were orders. Accordingly, he proceeded to the Swiss capital; in Bern he had personal interviews with the President. Shortly afterwards, anyone observing closely would have seen the Commander appear as a civilian, with a beard and mustache more resembling those of a French aristocrat than of a Swiss gentleman. How he managed to get inside the fortified lines and finally reach the besieged city of Paris, no one was ever told.

As Swiss Ambassador with plenipotentiary powers, he was received by Emperor Napoleon III. This ruler and his Finance Minister had a long interview with him and, at its end, they consented that he withdraw the gold that Switzerland had placed in France for safekeeping. Adelrich, being a man who could keep a secret, never divulged, even to the intimate members of his household, how he had been chosen to go to France on this dangerous and crucial mission, nor did any one learn how he had transported the money safely across the Swiss border. Only very much later did one of the Swiss Presidents mention the fact that the nation owed its economic life to Adelrich Benziger and his heroism.

That mission was so successful that within a few weeks Commander Benziger was again at the front line. The fighting was fiercer than ever along the Swiss-Alsatian border and Adelrich saw to it that Swiss neutrality was maintained, as the entire Swiss army was now under his command. He gave orders to rescue and save both French and German wounded who crawled into the neutral zone.

The Swiss now began to breathe more easily; with sufficient money, in the form of gold, they could buy necessary food from Italy and Austria. The threat of starvation passed.

However, there was soon another mission for Adelrich Benziger, this one equally secret. Government officials were receiving conflicting reports from and about France. The triumphant Germans were boasting that soon all of France would be theirs. Adelrich arrived in the hard-pressed French capital and learned that what had seemed to be mere rumors were, in fact, shocking realities. All means of communication between Paris and the outside world had been cut off by the attacking Prussians, and Emperor Napoleon III had been captured and made prisoner. The city had been so successfully surrounded that within the capital people were dying by the hundreds. Death and starvation stalked every alleyway. The civilian population survived only by consuming the bark of trees and by boiling grass. Those who were more fortunate ate rats!

When Adelrich crossed the lines and slipped into the strangling city, he immediately called on his friends, offering them aid, then returned to Switzerland to report in person the stark tragedy of a courageous and starving people.

In a short time, he was back in the capital in charge of distributing food and clothing. The Swiss government, on his recommendation, shipped trainloads of supplies to relieve the appalling shortages. Adelrich was still in Paris when, on January 28, the armistice was signed and a nation's face was changed: France had lost Alsace and Lorraine and the last vestige of a Napoleonic Empire vanished. France was to become a republic.

By the end of the war, the horrors and insecurity which Adelrich had witnessed gave him an immense longing for retirement. Having refused all honors, he returned to the burden of everyday life and found that the onus of running his huge business very nearly single-handed was almost more than he could shoulder. While he was ever a man of vision and daring, his partners followed his leadership somewhat reluctantly because his open-mindedness and modern approach to enterprise frightened, even shocked them. The Swiss, as a people, were conservative, seldom leaders in great world movements. They preferred to wait, to see, to take the safe course.

Every summer, the Benziger family retreated to a chalet in Gersau which they leased. There, on the Lake of Lucerne, better known to the locals as the Lake of the Four Cantons, the children played and rejoiced. Adelrich joined his wife and family whenever he could snatch a brief interlude from business affairs. However, he now longed to own a plot of his own on that particular lake. He had chosen a site that lay near the heart of its most historical landmarks. As all land in Switzerland was at a premium, owners of vast estates could be counted on one hand, but the Governor was weary of being in the public eye, and his craving for solitude and privacy prevailed. In Canton Schwyz, acres which had been retained in families for generations were worth their weight in gold. Prior to the Prussian War, Adelrich had had a friend open negotiations on his behalf. Several years were required before all the necessary 240 plots of land, owned by more than 100 people, could be bought and the deeds, at last, placed securely within his own hands. Now the Brunnen land was his.

Adelrich envisioned his own dream villa set high on a dramatic promontory above the lake, jutting out so that from his mountain retreat he would be able to see the land bordering all Four Cantons. Perched steeply on granite rocks, his aerie would overlook Lucerne on one side, Flüelen on the other. Opposite his home would lie the cradle of Swiss liberty, Rütli, where three great Swiss patriots had sworn to die rather than continue to be slaves under Hapsburg tyranny. All year-round he would face the majestic, snow-cropped glaciers of the Uri-Rostock.

Two years before the outbreak of the Franco-Prussian War, the Benzigers had moved to the newly-acquired estate. On it was situated then only a single primitive cottage. During the summer months the family camped out, thoroughly enjoying the wilderness which now was their sun-lovely Brunnen.

Then landscape gardeners were hired. Trees were planted along the mountainside. Some of the pines came from Oregon in America, the maples from Canada and the graceful birches from China. Adelrich had loved the American wild flowers, so seeds were sent from New York so that he could plant goldenrod and Michaelmas daisies. Thousands of wild cyclamen bulbs were imported, along with lilies of the valley, primroses and violets. For Switzerland this Garden of Eden was extensive beyond belief.

Soon architects submitted plans. Iron girders had just come into popular use in America and so Governor Benziger utilized this advanced type of construction to create a fireproof and solid home. On the second floor, he installed a tile bathroom for which the tub was imported from the States. To the Swiss, bathtubs were a contrivance solely for foreigners' use. Local tongues wagged when the people learned that the tub in the Benziger villa was not only of cast iron, but large enough to accommodate four children bathing at the same time!

A rocking chair, another curiosity unknown in Europe, also came from America, to claim a prominent place in the Governor's office. Comfortable steamer chairs, such as Adelrich had enjoyed while crossing the ocean, invited relaxation on the spacious verandas, where incomparable views were available of the entire length of the Lake of Lucerne. Roses of many kinds were planted along the driveways, Japanese wisteria at the sides of the house. This great country home, appropriately enough, was named in honor of Gutenberg, the father of printing. A statue of him was awarded a place of honor in an especially-built niche at the front of the house, and so the estate came to be known as *Villa Gutenberg*.

Because of the delays caused by the war, it took many months before the home could be completed. Every detail was of the utmost simplicity, yet of the finest craftsmanship. The cherry-paneled dining room was enhanced with exquisite wood carvings depicting wild life. The parquet floors in some of the rooms were inlaid with as many as 15 kinds of wood. The carved wooden chairs, prevalent in every Swiss home of the day, underscored the dominant motif.

To the *Villa Gutenberg* came many interesting men of the era. Among the first was George Page, the American Consul General from Lucerne, who had become one of Adelrich's close friends.

Shortly after the Benzigers took occupancy of the Villa, he came with his wife and baby to be a guest. The conversation turned at one point to the fact that one of the greatest tragedies of the War had been the untimely death of babies as a result of a lack of milk. If France could only have obtained a steady supply of it, these infants need not have become victims. George Page was struck by the wealth of Switzerland's dairy resources; he felt that if milk could be canned, this country might then dispose of its surplus supplies with great profit to herself and to the benefit of the rest of Europe. He invited Adelrich to look into the possibilities of such a project. Together they combed the countryside for a suitable factory site and found one in Cham, on the Lake of Zug. The Governor then solicited the aid of his friend, Henry Nestlé, who had been the inventor of Nestlé Baby Food. All Swiss city mothers began to raise their infants on this dried milk product. In the newly-built office of Governor Benziger, the Nestlé Milk Company came into being. The first stockholders held their organizing meeting there, formulated plans for the future and set into motion the business which was to revolutionize the feeding of babies and bring milk within the reach of non-dairy countries.

While Adelrich was fully occupied with the war and with his estate, his youngest son and the boy's cousin Franz were chronically involved in their inevitable mischief. Instead of Kümmel, this time they succeeded in buying a supply of dynamite from the workmen, the Italian artisans who were building a landing dock by the lakefront. The boys proceeded to fill bottles with the dangerous explosives which they detonated with thunderous results. The entire countryside for miles around felt a severe jolt and the workmen fled in terror. Mrs. Benziger just happened to be looking out of the new terrace windows at the moment of impact and saw August and Franz fleeing into the woods. That usually calm lady followed them in hot pursuit. She sternly ordered the boys to empty their pockets and remove their pants. When a mass of gunpowder fell to the ground, she made them collect every particle and dump their precious cargo into the water. Late that evening, Mrs. Benziger told her husband of the episode. He at once demanded a severe spanking for the culprits, but she pleaded with him, reminding him gently that another 14 years of patience would still be required on his part, for it would take that amount of time to make a man out of a child!

Seven-year-old August and his favorite brother, Adelrich, later to become a bishop, remained in Brunnen later than usual. September of 1874 was a beautiful month, much milder than would be expected, and the air was filled with anticipation of festivities. The boy's father had felt concern that the villa in Brunnen had never been blessed. Accordingly, he had invited the Prince Archbishop of Salzburg and his companion, Abbot Fichten, to be his guests for the dedication ceremony. The Benziger children had gathered laurel leaves and made wreaths under the watchful eyes of their gardener. These were then hung over doors and windows and along verandas, and the Swiss flag fluttered from the rooftop. Both Adelrich and August served as altar boys while Mass was said in the living room. This was a red-letter day in the lives of all the family. Their new home was complete and dedicated to God.

While the problems of war and building waned, Governor Benziger experienced many scholastic conflicts concerning the education of his youngest son. His first struggle on this subject came with his wife and two daughters. They felt that August should have more time to play, that late hours of study and practice were harmful to one so young, but their protests were in vain. At the age of five, August had been placed under the tutelage of the monastery organist as a music pupil. Hour after hour he practiced until, by the age of eight, he could play Beethoven's sonatas with ease. At the same time, he spent hours in the factory with Professor Nauer, mastering the technique of pen-and-ink drawing. During the summer holidays of his eighth and ninth years, he was sent away from home to be a paying guest under the roof of Professor Stucki at Näfels, to develop his skill in the techniques of etching. Upon his return, he promptly became the bane of all his masters, who dreaded his new talent far more than they had his pranks. With pad and pencil, he drew such realistic caricatures of his teachers that few possessed the courage to punish him.

A steady correspondence now ensued between the monastery and the child's father. The monks criticized a system of upbringing whereby the lad's talents were singled out for special attention and opportunity given for their development. They strongly disapproved of August's many activities which, they claimed, led to distractions in class. There was also the inevitable hint of jealousy and the suggestion that the boy might appear different from other village children, to be more favored than they. When father and son had a heart-to-heart talk, threats of being sent to boarding school emerged. These were counteracted by the womenfolk at home. Even at this early age, August had a way with women, most of whom were conquered by the sight of his apparently "innocent" delft-blue eyes. His older sister, Marie, came to his rescue by offering to tutor him daily before class; Anna, the sister who was about to become a nun, did all she could for him before she left for her convent in Bruges; Rosalie, the old nurse, as well as the cook, the chambermaid, the serving girl and the scullery maid were willing to give the boy anything he desired. Even his usually very level-headed mother was often swayed by his magnetism. All seemed to be at his command without his ever being conscious of this fact, to be at one in attempting to save August from what appeared to them as the too-great rigors of boarding school.

Truth to tell, the Governor suspected the women to be right and, he told himself, there was a distinct advantage in keeping so young a lad at home, one who was a bundle of nerves and who had an extremely delicate constitution. Also benefitting August's cause was the fact that the local school was conveniently located just opposite his home; with the time saved from the necessity of travel, it would be possible to keep the arts and music classes injected into a course that was otherwise purely classical.

One weakness plagued August throughout his life: a deadly fear of the oral recitations which were then much in vogue. He was never able to stand before an audience, either to recite his lessons or make declamations. When required to do so, he would feel his knees buckle beneath him, or he would turn pale, become weak and grope for his desk for support; his austere teachers termed this reaction affectation. Anyone, they told him, could learn by rote and then recite a lesson. No excuses were plausible, no exceptions made; nevertheless, sensitive to the utmost, August was never able to recite the zoological and botanical names in the class of Pater Ludwig Stutzer.

On one occasion, his father had been away on a trip to Paris. During his absence, August had been confined to his home for a three-week period as the result of a stomach disorder. A few days after he had returned to classes, Father Stutzer, who taught Latin and natural history, requested the boy to deliver a note to his father. August ran happily to the Governor's study, hopeful that the message contained the welcome news that he might be promoted to a higher class.

The Governor generally took pleasure in his son's impromptu visits; however, on this day his smile turned quickly to a heavy scowl as he studied the contents of the letter in his hand. Then he read aloud:

Stift Einsiedeln, December 22, 1879.

. . . Your son takes life far too easy. Of course this only happens during your frequent absences from home. August shows absolutely no interest in Latin or natural history. All his masters come to me and complain about the flightiness of his character. There is no solidity to his make-up. He seems so frail in health and complains so much about his stomach and having headaches. I wonder how much of this is real or make-believe. . .

August wept in helpless frustration as he had hoped that the letter contained good news. His father, ever a man of few words, said nothing. Instead, he took a long quill pen, tested it, then hurriedly wrote an answer, shook white sand over the wet ink, then handed the reply to his son.

"Here! I want you to see my answer."

August held the page tightly and read:

MY DEAR FATHER:

I have just received the letter from Pater Ludwig. You probably know that August has been absent from school for three weeks due to a stomach ailment. In the past, he has often brought me letters from his teachers, always thinking they were pleased with him. Instead, they now write that he is flighty. He has cried much as a result of these criticisms. I am sorry to learn the bad news about him. I fear his not being well may have been the cause of this relapse.

Personally, I have experienced the same reactions with August. Sometimes when I've asked him to recite his lessons, they were so poor that he did not know a single word. The more exasperated or annoyed I became, the less he could remember. He would leave my study for his sister's room. Marie, our eldest, would ask August the same questions. He could then recite the answers without a single error. I sincerely feel that August is not being helped by all this misunderstanding."

August, who was never overly-demonstrative, nestled near his father in relief. He then learned that he would not have to return to his regular classes; his father had other plans for him. In Sarnen there was a Benedictine school, a branch of the Muri-Gras

Abbey. *Pater* Keush, whom August had met, was in charge of the studies there and had promised that when the time came for a change of schools, he would personally tutor August in Latin.

Mrs. Benziger wept as she hurried about packing her son's belongings. She would miss her little mischief-maker. She kissed him and then said:

"I'm afraid we're about to lose you for all time. You will never return to us for you are so like your father. Yet I am convinced that whatever you do, you will do well." She went on with resignation: "You boys seem only loaned to us for a temporary period . . . Always be a good boy, August, and never forget to pray for me."

School days in Sarnen were happy and filled with useful study. Here August was a success. Although he still played pranks, the priests at the school were not as dour as those in Einsiedeln and, as a group, had a keener sense of humor; consequently, they managed to control the boy smoothly without constant recourse to parental assistance.

Pater Rudolph, one of the priests who supervised the school's study periods, was addicted to snuff. One evening, August managed to replenish the priest's supply with a very potent mixture and gave each of his classmates a pinch of the product for which Pater had become notorious. That night, when the priest partook, the hundred boys immediately followed suit. Sneezing and wheezing filled the room. The nasal concert ended in a round of hearty laughter, the priest himself joining in while holding his sides and yielding to uncontrolled mirth. The incident might well have played havoc with future conduct marks had the jolly Father not been such a rounded human.

In April 1881, the Father Director of Sarnen wrote to Governor Benziger:

> Your plans for August to study English, Italian, physics, mathematics and science will be carried out to the letter. Only please bear in mind that it will require several years' time before August will be ready to leave us for foreign lands to pursue the study of art. Pater Keusch feels that your son has a tremendous amount of quicksilver in his make-up. Do not expect us to make a student of him overnight. Great patience will be needed before any real results will be seen . . .

Although his mind was developing, his body again complained. August was often to suffer from severe toothache. As there was no one in Sarnen capable of extracting teeth, he was sent home for dental care. In the entire Canton of Schwyz, there was not a dentist to be found anywhere, so cavities could never be filled. Children went to school with swollen cheeks and flannel kerchiefs tied round their badly-distorted faces. Homemade poultices were often applied to the sore spot in an effort to reduce the swelling and relieve the throbbing pressure of the abscess, but beyond this treatment, little could be done. When excruciating pain finally became unbearable, it was the village barber who was called upon to perform the extraction. Using a sturdy pair of pliers, the "dentist" administered a sudden, strong jerk. If he possessed sufficient strength and dexterity, out came the tooth.

August had been sent to the Einsiedeln barber to have four molars extracted, and returned home in an agony of bleeding gums, swollen jaws and aching nerves. All four teeth had been broken, and the jagged roots remained to plague him for years. Not until he was in his 20's, while on a visit home for military service, did a Zurich surgeon attempt to bring him relief. In a hotel bedroom, Professor Kaufman administered merciful laughing gas, then operated for the removal of the deeply-embedded fragments. It was small wonder that Swiss children held a lifelong dread of dentists. Toothaches were borne in stoic silence; anything rather than endure the tortures of the inexperienced barber!

Back from Sarnen for the holidays, August rejoiced to be with his family. Brunnen itself was to him a veritable heaven on earth, but July 28, 1881 was clearly one of the most notable days in the lives of the Benziger children. Their father had always been an ardent admirer of King Ludwig II of Bavaria, and considered him to be one of the greatest patrons of art in the 19th century. On this particular day, the Governor had given his children a complete holiday—with no music, drawing or French required of them. They gathered in the village and waited with excitement for the lake steamer to land its royal passenger, for Ludwig was scheduled to pass through Brunnen *en route* to a hotel in Axenstein!

Many Germans openly called their monarch "The Mad King of Bavaria," and ridiculed the sensitive ruler who sought to bring democracy to his people. Many years before, Ludwig had come to Switzerland as a student pursuing the study of that country's laws and customs. While there, he became passionately fond of

Schiller's rendition of the thrilling story of William Tell for, to him, it represented a magnificent recounting of an exciting and inspiring historical event, a heroic struggle for liberty, but most of all, Ludwig loved the Lake of Lucerne with its noble historic associations. That was why he now returned, a man of 40, to be near Rütil, the cradle of democracy, Tell's Chapel and the Schiller Stone. He longed to become imbued with the courage of the men of the past who had succeeded in molding a powerful republic from four small states, and he gained inspiration from having the opera *William Tell* performed in his Munich *Hoftheater*.

By his critics and enemies, Ludwig II was termed eccentric, extravagant, a spendthrift. The king felt, however, that he never lavished riches on himself but, rather, disbursed a steady stream of money for the purpose of enriching and beautifying his kingdom. Never since the days of Louis XIV had Europe seen such a renaissance of art and music. The king studded the Bavarian countryside with fairy-tale castles, choosing the most artistic available sites for their settings. He embellished parks, boulevards and town squares with monuments of rare quality.

Ludwig II excelled, not only as a patron of the arts, but also as a poet, artist and musician. It was his marked musical talent that enabled him to appreciate the efforts of a promising young composer, Richard Wagner. As head of the House of Wittelsbach, he defended Wagner as one of the great Teutonic composers and, when some Germans threatened to exile him, the king personally rushed to his aid and protected the man dubbed a radical and a liberal. He even went so far as to give Wagner an opportunity to develop and perfect his operatic scores by having them first played and enacted in his own castle. Whether one is in unison with Ludwig's tastes and commitments or not, it is impossible to doubt his sincerity and generosity in furthering them. He erected a special music hall in Bayreuth so that annual music festivals might be held there. When no one would attend performances of the scorned Wagnerian operas, he lent his moral support and patronage by his personal appearance at all such events, and over 200 operas were performed for the appreciation of Ludwig and his entourage.

This royal patron of music and art suffered keenly. Narrow-minded, jealous members of the House of Wittelsbach sought to have him deposed, but he was far too popular with his people for this abasement to be possible. To them, he was like a storybook king rather than a person of flesh and blood, and they preferred romance to politics; but gradually Ludwig discovered that he could trust but few. Among those who remained faithful to him was his relative, the beautiful Empress Elisabeth of Austria.

On this 28th of July, 1884, Ludwig had come *incognito* to Lucerne by special train, hoping by this means to evade publicity. Bitter was his disappointment when he found that everyone in the area seemed to have had previous knowledge of his personal plans. Angered by this invasion of privacy, he decided to return at once to Bavaria.

On July 29, August was busily assisting the gardener, Schmid, in picking flowers for the villa, his specific assignment being to select appropriate blossoms for the various niches and shrines that abounded in the garden. August noticed that the dogs were barking. (People had tried various pretexts to gain admission to the grounds, so Governor Benziger had been forced to order three St. Bernard puppies in order to preserve his right to seclusion.) As the boy turned, he encountered Mr. Gransee, the manager of his father's little hotel, the *Mythenstein Pension* which faced the lake below *Villa Gutenberg* and contained 50 rooms for summer visitors. Eyeing the fierce dogs apprehensively, Mr. Gransee asked August to accompany him and his companion to the villa as a safety measure, explaining that the gentleman was anxious to see the governor on important business. Always happy for the opportunity to meet new people, August led the way up the path. The Governor, for his part, did not welcome this unexpected intrusion; he planned to leave that afternoon for Einsiedeln and there were many pressing matters requiring his attention prior to his departure. However, Mr. Adolf Ledermann from Munich was introduced, and Adelrich learned from him what was wanted. He replied curtly that his home was certainly *not* for rent. Thoroughly annoyed at being disturbed by such a senseless request, he hastily excused himself and withdrew to his office.

Later that afternoon, August was again out-of-doors, this time helping to harness the horses as Sep was preparing to take the Governor to Einsiedeln and hoped to reach his destination before dark. The boy was quite amazed when he saw that the same stranger who had asked that morning to rent the villa had returned. "I'm sorry to disturb you," the man said, "but I've brought a friend with me. We hope to persuade your father to change his mind." August shook his head soberly; there seemed little point in re-climbing the hill as Adelrich was not in the habit of changing his mind. "My father has told you that the house is not for rent. Besides, I doubt that he'll be able to talk to you as he plans to be on his way to Einsiedeln very soon." With typical German persistence, Mr. Ledermann continued: "Perhaps I should explain that Mr. Zanders, who accompanies me, and I are both Royal Emissaries. The King of Bavaria has sent us with a special request. Here, lad, take this card. Your father will not refuse to see us now."

August accepted the card, then gasped and sped up the hill to the villa. Panting, he reached his father who was just beginning to descend the hill. "Oh, Father! Father! Wait! The King of Bavaria wants our villa. Look! Here's his visiting card!" Thinking his son was up to some new prank, the governor remarked crossly: "August, can't you see that I'm in a hurry to make Einsiedeln before dark? Besides, the King of Bavaria arrived only yesterday and is most comfortably settled up at the Axenstein Hotel where he has every luxury." Governor Benziger regarded his youngest with annoyance. "What puts such strange notions into your head anyway?" By this time, Mr. Ledermann had come near and overheard the Governor's remark. Wasting no words, he revealed his mission: The King had sent him and Mr. Zanders, who served as Treasurer of the Royal Household, to say that the King had been greatly disappointed with Axenstein; he longed for privacy. Instead, he was followed everywhere by Swiss police, the guests stared at him as a curiosity, and the hotel servants hounded him with attentions. The King detested all this turmoil and publicity . . . His Majesty had been grossly misinformed of the facts; he had thought the Axenstein Hotel to be a castle. Ludwig never sojourned in hotels! Accordingly, he had brought along 12 of his own Royal Staff, including two Munich cooks. *Villa Gutenberg* having been pointed out to the King as he had passed on the steamer, he had been captivated immediately by the solitary dwelling perched so high that it overlooked the whole lake. His Majesty had remarked *Villa Gutenberg* was situated on the exact spot where he would like to live were he to build a residence for himself.

When Governor Benziger was told to mention any price whatsoever, and that it would be his for the asking, he was deeply offended, but he replied quietly: "I have always been a great admirer of your sovereign. This is my home. If his Majesty is willing to reside in my humble abode, I shall be delighted to have him as my personal guest. We naturally would never consent to payment of any kind. The honor is entirely ours." Then he added graciously, "Whenever he wishes to do so, your King is most welcome to move in."

Adelrich, who was always magnanimous to his friends, remained in Brunnen until the family could be moved to other accommodations. Within 24 hours, the villa was spotless as everyone concerned worked throughout the night. By dawn of the following morning, Mrs. Benziger, her children and the cook had been established in the gardener's chalet, although it was so cramped for space that there was no room for any of the other family servants.

Schmid, the gardener, was given strict orders that no one—absolutely no one—under any circumstances, was to be allowed to trespass or be admitted to the King's presence without written authorization. The servants of the Royal Household took occupancy of the villa and, by evening, His Majesty dined in regal comfort on the cool and spacious veranda.

August was right in his element. He had such a winning way with people that strangers welcomed the appealing boy. Without ever seeming to intrude, he was always near at hand to tell the whereabouts of anything that might be needed. The two Munich chefs could never have done without his useful services. Consequently, he became Royal Errand Boy, dashing about on his serious missions, yet largely managing to keep out of sight. He brought ice from the family icehouse, and bottles of French champagne to be cooled in readiness for dinner, though he must have thought it odd that His Majesty took only one meal a day, that one served at five o'clock in the afternoon.

The King was abstemious, though he was a gourmet. He knew and appreciated fine cuisine and, in turn, received it, so specialties were ordered from Zurich to please the royal guest. The King did not demand a large number of dishes, but preferred to eat heartily of one particular gustatory treat. At the conclusion of dinner, he would send for his two bottles of champagne, take a single glass from each, then dismiss his private valet, George Huber, with the request that champagne be shared with the rest of the household.

A night-light was always kept burning on the table next to Ludwig's bed. On a silver tray, a small silver goblet was laid out containing a portion of the finest cognac. Other than this, he never touched alcoholic beverages. However, the best vintage wines were ordered, and a generous supply of Munich's favorite Hofbräu beer was dispatched to *Villa Gutenberg* in large barrels, as Ludwig wanted his entourage to have all the comforts of home. There were few kind or thoughtful touches of which he did not think.

The members of the royal Household consisted of 12 persons, one of whom was Joseph Kainz, the renowned Hungarian actor. At the age of 23, he had already acquired a leading part as Bavarian *Hofschauspieler* and was tremendously popular. When King Ludwig had seen him a year before in one of Victor Hugo's tragedies, he had been so touched that he had sent backstage as a gift a huge sapphire ring.

The King's prodigious memory had been trained from childhood. He could recite extemporaneously all of Schiller and Goethe and large sections of many Wagnerian operas. When, at the age of 17, just after ascending the Bavarian throne, he had first seen *Lohengrin,* he at once wrote to Wagner, congratulating him and begging him to present himself at court. Bavarian nobility frowned on such an act. Was not Wagner a Protestant, a musical revolutionary to be banned and shunned? Nonetheless, Ludwig became the Wagnerian angel. He soon had every script submitted to him; and he read and corrected each one. He knew by heart, eventually, the *Meistersinger, Rheingold,* the *Walküre, Tannhauser* and *Parsifal.* What he liked best was to have parts of these operas acted in one of his palaces, but he had to be careful not to call too many actors and singers for the chorus or ballet; otherwise, the Bavarian nobility, aroused at his extravagances, would put an end to his artistic endeavors.

Ludwig now had Kainz to himself, away from the prying eyes of envious courtiers. At last he had a companion with whom he could compete, who knew as many plays by heart as he did. However, Ludwig had not confined himself to the theater; his memory had assimilated philosophical and historical works as well, and he had memorized many, many books on the history of art. There was little this authority on Roman or Renaissance architecture could not describe; dates and names were as familiar to him as were those of his Bavarian statesmen.

Nevertheless, the stay in Brunnen was not to be all play. Daily a special courier came from Munich, and the large mail pouch was delivered in person to the King. All through the night, he and two secretaries worked and studied by candlelight. By dawn, a tired monarch was ready for bed.

He usually rested until 11:00 when the snap of a whip and the clip of hooves on the gravel announced that the four-in-hand had arrived at the villa door. Ludwig was always accompanied by Kainz and by Hesselschwerdt, Equerry of the royal Stables. Together they drove along the famous Axenstrasse, that granite road hewn out of the Axen Mountain, skirting, winding and tunneling in and out along the rocky banks of Lake Lucerne. On the opposite shore rose the sky-reaching chain of mountains, topped by the snow-peaked glacier of the Uri-Rotstock.

Often a specially-chartered steamer would await the royal party. The side-wheeler cruised along the rocky coast, while on the upper deck a string quartet played melodies chosen by Ludwig. As the steamer passed the William Tell memorial chapel, erected to commemorate the Swiss liberation from the tyrannical Hapsburg monarchy, a place dear to the heart of every Swiss, Ludwig relived the story that Schiller had dramatized.

Regularly, when the 5:00 dinner was served on the veranda, Brunnen and its dramatic lake filled the monarch with mystery. He was so enchanted with the history of the place that with the coming of twilight he would go to the villa's private beach. There he might take a rowboat and, with Kainz, recite the words of Schiller's *William Tell*. While others slept, they would be rowed across the lake surrounded by looming pine tree sentinels. These forays were accomplished only at night in order that Ludwig might avoid the curious stares of sightseers.

In the forest clearing of Rütil, on the edge of the rocky shore, was a steep landing. Although an hour had been spent reaching this spot by boat, the king scaled the rocks, then climbed the narrow winding walk that was overhung by birches and larches. The trail led uphill until it opened out into a broad meadow. Here, hemmed in by sheer mountain walls, was a quaint old house. A Swiss ranger in charge of this hallowed ground greeted the king. With hands behind his back, the pale, black-bearded King of Bavaria walked about as if in a dream. To him the simple peasants and shepherds who had fled to the Rütil meadows in 1291 were living beings. He longed to be counted among those great lovers of freedom, a Walter Fürst from Uri, Arnold von Melchtal from Untetwalden and a Werner Stauffacher from Schwyz. He envied their courage when, on that fated August first, they had sworn in solemn oath to free their lofty country from tyrants.

In Bavaria, King Ludwig was sneered at as a dreamer and visionary. In reality, a few thought, he was far ahead of his times. He had the soul of a poet and dramatist but, for him, never was anything more moving than the midnight scenes enacted in the Rütil meadow. So he suffered, and longed to free his own people, for in this cradle of Swiss liberty where democracy had been born, he sensed that in Bavaria too much time was wasted in politics, and too little spent on art and music.

His Majesty, once returned to the Benziger estate after one of these outings, and fearing to disturb Mrs. Benziger and the children sleeping in the chalet, would get out of the carriage and walk up the steep mountain road that led to *Villa Gutenberg*. August was carried away by the magic of this visit. Here was a ruler who had a fortune at his command, steamers, horses, servants at his beck and call, and who was yet sensitive and considerate enough to be deeply concerned about the ease and comfort of his host's little family. August might pretend to be in bed, but often, in reality, he hid in the stable in the early morning, waiting to catch a glimpse of such a king.

Kainz held the carriage lantern and led the way. The hidden boy could tell which of the many paths they took from the sound of the pebbles and, later, by the creaking of one of the great villa doors. Crouched in darkness, he waited until the long, fat candle in the dining room was lit and Ludwig settled down with his two secretaries to cope with the state documents which had arrived that day.

Each morning, the two Benziger daughters carried carefully-prepared bouquets to His Majesty. They would ring the villa door-bell and wait, for it was usually the king himself who came to thank them for their thoughtfulness. It was with genuine appreciation that he accepted their flowers, and sometimes he would ask the girls to help him arrange them in his study or dining room. The king, in turn, would send his courier to the simple gardener's chalet, where the messenger would inquire about the health of Mrs. Benziger and her brood. He brought respectful greetings from the king. Although nothing could have been more correct, more formal, more gracious, there was also a note of real care and concern. Ludwig was, in any case, as mindful of court etiquette as if he had been in residence in his own royal palace.

On one occasion August was again helping Schmid, and they were standing next to the compost pile. The king happened to be taking his daily walk through the estate, and he seemed to enjoy sauntering about the premises, admiring the cyclamens which grew wild among the rocks, the periwinkles or the plentiful roses which garlanded the many shrines throughout the park land. On nearing the compost pile, Ludwig stopped short, shock and amazement written all over his sensitive face. In a loud and imperious tone he demanded that the Royal Equerry, Hesselschwerdt, at once remove the flowers lying there. The faded bouquets, given the preceding day by the Benziger children, had been tossed upon the ragged compost heap. "Have those flowers collected," he ordered. "They are not dead! I do not wish to hurt the feelings of those charming young girls. They take trouble to pick flowers and bring them to me daily. Those blossoms are to be cared for; then, when I leave, I wish to take them with me to Munich as mementos of happy days."

But the fairy tale eventually had to have an ending; still, no one enjoyed it more while it lasted than August. The king requested that before his departure all the members of the Benziger family come to the villa for a final farewell. Until then, respecting the wishes of the monarch for absolute seclusion, Adelrich had stayed in Einsiedeln, even though he had left his family in Brunnen. On this occasion, however, he returned to call on the king in the villa.

In *Villa Gutenberg*, Ludwig knighted the head of the house and was lavish in his praise. Never had such extraordinary courtesies been shown him, never had he enjoyed such a perfect holiday. He had relished the utter simplicity and austerity of the Benziger summer home. This had been an enchanted interlude; he nurtured a profound dread of returning to the chaotic bunglings and misunderstandings of Bavarian statesmen.

As the king pressed the hand of Mrs. Benziger, he placed in it a white satin box bearing the royal coat of arms. Inside was a magnificent brooch shaped as a cross and ornamented with 150 priceless diamonds. Marie and Anna were presented with ivory brooches bearing miniature reproductions of the Sistine Madonna, likewise surrounded by diamonds. All three sons, Albert, Adelrich and August, received large gold watches. On the back of each handsome timepiece was enameled the deep royal blue of the House of Bavaria; mounted regally with diamonds was the letter "L."

On the day of final parting, the Benzigers went en masse to the village boat landing. There they waited to wave farewell to this guest they had come to love and revere. Bags, trunks, assorted pieces of luggage were placed aboard the steamer, followed by the valet and other members of the royal household carrying faded bouquets which had adorned the king's quarters. As Ludwig left the carriage, Marie and Anna curtsied, then held out to the monarch the loveliest of their bouquets. Tears filled Ludwig's eyes and those of the Benziger girls as they made their slow parting gestures. The king, clasping the flowers, crossed the gangplank silently, then hurried to the top deck. When last seen, he was waving from the side-wheeler, not to the crowds of onlookers but to his valued, newfound friends.

Although the Benzigers now resumed their life in the villa, there was a great feeling of emptiness, for they all missed the presence of this extraordinary man who had come among them. His gentleness, his self-effacement, his personal interest in their welfare had brought him very close to them. A hundred different tales were circulated of things that had happened during his visit—some of the "facts," perhaps, slightly embroidered, but one thing is certain: for the inhabitants of *Villa Gutenberg,* their home took on a new atmosphere, hallowed by the memory that a great man had come into their midst, that he had loved their way of life, that he had shared the simple pleasures of country living. In the bedroom he had occupied, they found a photograph on which was written in his own handwriting: "Here I have spent the most carefree nights of my life." In the dining room was found an impressive stack of boxes filled with Havana cigars. The card read: "To the most gracious and generous host, in memory of the happiest hours of my life." The kitchen had been cleansed until it shone and there, as further gifts, the tables were laden with a supply of delicacies sufficient to last a week. When the cellar was inspected by Mrs. Benziger, she stared in amazement. The three large wine cellars were filled with rare vintages. Over 800 of the choicest and rarest wines had been carefully stacked. Several barrels of Munich beer were laid away, as well as choice brandies, old cognac and liqueurs. The entire contents of the cellar had been entered on a proper wine chart, a lasting reminder of regal generosity.

Only five short summers later, on June 13, 1886, grief came to the hearts of all the Benzigers in Brunnen. On that day the agonizing news reached them that their loved King Ludwig of Bavaria was no more; he had been drowned!

Many years later, August was to meet a member of the royal entourage. He revealed the fact that schemes and seditious plots had been laid in order to assure the monarch's overthrow and that a few years before the actual tragedy took place, every effort had been made to brand the king as a schizophrenic. To achieve their goal, his enemies had kept the monarch in solitary confinement; later, then, it would be easy to drill holes in the bottom of the boat in which he and his doctor went rowing and he could be lured into the middle of his private lake. No one, they believed, would ever know the inside story.

Ludwig's enemies may have been treasonous to the gentle, well-meaning king. To the Benzigers, however, he would always be remembered as a man who was interested in the welfare of his subjects, who thought so much of his servants that he saw that the royal kitchens had the latest modern conveniences, that his retainers had the same foods as he, and were treated with respect and consideration. All the same, Ludwig was officially blamed for all the woes that fell on Bavaria.

Seventy years later, the fascinating castles and historic monuments that he had built, and which the Bavarian royalty claimed had impoverished the nation's coffers, actually helped to fill them. *Neuschwanstein* Castle, *Herrenchiemsee* Castle and *Linderhnof* Castle had been planned in their minutest details by the man the Bavarians called "The Mad Monarch," and tourists and architects from across the world came to admire them—and pay admission to enter them. His theaters which had been ridiculed became the meeting places where astonished audiences crowded to hear Wagnerian operas. In the end, at least one Benziger felt, Ludwig II would be one of the few Bavarian monarchs who would be understood by the outside world—yet his short-sighted subjects had held him up to public ridicule.

In the hearts of the simple Bavarian peasant folk, Ludwig remains a legendary character. To the Benzigers, he was ever a noble human being and an inspired king.

CHAPTER 5

Student Days—Munich and Vienna (1886-1889)

The great out-of-doors had always enthralled August. He and his boyhood companions kept secret their knowledge of where to look for the frost-nipped hazelnuts, or the opportune moment to pick the green walnuts so that their juicy skins would fall apart with the crunch of a heel. They could never wait to claim their prizes so their brown-stained fingers were the tattle-tales that let everyone know that walnut-picking was in full swing.

August passionately loved the spring in Canton Schwyz. After a cold, bitter winter it brought its laughter and gaiety—spring with its cherry and pear blossoms. Cherry blossoms fluttered against a backdrop of snow-capped peaks, bright verdant hills, while underfoot the cowslips and wild narcissi danced in the breeze.

Midsummer was his favorite season. Then August and his many cousins banded together to pick the dark, juicy cherries from heavily-laden branches. Along the shores of the Lakes of Zug, Ageri and Lowerz, they busily climbed their ladders, each carrying a two-pound oblong basket attached to his belt. Into it went handfuls of the luscious black fruit the various uncles had invited the boys to pick. These were the famous cherries used in making the native Swiss drink, *Kirschwasser*, more commonly known in dialect as *Chrisiwasser*, or plain cherry brandy.

The word *Chrisi* filled every child with a year-round longing for the wonderful plump, dark fruit. Usually more was eaten from the basket than was brought home in the hampers. The boys' livid tongues and purple lips and fingers divulged just what had happened to most of the *Chrisi*, yet no one scolded as old and young rejoiced that the crop was plentiful. Besides, cherries were considered a cure-all for every ailment, even growing pains!

Invariably the children swallowed the fruit, pits and all. August was a typical feaster as he was always in a hurry; the only time he refrained from swallowing the pits was the moment of competing in a contest when the boys vied with each other in a game of spitting the little stones at a target and winning prizes for the best aim.

The women collected, dried and packed the pits into linen bags to use them when winter came as heating pads to warm damp beds, or allay aches and pains. Some cherries found their way into the shining copper jam pots and long hours were spent stirring the fruit with the exactness required to make the noted *Chrisi confiture*.

The last month of summer meant the picking time of the tiny, bitter pears that were not generally edible. Large pear trees lined many roads and farms and provided an abundance of fruit that the peasants crushed in presses. This pear cider, called *Most*, was the popular beverage of the field workers; to the Swiss farmer it was what the *vin du pays* was to the French, or *Chianti* to the Italians. Domestic and day laborers each received a portion of this beverage with every meal, so the making of it was a serious undertaking in the life of every peasant. An abundant supply meant as much to him as a well-stocked cellar would to the French or Italian. Water? Why, no Swiss every drank water. Water was used in the making of soups, or occasionally added to milk. Water was intended for cattle, not for human consumption!

August liked this way of life at his boarding school in Sarnen; it was cozier, more friendly than had been that at the huge monastery of Einsiedeln. It was more inserted into the simple village life. The boys were often called upon or permitted to go on errands for the monks who, like those in August's native village, belonged to the Benedictine Order. On several occasions, when the Brother Sacristan was too busy to do so, he permitted the young Benziger to climb the monastery tower and toll the "Agony Bell," the sound of which conveyed to the villagers the solemn news that someone was dying. August knew that the "Anointing" or "Agony Bell" had to peal long and loud. At its sound, a priest wearing stole and surplice, accompanied by acolytes bearing lighted torches, and a crossbearer then formed a procession to the home of the dying villager. Sometimes August joined the assemblage as all prayed with the priest carrying the Holy Viaticum, the sacrament of the sick.

When the "Agony Bell" rang out, everyone reverently made the sign of the Cross and, as the crossbearer came into view, men and women, rich and poor, knelt in the fields or on the sidewalks in support of the person who was entering one of life's great, decisive moments. Bells spoke a vivid language of their own. As they tolled, they passed along news much faster than the notices that were posted on church doors or at county courthouses. So precise were their messages that, from the number of peals, everyone could tell whether the departed person had been a man or a woman.

In Einsiedeln, August had learned to dread the *Wetter Glocken*, the "Storm Bells" which rang out from the church tower to foretell the coming of great winds and threatening weather. He had heard the monastery bells of his home terrain ring loud and harshly as they had clanged the terrifying news that his father's factories were on fire. Now, on the Lake of Lucerne, the boy became acquainted with the ferocity of the *Föhn* Wind, the warm, unpredictable African sirocco that swept across his country without the slightest warning. Storm bells could mean stark tragedy. Farmers rushed to their stables, to their homes, the villagers to their stores or hostels. Everywhere fires were watered down, stoves extinguished. Not even a lighted pipe or cigar was permitted since burning embers could be blown tremendous distances. Every year, villages, forests, whole towns were burned to the ground as the result of carelessness about wanton sparks, so much so that it had been necessary to impose severe fines and even prison sentences for neglect. The *Föhn* bell both heralded and warned of the coming of spring. At the same time, the oppressive desert wind served to blot winter snows from the mountain peaks and whip the lakes of the Central Swiss Cantons into seething cauldrons, but the treacherous *Föhn* could even descend in midsummer! Yearly, tourists were drowned because they did not believe it possible for any landlocked body of water to be lashed into mad fury.

The "Storm" bell also sounded urgently to alert villagers and visitors alike of the dangers of an imminent avalanche, or tolled the coming of a flood.

Eventually, although August loved this world of cherries and pear blossoms and heralding bells, there descended upon him the need every Swiss had to master several languages, and French was a prime requisite. Although he had become a favorite with his Sarnen classmates and teachers, he had to bid farewell, and transfer to a school in Savoy. The color of his life was to change drastically.

During the course of his existence, he had met many priests. There may have been occasions here and there for a slight disagreement with a few, or some ill-favor resulting from his love of pranks, but never until this time had he been confronted with any who were unworthy to wear the Roman collar. Unfortunately, August's father had not personally investigated the background of the men to whom he now entrusted his adolescent son. The boy wrote accurate accounts home to his parents but, for obvious reasons, his letters came to be censored, censured or actually destroyed.

One of the French teachers had been guilty of taking the teenaged Benziger to a local tavern where the older man had not only displayed open drunkenness before his minor charge, but had had the further bad taste to boast blatantly of the women whose conquest interested him. Had August not come from as solid a home background as he had, his mental attitudes might have been irreparably damaged by shocking disillusionment. Furthermore, his parents were billed for classes which he never attended and were charged for food which never appeared. Fortunately, his older sister, Marie, stopped by to visit her brother in Savoy while she was on her honeymoon trip. She was aghast at what she witnessed with her own eyes! August was emaciated, and suffering severely from rheumatism and hunger. Marie notified her parents at once, packed her brother's bags and took him back to Einsiedeln, threatening to denounce the staff of the school.

English Catholic schools were austere. They were also extremely poor. The English Reformation had left most of the ancient monasteries so impoverished that years of hard and costly work would be required before any significant restoration could take place. The result was that August and his classmates were almost always hungry. Seeking to find a solution to this problem, the boy joined a group of other daring pupils who knew where the school larder was located. Midnight raids were held during which piles of apples were consumed and the contents of jam jars satiated hunger. One evening, to everyone's confusion and dismay, the band of foragers was caught by no other than the Father Prior himself! (Although he had recently been installed as Abbot, the boys still referred to him as Father Prior.) This tall, ruddy-complexioned Englishman, one of his country's outstanding authorities on biblical and historical matters, could be most severe, yet, coupled with his strictness and stern meting out of justice was a remarkable sense of humor that endeared him to his friends and students alike. Abbot Gasquet had also known the pangs of hunger in lean years, so he swore the marauders to secrecy, ordering them to report to his cell before retiring. From that time on, nightly visits were paid to his study for rewards of sugared buns and apples. Never again did the students complain of insufficient food. In appreciation, the former nocturnal prowlers affectionately named their abbot, "Jellybags."

But not all was food and fun. In the art course, August worked with concentration, and won first prize. The teacher had taken his pupils to sketch the lonely moors, purple with heather, and to the rolling countryside dotted with lovely village churches which were surmounted by towers dating back to the time of the Norman Conquest—and then there was the Swiss boy's first intimate contact with the sea. He was captivated by its grey-blue vastness, by the chalky cliffs and dunes, by the sailing vessels anchored in peaceful coves. All of these stirring, indelible impressions would resurface in the etchings and engravings which, in later years, were to bring him many honors. Together with art, August also loved music and could hardly tear himself away from the piano; every free moment was spent in practicing. When the first year of school had ended at Downside, it was he who had won the gold medal for musicianship.

Mastering the English language had its share of pitfalls. Governor Benziger had left explicit instructions that his son was to receive special tutoring in this subject. Always weak in spelling, August was instructed to devote at least one hour each day to the writing of essays, and so creative writing was to become the bane of his existence. Daily, weekly, monthly there were compositions to produce without respite—to which a growing stack of notebooks attested. These were sent back to Einsiedeln regularly so that his father might survey the rate of his progress.

On June 1 of the ensuing year, a discouraged footnote made its appearance: "Very little for one hour of composition." The English teacher had then suggested that his pupil comment on Sunday's sermon by way of a subject. In August's neat, meticulous handwriting, the following essay had been written:

> I am not at all able to write about the sermon of today.
> Why? I will try to explain why this is most difficult. My

brother, Adelrich, and I went for a walk just before High Mass. When we heard the bell ring, we were just halfway round the shrubbery.

My brother, a very strict observer of the rule, said, "There remains only one thing for us to do so as not to be late. Let us charge home as quickly as possible."

Thanks to my brother's good advice, we were just in time for Church. After reading the Gospel, one of the Fathers—the very one whom I can never understand when he speaks in class—got up to preach a sermon. After listening for fifteen minutes and not understanding a single word, I became very tired and fell asleep. That is all I know about the sermon.

The English teacher gave his Swiss student a "C" and noted tersely: "A very clever excuse. Do not try it again."

Fearful that his sons might speak the Swiss dialect and thus lose much of the language facility acquired during their current term, Governor Benziger decided that the boys should not see each other over the Christmas holidays. August was sent off to stay in a dreary boarding house in London where he spent all of December 24 sight-seeing and getting acquainted with the city's major historical monuments, but he also made a thorough study of the Tate Gallery and so gained his first insight into British art. At the National Gallery, on Trafalgar Square, he found displayed some of the finest Italian old masters and paintings of the early Flemish school. Unfortunately for August, most public buildings were closed on Christmas day, and no provisions whatsoever had been made for him for the celebration of the feast. Suffering from homesickness, entirely alone in the museum except for the guards on duty, he made the rounds of the exhibits until the closing hour.

At 15, August's elegant manner of dress stamped him as a young man of means. He held himself well and was extremely handsome with his newly-acquired sideburns. Sketchbook in hand, he left the museum and emerged into Trafalgar Square wondering what to do that evening. He had not noticed that a woman had followed him closely for some time. Unexpectedly he came face to face with this attractive brunette who not only sensed his lonely plight but at once agreeably offered to show him London's sights. The young man, unused to the ways of some city folk, hastened to accept this seemingly friendly gesture. While he had been properly cautioned about the perils of talking with strangers, he still had not the faintest suspicion that he was falling into a trap as old as the human race. Only when the day came for August to return to school was he struck by the full impact of what had taken place. He lived in an age when questions regarding sex were never voiced; neither home nor school had prepared him for the decisions that lay ahead. "Nice people" simply did not talk about such matters; this was the attitude that was supposed to dispose of the matter for all time.

August returned to Downside much the sorrier for his hapless experience. Months were required before he could calm his troubled conscience. The teenager who had once been deeply religious now shrank from approaching the sacraments, and he dared not discuss the sordid London episode even with his most trusted friend. Struggling bitterly within himself, he dreaded the time fast approaching for him to perform his Easter duty. In acute embarrassment, he refused to confess to any of the Downside monks. Finally, he summoned sufficient courage to seek out the village priest who was a total stranger; only then could he bear the thought of baring his soul. The grueling ordeal, the battle within his own conscience, had left him haggard and unhappy; he resolved never to find himself in that position again.

Once August had achieved command of the English language, his father decided that it was necessary for him to renew his acquaintance with French, and the young man sadly bid farewell to Downside. He had won all the honors in art and music and, though he never really understood the English people, he dearly loved the Abbot and made of him a lifelong friend to whom he often turned for help and advice.

It was to Belgium that he was now sent, as that country was considered the center of Gothic art, especially the little town of Ghent renowned for its Van Eyck School of Drawing. Here August was enrolled at the *Académie Saint-Luc* so he might make progress in the art world and, at the same time, continue with his French lessons.

In England, he had made such strides in piano that his Ghent professors, on hearing him play, insisted that he enter their annual music contest. As a result he won not only the coveted *Grand Prix* but also the Brussels Conservatory Award. Proudly August wrote home sharing the good news that he had come away with flying colors, but a special delivery letter soon arrived from his father. Instead of congratulations, he was being condemned for wasting precious time on music. Had he not been sent to Ghent to study art?

Within hours after the Governor's decisive message, August was again packing his bag. His worldly possessions were few as his father would have considered it folly for his sons to own more than two suits of clothing. One dour black suit served for working days; a second of better quality for Sundays. Into his traveling bag went two little black bow ties, several black wool socks knitted by his mother, woolen underwear and one extra pair of black *Hochwasser Hosen,* the tight-fitting pants that came above the ankles. It was as simple as that; August, the art student, was once again ready to move.

L'Institut Saint Louis in Brussels became his next abode. He attended classes in French, but his art instruction was under the immediate supervision of a family friend. M. Stallaert was head of the Academy of Fine Arts as its *Monsieur le Directeur* who taught the technique used by the Flemish masters. August spent many a profitable night in the private studio of this teacher; there priceless secrets used by the Flemish artists were unfolded before his eyes. According to this technique, the foundation for any portrait had to be sketched by the artist in black and white. Once the human form had thus been delineated, the highlights were brushed in with brilliant colors. This was a simple approach as solid as a bas-relief.

Although August had renounced all musical instruction in obedience to his father's wishes, his mind and heart were still nourished by concerts at the Brussels Conservatory of Music. Shrewdly sensing that this, rather than pictorial art, might in the end triumph and steal his talented son away from him and his designs for his future, Governor Benziger laid plans for Father Kuhn to take August on a Rhineland expedition. This Benedictine, Adelrich's wife's cousin, and the priest who had christened the boy, had become a noted authority on the history of art and was about to index the castles and churches of this area, and to visit the museums of Germany. August was to assist him. In this congenial atmosphere, the young man expanded and began to be himself. Fortunately, the learned professor and the eager student got along famously together. They covered a wide field with their comprehensive program of study, saw fascinating historic sites, and altogether had a stimulating and successful trip.

When the holidays ended, August was informed that Geneva was to be his next stopping place. Geneva was nearer home, and a far safer place for him to continue his education if he were to be weaned from thoughts of a career in music. In the conservative atmosphere of the French-Swiss metropolis, August could be tutored by the noted pedagogue, Dr. Gross, an erudite gentleman who only accepted two or three noblemen annually as his pupils, and trained each one individually. This mentor's tuition fee was exorbitant, yet he was able to provide what was most needed to conclude August's classical education. The Governor wanted his son to crowd as much basic instruction as possible into the coming months so that the future might be entirely devoted to art and its interpretation.

August again threw himself wholeheartedly into this new form of student life. Under the careful tutelage of Professor Gross, he continued his studies and attended lectures at the university. His painting was by no means neglected. Ravel, a follower of Millet, finally agreed to accept the Einsiedeln scholar as his pupil; from him August learned much about background technique and landscape.

Finally, emancipated from the humdrum activities of boarding schools, August emerged as Geneva's most-talked-of bachelor. Genevans were as socially-minded as Parisians, and the residents of this cosmopolitan city dressed well, very well. Vastly different from the stolid German-Swiss, the sophisticated populace was pleasure-loving, cheerful and romantic. Their parties and balls were brilliant events, and the coarse jokes currently in vogue among the students of Zürich or Bern would not have been considered *comme il faut* in Geneva. This was a time of psychological release for August. In the classroom as well as at play, this 18-year-old enjoyed enormous popularity. While he was in England, he had learned to fence; now he tried the "bicycle-built-for-two." On crisp nights, when the Lake of Geneva was frozen, he joined other skaters with graceful exhibitions of his skill on ice. Fun entered into his life easily.

One day, the students of the Ravel School of Design conspired to draw a poster in which to depict the many-sided Benziger. In it, the Swiss student was shown with his large dish of whipped cream, and the mug of beer he relished; added to this design were the visiting cards which he had left when calling on the prettiest debutantes. Then, as if to stress that at no time did he neglect the purpose of his being at the art center, there was added the design of a palette and easel.

August had a favorite saying. This he repeated daily for the benefit of the pretty flirts who pursued him. He managed to charm his feminine listeners, yet he reminded them in no uncertain terms in his now exquisite French:

> Point de bonheur sans mélange,
> Tôt ou tard la déception.
> Toujours on crois aimer un ange,
> Mais souvent c'est un démon.

> (There is no joy that is ever unalloyed;
> sooner or later one is deceived.
> Always one hopes to be in love with an angel,
> But more often it's a devil.)

News spreads swiftly in such a small country as Switzerland. The Benzigers of Einsiedeln soon learned of their son's social success and certain jealous citizens in Canton Schwyz openly resented it. Why would so prominent a Catholic family send a promising son to be educated in the Protestant Canton of Geneva? Broadminded and tolerant Governor Benziger had many friends in Geneva. He had done more than any other Swiss of his day to bring together the Catholic and Protestant factions, yet he fully realized how delicate this subject was. It was not because of sect considerations that he made his next decisions but because of academic ones. It would hardly do for August to fall in love at the outset of his artistic career as he had still ahead of him several stiff art courses to be completed. With these things in mind, he went to Geneva. Overnight the fun, the parties, the merry dances and social whirl ended. The bright bubble burst. August was whisked away to Munich.

In the Bavarian capital the Governor also had friends. Many of his artists and craftsmen came from that city, and he resolved that from now on nothing would be left to chance. Day after day, father and son made the rounds of outstanding schools to discover where, henceforth, August would learn to paint, to draw, to produce his own lithographs and photographs.

Great German and Swiss artists had been hired to produce the religious paintings that had been uppermost in the thoughts of Adelrich Benziger. Half of those on the payroll were members of the Düsseldorf school, but no matter how well-established their reputations might be, each sketch they submitted had to be returned two, three or four times, until what the head of Benziger Brothers had conceived in his mind had been faithfully depicted on canvas or paper. Adelrich knew little of the intricate technicalities of creative art; nevertheless, he knew exactly what he wanted to buy and how it should be attained. He had spent a fortune in fighting the baroque *frou-frou* of his century. Now his son was to take over the aspect of his work which he himself had never been able to master. August began to make original sketches and to examine and correct the work of others as he was one day to take over this department of the firm's production and make it the finest in the ecclesiastical field. Adelrich the revolutionary had met nothing but opposition to his methods. Impatient for results, he sought to have his son bypass the long, successive years of training required in specific fields in order to become well-rounded in all the arts and crafts simultaneously, and to prove himself to be of professional caliber as soon as possible.

Professor Haab, head of the Munich Academy of Fine Arts, protested. This accelerated procedure would be sure to destroy the student both mentally and physically. It required from eight to ten years to produce an artist. Lithography, photography and engraving were all distinct professions, each necessitating years of study before skill and technical mastery in them could be achieved. Adelrich was demanding an unreasonable feat of a single human being. To gain versatility in half a dozen subjects was entirely out of the question, a superhuman task unrealizable by anyone. However, Governor Benziger would listen to no one; he had made up his mind, and compromise was not in his nature. This time, he felt he was right. Accordingly, he immediately enrolled August in eight separate Munich schools, each completely different from the others, each providing something special to perfect his education.

The *Kunstgewerbeschule* offered useful classes in bookbinding, jewelry, sculpture and gold lettering. Here August learned the details of copperplate engraving from Dr. Raab who, prior to founding his own school in Munich, had pursued his trade at Benziger Brothers in tiny Einsiedeln.

In the Ferdinand Barth School of Decorative Design, Professor Barth made a decided exception in August's case, deviating from the school's policy by accepting the Swiss as a part-time student to attend a single hourly class each day. Here the young man was taught how to reproduce on canvas such objects as flowers, draperies, jewels and landscapes.

The *Nauen School of Drawing* was to provide a most rewarding period of instruction. It was under the personal tutelage of Professor Nauen whose classes in charcoal composition August attended that the student produced some of his most accomplished sketches. Molding in charcoal on white paper, he skillfully depicted heads that were to win him honors in both Vienna and Paris. It was at this time that he first created masterpieces that commanded the attention of those who saw his work, images of the gentle profile of a kindly Christ, of an arrogant young peasant bursting with life and energy, of a tired, wrinkled old woman worn out with work.

Yet he could never have achieved this success without having attended classes in anatomy. His father felt that he must know the human form thoroughly—each muscle, bone and anatomical detail; only then could the artist create lifelike beings. For the acquiring of this knowledge, August had been entered in the anatomy and surgery classes at the University of Munich, where he also assisted at operations and even studied at the morgue.

Finally, Professor Haab, who was still holding out against such a crushing schedule for the young man, relented, and August was enrolled in the Munich Academy of Fine Arts. Here the renowned Andreas Müller became his favorite professor. Under his strict supervision, August worked eagerly in the classes on religious art, although the teacher's method of instruction was unsettling: the master read scenes from the Old Testament, then gave his pupils 15 minutes in which to sketch a completed work. Quick thinking and trigger-quick action were required! For August, this was a vitally important subject as his father had decided that his life was to be dedicated to religious art. He sketched Tobias and Abraham. Sometimes he switched to New Testament subjects and did interpretations of the Last Supper, the Agony in the Garden, the Sermon on the Mount or the Descent of the Holy Spirit. When classes were over, he would visit Professor Müller in his private studio. Often large portions of the night were spent there in discussion, criticism or study and it was in this manner that the aspiring artist became an excellent draftsman.

Fortunately, during these years, rapid progress was being made in printing and photography as two friends of Governor Benziger had developed new inventions. By 1870, Hanfstaengel had worked out a method for reproducing the masterpieces displayed in European museums, one which combined photography with lithography. Paintings of the masters, which formerly could only be viewed and studied by a chosen few, could now be produced and made available to all. Obernetter, another friend, had invented a process called heliography.

Tremendously interested in all such advances, August's father made a special point of visiting these two gentlemen, and paid Hanfstaengel a substantial fee to introduce his son into the use of his method of reproduction. Obernetter was most anxious to have his invention bought by printing firms, so he personally undertook to supervise the special studies which would, in time, enable August to introduce heliography into both Switzerland and France.

This herculean program of instruction would have ruined the disposition of most talented students, yet young Benziger worked steadily to keep pace with the ambitious demands made on his limited energies. True, his father had placed large sums of money at his disposal and he wanted for nothing, so he enjoyed the best in food, lodging and working materials. He also loved the nature of the work. All of these factors were rare advantages as most other artists and students were severely handicapped by poverty. August, however, was far from being a free agent as he was required to render a strict accounting of every penny he spent and to carry out the dictates of his father to the letter, since he lived in an age when young people were expected to submit with unquestioning obedience to the wishes of parents and teachers alike.

Still, he quickly felt at home in Munich, a cheerful and friendly student city. Though he refrained from joining a fraternity, each group of students held out welcoming hands to him and he saw many of them daily. Usually at eleven in the morning and at five in the afternoon, he would gather with other students for his stein of beer. Mondays, he visited the *Augustinerbräu,* Tuesday, the *Löwenbrau;* Wednesday, the *Hofbräuhaus*, and on Thursday ate his favorite white sausage, *Weisswürstel*, at the *Bratwurstglöckerl*. On Fridays, he joined the medical students with their colorful caps at the *Salvatorkeller* and on Saturdays met with some of his professors at the *Franziskaner*.

The beer houses served excellent food. In each, a *Stammtisch*, or reserved table, was set aside for steady customers, and each waitress hovered over her *Stammkunde*, or client, with maternal solicitude and knew each student's favorite dish. The steins of the old and valued customers were filled to the brim with good brew, topped by only a small cap of foam, but newcomers were often cheated. Their beer was mostly froth! Tremendous barrels from famous breweries were rolled into the beer hall and, in winter, the brew was warmed by means of a hot poker thrust into the cold, amber liquid. In more exclusive establishments, a waitress held a container filled with hot water in immediate contact with the stein in order to bring its contents to room temperature.

When the 11:00 portion of liquid was consumed, there was often insufficient time to eat a full-course meal, so August would call for his *Radi* and *Semel,* his radish and roll. The big white radish was of primary importance since it helped to keep the hungry students sober. It was sliced paper-thin, sprinkled with salt and then pulled out to astonishing lengths like an accordion.

An eagerly anticipated festival was the *Oktoberfest.* This harvest feast was celebrated in Munich with considerable pomp, as on this occasion the high-nosed Bavarian nobility from *Schloss Nymphenburg* and the *Residenz* deigned to rub shoulders with the plebeian tradesmen and workers. It was also the season when the aristocracy condescended to engage in "platonic love affairs," so from September 15 until the first of October, the *Theresien-Wiese* on the outskirts of Munich was turned into a fairground. Monstrous barrels of brew, drawn by heavy white horses decked out in silver harnesses and tinkling bells, were hauled across the city and placed at a strategic spot in the park for everyone to enjoy. Whole oxen were roasted on spits over a yawning pit. Throngs of Bavarians arrived to dance, feast, laugh and sing, while royalty and peasantry exchanged partners in the numerous and colorful folk dances.

Not long after came the opera season, to be followed by *Fasching*, a Teutonic form of *Mardi Gras* celebration which once again provided for the mingling of the social classes. All of Munich masqueraded for Shrovetide in a six-day carnival during which the Bavarian capital went mad. Studies ceased. Students took over the town. Lovemaking, wild revelry and a reigning mood of utter abandon lasted until the ushering in of the penitential season of Lent. Then at the sober clang of midnight before Ash Wednesday, reputable citizens put their escapades behind them in order to begin a 40-day period of penance, making atonement for their libertarian deeds.

This carefree and happy existence left a tremendous impression on August. Here, in a world apart, were a people who lived art, understood music and enjoyed as many pleasures as could be garnered from their world.

Although he sent his father weekly detailed reports of his progress, and also turned in to him sketches to be corrected, life seemed sweet, if not always easy, for the student until, once again, the Governor arrived unexpectedly in Munich. He informed August abruptly that he was needed at home and was to begin his apprenticeship in the factories immediately. The earnest young art student had set his heart on at least another two years of schooling. He was stunned at his father's decision which threatened to put an end to all his dreams and plans. August pleaded with him that the two-year course he had taken thus far had been merely an initiation into the six years of advanced training which should now follow. He was just beginning to find his way and, to date, had not reached professional status in any of the many trades and crafts for which he was preparing. It all took time; the process could not be hurried.

Noticing his son's disappointment, Governor Benziger paused. He had come resolved to prevent his enrollment in any further courses; still, he did not want to suppress August's artistic inclinations with a definite and conclusive "No." He decided to solve the problem by driving a shrewd bargain with him. The elder Benziger wanted August to have an art background for the purpose of electing and correcting the material submitted to Benziger Brothers; he had no intention of allowing his prize son to escape into an uncertain dream world of the creative free-lance artist. Adelrich was determined to nip this kind of nonsense in the bud. His son would have to take his chances in a much more difficult environment, strenuous enough to prove a deterrent to his more directly creative aspirations. He could continue his studies with one proviso: that he obtain admission to the school of composition of the Vienna Academy of Fine Arts. Its director, Ritter von Trenkwald, was the most exacting master in Europe. Of the thousand applicants who annually struggled with the entrance examinations, only 30 were deemed worthy of acceptance.

August took up the challenge. His career was at stake. He must win for art's sake or lose everything, only to become a business executive shut up in the cultural bleakness of an Alpine village. In his time of need for psychological support, he sought the advice of Andreas Müller; to him he could unburden his heart. Doubt and fear had gripped him; should he or should he not enter the competition? Andreas Müller proved a pillar of strength at this crucial time. He firmly counseled his pupil to leave at once for

Vienna and to lose not a minute in applying for the entrance materials. He then scanned all the sketches made by August during his time in Munich and aided him in making a wise selection of the drawings most suitable for submission.

Tentative with inner doubt and fear, the young man approached the *Kompositionnschule.* As in a nightmare, the dreaded experience was somehow lived through. He filled out the application forms, took the entrance examinations and left his drawings to be voted on by the jury. Then, with as heavy a heart as he would bear in all his life, he bade good-bye to the fair city of Vienna with its graciousness, beauty and charm to board the Arlberg Express for the return trip to Einsiedeln.

Once back home, the aspiring artist soon abandoned all hope of having succeeded in the contest. He had taken the examinations with men who had already devoted eight, even ten, years to art. To nurture thoughts of being accepted by the Academy under these challenging circumstances was sheer folly. August adopted a realistic attitude, resigning himself to making the best of the present situation. He replaced his father as much as possible, took as lively an interest as he could in the happenings at the Benziger factories. He helped with the printing, worked on the newest lithographic prints and lent a skilled hand with the bookbinding. In addition, he edited the magazine, *Die Alte und Neue Welt,* which went out to some 80,000 subscribers. At night, August studied the compositions submitted by artists under contract to the firm. In his subconscious, he could hear his father repeating over and over: "A good picture speaks every language. Good religious pictures are universal messengers. In order to reach the minds and hearts of men, art must be of the highest quality, must appeal to the soul as well as to the eye."

Gradually, he became anxious for the return of the sketches he had submitted while in Vienna and wrote to a friend requesting that his drawings be mailed to him. By this time, the fall term had begun. The reply from Vienna was to prove a turning point in his life. He tore the letter open, then, without reading it through to the end, rushed with abandon to his father's office. Radiating joy as he handed the envelope to Governor Benziger, he stammered: "Father! Father! Just think of it. I've passed the entrance examinations!" His father grew ashen. "Read me the contents," he said quietly.

Dear Friend:

Whatever is the matter with you? Naturally I am not returning your drawings, for they are held in the studio of Ritter
von Trenkwald. They are to remain here until you arrive.

The Director is much upset by your indifference. Of all the
thousand applicants, you, alone, won the much-coveted
scholarship. A free studio has been reserved for your use.
Until you are forty-five, it is at your disposal. This is your
award—offered you in the name of your patron, Emperor
Franz Josef.

August halted in dismay. He could not believe his eyes as he
saw his father, head bent with grief. Could this be the man who
had commanded armies, who held the destinies of thousands in his
hands, weeping like a child? He listened to his father's words
numbly, scarcely comprehending:

I cannot permit you to become an artist. I will not allow
you to continue with a profession that makes of all who
embrace it needy wretches. You will become like the rest.
Artists spend their lives struggling. Few earn enough to support themselves, let alone a family. I have pinned all my
faith on you. If you defy me, you will die of hunger—*ein
Hungerleiderer.*

I had hoped you would fail . . . that of your own volition
you would see fit to renounce your artistic career. How
strange it is that, even before you were born, I prayed God to
give me a son . . . a son who had *die Kunst.* Never . . . never
did I dream that this would happen to me. I feel as if I were
about to lose you for all time—just as I have come to depend on you to aid me in carrying the burden of this firm.

August was stunned. He had had no notion that things would turn
out this way. Until now, his father had always been the one to
urge him to study and aim for success. He'd tried his best to
please him. He gathered his words together:

Look, Father! There's no use in my staying here any longer.
I need at least two or three more years of basic training before I can prove of any real value to you. Since you feel as
strongly as you do about my becoming an artist, I'm willing
to compromise. Even though I've won this prize I never
dreamed of getting, I promise not to go near the art schools.

But, do give me my chance to study lithography and photography. Let me learn the technical side of the business. Until now, it has always been the artistic side. However, I'm willing to forget all that—if this is the way you want me to be. Then, after I've finished school, I can come back to carry out your wishes.

Adelrich nodded in agreement, and told his son that he was right, that he would have his chance to go to Vienna and resume his interrupted studies for two more years. His funds would be taken care of, but he was never to forget his part of the bargain as "I do not want an artist in the family."

August's arrival in the festive capital of Austria was dampened by the realization that he was barred for all time from the Art Academy. Not once was he able to summon sufficient courage to call on the *Herr Direktor,* and the studio designated for his use by Ritter von Trenkwald remained empty. Putting temptation behind him, he enrolled at once as a student at the K. & K., officially known ad *Die Kaiserlich Königliche Lehr und Versuchsanstalt für Photographie und Reproductionsverfarhen.* This fine institute for research in the field of reproduction was under the personal patronage of Emperor Franz Josef and had become a prominent center for the dissemination of technical knowledge. Austrian paper money was printed here, as well as maps of the Austro-Hungarian Empire. Chemists, inventors and pioneers in the techniques of color photography congregated within the school's walls.

In a letter dated October 10, 1888, August wrote his father:

> I have just started my lessons at the Geographical Institute and the *Kaiser's* printing presses. This Institute is definitely the best in Europe. The most up-to-date equipment, the most modern machinery and the very newest inventions are used here.
>
> I am carefully taking notes of all I learn. I have just started the course in map-making. These are copied by means of heliogravure, which has been revolutionized by the use of galvanoplastics. You need no longer worry about me, dear Father. I haven't very much free time.

Young Benziger threw himself into the task with the same élan he had displayed during his study of music and art. Lithography, printing, photography and publishing—these would be his future fields of endeavor. He soon won prizes in photography and was invited to join an excellent photographic society, one of the best in Europe. In 1889, during his last year of study in Vienna, his name had been added to its roster as the two hundred and first member. His work was exhibited, winning prizes and general praise both for himself and the Vienna Photographical Association. Even at this early date, August felt that photography and engraving would one day be combined, that in time, the process of heliographic engraving would become photoengraving.

Now came more advanced courses in the use of the daguerreotype and the tintype, followed by experiments with glass negatives. Husnick of Vienna had finally invented the dry plate film made of gelatin, and Professor Gros, in charge of the courses in photography, had requested of him a large supply of this substance so that his students at the K. & K. might experiment in producing the first lifesize photograph ever to be made. As subject, a negative of a picture of the Prime Minister was to be enlarged. In hushed excitement, the students and professor worked painstakingly day after day. As it was necessary for the masses of unstable gelatin to be properly dissolved, the process was a touchy one requiring both a precise temperature and an accurately-compounded solution. When the gelatin had set, the crucial moment for the pouring of sensitive silver salts arrived, and they had then to be spread over the huge area of the hoped-for lifesize portrait.

"Work Time" meant nothing to the excited Swiss student, and so he bribed the night watchman to let him remain in the building after closing hours. Step by step, he followed his carefully-made notes. Each minute instruction was studied and then carried out in proper sequence. By dawn, August was ready to pour the critical solution over the gelatinous surface, but suddenly the solemn silence of the dark room was broken into by the sound of deep breathing. The young man could feel hot breath pressing against his neck—and he sensed deep-seated anger. Turning, he saw the outline of Professor Gros and heard him shout: "Wretch! See what you've done. You have ruined one of our most expensive experiments!"

Minutes seemed hours as pupil and professor waited tensely. Then, shaking with indignation, Gros finally summoned the courage to look at the sensitive mass and turned pale with relief. In a barely audible whisper, he muttered: "Benziger, you're a genius. You're a real credit to this Institute. I, myself, could not have done as well. Thanks . . . thanks, my boy. The experiment is a tremendous success."

By this time, August had mastered lithography and the new three-color plate process called chromolithography. He had also worked in Einsiedeln with the cumbersome 28-stone method of reproduction, which was almost prohibitive in cost. Finally, the eight-color plate method was imported from France by Governor Benziger and his son was fascinated by it, but not many were able to understand it as thoroughly as he, as it involved complicated chemical research.

In Vienna, the students were schooled in the use of all available tools of their trade. Crayons, *touche,* scrapers, needles, blades and brushes all had to be handled in an expert and professional manner. During class and work hours, August avoided wasting time like many of his lighthearted Viennese classmates who had come to the Institute to learn printing but preferred their fun. This was inevitably a fact of which the professors took note. Even then, during his student days, as throughout the rest of his life, he had a remarkable way of separating work from recreation, although he was by no means as naïve or inexperienced in fun-making as his mentors believed.

Vienna, in the Gay Nineties, was no less than fabulous, especially when spring fever was in the air. The populace danced in the parks bordering the Danube, while the élite held elaborate balls. Sundays were leisurely and well-utilized by such a skilled equestrian as August, who never had any difficulty in finding a group of lovely young ladies to escort. The nobility, who owned the finest stables and prided themselves on their spirited horses, liked to invite the handsome Swiss student to join their riding parties. Sometimes it might be just a small outing through the *Prater,* a five-mile wooded trail that skirted the Danube, that was planned, or it might be a weekend at a shooting lodge, or a hunting party at a country castle, as the outskirts of Vienna were honeycombed with magnificent properties where there was revelry and feasting.

Sometimes in the heart of Vienna, or even in the country near Pressbaum, riders would stop in respectful awe for the Imperial equipage to pass. Most often the bearded, genial ruler in the open carriage would bow and smile, and the riders become elated at having caught this fleeting glimpse of their Emperor who seemed to be the heart and soul of Vienna.

Born flirts, the Viennese were past masters at the subtle art of lovemaking. To one raised as August had been, this ambience provided a new experience. At least a dozen *Fräuleins* refused to accept a simple "no," and did all in their power to ensnare the handsome, mustachioed Swiss student in a madcap *amour*. They wanted gaiety, fun, the pulsating excitement of being caught up in a rapturous love affair. They sought love for love's sake, asking nothing in return except to be the apple of some youth's eye just for a little while. This light-hearted promiscuity shocked August at first, although to him, as an artist, there was nothing more beautiful than a handsome woman. Still, he kept his distance and refrained from joining his friends and classmates in their revelry, aware that lovemaking exacted its toll, held its pitfalls and might lead to serious consequences.

Eventually, however, he too was caught by the contagious spirit of the Viennese who sought pleasure wherever it could be found.

The palette of pleasure, he learned, could be many-hued. It was at this time in his life that he met the lovely, sad-eyed Empress Elisabeth at a ball and spoke with her about her much-loved cousin, Ludwig II of Bavaria, of whose visit to *Villa Gutenberg* all of the Benzigers had loving memories and whose death in tragic circumstances they mourned. It was at this time, too, that August became the mysterious Prince Charming at the masked ball presided over by the Bürgermeister and his charming, if quite naïve, daughter, Mitzi. It was a lustrous time in his life, and still held unexpected incidents in store in which both joy and tragedy would blend.

During Shrovetide and at various receptions, August had met the charming Baroness Vetsera and her two lovely daughters. The Baroness's husband, it was buzzed about in intimate circles, had been designedly sent by the Emperor on a long and hazardous mission to far-off India, and the incipient *cause cèlébre* developed into a full-blown scandal.

From the moment August had been introduced to Baroness Vetsera, he had been intrigued by her vivacious daughter, Marie. Though the girl was only 18, she had been seen by many as the most outstanding belle at the *Faschingsball;* August kept recalling her face. Now was his first opportunity to enjoy a *tête-à-tête* with the fascinating young Baroness. When not dancing with Mitzi, the Burgermeister's daughter who was his hostess, the young Swiss

Prince Charming of the night would slip off to catch this lovely newfound creature in his arms and waltz her away. The artist he was could not keep his eyes off her flawless ivory complexion; her eyes seemed filled with star-slivers; her rich, long brown hair was velvet. He could not quite make up his mind whether Marie Vetsera reminded him of an Irish colleen or a Greek goddess. As they danced, his petite partner gave voice to her secret hope: "Do you think it possible that the Crown Prince will come to the ball?" She had heard so much about the heir to the Hapsburg throne from her mother that he had already become her idol. August laughed at the young girl's eagerness. He told her that she was like all the rest of the Austrians, and that there was not a woman in the Empire who had failed to be attracted to Rudolf von Hapsburg. He was the toast of the whole realm, but, August honestly told his dancing partner, he hoped that for his own sake the Crown Prince would not appear, as she was the one person whom he wished to see again. He hoped they would meet often.

Crown Prince Rudolf had been married seven years earlier to a member of the Belgian royal family. This purely political alliance had resulted in great unhappiness, as Rudolf's wife was madly jealous of his attentions to other women and acutely aware of the measure in which they were attracted to him. The royal couple had been estranged for several years. While the prince had a brilliant mind and handsome physique, he had very simple tastes and longed for privacy and a measure of solitude. Court functions were, generally, not to his liking. During August's brief interlude in Vienna, he had often met Rudolf. By coincidence, they happened to have a *Stammtisch* at the same coffeehouse, and the heir to the Imperial throne enjoyed sipping his brew with the foreign art student.

As August recently had been swept off his feet by his first dance with the diminutive young Baroness Vetsera and had begged the popular lady to save her last few dances for him, he set off eagerly to claim his partner. When, however, he glimpsed Marie Vetsera waltzing away in the arms of her enchanted Prince Rudolf, he knew that he was the loser in this quest. As a result of his initial encounter with Marie, the Crown Prince felt just as had the Swiss artist a few hours earlier. This girl, approaching womanhood, had bewitched them both with her pristine simplicity, her charm and her intoxicating beauty. Neither of the men fully understood what had taken place that fateful night. Each of the romantic

suitors had fallen under her spell and both had plunged precipi-
tously in love with the same infatuating Lorelei: the tragedy of
Mayerling had begun.

Invitations to the Hofburg festivals provided new thrills each
time they were accepted, especially as Emperor Franz Josef presided at the balls. Once inside the imperial palace of Schönbrunn,
August wondered if this fabulous pageantry was real or make-believe. There were nobles in brilliant uniforms, stunning ladies of
royal lineage aglitter with the sparkle of precious jewels, their
handsome evening gowns trailing on the marble or parquet floors.
This must be a fairy tale come true, embellished with all the romance of deep bowing, the clicking of heels, the kissing of hands,
the low curtsies of ladies scented with exotic perfumes. In the
background, the playful tinkle of fountains blended with the soft
refrains of musical airs. The lights of thousands of candles blazed
from the crystal chandeliers, and guests paid little heed to the hot
wax that occasionally dripped onto impeccable uniforms or gowns
with low-cut décolletage. The important thing was to be invited, to
be able to participate in the laughter and fun within these enchanted walls!

Countess Lela von Fesztetics, a favorite at court, was present.
She was also a family friend. August had frequently spent Sundays at her *Schloss* outside of Vienna, and she had insisted that the
young Swiss escort her to one of these balls, as her husband was
out of town and she could not go alone. Once arrived at the gala,
they had just had their first dance when an equerry of the imperial
household bowed low in their presence. August, thinking he was
addressing Countess Lela, paid little attention. Young Benziger,
however, heard that *he* was wanted. Questions were never asked in
royal palaces, and, though he had no notion by whom or for what
purpose he was being sought, he promptly excused himself and
followed the equerry through winding corridors. Moving along, he
recalled that he had noticed a mischievous twinkle in the eyes of
Countess Lela as he had taken his leave of her, kissing her hand as
was quite the proper thing to do when separating from one's partner. Then, August was caught up short when he noticed that his
guide had come to a halt outside of what seemed to be a conservatory. Two pages in pale blue uniforms bowed low, then opened the
glass doors. He was greeted by a nobleman who said solemnly:
"Your Royal Highness, Herr Benziger is here."

August found himself in the presence of a reclining woman whose elegance left him breathless. With languid grace, his queenly companion held out a richly jeweled hand, and the young man bent low to kiss it. She was surrounded by exotic flowers and subtle music. The lady was apparently a foreigner and had a strange, unfamiliar accent. *"Mein Herr,"* she said, "will you dance with me?" Never before had he seen anyone as ravishingly beautiful as she. As he was certain that an error in identity had been made, he sought to explain who he was. The noblewoman left no uncertainty in his mind. "Apparently you do not recall me," she said. "I was disguised in a costume of Queen Elizabeth at the *Faschingball.*" August chuckled: "Were you the young lady who danced with me so often the night we all masqueraded?" "Yes," she replied. "To me you were another Walter Raleigh. You made a perfect nobleman, dancing so exquisitely that I couldn't forget you. I have been haunted by your memory, and I want you to come with me to Petrograd; you must come to the Czar's court. There every ballerina will fall in love with you as you dance like a professional. No one can make me believe that you learned the art of waltzing here in Vienna!"

The next thing August knew, he was escorting this overwhelming lady through the countless corridors. Suddenly, her pungent oriental perfume seemed familiar; its fragrance brought back provocative memories. This was the temptress who had tried energetically to entice him into joining her once before—when he had been at a masked ball at the *von Fesztetics Schloss.* She was the glamorous lady of Russian background. At that time, it had been only with the greatest difficulty that he had succeeded in eluding her wiles. This time, loose ends came together in his mind. Seditious little Countess von Fesztetics had fashioned this situation. Instinct warned him that this woman meant trouble, and he earnestly wished that he had had some previous inkling of the plot so that he could have avoided coming to the Imperial Palace.

When they reached the ballroom, the lady with the alabaster skin, raven-black hair and smiling eyes laughed with satisfaction. "Now at long last, I can have you all to myself! I can dance with you! Just with you!" Before he knew it, this wispy something was floating through the air light as a feather, agile as a butterfly. Carried away by the music, they were both unmindful of anything but each other. All of a sudden, August realized that they were dancing all alone; everyone else had stepped back from the huge ballroom floor. Dismayed, he whispered: *"Hoheit*, we must stop. Everyone is watching us. Why, even the Emperor is smiling. This will never do!" Laughing, his partner tossed her head of black curls: the diamonds of her tiara sparkled like moonlight on water. "Nonsense," she said, "continue to dance. I have longed for a moment like this. It is high time that the smug Hapsburgs know that we, the Russians, can also dance. We can outdo them at their own waltz. They feel that they are the only ones who possess magic toes. Let us show them how wrong they are!"

August needed no second invitation. When the music finally stopped and the waltz came to an end, the dancers were greeted with wild applause. Even the Emperor joined in the congratulations.

"Lead me, my charming cavalier, to the Emperor!" his partner said. The starry-eyed *danseuse* touched her fingertips to his white-gloved hands, and he held her arm as they advanced to the throne, the crowd of admirers giving way to the handsome couple. August bowed low, very low, as though it were an everyday occurrence for him to greet a reigning Hapsburg; simultaneously, the princess made her deep curtsy. Once again there erupted enthusiastic applause. Then, August led his partner back to the conservatory. Liveried waiters brought the couple champagne and offered long-stemmed glasses. The lively lady drank a toast to her escort, to their triumph.

When the evening finally came to an end, August escorted the blazing Russian to her coach. Two ebony stallions harnessed in silver were drawing the carriage that bore the Czar's coat of arms. She whispered a few words to her escort, then entered and seated herself. August acted as though he had not understood what she had said, and merely bent low, kissed her hand again, and backed away. A lackey holding his silk hat and evening cape, stood at attention. A gentleman in waiting took these things, then asked: "You are escorting Her Imperial Highness home?" His eyebrows were raised quizzically. All eyes became fixed on this woman whose conduct seemed less than becoming. Her smile faded; her crimson lips tightened. There was a deadly silence, an interminable wait as the liveried footmen and coachmen took their places. The door was closed. When the proud lady leaned out of her carriage window, her glance reproached August for being less than gallant. Slowly the horses moved away, there was a faintly fluttering handkerchief in the night and then she was gone. August exhaled as he mopped his brow and beads of perspiration surfaced. Never had he seen anyone or anything as entrancing as this woman, or so provocative.

Only once again was he to glimpse this will-o'-the-wisp. One day he happened to be hurrying along a narrow cobblestone alley in the heart of the "old city," which was filled with rushing humanity at the noon hour when August was returning from St. Stephan's Cathedral. Under his arm was a collection of sketchbooks since he had visited the cathedral for the purpose of correcting a few etchings. The sudden clatter of hooves on that restricted thoroughfare made him spring back as there would not have been enough room for both him and the carriage. As he looked up, a familiar sight sprang before his eyes and he recognized instantly the handsome equipage, the jet-black horses, the well-fed footmen. As though by some prearranged signal, the coachman reined in the horses. As the carriage door opened, August's lady of mystery exclaimed: "Ah, *mon cher ami!* This time I will not let you escape so easily. We have searched the whole town to find you. Where have you hidden yourself?"

August smiled in disbelief. "*Hoheit*, nothing would give me greater pleasure than to join you—but you have surely mistaken my identity. You take me to be some Bohemian nobleman. I am only a simple Swiss. I came here to study. I'm just a poor student, *sans* uniform, *sans* title, *sans* anything. You, as sister of the Czar of Russia, can have nothing in common with an ordinary person like me!" The words were spoken with such sincerity, such feeling that the lady's eyes filled. "I beg you to reconsider," she replied. "You are the first person ever to have turned down my whim. You do not know what this means to me." August stood with one foot inside the richly-upholstered vehicle, bowed, placed his lips on her hand, then quickly backed away.

In a moment, it was all over. The door had closed, the clatter of hooves grew fainter. The puzzled student resumed his way down the narrow alley as a strange mood of uneasiness came over him. Just ahead, a young boy was in the process of placing a bouquet of flowers at a votive shrine where a small vigil light was burning at the feet of the Madonna. August caught himself murmuring a little prayer. As if by magic, he was suddenly transported back to Einsiedeln. He could see his mother sitting by her bedroom window, gently fingering her Rosary, and he felt that it was her prayer which had once again saved him from yielding to temptation.

It was time to stop by his favorite coffeehouse which was located in the center of town and there, at his own marble-topped table, he sipped his *Mokka*. He liked his black brew to be served *Schwarz mit Obers* which, in the quaint dialect of Vienna, simply meant black with whipped cream. An adjoining table had been marked by a brass plate indicating that it, too, was a reserved *Stammtisch*. The coffeehouse also happened to be the favorite of Rudolf von Hapsburg, and almost daily he dropped in, often joining August and his classmates. The 29-year-old heir to the throne was a quiet, modest person, but also extremely democratic and very much at ease with these companions. Although he was brilliant of mind and handsomer than most men, his eyes were sad, and he was shy with strangers.

When alone, August and the prince would often talk about Rudolf's cousin, Ludwig II. Like the King of Bavaria, his kinsman felt that the changing times needed reform in government, and he was acutely aware of the fact that no one could be sure about the political future. His father, the Emperor, might manage to hold together the much-divided Empire, but what would happen later to the Austro-Hungarian people? Could a decadent nobility prevent a revolution? Faint strains of unrest could already be heard. The Swiss! Ah, yes, the Swiss had real democracy. Ludwig of Bavaria, while visiting there, had seen the handwriting on the wall, and had returned home to secure equal rights for all.

On many other occasions, Rudolf spoke to August of the enchanting Marie Vetsera. Had they not both been taken captive by her loveliness on the same night? Rudolf's current liaison with her was no longer a secret; in fact, the court could speak of little else. The romantic attachment was the leading subject of conversation, not only in Vienna, but all the way to Budapest.

Long before Rudolf had met the Baroness, he had contemplated renouncing his claim to the throne. He and his father did not see eye-to-eye on many subjects and, now that he had fallen in love with Marie Vetsera, it was rumored that, if the Crown Prince could, he would divorce his unpleasant wife and marry the captivating Marie. The Emperor had always been willing to close an eye to any alliance. Mistresses? They were to be had by the dozen. No one took the trouble to condemn a custom which had been widely-accepted for centuries; in his view, it was a lesser evil than divorce. Beside, divorce in so Catholic a country as his was out of the question.

August knew that Rudolf was suffering; pain was clearly written on his face. Here was a man of great ideals, a lover of freedom and of the out-of-doors who was, at the same time, a non-conformist according to the standards set by tradition for royalty. August also knew that this evening the Crown Prince was to participate in a family farewell dinner, as the newspapers had carried a list of the Imperial engagements. The prince's parents were to leave Vienna in a few days, and he was to be present at the gathering, together with his wife, Princess Stephanie, although everyone was aware that they lived in different sections of the city and that the marriage had been a failure.

On this afternoon of January 29, 1889, Rudolf dropped in and joined August at his *Stammtisch*. He looked very tired and spoke of needing a rest. He was also extremely worried. Looking handsomer than ever in his gray-green Tyrolean jacket, ornamented with carved horn buttons, he told his Swiss friend that he had given orders that the Royal Hunting Lodge at Meyerling was to be prepared, as the weather was excellent for the chase. They both left the *Kaffeehaus* at the same time, August to return to his classes, the heir to the throne to his carriage. As he wanted to avoid the public view, he asked August to walk to the corner with him since it was there that his horses and coachman were waiting. They bowed low, bid the customary farewell, and parted.

August had one distinct impression: Crown Prince Rudolf was very upset. He pondered about how it would be possible for him to get to Mayerling, some 30 kilometers distant and be back in time for the Imperial dinner, and concluded that one person would not be there. Apparently the Crown Prince preferred the solitude of the Hunting Lodge to court festivities and farewell preparations.

August, having gone a few paces, was about to cross the street when he heard a carriage come around the corner, stepped back to make way for the horses and suddenly recognized Marie Vetsera seated inside. She was alone. The young Baroness nodded graciously. Of all the girls he had ever met, this one was certainly the loveliest and the most unsophisticated.

The following evening, he went to dinner at the home of a prominent lawyer about whom it was known in confidential circles that he was the Emperor's most trusted adviser. Earlier in the day, August had wondered whether the hunting at Mayerling had been good. It should have been, since the weather was cool and brisk. No need to puzzle whether Marie Vetsera had joined her Rudolf; that was a foregone conclusion. During the course of the evening, the conversation turned, as it inevitably did in all Viennese drawing rooms, to the heir to the throne. August's deepest sympathies lay with the Crown Prince. He also felt a bond of compassion for Marie Vetsera, whom he had known as a very modest, timid but brilliant person. She certainly was different from the many brazen Viennese coquettes who made a game of stealing kisses from any nobleman who came along.

Before the dinner had ended, a courier from the imperial palace requested to see the host, who left the table, returned hurriedly and explained that he would be absent for quite a while: the Emperor wished to see him at once; he hoped the news was not bad.

August was not to meet this host again for over a year, and then in far-off Paris. No sooner had the head of the house left than the Extra editions of the paper were being hawked in the streets of Vienna. Shattering headlines appeared on all of them. Crown Prince Rudolf had been murdered that very day by his paramour!

The whole pathetic truth finally came to light and a shocked, saddened nation learned of the great sorrow that had befallen the imperial family. Crown Prince Rudolf was, indeed, dead. No one could or would believe that he had taken his own life. The young heir had gone to Mayerling to keep a love tryst, a double-suicide pact. He and Marie Vetsera had plotted to die together!

On the morning of January 30, attempts to rouse His Imperial Highness had been made by the valet. The huntsmen were ready, the weather was perfect. There had been no answer to the heavy knocks on the chamber door and, on forcing entry into the Crown Prince's bedroom, the household had found Rudolf fully-dressed, hunting boots on, slumped over the foot of his bed on which, laid out in all her youthful glory, was the girl he loved. She, too, was dead. Her luxuriant brown hair was loose, and in her hands she held a fresh red rose. The Crown Prince had shot her, then used a second bullet to end his own hopelessly-tragic life.

August had remained dreadfully perplexed about the suicide pact, and well might he be; the Mayerling tragedy had rocked the entire Austro-Hungarian Empire. There was something about the tales circulating, the newspaper reports, that did not ring true. He had known Rudolf von Hapsburg and he had also known Marie Vetsera, and he could not understand how two people so radiantly in love as they would seek to end their lives. Rudolf usually displayed such clear-headedness in his thinking that surely something dire and unexpected must have taken place to change his outlook radically. August knew that he had been upset on the day they had met at the coffeehouse. He also knew that Rudolf was heir to the throne that was the most colorful in all of Europe. The Emperor was looked on with affection by his people, and especially by the Austrians, who were passionately fond of Franz Josef. He was not only head of the realm but to each he was a personal friend, a paternal ruler they admired and to whom they looked up. Now the only heir, his anticipated successor, was dead.

It was to be a year later when August learned the details of the tragic story. His host on that fateful night, the Emperor's legal adviser, was in Paris, and the young Swiss had gone there to join his father. At dinner this gentleman had divulged in utter confidence the secret knowledge that had become his, as he knew that August had mourned Rudolf and that he had admired Marie Vetsera very much. He himself had been sworn to secrecy when, on that fateful night, he had been called to give advice to a brokenhearted monarch.

Crown Prince Rudolf, he said, had previously approached his father, pleading for permission to renounce all claims to the throne. He told Emperor Franz Josef that he intended to seek an annulment of his marriage to Princess Stephanie, and that he planned to marry Baroness Marie Vetsera whom he loved passionately. The Emperor had become enraged and refused to listen to his son. After several repeated scenes on this subject, spread out over a period of time, Prince Rudolf had defiantly stated that he was determined to overrule all parental objections. He told his mother and father that he had waited long enough, that he was in love, that he would take the required steps in Rome to seek an annulment of his marriage— then he would renounce his right to succession and leave his country forever. But . . . he would . . . marry . . . the girl he loved . . . he would marry Marie Vetsera!

The very day a sad, brokenhearted father was to be given a farewell dinner, he had been forced to reveal the truth to Rudolf. Never would he be able to approve of his son's designs. Rudolf would never be able to marry Marie. He would gladly give his royal consent to any plan that might lead to his son's happiness, and Rudolf could marry whomever else he wished, once he had an annulment—but . . . never, never Marie.

Marie Vetsera was his half-sister.

CHAPTER 6

Interludes
(1889-1890)

After this time of tension and soul-searching, August yearned for a period of quiet and calm, but not of inactivity. An unexpected opportunity for just what he needed presented itself. In recognition of his father's many services, the French government wished to honor Adelrich and did so by naming him Vice-President and member of the jury of the Paris World's Fair of 1889. France also officially rewarded his distinguished service by presenting him with the coveted *Légion d'Honneur*. Considered to be one of Europe's most progressive publishers, he had justified this reputation by modernizing his factories and importing from America its latest inventions. His Parisian associates were delighted, and invited him to be their houseguest; at the home of Charles Lorrilleux, he was almost as much at home as if he had been back at Einsiedeln.

Once in Paris, Adelrich realized the enormity of the task now confronting him; he had the challenging assignment of sorting, classifying and selecting the suitable books, pictures and engravings for display at the Fair. His pavilion was dedicated to printing and the field was all-encompassing, demanding many more decisions than he could possibly reach in the brief time left at his disposal. Feeling inadequately suited to judge the true merits of the diversified material submitted and to allocate the important prizes to be awarded, and also being a man of integrity, he admitted that August was far more qualified than he to act in the role of judge.

Soon a telegram reached his son in Vienna. He was to assist his father in judging the entries, then return to Austria afterwards to resume his studies. Now August would have full opportunity to show whether his years of working in design, lithography and photography had been worthwhile. There followed wonderful weeks which the two men spent together. Daily they worked under the shadow of the Eiffel Tower which had been erected to prove to all who visited the World's Fair that a turning point in progress had been reached. Science and mechanics had come to stay.

The Fairgrounds were spacious. The *Palais des Arts Liberaux* housed the exhibits of printed material, photography and bookbinding where the Benzigers, father and son, worked all day long. Not until the builders and carpenters had left at night did the two take the *fiacre* to the Lorilleux home. Laden with books, pictures and notes, they again worked steadily until two o'clock each morning. When the labor of cataloguing and judging had finally ended, Governor Benziger left at once for Switzerland, and the time had also come for August to return to his classes in Vienna. His new Parisian friends protested vigorously that it was wrong to leave before the opening of the Fair and insisted that he stay on a while longer. The elder Benziger realized that in doing so there was a valuable opportunity for his son to meet his French business *confréres*. All were publishers of high-standing, men of vital importance such as Lorilleux, Didot and Hachette. As nothing in August's upbringing was ever left to chance, a carefully-combed list of 150 prominent Parisians he should meet arrived. Also detailed were interesting places for the student to visit. Every week, the dutiful son was required to mail his father a report of events that had transpired, but he was firmly warned not to visit wealthy friends over weekends. Attractive daughters were then quite fatal. August would do much better to fill his mind and sketchbooks with useful data, as silly flirtations were a waste of time.

Prominent men were to be visited during the working week and, under no conditions, was business ever to be discussed before a meal had been consumed. The French required at least one or two glasses of wine before the shrewd Gallic tongue was loosed. When the black coffee was being served, a few well-pointed questions might then be asked.

Adelrich also insisted that Sundays should, by all means, be devoted to work. First, attendance at early Mass—then, sketchbook in hand, a study of church edifices and worshippers should be made. Not a moment of his stay in the French capital was to be wasted. August, consequently, recorded everything he had seen. He sketched busily, and also sent home to Einsiedeln the names of significant photographers, engravers, publishers, libraries and religious goods stores, together with a summary of his impressions of them.

In Tours, he had made a visit to the House of Mame which he considered to be, by far, the most outstanding Catholic publisher in France. He also was privileged to have dinner with Monsieur Marinoni, owner of the *Petit Journal,* which boasted over 360,000 subscribers. The President of France had personally told the Swiss student one evening that Marinoni, who also owned *Figaro,* was the greatest opinion former in France.

August learned that the Didots had a 28-year-old son who operated their Paris bookstore, and that another son, 24, was in charge of the paper factory and bookbindery outside of town. One of their sisters, an invalid, prayed for August's soul every day, she said! Didot and his associates had enormous annual incomes, young Benziger learned, and he came away with the impression that their business was far too large, and that entirely too much money was being made!

While he filled his sketchbooks and notebooks, no one knew better than he how to combine business with pleasure. On Sundays he would visit the St. Cloud home of the famed composer, Charles Gounod, and there, spellbound, hear the master play. Here he also met the dramatist and novelist, Alexandre Dumas, *fils,* as well as other outstanding artists and writers of the day.

As he had always admired the draftsman, William Bouguereau, August enrolled in classes at the *Académie Julien* in the Faubourg Saint Denis. Bouguereau's forte lay in the creation of unsurpassed flesh tints and massive paintings of nudes which were exquisitely lifelike. The periods of instruction under the tutelage of this master filled the student with great respect, and an inspired and close friendship developed between them. Bouguereau delighted in the accomplishment of each of his pupils and, as August proved to be far more gifted than most, after barely six weeks of attendance, the master encouraged him to take the composition test. This was the most grueling competition held during the term; among the 150 competitors, August succeeded in placing fifth highest in the group. Once again, therefore, Governor Benziger was seized with anxiety for his son's future. On learning that August had won still more honors in painting, he immediately sought some legitimate excuse to remove him from Paris at the earliest possible moment.

Along with painting and music, a third in the list of August's God-given talents was expert horsemanship. All his life he had been able to do with any mount whatever he liked. Although his father did not realize the fact, August's artistic career was not the only stumbling block to Governor Benziger's plans for a successor to his printing and publishing dynasty. The issue had not yet been forced, but there was ever the possibility that August might one day decide to make a lifetime career of serving as an officer in the Swiss Army.

Switzerland observed a strict program of compulsory military service. The only acceptable excuse preventing one from performing this inevitable stint in the army was residence in a foreign country. If August should return to Einsiedeln, local draft officials would surely call him up for duty at once. As the lesser of two evils, the Governor decided that the time had come for this son to fulfill his three months of required military training. Yet again, August packed his bags to return home. In order to determine his aptitude as a horseman, a three-weeks' course in the Mounted Scouts of the Zurich Military School came first on the agenda. After passing these rigorous entrance examinations, he was then declared a fit and proper candidate to attend the Officers' Cavalry School. In May of 1890, his name was entered on the advanced school's roster of recruits under the leadership of Colonel Willie. The next few months were to prove extremely difficult since, as an artist and student of the arts, he had been able to find little time for sport or exercise. The physical fitness of the other 18-year-olds was in marked contrast to that of this urbane, softened man of 23.

Yet August, like every Swiss, looked on preparedness as the keystone of Swiss freedom. The neighboring nations were forever at each other's throats and, among them, needless wars throughout the centuries had retarded progress. Although the Swiss hated war violently, they prided themselves on being able to arm every male literally at a moment's notice. Every citizen from the age of 18 to 65 kept his uniform, arms and vital defense equipment in his own home. The Swiss house was the nation's arsenal of democracy as the government could trust every able-bodied voter with arms; the mere ringing of the *tocsin* mustered city and countryside.

Though the next few months were to be spent close to his home, August might very well have been in training at the opposite end of Europe. A series of letters sent to his father gave inklings about daily affairs. For one thing, the candidate ran out of money.

An itemized statement received by Governor Benziger bore mute testimony to the fact that August had certainly not let grass grow under his feet; he had worn out two pairs of riding breeches, his saddle had been patched, two pairs of riding boots had each been resoled three times. He had also acquired a new pair of boots, and bought two spurs at five Swiss francs each. For a fastidious young man with an international reputation, the art student would appear to have entered into the spirit of the war games with exceptional vigor. Further, he sent home a note warning that the horse he would be required to buy would be expensive; he was to contribute 1,500 Swiss francs, and the sale was to be held that week. He would have preferred a smaller, less-expensive mount; however, his superior officer, knowing him to be well-to-do, felt that he could afford the cost of the black mare. The army would donate the balance of the money due. Then, over a period of 10 years, the horse would be at the disposal of the army whenever needed, even though remaining in the custody of its owner.

At this time, August had written home a very serious letter criticizing the conduct of some of the officers at the Cavalry School. The Swiss colonels in charge had received their training in Berlin and carried with them the spirit of brutality common to the Prussian army, but completely foreign to the military forces of a democracy. August had found it necessary to report that some men had been horsewhipped outrageously, while others were forced to such indignities as crawling on all fours in imitation of a horse.

Even trivial offenses met with severe punishment. One poor soldier had been forced to swallow a quart of vile liquid which nauseated him for days. Another, a strapping big peasant, suffered agonies from an acute abscess caused by his saddle and was not permitted to report his illness. Instead, Colonel Bachoven reprimanded the burly farmer for straddling his horse in such poor form as to cause the wound. Curtly, the colonel commanded this unfortunate man to dismount. Two other recruits were ordered to yank down his breeches and flog the victim with riding whips. Weber of Wadenswil, son of a noted brewer, who was at that time engaged to the daughter of President Hauser, had been one of those forced to administer the lashing. Ever-increasing rumbles of protest were heard throughout the ranks, but few of the men dared to air their grievances to those in authority as they feared harsh disciplinary action by way of retaliation. August, however, could not be intimidated. He was unafraid of the possible consequences of exposing these evils, and wrote to Governor Benziger, suggesting that the president of Switzerland investigate conditions at the Cavalry School at once. If President Hauser were to learn of these abuses, they would surely come to an end.

In July, these heavily-equipped recruits were transferred to the High Alps for maneuvers. One night the alarm sounded and instantly the troops became ready for attack. Amor, August's black mare, was held by his orderly. Colonel Bachoven, making one final inspection of men and equipment, shouted: "Benziger . . . stable police." August dismounted at once in order to pacify his restless horse, as there was nothing this mare loved better than the smell of gunpowder and the roar of battle. Then he set about the heavy task of cleaning out the stables, hauling manure, filling mangers with fresh hay, measuring rations of oats, providing water for the stalls.

The louder the gunfire, the noisier, more impatient Amor grew. In the dimly-lighted stable, a familiar voice was heard. It was that of the cavalry blacksmith, a jolly Swiss who had once volunteered in the American army and had saved sufficient money to return to his native soil. Having grown homesick for army life, he had joined the Swiss cavalry and resumed his work as blacksmith. Forthright and outspoken, he had questioned the motivation of Colonel Bachoven in leaving such an accomplished man on stable police duty. He urged August to remount Amor and be off before the animal, eager for action, kicked out the stall walls and injured herself. August demurred, declaring that he would never dare to defy the colonel's orders. "In that case," the blacksmith declared, "I'll take your horse for a run." As the smith was a soldier and August only a recruit, the smith's word outranked his and August had to comply, but he warned that the horse "could be pretty mean at times." The smith felt assured of his own prowess and tore off into the dark.

Dawn broke. In the eerie morning twilight, a bedraggled soldier limped back to the stables, clinging to a sorry-looking horse. Amor was an appalling tangle of sweat and blood, and three of her shoes were missing. The blacksmith almost wept. He had had a nightmare ride on a horse that dashed headlong into the jaws of death where 4,000 sharpshooters were firing real bullets. Further, he felt that he was done for militarily and would be thrown out of the army as soon as Bachoven discovered the identity of the man who had been in that saddle. August's heart went out to the poor fellow, and he agreed to keep his mouth shut.

When the soldiers returned from the *Allemein,* there was excited talk on all sides; a phantom horse had terrified the troops. August had not long to wait for repercussions. He was immediately summoned to Headquarters, where a grim-faced row of officers faced him. Colonel Bachoven shouted furiously: "Benziger, you disobeyed orders. You were riding across the *Allemein.* I know your horse!" As August denied the accusation, he was called a "first-rate liar" by his commanding officer, who then ordered four soldiers to come forward and handcuff the insubordinate man, take him to the *cachot* (the place of incarceration) and put him on a regimen of bread and water and of solitary confinement in order to teach him honesty. August was led to a dungeon lacking both light and fresh air, where the stench was almost unendurable.

Within a short interval, the astonishing news of August's arrest had spread throughout the barracks, and his companions-in-arms promptly set about bribing the jailer for a chance to visit the prisoner. It was not long before bread and water were forgotten penalties; August soon found himself feasting on wine, sausage, fruit, cheese and other delicacies smuggled in by his friends. Nothing before had caused such a sensation in the ranks as did this incident, yet fear of Colonel Bachoven was so great that plans were laid only under the cover of secrecy. On August's second day in prison, several of the ringleaders brought as choice contraband a candle, pen, ink and paper. They insisted that the accused immediately write the facts to his father and reveal the entire truth. Once the letter had been completed, it was conveyed secretly into the dark and dispatched to Einsiedeln. Four days later, August was again led before Colonel Bachoven, and again accused of insubordination. When he once more denied having ridden on the *Allemein,* Bachoven was infuriated, yet, not daring to order the prisoner flogged, he pointed to him and said in a scathing voice: "To the *cachot* until he confesses."

Great was the consternation of the Benziger family on learning that their son was not only in jail but was also being held in solitary confinement. Within a matter of hours, the head of the house was on his way to the Swiss capital. Upon arrival in Berne, he wasted no time in marching straight into the offices of the President of the Republic, handing Mr. Hauser the incredible story as revealed in August's several letters, and demanding an immediate investigation. The perpetration of such outrages against his own son, as well as the sons of other honest citizens, positively had to cease. The case was to be given nationwide publicity.

Six days spent in a dungeon seemed interminable to the sensitive Swiss artist. Six days of being treated like the worst kind of criminal had left their mark on one who, until then, had believed in the justice of his leaders. On the night of the sixth day of his incarceration, the jailer suddenly unlocked August's cell. As the sound of the clinking keys disappeared into the distance, he learned that he was, at last, a free man, at liberty to come and go as he pleased. No explanation for his unexpected release was given!

The Swiss President at once sent for Colonel Willie, who was in charge of the Military School, and summoned the members of the Colonel's staff into conference. The officers hotly denied that recruits had been punished and that there had been any abuses, and they swore to a man that the report turned in by Benziger was false. At this unexpected turn of events, Governor Benziger quietly sought the aid of a prominent attorney; in his official capacity as Senator of his Canton, he *would* reach to the bottom of this scandal. The fear of reprisal was such that only after the soldiers had returned safely to their homes following their period of duty was the full truth revealed. President Hauser heard the unpleasant facts from his own son-in-law. Weber, the soldier who had been forced to whip an ill recruit, now felt secure. The whole ugly story came to light.

When the three months of military training ended, there were solemn commencement exercises presided over by Colonel Willie, Chief of Instructors. When August's turn came to march up to his commander, his rating was read aloud: "Lazy. Stupid. Not at all fit for military life." Further, this young recruit discovered that he had been given the grade of 4-, the lowest of all possible scores. Since these marks and ratings were entered into the record book for all time, and had to be turned in annually to the Military Commission, the situation was a serious one for him. Voluminous correspondence now ensued between Governor Benziger and Colonel Willie. Eventually things were hushed but, although the Army refused to affirm that its officers had been either brutal or unjust, the colonel saw fit to resign.

Throughout Canton Schwyz, where August was well known, it was now imperative for him to redeem his honor, so he tossed his gauntlet into the ring by reenlisting in the army. Although he would once again start at the beginning of the course, and the rigors of basic training would have to be endured, nothing mattered to him except proving how wrong Colonel Bachoven had been.

From the moment he reenlisted, each officer seemed to try his utmost to demoralize August. He became everyone's errand boy, was the much-used doormat trampled upon by everyone. His long hours at "stable police" or "kitchen police" duty seemed endless. But then, as in the past, he became the idol of the younger recruits since they saw that he was a masterly horseman who rode as superbly as his commanding officers. No one could find the slightest fault with his military appearance or his performance of duty. In the end, he would stand at attention before the assembled troops and hear his commanding officer declare "It is my duty to inform you that you have won the highest honors. I shall see to it that our Government in Berne is informed of the distinction. . ." Never again was August to entertain aspirations to a military career.

Years later, President Hauser invited August to a party. Having served four terms as President of the Republic, he was being given a huge banquet in Lucerne to celebrate the auspicious occasion. At its conclusion, an excursion on a lake steamer was planned. Bands played, crowds congregated. Colonel Weiss, an old family friend, approached August, saying that Colonel Willie had asked him to bring young Benziger to him. Naturally the suggestion was met with less than enthusiasm; however, Colonel Weiss began to grow annoyed, saying that he was being placed in a very embarrassing situation. The former recruit had no choice, and so followed Colonel Weiss to the steamer's sundeck.

On seeing them approach, Colonel Willie stepped forward and extended his hand. The Swiss are notorious handshakers. On greeting, on meeting, on parting, it is considered good etiquette to shake hands energetically. To neglect to do so is an act of rudeness, and to disdain to shake a proffered hand is equivalent to a slap in the face. On occasion, such behavior can even lead to a duel. August coldly regarded the outstretched hand. With seething sarcasm, he retorted: "*Herr Oberst* Willie, neither of us needs an introduction. We have met all too often in the past. Unfortunately, we know each other far too well." Willie looked squarely at August and said that he wished he had really known the young man. Had that been the case, he averred, he would have insisted that he join his staff at the very beginning. Such sentiments infuriated the young man. The statement seemed to him to have been made in a jocular vein and had the effect of being like salt rubbed into an old wound. The retort was swift. It was pointed out that this was no time for pleasantries, that that offer might have been flattering in the past but since its maker had been responsible for August's failure in the army, he should know that he was responsible for a young recruit's never wanting to see another uniform. He added that Willie had sheltered unworthy officers, men who made grave mistakes. The young Swiss's eyes blazed contempt.

Colonel Willie was quick to reply: "Benziger, you're absolutely right. Yet, don't forget that I, too, had a duty to my men. I was obliged to protect them, just as you felt it necessary to defend the honor of that blacksmith who was your companion-in-arms." Amazed by the honesty and sincerity of Colonel Willie's explanation, August could feel the tension between them relaxing. With a wry smile, he consented to shake hands with his former enemy, thereby accepting the Colonel's apology; thereafter, the two men became friends.

During the course of the afternoon, August spent many hours with President Hauser. He could not help noticing that Colonel Willie continually edged nearer to their intimate group in an apparent attempt to join the presidential party. Invariably he failed as President Hauser flatly chose to ignore his presence. Had not President Hauser been forced to request the man's resignation because he had harbored officers unfit to wear the Swiss uniform? It was inevitable that the President and Willie would finally come face-to-face; then the President promptly turned his back and refused to accept the offered handclasp. Willie looked first at the President and then at August Benziger. Earnestly he remarked: "Mr. President, I only wish I had possessed honest enemies—enemies such as you and Benziger have been. Had that been my case, things would have gone much more favorably with me." President Hauser, too, was touched by the Colonel's forthright attitude, by his spirit of contrition. He commented later: "Willie has been a big enough man to see the enormity of his errors." Shortly after this incident, Colonel Willie was reinstated to his former rank in the army. During World War I, he was named to the highest post of honor assigned to any Swiss citizen: in 1914, he was made a General in the Swiss Army. Only in time of war does the Swiss Government ever appoint a General, as, during such a time of national crisis, he supersedes even the President in authority. His word became law.

Having completed his term of military duty, August found the return to Einsiedeln a joyful occasion. This was the first time he had come home to stay, and everything was in readiness for his assuming much of the responsibility for carrying on the family business as Governor Benziger was in poor health, suffering from a stomach ailment. In a community as tiny as this, many commented on the artist's aristocratic bearing. The mere sight of this dashing young man at Sunday Mass caused, on occasions, noticeable excitement in the left-hand pews where the Swiss wives and daughters sat separately from their menfolk ensconced on the right side of the nave. Everyone knew that one day August would inherit Benziger Brothers, as one of the three boys had gone to Belgium to enter the Carmelites and another had retired to Solothurn. Now there remained only this last son, the one on whom the proud *Landammann* pinned all his hopes. In small mountain villages, jealousy was often displayed; the locals felt that the young man who would one day head the firm should marry one of his own place and kind, and they were fearful that this eligible bachelor might conceivably slip away. Loose tongues asserted to the Governor that, on occasion, his son had deviated from exemplary deportment and, although these were merely rumors without substance, *Landammann* Benziger decided that it was time to have a long discussion with his son.

With typical determination and thoroughness, he pursued his chosen topic in great detail. He thought it might be wise for August to look into the possibilities of marriage in the near future in preparation for his entering into the publishing business. Why should he not move next-door to the *zum Adler*? That building could easily be converted into a suitable home, and there August could enjoy the privacy of his own quarters; there was place for his office there and even a reception room where he could meet the salesmen. He hoped and prayed that his son would marry a good Catholic, a deeply religious woman with a fine disposition. Money was not essential. The Governor hoped his son would give the matter serious consideration. These were specific instructions. Should he marry someone outside the Catholic Church, he would be cut off from the family but, if he married the right type, he would receive as wedding gift an estimable sum of Swiss francs. In short, the father wanted his son to have all the comforts, to know no wants, to be able to carry on the family traditions. The conversation ended quietly, the son responding that he had as yet no intention of marrying, and that he still had a great deal to learn in the world of art. Besides, he was quite content under the parental roof, and liked being close to his lovely mother. If he could be useful to his father, he would do all in his power to please him.

Little by little, it became evident that the Governor was ill and that his state of health was worsening. The doctor advised him that he should leave at once for a long rest; perhaps a cure at Vichy would help him. Together doctor and patient left for France.

During this period, August took over the business and his first opportunity to exert real authority. Benziger Brothers was thriving and Adelrich widely regarded as a genius among publishers, who had revolutionized business methods not only in Einsiedeln but throughout all of Switzerland and much of Europe. His entire fortune he poured back into the firm each year in order to promote religious art and books of the highest caliber. Sharing the ideals of Pope Leo XIII, the pope of the working man, he paid his workmen and artists generously, and maintained that others should do so as well in order to promote a new social order. As many of these men were situated not only in Switzerland, but also in Germany, Austria, France and Italy, his practices gained widespread attention and application.

A top-notch salesman himself, he was a staunch adherent to the principles of right advertising, and his agents were required to return to Einsiedeln periodically for a review of the latest selling techniques. His representatives were sent as far as Latin America; branch offices were established in New York, Cincinnati and St. Louis. It was a Benziger theory that no matter how renowned an author or artist might be, no book or picture ever sold itself. August felt that he had much to live up to, but exhausted from work, spent each evening with his mother. After dinner, the assembled household would say the rosary before the family shrine; then, while *Frau Landammann* sipped her linden tea, her son would review the outstanding events of the day. Only then, after she had finished her *tisane* and retired, did August return to his father's office to sort pictures, correct drawings and make plans for the following day.

As the weeks slipped by, he felt as though he were being smothered by an inexplicable feeling of uneasiness. He had everything the world could offer him; he was surrounded by wealth, affection, even adulation. Prior to this time, he had never seriously entertained any idea other than that of following in his father's footsteps. Now the mere thought of what faced him, of years spent in Einsiedeln, filled him with repugnance. His aversion to the world of business grew to alarming proportions, and he was sickened by the contemplation of taking over the vast machinery he was now controlling. Attempting, without success, to discard these feelings, this sense of oppression, he began to feel out of place, like a character miscast in a play. There arose in him an overwhelming longing to return to his drawing and painting, to his circle of artist friends. He had grown to love that vivacious world of make-believe which had freed him from his shell of shy reserve and made him a man capable of relating to all men.

During the years of his adolescence, had he not literally breathed art? Now, by contrast, Einsiedeln seemed listless, drab. Einsiedeln was dead. Were it not for the chanting of monks, the noise of his father's factories, the sounds of thousands of devout pilgrims coming to honor Our Lady of the Hermits, it would, indeed, be a place without hope, without so much as a horizon.

In December there was great rejoicing when Governor Benziger returned from his Vichy cure and immediately resumed his duties as head of the business. A perfectionist, he voiced instant disapproval of certain paintings which his son had accepted. Adelrich had always been exacting, even severe with August. He demanded that, in the choice of paintings, there should be more dignity, less of the ethereal; the coloring should be more sedate, less flamboyant. Instead of faulting his artists, he let all the blame fall on his son for lacking maturity. He had shown a want of proper judgment in accepting work that was modernistic in concept and execution; he had been blinded by the type of art emanating from Munich, and even Vienna, which lacked restraint and good taste.

From the time he had left home, August had looked forward to the time when he would once again be able to spend Christmas with his parents. How he had missed his wonderful mother! The atmosphere of home, the bright candles, the preparations, the fragrant aromas that wafted from the kitchen where all the womenfolk congregated weeks ahead of time to concoct sugar delicacies surfaced in his memory. However, on December 21, a mere four days before the great feast, Governor Benziger sent for August. He had been far too busy with his factories to talk things over quietly with his son. When he told him that he required more artistic training, the young man agreed. He had spent, the Governor said, far too much time on externals; what he now needed was austerity, the

depth of vision which only the Düsseldorf School could provide.
As soon as the Christmas festivities had ended, he would expect
August to pack his bag for the Rhineland in order to study for the
next year under the tutelage of Friedrich Stummel. Only then
would he be qualified to judge the work of contemporary artists.

With no warning whatever, the Governor now began a bitter
tirade against the immorality of the French. His last trip there had
convinced him that it was no place for any young man to go; he
had learned, he felt, a good bit about the low moral standards of
those attending the *Académie Julien*. He had heard that a single
Parisian model had infected 60 of the students. The painting of
flesh-tints and nakedness which Bouguereau encouraged could lead
to nothing but tainted morals.

In vain August remonstrated. Everyone knew what went on
in French art circles, but that did not mean that every student was
immoral. He tried his best to convince his father that he was
wrong, and realized then and there that someone had prejudiced
him while he was recently in Paris. Now he understood why, upon
his return to Einsiedeln, his father had disapproved of all his efforts to encourage some of the newer artists.

Benzigers were known for their wills of iron and hot tempers.
Adelrich, especially, had been born to command, not to lead by
gentle persuasion. August felt that he should have been taken into
his father's confidence, that man-to-man they should have discussed this matter openly. Why had his father gone ahead and
made arrangements with the Düsseldorf School? Was he not old
enough to make his own decisions? That first of January he was
going to be 24. A great welling up of despair overcame him and
he knew at that moment that Paris, Paris alone, could give him
what he needed. Yes, Düsseldorf might be an excellent school of
religious art, but first and foremost he had to learn to build a
human body—to create living images—to make his characters on
canvas talk and breathe and see. He would go to Paris *and to no
other place!*

On occasion in the past, Adelrich had been haunted by the
stark realization that his son might still long to become a creative
artist. In essence, this is what he said to him at this time: We
have gone over all of this long ago. Before you left for Vienna,
we discussed a similar situation. Now you are about to renounce
your high ideals. You plan to become an artist? Are you willing,
then, to gamble with hunger, probable failure and becoming a so-

cial outcast? You need not count on me to support you any further! As the future head of the house of Benziger, you have no choice. You either go to the Rhineland or pack up and get out.

August was too hurt to reply. There was nothing more to be said or done. He would have to act. He left the room, climbed the stairs to his room, slowly packed his bag, then came down. On the way to the front door, he met his gentle mother. There was no need to tell her. He knew she had heard, she had seen, she had sensed the tragedy that had come.

There were tears in her eyes as she clutched her son's arm and pressed something into his hand. "August, you will need this for the hard days ahead. I have expected that this would happen. I have lived in dread of this day, but it was bound to come. These 2,000 francs will help put you on your feet. For a long time I've been saving from the household money to help you gain your independence. You are so like your father. I have faith in you. I know that whatever you are determined to do, you will do well."

August hesitated, fearing that she might ask him to wait. Knowing and loving him, she did not do so, but added that his father wanted to know how much he would need monthly. "He will send sufficient money to get you through."

He shook his head. "I refuse to be tied as in the past. I cannot continue to submit my sketches, or to be treated like a schoolboy." Her lips were drawn tightly in a grim line. "Would 250 francs be sufficient for classes, room and board?" Only then did August realize that once again his mother had played the role of intermediary; she must have pleaded with his father. He hesitated. Should he accept or refuse? "Thanks, mother. That will be a great help. It will give me the chance I need to study." She replied: "Father wants me to tell you that he is willing to let you have this sum for the next three years. After that, you will become independent and make a name for yourself. You may no longer expect to lean on him."

In return, he made a promise to her: "Mother, I hope that I will only need assistance during the next two years. If, at the end of that time, I fail to be self-supporting, I shall return and stay at home. I will then replace Father in whatever capacity he designates."

The postilion horn was blown and the horses had come to a stop at *Pfauen Inn* next door. August knew it was time to run if he wished to catch the coach. Hastily, he leaned down, caught the tiny woman in his arms—then fled—calling as he ran: *"Auf Wiedersehen! Adieu! Adieu! Adieu*! I will write you from Paris!"

CHAPTER 7

The Maturing Artist
(1890-1892)

The Basel Express came to a halt at the Paris terminal. August pulled down the compartment window and looked the length of the smoky *Gare de l'Est*. In a matter of seconds, a burly "blue cap" caught the bag from the train window and strapped it to his back. As August jumped into a waiting cab, he instructed the driver to go to *L'Académie Julien* in the Latin Quarter. Only then could he sit back and relax. The ordeal was over.

On reaching his destination near the banks of the Seine, he learned that the school holidays had just begun and that the classrooms would remain deserted until the New Year began. He was in urgent need of a studio and it was going to prove extremely difficult to find one, so he first began what seemed in fact an interminable hunt for lodgings. Up one street he went and down the next, only to be filled with disgust at the filth and poverty which met his eyes. Finally he did stumble upon the very thing for which he had been looking, and was fortunate enough to lease an *atelier à la mansarde* on the Rue Saint-Jacques which was everything that a struggling young painter needed—a little attic workshop to call his own. As he puffed up the six flights of steep stairs, he gazed upon the shabby garret with deep satisfaction. What more could anyone want? His studio had clear north light, a clean couch and a warm wood stove in the center of the room.

Living in Paris proved far from inexpensive. The monthly tuition alone at the *Académie* was 100 francs, and then there were such costly items to purchase as canvas, sable brushes, oil paints, varnish. For the first time, August knew the bitter taste of poverty and what it meant to be hungry, as there were days when he had nothing but a crust of bread to munch. Pangs of hunger were especially difficult to endure for this young man who had suffered

113

through most of his student days from nervous indigestion and migraine headaches. Furthermore, his studio usually remained unheated as he lacked both time to get wood and money to hire someone to keep the fire going.

The Latin Quarter, dedicated to the students who filled its streets and cafés with laughter, animation and talent, was honeycombed with modestly-priced restaurants. August found a most satisfactory one near his *atelier*. There, for a few sous, he could order a frugal meal, a *pot-au-feu*, which was easily digested and served to warm his half-frozen body. This establishment of *La Mére Blanche* catered solely to artists. Its *patronne* enjoyed their Bohemian manners, their ardent love affairs, their tremendous appetites, and she had been particularly attracted to the tall, blond newcomer. He ate sparingly, remained more polite, more reserved than the others of her *clientèle*, invariably ordered the most inexpensive meals though, strangely enough, he was attired in costly clothing.

Mère Blanche watched this new arrival who politely, if somewhat disdainfully, had turned down the advances of the *demimondaines*, the brazen young women of doubtful reputation who prided themselves on making conquests of homesick students. However, this artist had never ignored the affectionate nudges given him by her flea-bitten mongrel, and had petted Bouffon kindly. She also noted that nothing escaped his expert eye, and that he was able to sketch passersby on her mimeographed menus swiftly and with great skill. This young man had definite ability.

One evening, when there were few guests in the house, Mère Blanche felt that the time had come to approach him and tell him that he had great talent and depth of feeling. She inquired whether or not he would do her the favor of painting a portrait for her. She had waited for years, she said, to find a suitable artist among her guests. "You are that man, *monsieur*! Name your price. The order is yours." Flattered beyond words, August rose, bowed gallantly and thanked her for her gracious offer. Only *he* knew how urgently he needed the money, needed everything, above all the security of knowing that he could have at least one meal a day. He had come to this restaurant because it was cheap and clean, but had noticed little about the *patronne* and so was startled by her request, vital as it was to his well-being. He was astonished by the turn the conversation now took.

Mére Blanche was clear: "I want a full-sized painting. The more I see of human beings, the better I like dogs. That's why I want Bouffon to be immortalized! She is to hang over the mantelpiece in a place of honor." August started to throw back his head, to roar with uncontrollable laughter, but, always a gentleman, he caught himself just in time. So it was a dog he was to paint—not *madame la patronne*!

Remembering his empty stomach, he decided that a dog was a far better subject than none at all. Here, to say the least, was a challenging opportunity to show what he could do. Inwardly he chuckled. What would his father say if he heard that, instead of saints and religious subjects, August, in order to live, had to paint animals?

Now he became engrossed in trying to discover the salient features of the black-and-white mongrel. This portrait would prove to be unusually difficult as there were few, if any, redeeming points. Sketches by the dozen were submitted for Madame Blanche's approval. Happily, she chose her favorite sketch. The ugly, nondescript dog, her pink tongue hanging to one side of her mouth, almost barked. August had caught the half-cocked black ear, the white one drooping in mournful contrast, the inquisitive twinkle of her eye, realistically appraising each of the restaurant's customers, and transferred these features to canvas. Thus, for all time did Bouffon, the funny little clown dog of mixed parentage, join the ranks of canine immortals.

From the day August started his portrait of Bouffon, a new era dawned in his life. Gone forever were the pangs of hunger. Since he had refused outright to be paid a specified sum for his painting, the *patronne* had taken it upon herself to see that her client never went hungry again; the best food in the house was reserved for him.

Days and weeks slipped by. Bouguereau required much work from his students and August spent long hours producing and perfecting his sketches. Sometimes there were nights when he did not get to bed at all. Hovering over a flickering candle or smoky kerosene lamp, he would sketch in spite of the atrocious light, the stifling odors. Although the stove had been lit, by dawn the room was always freezing, and his numbed fingers and painful chilblains were constant reminders of the price to be paid for his independence.

Doubts began to torment him. How could he possibly survive this way? Would he ever be able to achieve his goal? Had the moment come for him to abandon his art and, sensibly, look for employment? No one knew better than he how urgently he needed this art course. His flesh-tints were still poor. Up to this time he had merely been aping the methods of others. Now Bouguereau had instilled confidence in him, had taught him to put the personal element into his work. Groping, struggling, confused, the artist now prayed for light and the strength to take the right step.

Early in February, a foggy mist had settled like a pall over Paris, and nightfall came earlier than usual. From his cold attic, August watched the busy corps of lamplighters at their work. Hundreds of men dressed in blue smocks, carrying ladders and flickering tapers, were on the move, each covering a territory of 10 kilometers on foot. The *allumeur* would first light a weak flame, turn it up to shine brightly, then scurry to the next corner to repeat the process. Now the city was bewitching, as hundreds of street lanterns, one by one, burst into light. The banks of the Seine loomed eerie and mysterious.

August's imagination, piqued by these wonderful men who brought light into darkness, had catapulted him to his easel where he rapidly made a water-color sketch of the portly *bonhomme* who had stood beneath his window only a minute before. "The Lamplighter" became August's second Paris portrait.

The sketch was interrupted by loud shouting on the staircase. The door was flung open, and a heavy-bundled figure fell into the artist's arms producing a fusillade of imperatives, interrogatives and expletives such as only the French can muster: "What an atrocious place! These six flights have given me a heart attack—they are certain to be the death of me. *Parbleu*! What do you mean by burying yourself alive on the sixth floor. *You*! Settled in an attic! Have you lost your wits? Are you completely out of your mind?" "Papa Lorilleux! How wonderful to see you!" August exclaimed as he assisted the elderly gentleman to the couch. The old family friend was in a bad mood, still struggling to catch his breath. "Don't stare at me, you idiot! Get me a glass of brandy at once. My poor old heart can't stand this shock." August ran to fill a glass with ordinary wine, apologizing for its poor quality.

M. Lorilleux went on with more concern. What under the sun possessed August to come here? Why had he hidden from everyone? "I've even been to the Prefecture of Police. No one was able to help me in my search—until today. I met Bouguereau at the *Académie* and he gave me your address." Papa Lorilleux's voice softened. "This is not a very nice way for you to have treated your friends, August. We have missed you as we would our own son."

August was overcome with emotion and explained that no one regretted this situation more than he, yet there was no other course of action possible. "I can no longer impose on my father's friends. I must stand on my own feet. It is high time that I make a name for myself instead of clinging to the family reputation." He went on to explain that he and his father no longer saw eye-to-eye, that his father wanted him to study in Düsseldorf but that he himself felt that there was nothing to be learned in Germany that couldn't be better learned in Paris. "The warmth of French art appeals to me. This is where I belong."

M. Lorilleux said nothing as he listened to August's sincere plea, though deep in his heart he was in accord with the thoughts of the young artist. Asking for a candle, he pointed to a letter, saying that it had lain on his desk for a month, but that he did not know where to deliver it, and that August's parents were extremely worried about their son. The letter was dated Einsiedeln, December 22nd, 1890. August read:

MY DEAR SON:

Only yesterday you left us, dear August. I had hoped to see you finish your studies in Düsseldorf, for at that school you would have acquired a precise and more austere technique. This would have been more in keeping with the religious spirit it is necessary for you to acquire. By going to Germany, you would have saved yourself much time.

You have made up your mind about Paris. I wish to remind you that you must now improve your drawing. Once you have done this, then you may apply for a position with any publisher, where you will be able to work as an illustrator, photographer or chromolithographer. Drawing, in itself, will supply you with all the aspects needed for any of the graphic arts.

I have always prayed that God would give me a son, possessing talent for art. Now, instead of becoming a publisher, I greatly fear you will become an artist. God heard my prayer, only He has not answered it as I had hoped. Enclosed, dear August, you will find the 250 francs promised. Every month I will send you the same.

August was deeply touched. Although he sympathized with his father's viewpoint, there were questions in his mind. Where were the opportunities for advancement greater than right here? Was not Paris the center of the art world? Then August shivered involuntarily, thinking of damp, dreary Einsiedeln. Would he ever be able to bury himself there again? Had he not outgrown its confines artistically? How could he now forsake all that he loved here for a purely commercial career? Papa Lorilleux sensed August's severe inner struggle and broke the silence as he rested his hand on the student's shoulder: "Hurry and pack your belongings," he begged, "and let's get out of here before I die of pneumonia. I insist on taking you back with me to the Rue Sugère." August demurred. He had leased the studio for the winter; he was very near his school; he had fine northern light, but Papa Lorilleux was not to be denied. He would have workmen elevate the roof to provide adequate northern light in a section of his home. August would be able to come and go as he pleased. "Young man, you shall have your northern light, your private studio, your solitude. Now, no more of the matter! Do you hear?"

August knew that this trusted friend meant every word sincerely. He had no choice. With overflowing gratitude, he escorted his benefactor down the interminable flight of stairs. While his new studio was being prepared for occupancy, he was presented with a house key and made to feel at home, and he returned to the Lorilleux household each night to sleep in warmth and comfort— then, early in the morning, he would return to his attic studio to apply himself to his usual long hours of work. By the first of March, the new studio was ready for its artist. As the moving of stretchers, easels, canvas and paints was accomplished without August's knowledge, he was utterly astounded when he stepped into the room and discovered all of his familiar Rue Saint-Jacques equipment transplanted to this new and attractive setting.

The first morning when he awoke in his new studio, loud words spoken by his host thundered in his ears: "You lazy, lazy loafer—what do you mean—still in bed at this hour! It's late. You should have been up long ago!" August sprang from the depths of his blankets and threw the shutters wide open. Outside it was still pitch black. Looking at his clock in confusion, he discovered that it was just five o'clock. "Get out your paints, if you call yourself an artist. I want you to paint my portrait." August thought he was joking. He was not. "This is the only free time I have all day long. It's now or not at all. I have waited many a year to have my portrait painted, and you are hereby delegated to do the job." Then, chuckling to himself for having taken August unawares, jolly Papa Lorilleux tiptoed out of the room.

August determined never to be caught napping again. He spent most of the day preparing a suitable canvas and working on a few sketches and a final outline. By the following morning, he was ready. The next morning, Papa Lorilleux again entered the studio before daybreak, but this time he found the artist waiting for him. "*Me voici!*" the cheerful man exclaimed. "How do you like my attire? Are you ready to paint me just as I am?" August collapsed with laughter at the ludicrous sight which met his eyes. His benefactor stood before him in his rumpled nightclothes. No one in the world would have recognized this captain of industry. "You'd certainly make the headlines," roared the artist, "if I painted you exactly as you are at this moment—in your bare feet, your nightcap, striped flannel nightshirt and all!"

August concentrated every talent he possessed upon the task at hand. This portrait was a crucial test. During one of the early-morning sittings, he looked up from his palette and remarked happily: "Today is the 13th of April and I feel sure that it's my lucky day. Many of the most important events of my life have taken place on the 13th of this month. Your belief in me, Papa Lorilleux, is certain to bring success."

The artist who had begun the portrait with caution and hesitancy, now gained confidence as the sittings got under way. The old shackles had been left behind for all time. Since a bust was much more difficult to execute than a three-quarter-length portrait, here was an occasion to display his full range of artistry and technique. It was necessary for the head to be exceptionally well-delineated in order to command attention. Gratifying progress could be noted; the eyes became real, the lips lifelike. When Papa Lorilleux excitedly called his family to view the work, he and they could hardly contain their joy; here, indeed, was the work of a prodigy—they had a genius in their midst! August, the man of few words, had let his paint and canvas speak eloquently of his gratitude and affection.

As hours passed Papa was seized with impatience. It was late afternoon, and he paced the floor irritably, waiting for the paint to dry. Finally, snatching the portrait with frightening energy, he rushed off into the night—no one knew where. August and the family exchanged looks of bewilderment. What on earth had come over Papa? What had possessed this usually cool-headed and businesslike man to cause him to behave in this extraordinary manner? When he returned, he no longer had the painting. He moved about the room in a triumphant mood as he admitted that he had submitted August's portrait to the annual contest being held at the *Salon*. Not wishing to upset the artist, he had said nothing of his plan. The deadline for entries was the following day; small wonder that he had been nervous. The painting had barely made it!

The most exciting yearly event of the Paris season was the opening of the *Salon des Champs Èlysées,* which Parisian society attended on May 1 to view and discuss the latest paintings. The victors in this vital competition would be fêted, sought after, pursued. This was the single occasion during the year when artists joined the ranks of the aristocracy, being accorded the deference due royalty. Struggling students, artists standing on the brink of success, their talents freshly revealed, rubbed shoulders with dignitaries. Only in Paris was it possible for a newcomer in the art world to attain such heights overnight, since the French alone awarded the artists their rightful place among the professionals; their prestige was inviolate, as deeply respected as that of attorneys, judges, doctors or leading politicians.

For the Swiss student, May 1, 1891 became the turning point of his career and of his life. It was the day when knowledgeable Paris stood before his portrait and agreed that it merited Honorable Mention. Even greater than the thrill of his award was August's gratification at finding his work hung side by side with portraits executed by such eminent men as Leon Bonnat and William Bouguereau. Suddenly, overnight, his work attained prominence, and the Paris press was lavish in its praise, asserting that "This portrait of Charles Lorilleux shows that a real artist does not need to resort to ostentation in order to call attention to his paintings. It is amazing how a simple unassuming bust can achieve the effect created by Benziger." From that moment on, the Rue Sugère was thronged with clients. Hallo, one of France's leading art dealers, brought his keenest patrons to August's studio, and within a single year following his success at the *Salon*, the young artist booked 45 orders for portraits.

Neither the swift success nor the excellent grades he received at the *Académie St. Julien* elicited any comment from Einsiedeln. Governor Benziger had lapsed into an ominous silence, and the strained relationship between father and son grew increasingly acute with the passing of time. They left a marked effect on August's work. Time and again, he heard in a roundabout way of letters being sent by his father to his Parisian friends, and it was most disturbing for him to learn that the Governor was requesting these family confidants to set the young student on the right path and remind him of his duty to his parent. It was his father's hope that they might be able to dissuade him from continuing in his present career.

August was now confronted with the terrible ordeal of having to make a definite choice as to his future, one way or another. His heart and soul were engulfed by artistic aspirations, nurtured by the awareness of the recognition accorded him in recent months. The time for decision could no longer be postponed, and under these circumstances it was scarcely ethical to accept further orders. Should he continue to be an artist or enter the field of publishing?

Tormented with inner conflicts that turned his nights into agonies of indecision, August was seized by doubt. Was it fair of him to cause his kind but misunderstanding parent still more misery? His deep filial sense of duty forced him to give full consideration to the Governor's future welfare and happiness. Suddenly, an inspiration lit his mind. He remembered an impartial and unbiased friend of the family, old Alfred Firmin-Didot, who would be fair and sincere in his judgment of the case. As a publisher whose main interest lay in having his own children follow in his footsteps, he would understand the situation and know what answer to give. He could be trusted. August needed no further prompting. He speedily tossed his sketches, paintings and watercolors into a cab, only later to unpack them in M. Didot's office, explaining his mission and pleading that this successful businessman serve as a judge. Upon this shrewd Frenchman's verdict would hinge his future. "To be or not to be?" It was a frightening question.

Paternal, white-haired M. Didot was both flattered and sincerely moved by August's confidence in his opinion. As he had followed his suppliant's meteoric success with great interest, he carefully surveyed each example of the young man's work. Yes, he would gladly give his counsel. He could, he affirmed, fully appreciate the Governor's feelings, but his evaluation was clear-cut and to the point. "We old folks, who are trusted friends of your father, love him dearly. However, under the present circumstances, we feel him to be sadly misinformed." He affirmed that August's proven ability as a portraitist had decided his case for him. From the day the *Salon* had accepted his first painting, he had no alternative; he had an outstanding talent which must be put to use immediately. "Do not hesitate or delay. Mark my words: You are predestined to become one of the great portrait painters of the 20th century."

With grateful heart, August listened humbly and accepted the verdict, knowing that now there would be no turning back. The aching doubts vanished and a great peace filled him. He would take up his palette and brushes, as if for the first time, and dedicate the rest of his life to art.

As August prepared to return to his studio, he was detained by M. Didot who told him: "Your friend, young Louis Hachette, paid me a visit earlier this afternoon. We happened to be speaking of you, and both of us decided that we would like to have portraits of us done, just like the one you made of our mutual friend, Lorilleux." He added: "You can begin with mine right now—this very minute! Louis will see you tomorrow at 9:00 in your studio." Thus it was that August had two more excellent busts completed in time to be entered for the Salon's opening the following May. Once again he won honors—this time the coveted first prize.

Finally, the Swiss press, which, up to the present, had been reluctant to give August either coverage or praise, published a complimentary article about their countryman's achievement in Paris. The *Zürcher Zeitung* reported:

> Benziger wins awards and takes first place for his portraits of two prominent Parisian editors, Firmin-Didot and Louis Hachette. In that of Louis Hachette, it would almost seem as if one were gazing at a boy, yet it represents an adolescent of fine, delicate appearance. His clear, meditating eyes look at one so intelligently.

> The second portrait is that of a white-headed man of ripe age whose fresh, strong features and kindly, sparkling blue eyes amaze the onlooker. In conception and execution, these two pictures are entirely different, yet they are real gems of a highly-developed art.

August promptly received from his delighted older client, a most imposing check. Noting the large sum for which it had been drawn, he felt that a serious error had been made and at once rushed to M. Didot's office to return it. That amiable gentleman greeted his portraitist with a laugh. "*Mais, mon cher August,* there has been no mistake," he assured him. This was what he deemed a fair price for the portrait; the artist was entitled to every sou of the 2,000 francs. "From now on, I shall insist that you charge this sum for each of your paintings. Your work is well worth that amount. Time will prove my opinion to be right." Then he added thoughtfully: "Never throw away your talent for less, *mon ami*. Always place a high value on what you have to offer." Those who truly appreciate art, he affirmed, will gladly pay any fee for work that is worthwhile—or great.

The next four years, 1892 to 1896, were crowded with kaleidoscopic activities. Although the artist worked long hours, the sittings were alternated with nights crammed with dinners, dances and a full round of pleasurable activities. When the social season was at its peak, August made a point of attending several balls. It was important for a portrait painter to enter into circles where possible future clients could be found. For one who enjoyed dancing as much as he did, this Parisian nightlife was an agreeable necessity. Upon his arrival at a fashionable gathering, he first obtained a bird's-eye view of the evening's possibilities, noting where the young ladies were congregated, and then he pencilled quick sketches of the most attractive and outstanding, thereby augmenting the material in his sketchbook for future use.

In the small hours of the morning, when the festive affairs had ended, he knew exactly where to find the best *cuisine*. He invariably ended up in *Les Halles*, the great Paris marketplace, an area filled with ancient restaurants and bistros which was frequented by knowledgeable peasants. For over 800 years, these sturdy farmers had carted their produce into town, night after night, in order to sell it at auction at dawn. Anyone searching for August in the small hours of the morning might find him at the *Pharamond* or at *L'Escargot* savoring a few snails. More often he was to be seen rubbing elbows with the hefty peasants at the crowded counter of *Le Père Tranquil*, where everyone sipped the steaming onion soup noted for its marvelous restorative powers. Outside, in the frigid winter dawn, huge two-wheeled carts creaked beneath their loads of vegetables, masses of colorful flowers, clucking hens, squealing hogs. While the rest of Paris slumbered, these blue-smocked countrymen streamed steadily into the city, their one purpose to wrestle a living from the barren soil; they bargained, haggled, struggled over their produce.

Sleep counted for little in these days of ambitious, youthful drive; refreshed by only an hour or two of it, August would be up and at his easel. By 6:00, his faithful servant, Geneviève, would be stoking the embers of the little stove and then preparing his breakfast of three soft-boiled eggs, coffee and one lone croissant. This middle-aged *bonne à tout faire* (the French, feminine version of a Jack-of-all-trades) was paid five sous per hour and would never have dreamt of asking for more. She delighted in a sly little game which was played by herself and *monsieur l'artiste*. As she had been assigned the challenging task of shielding her master from scheming women, there was to be no breath of scandal in his studio. Certain signals, prearranged by August, would reveal that the current "sitter" was proving dangerous; he needed a chaperone at once! At this point, Geneviève would approach the easel wielding her feather duster. As a rule, dusting was something August never tolerated, especially while he was painting. The only excuse for this activity was that of guarding his morals and protecting his reputation.

To a handsome, eligible bachelor, Paris was one of the most dangerous capital cities, and the milieu of the portrait painter held, in itself, its full share of snares and pitfalls. Some silly, giggling young girls, older women both married and single, gay divorcèes, bored, restless housewives sought pretexts to stop at the studio. Despite these many distractions, August's success as a portraitist was phenomenal. In 1890 he had won the gold medal given at the Vatican Exhibit, and by December 21, 1892, he had been invited to become a member of Paris's *Cércle de l'Union Artistique* founded by Napoleon. He had finally been recognized as a genius, competed for major prizes and come away with honors. The French people had taken this Swiss to their hearts; they no longer considered him a foreigner and so, like his father before him, he was awarded the *Légion d'Honneur*. This official recognition made it possible for him to have direct contact with the greatest minds of France.

August was popular with the older, sedate set and was often called upon by some of his father's elderly business associates who found themselves enmeshed in liaisons from which they had urgent need of being extricated. They soon found that this young, experienced artist could be exceedingly helpful in untangling their clandestine affairs, affably rescuing them, these white-headed gentlemen, from their dilemmas. In France, no malicious gossip or shadow of doubt must ever be permitted to mar the sacredness of the hearth. The *foyer familial,* the home, and one's integrity and reputation had to remain inviolate, above reproach; and though it was the acceptable thing for a man to have a liaison, the gentle womenfolk of the household must never be given cause to suspect that a husband, father, brother or serious admirer could play the roué or be guilty of common sin! It was taken for granted that the male of the species belonged to a privileged class to whom all liberties were permissible—as long as one's escapades were hushed. On the other hand, by a queer form of logic, it was similarly assumed that women of good family naturally clung to the straight and narrow path, remaining at all times pure, chaste and virtuous.

One very close friend even proposed that August become betrothed to his 16-year-old daughter. When August recoiled in shock and dismay, the man's reaction was simple and unadorned. Certainly, he was told, no one would ever expect a man in the artist's position to remain constant for such a long period as would be required for the girl's maturation; this would be merely a *marriage de convenance,* simply a signing of the marriage contract— that is all. The father was quite ready to provide the desired son-in-law with everything he would need—money, an apartment, even a *maitresse*; all that was asked in return was that, when the right time came, the daughter would have a worthy husband and her parents a distinguished son-in-law. August explained that this arrangement would not be tolerated by the ecclesiastical authorities in his own country, nor could he himself think of signing such a contract. When he felt that the right woman had come into his life, he would marry her; in the meantime, he would remain unattached.

In spite of this type of experience, August continued to be fascinated by Parisian life where he had shared in equal proportions both the sordid and the beautiful. The quick tempo, the peculiar pulsebeat of this city suited him perfectly. He loved the broad boulevards with their acacia-lined sidewalks, their brightly-hued corner kiosks plastered with gaily-colored posters of operatic or theatrical programs. The awe-inspiring churches, the stirring monuments and exquisite homes all spoke to his artist's soul, as did the colorful people. There was suicidal Boris, a Roumanian whose life he saved, or an infamous baron overcome with fear that his scandalous activities, if discovered by his parents, would destroy them. And there was the Marquise de Toulongeon who lived on the Boulevard Malesherbes and who pleaded with him to join her at

Rimini. Her *palazzo* on the Adriatic was in the process of being remodeled. She felt that August was the very person to add some frescoes to the work in progress in her lovely, newly-designed chapel. After considerable persuasion, coupled with growing awareness that it was becoming a necessity for him to slacken his feverish pace, he decided to accept the invitation. Upon arrival, he immediately began his project, working with concentration on four enormous frescoes of the apostles; but not long afterwards, he had word from his *concierge* that it was vital for him to return to Paris. Business matters were accumulating. He promised the Marquise that he would return later to complete the work and hastened back to France.

Upon his return, a steady stream of clients set upon his studio. Although the French Impressionist School was gaining momentum, the Swiss artist proudly declared that he would remain a disciple of Holbein, to the great relief of his admirers. He had already made his name by the delicate brushwork of his facial features, the realistic flesh-tints which he had now perfected, the modeling of eyes that spoke, and he determined to remain upon this path. Work, work and still more work began to reap its harvest. Dr. Marion, his physician, frightened August into taking a much-needed vacation, to curtail this far-too-fast and demanding pace he had set for himself. He must leave for the High Alps; rest, quiet and freedom from all demands and tensions alone could ward off the nervous collapse toward which he was headed with leaps and bounds. Alarmed at the thought of illness which might incapacitate him at what seemed the height of his career, August immediately heeded his doctor's orders, packed his bags, canceled all engagements and rushed to catch the express train for the Engadine. He had purposely chosen Saint Moritz as the locale for his rest-cure because of the fact that, in summertime, it always attracted a cheerful international set. He was sick to the point of satiation with tiny provincial villages where everyone knew his personal business and took diabolical delight in criticizing his way of life. Saint Moritz was crowded to overflowing with interesting Europeans, plus a sprinkling of prominent Americans. In this worldly, cosmopolitan atmosphere, no one would be guilty of gaping at him as though he were a curiosity; here he could easily remain anonymous. The manager of the Victoria Hotel was a personal friend who found him a quiet back room where nobody could bother him, and so August succeeded in going his own way undisturbed. This was the first time he had ever fully enjoyed a holiday, and he planned to savor it to the full, carrying out his doctor's orders to the letter, relaxing in long, healing periods of solitude.

A keen observer of human nature, August derived an enormous amount of pleasure from studying people. It was his habit to select an individual's most outstanding features, then to jot them down pictorially in his ever-present notebook, sketching in details for future reference.

One evening in the dining room, his eye was held by the sight of an arrestingly beautiful woman, and he was puzzled as to her identity; however, he resigned himself to dealing with an unsolved mystery, for he had made a firm resolution not to engage in conversation with anyone while in Saint Moritz.

Still in pursuit of solitude, one afternoon after siesta he took a long walk in the cool forest. The silence of the trees and the thick bed of pine needles muffled the sound of approaching footsteps. Before he knew what was happening, the regal-looking lady he had seen not long ago had made herself at home on a bench quite near him although she could not see him. August, on an impulse, quickly pulled out his sketchbook and watercolors and began to capture her likeness. Fascinated by her manner but unwilling to introduce himself, he waited until she had slipped among the evergreens and then returned to his hotel. As he was just in time to dress for dinner, he hurriedly tossed his sketch into a trunk. Suddenly there was a knock at the door. A stranger inquired whether he might see the recently-executed sketch. Completely baffled, the artist asked: "What sketch?" The man explained that he had seen the sketch being done in the woods and wanted to purchase it. August demurred, asserting: "I never sell my sketches!"

Crestfallen, the gentleman introduced himself as the *Comte de Monjour*, Chamberlain to Her Royal Highness, Princess Laetitia Bonaparte. He happened to have been in the vicinity when the artist was painting, he said, saw the picture and had told Her Highness about it. She had requested him to offer whatever price the painter should ask, but insisted on possessing the portrait. August had no intention of parting with anything so unfinished and frankly told the Count so. By then the man was visibly upset. A royal command was not to be turned down, and he dared not go back without the coveted prize, so he followed August into his room while the artist continued to button his vest and attach his bow tie. Finally, in desperation, August looked once more at the elderly gentleman. He felt that he had to yield, although to do so was against his aesthetic principles. The man ferreted out the much-coveted painting, and then, without another word, rushed down the corridor as though his coattails were on fire.

The next morning, he was back again, politely informing *monsieur* that Her Highness requested the artist to visit her royal suite at noon that day. August hurriedly made enquiries about this noble personage. He learned that she was the niece of Napoleon III, had married the former King of Spain, Duke Amadeo of Aosta and, after his death, had remained a widow. Still in the prime of life, she was not only beautiful but also highly intelligent. Princess Laetitia, for her part, was charmed by her newfound artist and promptly ordered two portraits, one for herself and one for her favorite aunt, Princess Mathilde, the sister of Napoleon III.

Holidays were soon a thing of the past. Princess Laetitia arrived in the company of this aunt and, as the portraits began to take shape, the threesome joined in enjoyable conversation. By this means, August learned, he could explore the core of his sitters' personalities by encouraging them to talk on varied topics, forget themselves and thereby reveal their innermost interests and opinions. This was an enjoyable interim, but it was suddenly interrupted when the Torsch family from Vienna arrived on the scene. Gentle Miss Torsch was another of those young ladies with surprisingly strong wills and persuasive manners. Her parents had tried to induce her to marry but, contrary to European custom wherein all nice daughters did as they were told when it came to finding a suitable partner, she had insisted on living out her life in "single blessedness." Later, they learned that she had set her heart on just one man, and that was August Benziger.

Fraülein Torsch was painted exactly as she had come into the room. She had been wearing her new Paris creation, a straw sailor hat adorned with a demure white dove with extended wings. Her exquisite features were made increasingly lovely by a gossamer thin veil. These sittings, of course, were well-chaperoned, though the parents secretly hoped that the artist and sitter might "reach an agreement." The outcome was that Miss Torsch and her family returned to Austria after an exciting holiday at Saint Moritz, taking with them the fascinating portrait of the daughter, but not its painter!

Early one morning while August was putting the finishing touches on one of his portraits of Princess Laetitia, his *concierge* presented August with a visiting card. *"Herr Bundespräsident* Hauser wishes to speak with you," he said. As August did not know him, he was sure that there was some mistake, and made this fact clear, but the *concierge* persisted: "The President of the [Swiss] confederation has requested that I show him to your room. He wishes to call on you in person."

Hauser, a man of few words, was also a man of action; he had followed the *concierge*. Apologizing, he did his own explaining as he stood there in top hat, frock coat and striped trousers. August, surprised to see him arrayed as for a state occasion, stared, then bowed and shook hands. Hauser explained that he had been nearby and so came over to present the artist his congratulations and thanks on behalf of himself and the *Bund*. "You have, indeed, been an ambassador of good will wherever you have gone. Foreigners see a Swiss who is representative of the best," he added. Then he became more personal: "I admire you, you know." Why? Because he had heard a great deal about August from his young son-in-law, Captain Weber, who had served with the artist during the latter's trying times in the Army. This visit, as it grew in length, led to one of the most remarkable friendships in August's life. These two men had one strong bond in common: their great love of humanity embedded in their absolute sincerity.

Although President Hauser, the son of a simple tanner of Wadenswil on the Lake of Zurich, had risen from the ranks to become President of the Swiss Confederation and had received honors and high station, he still loved nothing better than to roam in the high Alps in search of mountain flowers. A lover of nature, he collected rare seeds deposited by avalanches and then planted them in his Berne garden. He longed for the day when the burdens of state could be set aside and he could devote his undivided attention to the enjoyment of nature.

Hauser gave August an order to paint his portrait on that day in Saint Moritz, but many years were to elapse before both President and artist could find time for a sitting. In 1897, August had moved into his Brunnen estate where Hauser finally came and sat for his portrait, a man of radiant, kindly humor, unperturbed by outside events. Only on one occasion had he come in a decidedly bad humor. His mood then was so evident that the artist could not delineate his features properly and felt that it might be wise to postpone the sitting. *"Herr Bundespräsident,* is there anything troubling you? You seem so upset that I simply cannot paint you with such a frown." What would posterity say, he queried, if he were depicted as the artist now saw him? Hauser broke into a broad grin, asserting that the only way in which August could make him feel better would be to help him rid the country of "crooks." He was sick and tired of corruption in high places. August let him go on about the things which preoccupied him, and the sitter forgot that he was being minutely studied. His inner spark shone through and August painted frantically while the *Bundespräsident* went on about an incident that had taken place in his office that morning.

He explained that just before leaving Berne for his sitting, he was attending to last-minute affairs in his office when his secretary announced that six gentlemen from Zurich were waiting for an urgent appointment, and that they represented one of the most important banks in their city; because of them he had had to miss his train for Brunnen. He had noticed that one of them was carrying a large suitcase with the utmost care, and he wondered why they had brought it into his office. They bluntly informed him that his annual salary as a member of the Federal Council was a mere 15,000 francs. Surely a man in his position needed a little extra money. What would he say to an additional 10 million Swiss francs? Naturally, the matter would be kept strictly confidential. All they wanted him to do was answer one question. So many of the railroads had gone bankrupt that the government had taken them over; they had heard that a certain number of these railroads could be sold to private owners. Which ones were they, and what was the asking price?

August was so fascinated by the story that he ceased to paint. "How did you rid yourself of these underworld characters?" Hauser's face blanched with anger, and he explained that, without so much as saying a word, he had walked to the huge window in his office and thrown it open to the cold of the April morning. Then, he merely pointed to the snow-capped mountains and said, while turning to his visitors: "Gentlemen! It is getting—too hot! You had better get out!" Hauser was laughing heartily by then. "Those scoundrels took the hint," he said. "They grabbed their bag full of money and fled."

President Hauser often visited August in later years, and was present for the opening of the Benziger's Grand Hotel. When Walter Hauser died in 1902, August mourned long and deeply for him. Fifty years after this friend's portrait had been painted, the artist received a letter which moved him profoundly. It had been written by the children of his friend:

> Thanks for your outstanding painting of our beloved father; his memory is ever before our eyes. Daily we gaze upon his smiling, genial, benign countenance, and are helped and strengthened. Never a day passes without our blessing the memory of one who made this consolation a reality.

CHAPTER 8

Triumph
(1892-1896)

In September 1892, August had terminated his stay in Saint Moritz where he had, in spite of his intention to rest, worked a good deal. Now he planned to spend a month with his parents at *Villa Gutenberg* before they returned for the winter to Einsiedeln.

Somewhat reluctantly, his father finally consented to pose for him during this visit. Adelrich had been skeptical about the results at the start, but he watched the gradual progress of his portrait with amazement and pride; he saw that his son had caught in oils his strength and energy. No, this son did not belong to the ranks of the average artist. Adelrich was satisfied.

August, who had always longed to portray his mother had, until this time, never been at home long enough to satisfy this aspiration so, when his father's three-quarter length canvas had been completed, he painted her as the self-effacing woman she was. He caught her expression of resignation not only in her facial features but also in her bearing, and depicted her simplicity in his delineation of her unpretentious black dress. She sat with folded hands, her serene but penetrating grey-blue eyes lost in contemplation; those eyes became the heart and soul of that picture. It was the portrait of a woman who had suffered much. After this masterpiece of composition had been achieved, even his undemonstrative father voiced his approval warmly. He knew deep down that August had won, that he himself had lost, and was big enough to accept defeat and congratulate the winner.

August, back in Paris, continued to complete orders throughout the winter of 1893. One of the more important was an ink drawing of 29 members of the exclusive club, *le Cercle Artistiques et Littéraire*. The experience of trying to get 29 outstanding citizens to find time to sit was not a calming one; some feigned excuses and others arrived at the club for sittings at midnight. When the remarkable ensemble had been completed, the club's president, M. Dramard, was so impressed with its excellence that he ordered a separate portrait of himself. The pen and ink sketch of the 29 heads, as well as the portraits of the artist's parents, were shown at the club's annual exhibition held on the 7th of February; the portrait of his mother won the first prize.

Curiosity prompted August to listen to the remarks of the exhibition's viewers, so he remained near his work without the public's being aware of his presence. Félix Faure, President of the French Republic and a keen lover of art, had been invited to participate in the opening. Accompanying the president was his Minister of Fine Arts, M. Poincaré. Faure, turning to him, asked the name of the artist who had painted "My Mother." Poincaré mentioned the name of Benziger and stated that he was a newcomer and a foreigner. Faure closed the fist of his right hand; through it he peered at the eyes of the portrait, studied them in detail and then exclaimed, "I have never seen anything like those eyes. They live." He went on enthusiastically about the face, its wrinkles, the hands which personify "composure and dignity." He wanted to meet the artist who "embodies the brilliant qualities of our best French Schools." When August met the president, he was told by him that his paintings "will give future generations a clearer perception of the type of people who live in our times."

Within 24 hours, August received an invitation from Faure inviting him to his home. From that time on, he was frequently present at the Èlysée Palace. The nights spent in the company of the president and his companions were lively affairs. A patron of drama as well as of art, Faure was constantly surrounded by the most talented and beautiful actresses of the day. Each *soirée musicale* or *dramatique* was an unforgettable event. Although August admired Félix Faure, he could hardly condone the financing of these women of "immodest conduct" by the head of the state; had they shown any desire to become respectable by marrying the men who supported them, it would have been a different matter. Instead, these well-known actresses clung vigorously to their irregular status and reveled in being in the public eye.

As a result of the February 7th exhibition, the world in which August lived changed. Only a few days later he had a prominent visitor while he was busily preparing a canvas for a projected work. (His foundation of black, white and brown was laid in with the same meticulous care as his most brilliant coloring; to the outsider it resembled a bas-relief and, though merely a base, was so lifelike that it looked as though a skeleton might step out from the canvas.) Hearing the studio door open, he turned to see who might be coming at this early hour, and found that he needed no introduction to this visitor. Time after time, he had seen Bonnat and envied those who studied under him at the *Académie des Beaux Arts*. Bonnat asked who had taught him to use colors this eminently rich in tone. "You have nuances that only the Flemish masters had!" August replied that he had taken Holbein as his ideal, then added: "But there is much that I can learn right here in Paris. I like the realism that is achieved by the French School; nowhere else in the world could I learn that." Bonnat questioned why he had never come to study at the *Académie des Beaux Arts*. The reply was direct: "There is nothing I would rather do than study under you, but every time I applied at the *Académie*, I was told that the enrollment list was filled and that for foreign students there was no hope." Bonnat studied the portraits on the easels standing around the studio and admitted that "the eyes of your mother have haunted me ever since I looked into them; . . . they have left me no peace. I want you to honor me by becoming my student."

Nothing could have pleased August more. From Bonnat he would now be able to learn new techniques in portraiture. This master who commanded the highest prices in Europe for his work used plain backdrops and his sitters virtually walked out of the canvas. It was this same quality which August had attained in the portraits of his parents, and so he felt encouraged that from Bonnat he could learn technique essential to speeding up his work.

For a time he attended classes at the *Beaux Arts* but later was invited to visit the master in his own home. Bonnat was a bachelor who had promised his mother that he would never marry during her lifetime. The elderly lady and her small, stocky son maintained a wonderfully vivacious household where many of the stars of the art world congregated. Every Sunday found August invited there for his noonday meal, as Madame Bonnat had taken a fancy to him. She was motherly, yet a person commanding attention, and at a time of frightful loneliness for August, she had made him understand the greatness of his talent and opened before him vast horizons of work. She made him promise to persevere, for she firmly believed that he possessed even greater talent than her own son and that with time and hard work, he would become the greatest artist of his era.

The Marquise de Toulongeon now insisted that August return to Rimini, this time to paint her mother, the Vicomtesse des Verges, and he found it difficult to resist her attractive offer; thus it was that, once again, he sojourned in the gorgeous *palazzo* on the Adriatic. Being relatively near to Rome, the marquise could not understand why he did not take advantage of the opportunity to visit the Eternal City, but August seldom had time for sightseeing. Then it was suggested that he paint Pope Leo XIII. Again he found an excuse. The pope had enough artists; besides, none achieved admission to the Vatican without permission granted by a special committee, a committee whose purpose was to censure, even forbid, the depicting of the aging pontiff as he really was. Leo XIII definitely felt that, as head of the Church, it was more in keeping with his station to be portrayed without his thick glasses, his stooped shoulders and his huge ears. August knew that he, as an artist, could never submit to any court of censorship; if and when he should paint the pope, he would paint his subject as he saw him.

On learning of his nearness to Rome, August's mother wrote enthusiastically. She hoped he would avail himself of this unique opportunity to visit the Vatican. Though the pope was old, no living man had done more for the poor than had he. He had long espoused the cause of the masses and in his encyclical, *Rerum Novarum*, had pleaded that the lot of the working man be bettered. World revolution could be prevented only by heeding his advice.

His mother's thoughts reached into his depths; he needed no further inducement and so bought a two-day round trip ticket, hoping also by this means to pacify all of his other "advisors." As to seeing the pope . . . well, he would glimpse him now and plan to see him at greater length on another occasion. This would be a flying visit; currently, more was hardly necessary.

Once in the Eternal City, he called on Monsignor Marty who was then chaplain of the Swiss Guards. He had often heard his father speak of Leo XIII as the pope who had knighted him and given him the highest honor a layman could receive. His Holiness had even asked his father to suggest the name of a man suitable for the post of chaplain of the Swiss Guards, and that was how the choice had fallen on that family friend of many years, the humble Father Josef Marty.

When Monsignor Marty saw August and learned of his short stay, he was horrified. Forty-eight hours precluded the possibility of seeing the pope, but early the following morning, the Monsignor came for August in person, saying that he had managed to get an invitation for an audience at the Vatican. "I will wait for you since you barely have an hour to get ready." For August, who always wore a frock coat and striped grey trousers, dressing for the audience was no ordeal; soon the two men were riding to the Vatican in one of the open Roman carriages.

As they alighted at the bronze doors, Monsignor Marty entrusted his protégé to a Swiss Guard from Canton Schwyz who led him through one marble corridor after another, up one flight of marble stairs to the next, until they finally reached the great hall, where the semi-formal audience of 16 people was to take place. As the venerable septuagenarian came into the room, all knelt. Spellbound, August watched each movement of this statesman whose every gesture and action denoted his royal lineage. The round-shouldered pontiff was so stooped that as he walked from pilgrim to pilgrim he looked very tiny, although in former days he had been a tall, imposing man. When the *Maestro di Camera* introduced August, the pope's face broke into a smile and he remarked in French, "Ah, . . . Benziger! Benziger is a familiar name . . . a name we like to hear within the Vatican." Then he inquired about the health of Adelrich and asked if there had been any news of August's Carmelite brother who had volunteered to go to India as a missionary in Quillon. No sooner had the pope moved to the next pilgrim than the artist instinctively reached for his notebook. He usually had one secreted in his vest but, finding he had none, he turned to a Salvatorian seminarian and begged for a sheet of paper. Then he began sketching furiously, completely entranced by the surrounding splendor, and inspired by the delicate parchment-like features of a wonderful, tired old man who, in spite of his high office, reached out to his people with the warmth of a great father. He forgot where he was and also forgot that it was forbidden to make any drawings of the pope; his trance was broken when a surprisingly heavy hand on his shoulder brought him to his feet. The enormous hall was empty except for a few Swiss Guards. Although he was not aware of the fact, they had been assigned the duty of protecting him should anyone be inclined to prevent him from sketching. Then, suddenly, there was a roar of laughter as Monsignor Marty, in his native Swiss dialect, said: "I knew it! I could have sworn that the moment you laid eyes on His Holiness, you would succumb to his magnetic charm." August needed no further coaxing to postpone his departure for Rimini.

Inside the Vatican, it was not long before busybodies had reported to their superiors that a friend of Marty had acted contrary to protocol and made a sketch without official permission. The news inevitably reached the ears of the pope, but Leo XIII, who had already heard about the incident from Monsignor Marty, brushed aside the report with a curt: "I have nothing to fear from any member of the Benziger family. My fate is perfectly safe in the hands of that young artist."

Though August was not superstitious, he always claimed that 13 was his lucky number, and on this 13th of October, 1894, he knew that he had come to a red letter day in his life. Monsignor Marty spirited him through hidden passageways to the elaborate Throne Room. There Leo XIII was borne into the audience hall by sedan carriers clad in red damask. The pope, in his white cassock, was seated in the *Sedia Gestatoria*, blessing the pilgrims. His vivacity was astonishing considering his advanced age. For a long time after the greetings and a talk which closed with a formal blessing ceased, shouts, cheers and "evvivas" echoed in the hall. When silence settled in, several cardinals surrounded August, and the *Maestro di Camera* and the pope's *major domo* joined the group. These members of the household watched spellbound, carrying on conversations in whispers as though fearing to interrupt the finishing touches. August realized that if any men knew this aging pontiff well, this audience did, and he smiled as he heard them remark that he "had caught that poignant, understanding smile," or that he had captured the "fatherly tenderness as well as the austerity and severity" of this man of God. They even laughed at the forbidden spectacles for, there they were, slipping halfway down the emaciated nose. The large ears and stooped shoulders merely enhanced the drawing, and all present, from the loftiest cardinal to the lowliest Guard begged for a copy. August promised to have faithful engravings made which would serve as his "thank you" to each one.

His sojourn in Italy had been highly successful; the name he had acquired as an artist in ecclesiastical circles was to bring him lasting results and, upon his return to Paris, records kept in an old diary of 1895 revealed that there there awaited equal success.

January 1st. Birthday dinner given in my honor by Charles
and Mme. Lorilleux. Supper *chez* René Lorilleux and family, Rue Sugère. Called on Dr. and Mme. Eugène Willemin,
as well as six other couples. Also called on American Ambassador, English Ambassador, two French statesmen,
Bonnat and Bouguereau.

A Paris custom required that on New Year's Day, visiting
cards be left at the homes of friends to which one had been invited
rather frequently during the past year. That accounted for the fact
that on the current January 1, he had been to no less than 13
homes.

Other entries in this diary indicate that on January 10, the
Archbishop of London, Cardinal Vaughan, had visited his studio
and invited him to London, and that Harris Phelps had also arrived
later with the American Ambassador, Horace Porter, in order to
commission a portrait. On January 13 there was a dinner in honor
of Princess Galitzin given by the Comtesse de Gontaut-Biron, and
the next day an "at home" in honor of La Princesse Amélie de
Boubon. Life, it seems, was never dull.

Another friend of the portraitist was a Swiss art critic for the
Zürich and Berne newspapers, Dr. Felix Vogt, who extended to him
frequent invitations and often came to the studio. In a note to the
Swiss press, he remarked:

This up-and-coming star is capable of concentrating on the
spiritual qualities of people whose exterior is by no means
captivating. Benziger's portrait is perfect resemblance. He
has shown the model in such a frank and natural manner that
one forgets one is in the presence of a painting.

This and other glowing reports sent to Swiss editors who had not
had the slightest interest in giving August publicity, finally won
over their curiosity. He was invited to exhibit some of his paintings at the Zürich *Künstlerhaus*; if he were really a genius, he
would be certain to make the grade; if not, this event would finish
him off very quickly.

During one of his frequent absences from Paris, the great
Papa Lorilleux died. Saddened by the passing of his irreplaceable
friend whose spontaneous generosity had started him on his Paris
career, August did all he could to console the bereaved family.
The Rue Sugère penthouse had welcomed him to Parisian success
but, after his host's funeral, he felt it advisable to move. His

growing clientele made it imperative for him to seek a larger place where he would not inconvenience his friends.

Léon Bonnat heard of the artist's resolve and suggested the empty studio of his deceased brother-in-law. Without hesitation, August accepted the offer, brought all of his furnishings and moved into number 13 Rue Washington. Thirteen was, indeed, always August's lucky number. How could good fortune fail to follow him now?

Everyone was delighted by the change—except the concierge. Since the transaction had not gone through his slippery fingers, he had failed to reap a handsome commission; besides, he was not sure it was advisable for so young and handsome a tenant to be left on his own. There were far too many attractive and flirtatious women coming and going from that Benziger studio. Art was surely not the only attraction. He had ways of proving that M. Benziger was not the type of tenant he wanted.

One evening, when August was dining at Boulevard Saint-Germain, his hostess approached him. In her hand she held a floridly-addressed envelope addressed to her in a woman's handwriting and purporting to be a note to her from August. August had his suspicions. He said little, acted speedily and confronted the concierge, demanding flatly to know whether he had been hired to censor the mail. After all, the purpose of a concierge was to control the people who came and went, not to scrutinize the post. When he produced the perfumed letter, the man's wife turned pale with fear and she blurted out that she had warned her husband that they would be found out. "It is illegal to do what you made me do." The concierge, irascible fellow that he was, shouted that he would denounce the artist to the proprietor, saying that his tenant had a coterie of pretty women and should be thrown out. No bully ever intimidated August. He went straight to the owner's apartment and presented his case, as well as the letter in question. The proprietor was so delighted by his tenant's honesty that he not only invited him to stay for dinner, but immediately fired the meddlesome concierge.

Not all of August's visits were triumphs; for example, once when he was invited to the Didot country home for a few days of shooting, he alone had bagged not a single thing. Walking around to the front of the chateau, he stood on the lawn with his host. From a nearby thicket there suddenly emerged an enormous hare. August raised his gun, aimed and killed the prize catch of the day, and others gathered round to praise him. Only years later did he learn that French politeness concealed the fact that he had shot the family's prize tame hare, an animal especially bred for the improvement of the species who, whenever he caught sight of Papa Didot, came hopping to be rewarded with his daily ration of raw carrots.

Returning home, he was told that the Austrian Ambassador to the Court of Italy, Baron von Wagner, wanted a portrait of his daughter. August remembered her as a charming, vivacious lady when he had first met her in Vienna, but now her parents were worried about her as, with the unreasonableness of youth, she showed no desire to meet any of the prospective candidates who came to ask her hand in marriage. She had made up her mind that she would marry the Swiss artist, and no other. Her parents, not knowing how to explain such a delicate situation, paid a visit to the Rue Washington studio and ordered a portrait. The sittings were a tremendous success. The headstrong baroness was painted with a natty toque perched on the top of her curly head; the high-necked blouse with its lacy frills softened her loveliness. When she unburdened her heart, August gave a weighty dissertation on marriage, listing at the same time, the disadvantages of nobility's falling in love with a mere artist. He convinced her that it would be better for her to give up her notions of becoming a spinster and marry one befitting her station, especially since he had no wish to marry and, therefore, would make neither a suitable nor a stable husband. The young lady apparently took his advice for, almost as soon as she returned home, she sent him an invitation to her wedding. The groom was to be a handsome Roman nobleman, the Marquis de Roccagione. Through this marriage, she became a cousin of the Archbishop of Bologna who would become Cardinal della Chiesa, and later Pope Benedict XV.

Foremost among August's paintings of this period were those of women: that of the haughty Duchess of Aosta with her wasp waist and dainty hands, one lifting her train and the other poised on the handle of an inverted umbrella; that of the cynical dark-haired Frau W. Baumann who went to his Paris studio insisting that she would remain there until he agreed to set up a branch studio in Switzerland; that of Frau H.C. Bodmer with her cape of boa feathers, or another of the sweet and simple Frau Ackerman holding her delicate-looking little son in her arms. When Henner, the Alsatian nature painter saw the portrait of the stunning young

Fräulein Maienfisch, he exclaimed: "Benziger, you have achieved a masterpiece of color technique." This had been August's first attempt to combine in one composition the out-of-doors with portraiture. Nor were all his sitters young. The representation of wizened Frau Koch-Finsler in her lace cap set on whitened hair above a wrinkled face bespoke the calm and dignity of old age. There were other portraits of women of high society intermingled with some depicting the contentedness of motherhood.

These stood in sharp contrast to those of the ruggedly individual Swiss men who, by comparison, seemed crude in their strength. There was one of Dr. Mende, head of one of the Zürich hospitals— opinionated and determined, and another of the austere surgeon, Professor Kocher of Berne, who had performed the first goiter operation.

There were clients who were also close friends, and August's closest at this time was Robert Schwarzenbach, who would leave him no peace until he promised to paint a portrait of his youngest daughter, Olga, a teenage fanciful girl. August depicted her in a red velvet smock open at the throat, to the joy of most observers, but not to her mother. This conservative Swiss woman insisted that red was a color used only by women of ill-repute, so the artist kept this portrait for himself and did a second. This time Olga appeared as a demure school girl with tightly-plaited braids and in a very drab dress, displaying none of the vigor or elan for which people had come to know her. But August kept and cherished the little lady in red and would never part with that portrait.

Schwarzenbach, the owner of silk mills in Switzerland, Italy and France, and a very civic-minded individual, conceived the idea of building a vast concert hall designed to become the center for musical performances in Switzerland. In order to get the project started, he volunteered to pay half the expenses, and invited such artists as Brahms and Paderewski to perform in the completed hall. Dr. Frederick Hegar, a Swiss composer, was in charge of festivities. Knowing that August was a friend of Brahms, he begged him to make a sketch of the musician as he played, but secretly, as it was known that Brahms violently objected to being photographed, to say nothing of being painted, as he wished to be remembered only by his music. This August did, sitting in one of the boxes and closely observing his dear old friend from his days in Vienna.

Each evening, as soon as the concert ended, the guests of honor retired to the generously-proportioned home of the

Schwarzenbachs. On this occasion, August was made responsible to see that his virtuoso lacked for nothing, and was instructed as to details: Brahms liked his large stein to be filled with at least a quarter of various liqueurs blended together—a little cognac, Bénédictine, Cointreau, Vodka, Kirsch and at least six or seven others. These were energetically mixed together, then sipped in very slow stages. Before the evening was over, Brahms was in the right mood. For a while, he toyed with paper and pencil and then, all of a sudden, he wrote out a composition. Once the work was on paper, he ran his fingers over the keys a few times; suddenly he broke into music and played until the rafters shook. Every now and then he halted to imbibe a small quantity of his potent concoction; then he would play once again as though his fingers were on fire. When he struck the last chord, there was a pregnant silence, then wild applause . . . only the great maestro never heard it. He had lapsed into unconsciousness. August and Dr. Hegar carried their slumbering genius to the safety of his bed.

The *Zürcher Zeitung* spoke in December of an exhibit being held in "Benziger's *Atelier.*" Reference was made to the aquarelle of Johannes Brahms gravely meditating, listening to the music, and to the portrait of Dr. Hegar. The art critic of that daily noted:

> Benziger denotes in his pictures the brilliant qualities of the French school, freshness of conception, vigorous coloring, easy touch, elegance and sureness of execution. There is no heaviness, no academical pedantry. . . . Only he who lives every day and every hour in the midst of life and in an animating artistic atmosphere such as that which surrounds the artist in Paris is able to observe and reproduce life in such a way.

One of the last Zürich portraits was that of August's niece, Anny Sonntag, a shy, pale, very blonde little girl. Loving to experiment with color, with this model he used a dozen tones of yellow. The soft yellow of the child's frock and of her light flowing hair contrasted with variegated yellows and browns, the browns of the nasturtiums clutched in her fingers and the great brown eyes wherein August had caught the warmth and tones of the Flemish school.

But the artist *had to* return to France; there was something so intriguing about Paris that he could not keep away from it for long. It was as though the city had entrapped him in some strange spell and he was invariably forced to return to this place where he was very much at home, surrounded by friends who understood him and whom he understood. One of his admirers, Prime Minister Léon Bourgeois, dropping in to welcome him back, brought along his favorite niece, a tall, lovely-looking child whom August could not resist painting. He caught her pensive, dark eyes, the sallow, distinguished face framed by dark brown bangs, her richly-hued hair surmounted by a large, dark blue hat. Uncle Léon was so thrilled by this composition that he immediately ordered a portrait to be made of himself.

A group of ultra-conservative French officials called the agreement a scandal. Why would a man in such high office employ a foreigner? Were there not enough French artists going hungry? Nevertheless, this painting was a great success, and the publicity caused by the carping officials merely attracted attention to the fine work of the artist.

During this Paris interlude, August frequently stopped at the home of the de Traverse family. One evening, the lady of the house, who had planned to entertain at dinner, presented her husband's excuses: M. de Traverse had just been called to the Elysée Palace on business and might have to be a little late. The half hour lengthened to several hours, and the hostess was seized with alarm, so August volunteered to investigate the situation. At that precise moment, M. de Traverse returned, ghastly white and extremely upset. The President of the Republic had had a stroke and was at death's door.

Only after he had been reinforced by a bit of cognac could M. de Traverse tell the somber if amusing story of what had transpired.

On reaching the Palace, he had mounted the great marble staircase leading to the quarters of the president. As he arrived, the personal valet rushed from the door, ashen and trembling. "Quick, quick! Get a priest. The president is dying. He has had a stroke and has not long to live." Henri de Traverse dashed down the staircase and into a cab, shouting orders to the driver to make haste with all possible speed. When they reached the Church of the Madeleine, only two blocks away, he roused the parish priest who hastened to get Anointing Oil and Holy Viaticum. Being led to the sickroom, the much-perturbed priest turned to the valet and inquired solemnly, "Is he still conscious?" The valet replied, "Oh no, Father. We have sent her home." The word "connaissance" which was used by the priest had a two-fold meaning. It could imply either a state of consciousness or an intimate human relationship. The priest had asked the question in all innocence, hoping that the president might still be conscious enough to make his confession. The valet, for his part, being aware of the president's weakness for all pretty women, and realizing that his master's last hour had come, had taken matters into his own hands. He had saved the highly-embarrassing situation by evicting the president's courtesan. The "connaissance" had been unceremoniously dispatched on her way.

August's reputation as an artist had certainly grown by this time, not least of all in clerical circles. On one occasion, the Papal Nuncio brought Canon Faralicq, the secretary of Abbé Chaumont, founder of the Priests of Saint Francis de Sales, to his studio. The two men discussed the necessity of having a portrait of the Abbé made, but unfortunately he was another individual unwilling to sit for an artist. Humble and sincere, he put no stock in pictorial immortality, although he was worn out in his struggle to make French Catholics realize the dangers of the anti-clericalism which surrounded them, and he probably had not long to live. He had formed a virile group of clergymen, one which was watchful and self-sacrificing and, within a period of 20 years, their numbers reached 2,000. As the anti-clerical French government had already confiscated monasteries and the properties of cloistered religious, it was clear that their survival depended on forming strong bonds with apostolic lay workers. These had to be trained and, once their education had been completed, the clergy would have to learn how to accept them, not merely reluctantly, but with love and trust and gratitude. This sort of idea was totally foreign to most of the basically conservative French, but the plan had worked well in England in 1631 when implemented by Mary Ward, who wanted lay workers living "in the world but not of it." Because her vision of the needs of her times created bitter enemies within the Catholic Church on the part of those who felt that women should not be allowed to live dedicated lives "in the world!" she was thrown into jail by Papal Order and her Institute was suppressed, but not until after it was seen by many to be the answer to contemporary problems. Mary Ward had believed that women had a contribution to make and *should* be allowed to work for the Kingdom of God without strict enclosure, without vows. Abbé Chaumont related to what she had had to say over 250 years earlier and adapted her insights to his own time and place. He felt that women, as well as men, should be able to seek key positions, and that their apostolic work should be felt in factories, offices, schools, hospitals and even in politics. In 1872, consequently, he founded the Association of the Daughters of St. Francis de Sales. These women wore no habits and worked in widespread fields at home and abroad, and their ranks included the single, the married and some lonely widows. In France, they assisted priests in the slums; in outlying districts they taught, helped the sick and became the heads of Catholic Action. Having provided for the clergy and for women, he finally organized apostolic work for married and single men along the same lines. Now, however, his secretary was gravely concerned about the health of the founder of these varied Institutes. The man suffered from dropsy and was almost unable to sleep at all. It was at this point that his secretary and Canon Faralicq called upon August to ask him to visit the Abbé. Perhaps he might induce him to sit for a portrait.

Abbé Chaumont possessed a disarming manner which enabled him to do whatever he wished with the most difficult characters, winning them over by his simplicity. August soon discovered that he was talking freely about himself, something he rarely, if ever, did. When he caught himself in the act and exclaimed in dismay, the old Abbé merely laughed and explained that he tried to look at each person from God's point of view. He had been endowed with keen intuitive power which enabled him to see through people as though they had been made of glass. The visit proved an astonishing success, ending with the good old gentleman's consent to sit for a portrait on condition that it be begun at once. "How soon can you begin? How long will it take for the work to be completed?" August realized that time was at a premium; he would have to cut short the length and number of sittings. "At least two weeks, Monsieur l'Abbé." The man with snow-white hair and stooped shoulders looked at the artist with penetrating eyes, pondered a moment and counted on swollen fingers. "Two weeks? Well . . . yes . . . two weeks might do, but you must promise me that you won't ask for a single day longer. Do you give me your word?" The following morning, the sittings began. Though the Abbé was only 59, he was so bent, so tired-looking that he appeared to be in his 70's. August felt almost as though he were in the presence of God, so holy and serene was this man.

While his physical condition grew worse daily, his mind remained clear, but he inquired with growing concern whether the portrait would be completed by the 15th of May. There were moments when even August could hardly conceal his anxiety. When the usually florid cheeks suddenly turned pale, the sitter would ring a bell, and at once a nurse would rush into the room to administer a powerful stimulant. After a few seconds, the Abbé would be able to look up and smile. Quite nonchalantly, with a wry little nod, he would exclaim, "For a few moments, I thought I was dying." Then he would mop his brow and watch the artist intently as he laid on the finishing touches.

On the 14th of May, August remarked: "Tomorrow is your last sitting. May I come again at the same hour?" L'Abbé seemed more pensive than usual. "Yes . . . but only for an hour. By 10:00 you must be finished." On the 15th they met again. August felt reluctant to say his farewell, so fond of this noble man had he become. When he remarked that he hoped to see him again shortly, l'Abbé had replied, "We shall see. . . ." Early the next morning, Canon Faralicq entered August's room looking greatly upset; the Abbé had passed on. Upon completion of the sitting, he had gone to the chapel as usual; later he had dictated a few urgent letters, held a conference and had been seized with a stroke. He had not been afraid of death but had once confided to his secretary his fear that he might die before the portrait was completed, even though he had promised to give his followers this last pleasure, a good likeness of himself for them to remember him by.

Cardinal Herbert Vaughan, Archbishop of Westminster, came for the funeral, and invited August to London. He had been approached by court officials who wanted to know if the Swiss artist would be able to paint Queen Victoria. The cardinal would recommend him to the Catholic Lord Mayor of London, who would be glad to help with the arranging of details. August, having almost more work than he could cope with at the moment, hesitated but, as result of the persuasive powers of the cardinal, he agreed to go to London to look over the situation. It was to be a visit of short duration. Sir Stuart Knell, the Lord Mayor, showed him about the city and took him with him to the Guildhall, where August sketched the bewigged judges with their long white curls and their formal robes of office, and also sketched his friend as he sat judging cases on the Alderman's Bench. Not long afterwards a telegram arrived from Switzerland; it came like a thunderclap. August's father was gravely ill; his mother begged him to return at once to Einsiedeln. Two days later, August was to have been presented at court, as Queen Victoria was anxious to meet him, but he immediately canceled all engagements, packed his things, took the first channel boat, and in France entrained for Switzerland.

Adelrich Benziger was a bedridden, desperately sick man, but at the sight of August he gained renewed strength. For hours on end the two talked and even laughed about the past, but the son sensed that his father's days were numbered. He longed to make one last portrait of him just as he was, propped up with pillows, a mere shadow of the dynamic man who was now being starved; the doctors insisted that the only cure for ulcers was absence from all food.

August now spent long hours in the sickroom, as all else had become immaterial for him. His clients in Zürich, Paris and London could wait for him; he was running a race with death. Some 40 sketches were made before he was satisfied that he had achieved a really striking resemblance in his profile of his distinguished, white-bearded parent reclining on his pillows, awaiting death. His mother was as delighted as was her husband as they saw that the miniature painting in oils was a perfect jewel, and the Governor left no peace until several thousand black-and-white engravings had been made of that painting. These he signed, then had his secretaries mail them to the hundreds of friends and acquaintances around the world who had sent him messages of solicitation and good wishes. To scores of whom he loved and revered, he sent this likeness and added a farewell note. In spite of the assurances given by his physicians, he knew he would soon go to God. His son knew as well.

Nevertheless, it became imperative for August to get back to Paris; an exhibition of his paintings was to be held, and prospective clients were besieging his studio. Although he seldom undertook more than he could complete in a reasonable period of time, he was now solidly booked for two years in advance. Furthermore, the prizes he had won at the *Salon* had brought him to the attention of the Americans. In the early years of the foundation of their nation, there had been little time to collect or even scrutinize art. Now, self-made millionaires who had cultural backgrounds as well as monetary success cried out for the beauties of Old World art, and were ready to secure paintings and sculpture to grace their homes. At this point, two ladies, Mrs. William Thaw, Jr., and her friend, Mrs. M. Husey, both from Pittsburgh, approached him and invited him to come to America. When August offered an overload of previous commissions as a reason to decline the invitation, Mrs. Thaw persisted. She wanted portraits of each of her four daughters. August still resisted. However, Robert Schwarzenbach, who happened to be present and who had already established his flourishing silk business in the States, looked at his friend in astonishment. In his Zürich dialect, he hissed under his breath: "August, you are a damn fool to turn down such an offer! America has a great future ahead of her. These people have plenty of money but lack art; you cannot afford to refuse. I sail in October. You can share my cabin!" August, on the strength of these words, reluctantly accepted the invitation, but promptly forgot the incident in the rush of urgent matters.

That summer, he adhered to his schedule of work, work, work, and was startled in September to receive a telegram from Schwarzenbach: "We sail from Liverpool October 6th aboard *Majestic*." August again hesitated. Now he had a perfectly valid reason for not going to America: his father's condition had not improved; in fact, it grew ever more precarious. He would go to Einsiedeln and present his dilemma to his parents. Adelrich, in his vast wisdom, would know what he should do. The ailing publisher had one brief sentence-worth of advice: "Go! Pack up and leave immediately." That settled the matter. The next few days were memorable for both men; father and son were drawn closer than ever before. Although Governor Benziger had often spoken in the past of his great admiration for America and its people, he had been somewhat reticent in revealing his innermost thoughts, but now he opened up secrets long hidden in his soul. "America is a land of opportunity. Had my father permitted me to remain in the States—as I longed to do—I, too, would have become an American." He added, "Go, and make a name for yourself in the New World."

August then notified his father that he no longer needed any financial assistance; he was absolutely independent. When he showed him his checkbook, Adelrich was dumbfounded. In the past year, through the medium of portraiture, the young artist had succeeded in earning as much as his father had in the publishing business. The Governor related the fact that, on his death, he would leave a stipulated sum of money to each of his children, including August who was also to inherit one of the houses, and August asked that it be one in which his parents had lived. He learned that he would receive the Brunnen estate. He then observed that his sister, Marie, had struggled financially for years; her marriage had proved to be an extremely happy one but it was not blessed with an abundance of material goods. He expressed the hope that his father would divide the portion of the money allotted to him amongst the other members of the family. So much had been invested in his expensive education in years past that, in this manner, he could now repay his brothers and sister for the many fine things which had been done on his behalf.

When August consulted with his father's physicians, he was told that the danger was not imminent. Since he would only be gone for six weeks, they were quite certain that, upon his return, his father would still be alive. At the moment of his departure, the Governor gave his son one last admonition, telling him that Americans have a very high moral standard. Their code of ethics, he explained, is not like that of Europe. Good Christians there really live clean, decent lives. They are not ashamed of chastity. Once you kiss a girl in America, remember, you will be expected to marry her. Take no liberties. Watch your step. The woman of America is an authority. She is a great power. Her word counts. These were wisdom-words for one who would find himself an American wife in the not-too-distant future. His mother promised to keep him posted on events but she, too, felt it advisable for him to go to the New World to look over the terrain. Their farewells were joyful.

Once again August took the train to Paris but this time secretly, with a heavy heart as he had definite misgivings about his father's health. October 6th found him in Liverpool where he boarded the English packet, *Majestic*, and moved into Schwarzenbach's stateroom. He thought of his father's crossing of this same ocean 54 years before—that time on a three-masted schooner. Now he and his friend were comfortably settled aboard a floating palace, a great luxury liner like a vast hotel containing every modern convenience.

August's shipboard companions were predominantly American millionaires who had sojourned in Europe and were returning to every state in the Union. Two groups of passengers interested him most, those from New York and Chicago. By coincidence, a Mr. Marshall Field, a Mr. F.R. Otis and Mr. and Mrs. Arthur Caton were seated at his table, Chicagoans all, who insisted that when the artist completed his work in Pittsburgh, he must come to Chicago and look them up; they would be happy to show him a thriving city which had really made progress.

August was astonished to learn that Mr. Field had left Paris in a state of agitation as the result of a highly unpleasant experience which had left him with extreme dislike of one Léon Bonnat. He was infuriated by this unexpected attack on his own master and leapt to his defense; surely there had been some mistake. Mr. Field was adamant. He continued his tirade about the fabulous price paid, the tedious length of the sittings, the unsatisfactory monstrosity that had been produced. He had, in fact, been so enraged by the whole procedure that he had thrown down the fee and then stalked off, leaving the insulting portrait of himself in Bonnat's studio.

August could not forget this distressing criticism of his master. At the first opportunity he had after his return to France, he made a point of seeing Bonnat. Without any preliminaries, he inquired: "Where is your portrait of Marshall Field?" Bonnat was vague, could not seem to recall what had happened to it, and brushed the question aside impatiently, as though it were a mere nothing. August persisted; he would not let the matter rest until he had the answer to some questions. Until that moment, no discordant note or harsh feeling had ever come between the student and master. Now August felt anger surge within him. Point-blank, he related the incident which had occurred aboard ship during which he had staunchly defended the name of Bonnat. Now it was only fair that he should see the painting in question and form his own judgment.

In the basement, with its face turned toward the wall, was the maligned canvas; he carried it upstairs, wiped away the cobwebs, then drew in his breath in shock. No likeness existed. The foreshortening of the arms was entirely out of proportion, the paint had been carelessly smeared on in a slap-dash manner. Could this possibly be the work of Bonnat? August rushed back to the studio. "Master," he exclaimed, "whatever induced you to do this dreadful thing to one of the world's major merchants? Field is a kindly man. Small wonder he left France upset." He made clear to Bonnat that it was imperative for him to arrange at once for another series of sittings . . . What in heaven's name, he asked, had possessed the artist to do anything so inhuman?

Bonnat, who had been spoiled and pampered because many people kowtowed to his whims, explained that Field had annoyed him. He was always in such a hurry to get things done. Bonnat required at least 45 days for his sittings. Field had refused to cooperate from the start; he, Bonnat, was accustomed to paint at a leisurely pace. No savage American was going to prod him into nerve-wracking haste and speed! In time, thanks to August's ministrations, Mr. Field returned to Bonnat's studio, a better understanding was achieved between artist and subject and, finally, a highly satisfactory portrait was completed. It was taken to Chicago and awarded a place of honor in Field's State Street store.

When the *S.S. Majestic* docked at the 10th Street pier, August and his companion drove to the Holland House, a white-stone, 10-story building which, until the erection of the Waldorf, had ranked first among the palatial hotels of New York. August liked what he saw of America; in fact, the impression was to leave lasting memories which were to change the course of his life. Having ascertained that adequate funds had been deposited in the local bank, he could afford to look about him and take his own time to plot his next move. If the Pittsburgh offer did not turn out satisfactorily, he could reverse his itinerary and return to France.

What August enjoyed most about the New World was the kindly hospitality and informality of the American home. Mr. J. Hood Wright was one of the partners of J. Pierpont Morgan, the renowned financier, who, with his lovely wife, had often dropped in at the Rue Washington studio. Mr. Wright invited him to make himself at home at their beautiful country estate overlooking the Hudson River as, of all his American acquaintances, they were probably the ones August knew best. Wishing to introduce him to their New York friends, they gave a huge banquet for him at the Waldorf, where he met not only J. Pierpont Morgan, but also Thomas Fortune Ryan, the Whitelaw Reeds, the Astors, Vanderbilts, Belmonts, Goulds and Whitneys. That first formal dinner was to remain for all time indelibly engraved on his memory.

Mrs. Wright had accorded him the place of honor at table where all sorts of new and exciting dishes had been savored, including oysters, lobsters and the fabulous *Terrapin de Baltimore*. Fascinated by the company and the food, August reached the dessert course without paying much attention to what the waiters had placed before him. He was quite accustomed to finger bowls as they were used in exclusive circles in France, and he had occasionally seen a great dowager lift a silver or cut glass one to her lips, then use it for the purpose of rinsing out her mouth! But until he reached America, he had never realized that tiny cakes of colored soap could be served for the cleansing of the finger tips. In talking animatedly with Mrs. Wright, August had toyed with the diminutive squares of pink and green "soap," forgetting what he was doing. Finally, he noticed that the cakes had vanished; he *must* have eaten them absent-mindedly! Hurriedly he rose from the table, excusing himself, and rushed to the dressing room barely in time to give vent to his violent nausea. When he returned, Mrs. Wright, seeing how pale he was, hoped to revive his spirits and improve his health. Meanwhile, she lifted a pastel-colored after-dinner mint to her mouth. August reached out his hand in alarm, attempting to stop her: "Surely you're not going to eat soap!" Mrs. Wright understood and laughed, and her guest learned through the lesson of the peppermints how cruel a trick the imagination can play on the uninitiated. From that time on, he decided to make inquiries about anything new he encountered, and not be too proud to admit ignorance.

Plans had been made and the tickets bought for the trip to Pittsburgh when a cablegram, signed by his mother, brought the sorrowful news: "Father died October 9th."

August had been three days at sea, and had not known. Apparently the message had reached the firm of Benziger Brothers 10 days before, and only now had the office succeeded in locating him. He felt that he had no choice but to cancel all existing engagements, pack his bags, and take the first boat back to Europe, but Robert Schwarzenbach rebelled. It was not at all necessary for August to change his current plans. A few weeks, more or less, could make little difference now. His father who had passed away would have wanted August to carry on as planned. He did.

Studio of the Artist

Sketches, 1888

Top row: an unknown friend; Marie Benziger; Zimmerman, the factory hand.
Center: Rika, his niece; Professor Stucky; Grandmother Benziger.
Lower: an unknown friend; Professor at Downside; Adelrich Benziger.

Man's Head

The charcoal sketches "Man's Head," and "Head of an Old Woman" (following) were awarded first prize for draftsmanship at the Salon of the "Champs Elysées," 1890.

Head of an Old Woman

Portrait of the Artist's Mother

Frau Landammann Benziger
This portrait of the mother of the artist won first prize at the Paris Salon.

President Theodore Roosevelt

The portrait was presented to the Chicago Historical Society.

The Hunter

Miss Helen Hatfield

Professor John A. Brashear

The Pittsburgh astronomer's portrait, painted for Charles M. Schwab.

Cardinal Farley

James Phinney Baxter

Miss Isabel Pereda

Mrs. Wallace H. Rowe

Robert S. Brookings

Mrs. Hutton and Children

Archbishop John Bonzano

CHAPTER 9

Portrait Painter
(1896-1897)

On his first crossing, August had met Josiah H. Penniman, a professor of the history of art at the University of Pennsylvania, and the two men were drawn together in friendship. As the professor had begged him to visit him the first time he passed through Philadelphia, August had agreed to do so, although he despised trains and the stopover involved the dreary prospect of traversing 250 miles of dismal track stretching through coal mining country when he resumed his journey to Pittsburgh. Still, he had accepted the invitation and there was no question of canceling it. However, it was to him that August was able to formulate with clarity and brevity his own philosophy of portraiture: "A portrait is not only the picture of a man's body; a real likeness must be a picture of that individual's soul as expressed by his body." August left with an order to paint Professor Penniman's portrait.

He was next invited to stay with the William Thaws in Pittsburgh. It was the same Mrs. Thaw who had seen his exhibit of portraits at the *Salon* in Paris, and she convinced him that he must come to her city and help further her dream of establishing an art center there equal to those in Chicago and New York. The well-to-do of Pittsburgh had long since moved away from the city proper which reeked of smoke and soot from factories and coal mines, so August found himself ensconced in the Thaw's luxurious home in suburban Allegheny across the river. However, sensing at once that he was viewed more as a curiosity than an entity by some in this setting, he excused himself as soon as possible, pleading the necessity for long and late hours of work, and succeeded in finding himself rooms in a small hotel in the Thaw's neighborhood.

Knowing that he could paint but a limited number of portraits in a given time, the artist soon found it necessary to exercise discretion in his selection of clients. The women of this city gave him trouble. As a man who prided himself on his stability, who had never kowtowed to anyone, August found his Pittsburgh experience of mercurial wives who were dissatisfied with his portraits more than exasperating. Once he was certain that he had caught the likeness in a painting, he flatly refused to alter his work. Ever a realist, he cleaved unyieldingly to what he saw as the truth, and he was especially adamant when it came to the matter of reducing his models' poundage. Certainly, August knew how to flatter women sitters and never failed to reveal their most fascinating aspects, yet he bluntly declined to portray a portly woman as a sylph. Consequently, at this time he resolutely turned his back on what he saw as feminine wheedlings and wiles to devote his energies primarily to portraying men.

There was something about American males that intrigued him. Their ability to accept defeat and failure and follow it up by persistent, repeated efforts to start anew stimulated his imagination. In Europe, these men and their heirs would have remained forever peasants or miners yet, in America, they had risen to the top with their horizons still unlimited. He praised the mettle of these pioneers who had come empty-handed from the Old World, risking their lives to carve opportunity out of the hard rock of the land.

Before leaving Pittsburgh, August had come to have deep respect for Mrs. William Thaw. She possessed innate refinement and longed to bring the best of Europe's artistic and intellectual accomplishments to her frontier town. Because the Thaws had amassed a fortune in coal, coke, steel and railroads, she sincerely believed that they had a duty to assume a role of leadership in arousing a genuine interest in art; but, meeting with little success among the Pittsburgh natives, she finally restricted her efforts to her immediate family. Elderly and young Thaws posed for the artist whose brush captured with equal facility the riches of youth and age.

Meanwhile, Marshall Field was on August's track again; he invited him to Chicago and assured him that he would find ample opportunities in this bustling lakeshore city for the practice of his art. Chicagoans were seeking a talented portrait painter, he said. The Windy City was quite the opposite of Pittsburgh in that it had managed to become a city with cultural interests in a comparatively short time, and its people had reaped their achievements, not through strokes of luck, but by dint of hard, back-breaking labor. Chicago was a city of enthusiastic lovers of beauty who had worked consistently toward bringing within reach of its citizens the best in European art and music. Only 60 years previously, it had been a Potowatomi Indian trading post but, by 1846, the swamp-lands adjacent to Lake Michigan had boomed into a promising real estate venture attracting a population of 14,000. The inhabitants believed implicitly in their city's future, especially because it already served as the railroad hub of the North American continent.

August was soon to meet an impressive group of men who, instead of competing with one another, worked side by side as a unit to achieve the ends on which they had set their sights.

His reception in this city was far different from that which he had received in Pittsburgh. Word of his coming had been circulated far in advance and newspapers carried articles announcing the arrival of this talented artist from overseas. Marshall Field personally helped August find a studio in dignified Steinway Hall. Among his first clients and visitors were friends whom he had met aboard the *Majestic*. Mrs. Caton took it upon herself to introduce her friends. A few years later, after she had been widowed, this lady who had been exceptionally kind and helpful to August became the bride of Marshall Field.

Mrs. Caton asked August if he knew anything about the Potter Palmers. Like the rest of this circle of Chicagoans, Mr. Palmer had risen from the ranks and, through carefully-planned real estate operations, had acquired enormous wealth. He was a patient plodder, achieving his reputation as a financial magnate in slow, steady states, advancing from the ownership of one store, to that of a hotel and then to an entire chain of hotels of which the Palmer House became preeminent. Potter Palmer had envisioned State Street as the major business center in the city and had handpicked the site for its development, the section later to become known as Chicago's famed Loop.

The gracious Mrs. Potter, at home in her mansion on Lake Shore Drive, was a collector of objects from foreign lands, and the rooms in her "castle" were filled with woodwork, tapestries, porcelains, and antiques from every corner of the globe; she took pleasure in becoming hostess to outstanding Europeans. Through her and her friends, August skyrocketed to fame overnight.

Mr. F.R. Otis, another of August's fellow passengers on the *Majestic*, was also involved in real estate, and there was little he did not know about property. August, who had heard so much about the high standards of American morals, was shocked to learn from Mr. Otis that his colleagues thought nothing of renting suitable homes to prostitutes. Though prostitution was legally forbidden and openly frowned upon, many houses of ill repute were in operation. From Mr. Otis's viewpoint, business was business; these clients paid well until raided by the police, and then moved along to other quarters. August deduced, therefore, that human nature was, indeed, very much the same the world over—although in America there was the notable difference that standards appeared to be higher than they were across the ocean.

On the northwest corner of State Street and Jackson Boulevard, Mr. Otis owned one of the tallest structures in Chicago and wanted August to see the incomparable view of the city and lake from the observation tower of his modern business building. The two men left the elevator at the seventh floor and climbed to the roof where a panorama of the countryside awaited them.

Two floors of the Otis Building had been leased to a merchant who specialized in ready-made clothing. Until the advent of this Henry C. Lytton, no gentleman dreamed of buying any garment other than one made-to-order. Henry Lytton became a leader in his profession. "Why should not the working male be as well-dressed as the millionaire gentleman?" he asked himself. In reply to his own question, he established his enterprise along unprecedented lines: mass production was initiated and became the fashion for the majority of American buyers. Clients came from a radius of a thousand miles, wanting to be outfitted with ready-made suits by Henry C. Lytton at his famous Hub store.

According to Mr. Otis, Henry Lytton was a provocative composite of high ideals and utterly bewildering notions. For one thing, Lytton did not believe that liquor and business should mix. As there had been a saloon in the basement of the building, he did not relax until he had succeeded in ousting the saloonkeeper. Subsequently, he moved his own wares down to those lower regions and initiated the famous "bargain counters"; he also stopped his salesmen from drinking, smoking or spitting while on the job!

Nobody knew better than Henry Lytton the value of advertising and he had spent over a million dollars in press publicity alone. A week before, he had tied up Chicago's traffic by blithely tossing fur coats from the roof as a daring promotional stunt. On another occasion he had filled the sky with a hundred colored balloons, each bearing gift coupons valued at a dollar or a hundred dollars. Show windows came into full use for a wide variety of schemes.

Many scandalized eyebrows were raised when Lytton invited young couples to be married in the Hub's display windows, offering as their reward the complete furniture required for a three-room apartment. During the Harrison-Cleveland presidential campaign of 1888, Lytton endeared himself to the fun-loving populace by making a wager with a prominent attorney at the Union League Club that Cleveland would win the election; the loser was to chop a full cord of wood in the Hub's windows. Harrison became president and Lytton, accordingly, proceeded to pay off his election bet. Police had to break a lane for the cable cars to move along State Street as thousands cheered while Mr. Lytton, in impeccable white tie and tails, reduced logs to kindling.

On their way out of the building, Mr. Otis took August through the Hub store and pointed out a jovial-looking man wearing a carnation in his buttonhole; he wanted him to meet Lytton, the optimist, "a quite remarkable man of tremendous drive and energy who will stop at absolutely nothing!" Lytton was swinging a jaunty walking stick as the two men approached, and in his hand he held a pearl-grey hat which matched his spats. He nodded in cheerful greeting. As he shook August's hand, he remarked that Mr. Otis had been telling him about his excellent portraits, and suggested that he himself might be interested in having one or two painted. August bowed in the Old World manner, acknowledging the gracious compliment and then dismissed from his mind the possibility of adding Mr. Henry C. Lytton to his growing list of clients. A few weeks later, a note arrived from the Lyttons, inviting the artist to their "at home" on Drexel Boulevard. The family had three sons and one striking daughter who had already made her bow to society. All were in the process of packing prior to sailing on a West Indies cruise. Upon their return they would like to have a three-quarter length portrait of the lady of the house. He would hear from them later.

Meanwhile, there were some other especially interesting Chicagoans August was about to meet, among them the Morris family. Nelson Morris, the son of a German Jew, had been born in Switzerland. Long before, as a child in Einsiedeln, August had heard his father lament the fate of the Jews in Switzerland. The supposedly tolerant Swiss prided themselves on the fact that they did not bar Jews from entering their country or engaging in any kind of business there, yet no Jew could ever hold public office. The owning of a business was made virtually impossible by the unwritten laws that ostracized them from every profession. While the Guggenheim and Morris families had fled from Germany to the Helvetian Republic, where they had settled in the Canton of Argau, prejudice within Switzerland had been so bitter there that they felt no hope for a happy future in that country. Disappointed, they had packed their things and migrated to America. Nelson Morris was a young boy at the time. August, meeting him many years later, liked this Swiss-American and Nelson, for his part, was happy to meet a full-fledged Swiss who was free from prejudice. They became fast friends . . . August was struck by this man's power of endurance, by his grit, his energy, his determination.

Although a millionaire when they met, Morris still rose at dawn. Daily he was the first to arrive at the stockyards where he bought his cattle while the rest of Chicago still slept, and personally supervised every detail, keeping well ahead of his competitors. Morris was the first to foresee the necessity of installing new methods of refrigeration and utilizing new methods of curing. In one morning alone, his firm prepared over 10,000 hogs for market, a staggering number for those days.

Knowing that the painter loved horses and sought the finest for his newly-acquired Swiss estate, he helped him buy eight beautiful steeds at an auction for less than $10 apiece! These were shipped to Europe to graze on the Brunnen land.

As both men were early risers, they often met for breakfast. One day August's curiosity got the better of him and he queried: "Tell me how it is that you, an orthodox Jew, eat pork? I thought your religion forbade doing so." Morris laughed. "God has been good to us," he explained, and went on to say that, through the medium of the hog, he had become a millionaire. How could he despise the heaven-sent animal? As a youth in his teens, he had reached New York penniless and unable to speak the English language. The relative who had promised to meet him did not appear, and work was impossible to find. He faced starvation. In an empty lot he had found a dead hog, skinned the animal and sold it. This transaction provided him with his first American money, and the beginning of his career. Through the slaughter of hogs, he not only made a name for himself but acquired a fortune. "That is why you find me serving bacon for breakfast. Just as you, a Catholic, can get a dispensation to eat meat on Friday, so I have a dispensation to eat pork!"

August made sketches of Morris's children, Maud and Ira. Ira was an attractive young man who was studying for the diplomatic service, and was also courting Miss Lytton. It was through him that August learned that the Lyttons had not left Chicago after all. Their son, Walter, had come down with the measles and the entire household was quarantined. There would be no winter cruise for any of them. August immediately called on Mr. Lytton and arrangements were made for him to begin the portrait of Mrs. Lytton; then began also those long hours when artist and sitter became as one in their interchange of experiences.

August learned much that pleased him. Here was a kindred spirit, a person with real insight and tremendous cultural background. To an artist who had found these qualities lacking in many of his New World subjects, Rose Lytton became particularly delightful. She had been a South Carolina belle. Her magnolia-like complexion delighted him. There was something ethereal and beautiful about this woman of strong, refined features and luminous, vibrant eyes. Her rich brown hair, crowned with a diamond tiara, was regal. A string of simple pearls encircled her lovely neck while the low décolletage of her black velvet bodice, set off by lace, served to focus attention on her loveliness. August captured her uniqueness with his brush. The phenomenal success of Mrs. Lytton's portrait led to four successive orders. By February 27, 1897, August was able to hold an exhibit at Thurber's. Fifteen portraits, all painted within the few months he had spent in America, proved that he was now established on both sides of the Atlantic.

Several commitments to paint prominent clergymen surfaced at this time. Both Bishop Cheney, head of the Anglican Church, and Archbishop Phean, the ranking Catholic bishop of Chicago, sat for August yet, among all the portraits he had been painting, one stood out as a *chef-d'oeuvre,* a likeness produced on a monster canvas 14 feet high. A demure, gentle, blue-eyed young lady, the very personification of womanhood, stepped out of a quiet green-brown background to present herself in her latest Paris creation. Her pleated purple ensemble was relieved at the throat by a white satin yoke and collar. Her seal cape was trimmed with sable, her blonde hair set off by a large white picture-hat perched on top of which were fragile ostrich feathers and a soft, white dove. This portrait of Gertrude Lytton was stunning.

With the coming of summer, August was obliged to end his Chicago stay. In New York, he learned that his Carnegie Hall studio would be ready for occupancy in the fall; in the meantime, he could remain in his regular suite at the Holland House. At this time, Vice President Hobart's interest in the Swiss painter's work ripened so he invited the artist to his home, and there gave him an order, not only for his own portrait, but also for two to be made of President McKinley. The president was a close friend of Mr. Hobart, and the latter wished to give him pleasure by presenting one portrait to the White House and the other to the Republican Party. These were to be begun in the fall.

Toward the end of May 1897, there was a surprise reunion with the Lyttons aboard the *S.S. Majestic*. August was returning to Switzerland to take possession of the estate he had recently inherited from his father; and the Lyttons, together with their children, were *en route* to Bad Nauheim in Germany, although Mrs. Lytton was suffering from an illness from which she was never to recover. She had consulted her brother-in-law, Dr. Simon Baruch, "Uncle Doctor" as everyone called him, and had been told that it would be advisable for her to go to Germany and place herself under the care of Professor Grödel in Bad Nauheim since both the patient and "Uncle Doctor" were staunch believers in hydrotherapy.

During the crossing, August was invited to join the Lyttons at their table where much merrymaking and laughter ensued. Nightly he and Gertrude danced. They both loved music passionately and she, having spent much of her youth studying it, could play Mendelssohn, Chopin and Beethoven with equal skill. Her father had a remarkable voice and Gertrude often accompanied him at the piano. At the ship's benefit concert, father and daughter performed; then August and she played several duets. The bond between them was increasing in strength. When the farewell party broke up, and the ship docked at Liverpool, August went to the Hotel Victoria and the Lyttons to the Savoy. The latter's 10 days in the metropolis were busy ones. Mr. Lytton's best friend, Harry Gordon Selfridge, was owner of one of London's largest department stores. A former Chicagoan, he and Henry Lytton had established stores facing each other on State Street but Lytton appeared to be on the lucky side of the street and Selfridge just the opposite. One day, on hearing his friend deplore his plight, Lytton suggested that Selfridge pull up stakes and start over again in London. There were no real American department stores there, and he felt certain that the novelty of the enterprise made the move worth a try. The risk had paid off phenomenally, so out of gratitude for the advice that had made him a wealthy man, every year Selfridge sent his friend in Chicago a copy of his balance sheet.

August eventually caught up with the Lyttons in Paris and explained his mysterious and unexpectedly long stay in London. It seems that he had been invited to paint a portrait of Queen Victoria and had gone to Buckingham Palace where he was received at Court. Then he stated his quandary: "If I paint in London, that will mean renouncing my American career; I will have to cancel my orders in the States and choose between England and America." Mr. Lytton was astonished. Surely, he interjected, after August's success in Chicago and his invitation to paint a second portrait of President McKinley, he would not consider residing in London. To Lytton's great relief, his reply was that his decision had already been made; he would not accept the English overture. "America is the land of the future. Besides, I have promised the Vice President that I would paint the second portrait of President McKinley in the fall." The Lyttons were relieved; they had taken quite a fancy to this artist with his cosmopolitan ways.

The next few days were busy ones. August escorted Gertrude all over Paris as he was familiar with his *Quartier Latin,* the art galleries, the cozy little restaurants where the best food could be had for a pittance. Her education was a liberal one in the Bohemian lifestyle. For the first time in her life, she felt that she had really begun to know Paris, the real Paris often foreign to American visitors. Benziger now reopened his 13 Rue Washington studio and, one afternoon, gave a huge reception for the Lyttons. There they met the current president of France, M. Maligne, and also Denys Pierre Peusch who had just won the *Prix de Rome.* The sculptor hoped the American would let him do a bust of Mrs. Lytton and, before she left Paris, he not only had completed the desired piece but also an exquisite bust of Beaumont Lytton, a lad of five with long corkscrew curls.

Evenings were always fascinating. The Lyttons, who were lovers of music, had their box at the opera, and August, in his long, flowing double-decker opera cape and *claque*, proved a most attractive escort. He, in turn, was highly appreciative of the handsomeness of his friends, and of their elegance and aesthetic sensitivity. Mrs. Lytton was exquisite in her heliotrope moiré evening dress, as was Miss Lytton in her *Bordeaux faille.* Arrived at their box, August gazed in admiration at Gertrude's off-shoulder, puff-sleeved gown, and remarked, "Mademoiselle, you are ravishingly beautiful tonight," and, bowing, placed a light kiss on her neck. Quick as a flash, Gertrude remonstrated: "I'd prefer it, Sir, if you did not forget your manners!" There was indignation in her voice, but the loge was dark—and no one saw her blush.

From Paris the Lyttons went to Bad Nauheim where Mrs. Lytton took the baths. Once the cure was over, Professor Grödel suggested that she take the after-cure in Switzerland on the Lake of Lucerne. It would be best for her to have a rest in a quiet hotel located at a high altitude. When the Lytton's name appeared in the Paris *Herald*, August learned that they were on his own lake, so he phoned and begged them to join him for luncheon at his villa. Arrangements were made for a meeting at Flüelen, at the opposite end of the lake, and a steamer took all to their appointed destination. At the Flüelen pier, a handsome pair of black stallions awaited their arrival and a coachman in livery held the spirited horses while August rushed to welcome his guests. He knew every inch of the famous Axenstrasse and explained that it had been hewn from solid granite. This road was one of the most beautiful in Europe, skirting and playing hide-and-seek with the steel-blue lake. Tunnel after tunnel yielded views, each lovelier than the preceding one. Suddenly their route swerved into a wide gravel road. "This is my home," August remarked simply. "This is Brunnen!"

The Benziger estate occupied the entire side of a mountain. A broad highway led to the top of a steep hill on which was perched a Swiss chalet, *Villa Gutenberg*, built at a dramatic bend in the lake and facing a semi-circle of snow-capped mountains. Mrs. Lytton voiced amazement. "Why, Mr. Benziger, you never told us that your estate comprised an entire park!" George, the older son, asked, "Is this rose-entwined villa your home?" August replied that it was, and that it was here that he had spent his childhood holidays. This alley of sycamore trees and its garland of pink roses had watched over his youthful pranks, and there was not a single tree that had not been climbed. What his brothers and sisters had loved best were the numerous apple, peach, pear and apricot trees, especially when they were loaded with fruit. The conversation was interrupted by the barking of what seemed to be ferocious St. Bernard dogs but, on hearing their master, they bounded forward like puppies. Several maids in black uniforms and stiffly starched aprons opened the villa door.

The Lyttons were delighted by everything they saw. To them, this home was a bit of enchanted fairyland, very different from anything they had ever anticipated. The Paris studio had been lavish with oriental rugs, silken draperies, handsomely-embroidered screens and antique furniture; *Villa Gutenberg*, by contrast, was the very embodiment of simplicity. Its panelled walls, its huge porcelain stoves, its dotted Swiss curtains and countless religious pictures all contributed to a deep home-like feeling while from every window breathtaking views of lake and mountain could be seen.

August explained that his mother spoke only German and that, as she was still in mourning, she would not join them until after-dinner coffee. "Mother is extremely shy," he added. "Even when my father was alive, she would never come to the table when there were guests." The table had been set with eight crystal glasses; just as many kinds of wine were served, a different vintage accompanying each course. Each time the wine was passed, Gertrude thanked her host and declined it. Finally, when the champagne was poured, August protested. He insisted that the maid fill her glass to the brim. "Today you're going to let me drink a toast—*à votre santé!*" He leaned forward and seized her glass, held it out to be filled, then determinedly put it down before her—with too much force. Instantly the glass shattered into a multitude of pieces. Gertrude was dismayed, and the old family maid, standing nearby, burst into sudden laughter. In her guttural Swiss dialect she made a comment loud enough for all to hear, but one that only the head of the house could understand. August seemed embarrassed; then, noticing that all eyes were turned in his direction, he interpreted for the Lyttons: "Elise says that this is a happy omen. It means good luck and a marriage."

After the sumptuous meal, all adjourned to the next floor. "Mother will be pleased to greet you in the salon." The door opened to reveal a demure little person, looking just like her portrait—humble and dignified. She cordially greeted her son's guests. *Demi-tasses* of coffee and little liqueur glasses of *Kirsch* were served; then Mrs. Benziger suggested that her honored guests might like to visit August's studio—and so that was done. The afternoon came to a close when the Lucerne boat tooted its warning. The horses were waiting to take the Lyttons to the Brunnen boat-landing, and August promised that he would spend a weekend at the Bürgenstock.

In honor of the Swiss national holiday on the first of August, Gertrude arrived at the festivities in a pale yellow evening gown adorned with sprays of mimosa, mandarin velvet and tiny velvet roses. She, who thoroughly enjoyed dancing with her stunning father and her athletic brother, now found that she had acquired a new partner. No, it was not August. She rose and felt herself swept off her feet as she twirled around the room wondering what had happened, for the man who held her in his arms spoke perfect English. She tried to focus some light on the situation by asking in a rather matter-of-fact voice: "Why, I thought you were an admiral in the Italian navy. How is it that you speak such beautiful English?" He skirted the question and remarked upon her beauty and her obviously happy family relationships. "How I envy you all. There never seems to be a cloud of discord to mar your days." Somewhat confused, Gertrude inquired hastily, "And you? Who can you be?" The reply was direct: "Of myself, I am no one. I am the son of the great Garibaldi." "You," he told her, "remind me of my mother." His mother had come from Brazil, and his father had seen her as a young girl while he was aboard a warship and had had no peace until he had landed, captured her and carried her off. Then he mused that their married life had been supremely happy—only there was too much fighting in Italy. He himself was the youngest son, born shortly before the last campaign, while his mother fought side-by-side with his father. She had died in the marshes, he told Gertrude, just as the enemy was about to track them down with bloodhounds. Admiral Garibaldi began to cough, then grew very pale. He led Gertrude back to her chair, bowed, kissed her hand and disappeared.

During the next two weeks he sent flowers regularly, with a card bearing his name, Manlio. Gertrude saw little of him during the day, since he spent these hours resting; however, night after night, she danced with him. It was on one of these nights that he told her that he was gravely ill.

The weekend before the Lyttons departed, while dancing with Manlio, Gertrude glimpsed August standing with her parents. August insisted on the next waltz, then told Gertrude most emphatically that he did not approve of her dancing with Garibaldi's son. To him, a staunch Catholic, all the Garibaldis were traitors, revolutionaries not to be met on a basis of any kind of friendship. She was much amused by August's agitation and chided him gently, asking him if he might not be jealous, reminding him that she was not a Catholic either. The Garibaldis, she protested, were patriots, people of singular courage; Admiral Garibaldi's history had fascinated and intrigued her. That night, August and Gertrude parted on a discordant note. The next morning, although the Lyttons had expected to see their guest once more, they found that he had taken the first funicular down to Lucerne, and had left a note explaining that urgent business matters had called him away. Gertrude had proven to be a match for him, to be one of the few women in his life who had not succumbed to his power and his charm. His vanity was piqued, and he doubted whether he would ever again care to see Miss Lytton. He was going to live in New York, she in Chicago. Fine!—and now, off to Carnegie Hall.

In New York, the 13th-floor penthouse was all that he hoped it would be. There he could find perfect lighting, quiet and solitude. The building, on the corner of Seventh Avenue and Fifty-seventh Street, was then one of the tallest structures on Manhattan Island, so August had a bird's-eye view of the entire city. To the north lay Central Park; to the west, the Hudson River crowded with the billowing canvas of sailing vessels. On the opposite side lay the distant East River. A few blocks away was "millionaire row," where society's Four Hundred lived in their brownstone mansions; Fifth Avenue had become the show street of America. At Fiftieth Street could be seen St. Patrick's Gothic cathedral, its twin grey spires jutting into the sky. In 1840, more than 50 years previously, a far-seeing archbishop had built a small frame church there in the woods to serve the many Irish immigrants living in shanties nearby. This poor congregation had saved its pennies and helped to erect the inspiring edifice, while many scoffed that it would never be occupied; it was much too far out in the country!

August was very happy here in his Fifth-seventh Street studio. Carnegie Hall, with its auditoriums and studios, was the talk of the town. For a price, artists and musicians could enjoy the best facilities that the New World had to offer. However, from the first days of his return to New York, Vice-president Hobart had left him no peace. He wanted the portrait of the president to be begun at once. Fortunately, August's first meeting with the Chief Executive was not at all as formal as he had anticipated. President McKinley was a kindly, quiet, fatherly man. When he heard the Swiss Minister describe the painter as one of his Republic's outstanding citizens, the president remarked wholeheartedly: "Though you have come to Washington for the purpose of painting my portrait, I trust

you will come to love our country so much that you will one day
become one of us and make America your home."

The president was honest and admitted that he had consented
to sit for a portrait only because the vice-president was a wonderful friend. Even so, he was hesitant; he had little time to expend.
Besides, he had had several portraits made in the past, and each
one had proven to be an extremely poor likeness. He smiled. "I
will give you a chance but if, after the second sitting, I'm not
pleased with what I see, I want it understood that I am free to
withdraw." The president's personal valet, who happened to be
Swiss, was placed at the disposal of the artist, and August was
given *carte blanche* to enter and leave the White House as he
pleased. To facilitate matters, he also received entrée to receptions,
cabinet meetings and conferences in order to give him fuller insight
into the man who was president. He made an intensive study.
When it came time for the sittings, the locale of the East Room
was chosen as it contained three enormous chandeliers which provided effective lighting. Almost at once, canvas, easel, palettes, a
life-sized mirror and dais appeared on the scene. A guard was
posted to make certain that nothing was touched between sittings
and that the artist was left alone to work at any time of day or
night so that the portrait could be completed as quickly as possible.
August was delighted.

President McKinley consented to allot several hours to each
of the first few sittings but, afterwards, these would be scheduled
at 8:00 in the morning and would last for only a brief interlude.
He was a man of utter simplicity, lacking any pretense whatever
and, after his first sitting, was perfectly natural and at home with
the artist. After a few days, he issued orders that during the painting time he would reply to the day's mail. Large stacks of letters
were brought and his two efficient secretaries would give synopses
of what each communication contained. Then, without hesitation,
the president would dictate his quick, precise, pithy replies. This
Chief Executive was a man of few words who knew exactly what
he wanted.

All of these factors gave the artist ample opportunity to come
to know the man he was painting. Thus, as he sketched, he not
only depicted the green-grey eyes of a man of thought, but also the
kindliness of this person of determination who displayed the careful speech and brilliant mind of a fine lawyer. Fearful of tiring the
president, August worked as rapidly as he could, and Mr. McKinley

took an almost childish interest in his speed and technique. Seeing the artist walk back and forth, staring critically into the mirror, the president left his place in order to see what Mr. Benziger was gazing at with such fixed attention. He was startled, as he looked into the mirror, to see not merely his own reflection, but the exact replica of himself on canvas. He turned to his secretary with an air of triumph and said, "Why, I can't get over it! Mr. Benziger has caught a likeness that is almost frightening in its accuracy. Do call Mrs. McKinley. I wonder what my wife will say when she sees this remarkable portrait." When the gentle, dignified First Lady arrived, she smiled with pleasure, then turned graciously to the painter and congratulated him, "You're the first artist to catch the deep fire burning within the soul of my husband." Then she straightened her skirt with simple grace, and sat down to watch the painting progress. From that time on, Mrs. McKinley often slipped into the East Room to watch the likeness take shape. August knew now that he was about to achieve what he had come to do: catch in oils the spirit of a man whom he had come to admire greatly.

Occasionally, one of the president's secretaries, the valet or a guard would invite him to explore another part of the White House or pay a visit to the Capitol where he had an opportunity to see the president in action, addressing Congress or receiving a committee of women. Here was a man who never spared himself. Usually standing while posing for August, on only one occasion did he request leave to be seated, saying that he was very tired. He had just shaken hands with over a thousand women who came to meet him. To every one he had spoken a few words. He was exhausted!

Gradually August learned more and more about the personal life of the McKinleys. Mr. McKinley's greatest sorrow had been the loss of his two children during their early childhood, and his wife had never recovered from the cruel shock. Further, although she presided at the White House with maternal charm, there were days when she was totally incapacitated as she suffered from attacks of epilepsy. The McKinleys were inseparable; he seldom left her alone for long, and was passionately fond and proud of her. In spite of her ailment, Mrs. McKinley attended as many functions as she could; however, instead of occupying the usual hostess's chair at the foot of the table, it was arranged by the president that she be seated at his left during large state dinners. In this way he could nearly always forestall a seizure. Noting the slightest symptom, he would rise quickly and lead his wife gently from the room as he wanted no one to see her beautiful face twisted by the dreaded convulsions. Mrs. McKinley usually wore a cashmere shawl across her shoulders so that, during these exigencies, her husband could cover her head protectively as he assisted her from the assembly. On one occasion, while surveying the progress made in the portrait, he noticed that his wife had forgotten the inevitable shawl, and symptoms of an onset were becoming evident. He hurriedly seized a newspaper and placed it tenderly over her head; then he and a guard led the First Lady from the East Room. August was deeply impressed by the gentleness.

When the president and Mrs. McKinley lunched, they often invited August to join them. Since Swiss men were accustomed to the continental habit of expending little attention on one's wife, the ladies, on the whole, expected to be taken for granted, although mistresses fared much better, receiving an undue measure of gallantry. For this reason, August was tremendously impressed by the kindness and respect with which Mrs. McKinley was treated by her husband. He always rose when she entered the room and would pause considerately until an attendant had assisted her to her chair; then he would pat her arm, and kiss her cheek gently as though he had not seen her for a long time. It was all genuine; there was no pretense. Here was the miracle of a really happy and united couple who lived for others.

Although he had been commissioned by Vice-president Hobart to paint a second portrait of Mr. McKinley, August delayed the sittings, quite sure that the president would be reelected, and besides, he was needed in New York. He made arrangements to return to the White House the following spring. Back in his Carnegie Hall studio, he was able to paint uninterruptedly. One afternoon, during a sitting with Mrs. Klingler, the wife of a Swiss embroidery merchant, the artist heard the door suddenly burst open. Quite unceremoniously, a strange-looking man strode in wearing a silk tophat perched above a coarse, heavy-set face. With infuriating nonchalance, the new arrival strolled about the studio as though he were in a public museum, examining this, peering at that. Outraged by such a flagrant lack of courtesy, August determined to evict this boorish caller at once—bodily, if need be. He uttered a strong protest to his sitter in Swiss dialect. "Watch me throw out this insolent wretch. Why, he hasn't even had the basic courtesy to remove his hat!" Fortunately, Mrs. Klingler had met the intruder and instantly recognized him as Richard Croker, the "head of Tammany Hall and the most powerful politician in America." Croker, with the audacity of a self-made man aware of the power he wielded, stood stock-still, squinted an eye and then walked straight up to the easel which held Mrs. Klingler's portrait. "By God, man, this is the finest painting I've seen anywhere. Looks just like the lady; neither compliments her nor makes her any uglier." He cocked his head critically, "In fact I'd say it's almost a dead-ringer!" Although August was irate, Mrs. Klingler had the poise to cover up the situation, observing: "If you think this is an excellent likeness, why don't you give Mr. Benziger an order to paint your picture? You'd make a most exceptional model, indeed!" Croker snorted at what he mistook as flattery, but early the following morning he returned. "How soon could you begin? How many sittings would it take?" The Tammany boss's blunt straightforwardness amused August by this time. Within an hour Richard Croker's portrait had been sketched in on canvas.

The artist could easily have made a grotesque caricature of this homely, beetle-browed leader, but for him, the man's distorted features merely constituted a challenge to his art of honest portrayal. As a portraitist, he was not content to peer at the surface but reached, rather, for the source of power beneath this man's exterior. The uncouth manners and crude ways were overlooked. August saw in Mr. Croker the master strategist who held in his hands as much power as any American had exercised—either for good or evil, and the portrait spoke precisely of who he was.

Now August returned to Chicago and the Lyttons were among the first to invite him to dinner. On this occasion, Mrs. Lytton asked a special favor. After the exhibition of his paintings in his studio, would he please paint the ring Gertrude always wore, before returning the portrait of her daughter? He avoided the question, declining to commit himself. Miss Lytton held up her hand and commented that the ring had never left her finger from the day she turned eighteen. Her father had given her this special circle of rubies, diamonds and sapphires because "she loved her America so much." It was his birthday gift to her.

A few weeks later, when Gertrude was in New York, she stopped off at Carnegie Hall one evening. To her amazement, the ring had not yet been added to the portrait. When she protested, August suggested that she return early the following morning; in the meantime, he would see what could be done.

Meanwhile, since the romantic tandem, or "bicycle built for two," had become all the rage, Gertrude went cycling with the brothers of her friends. In those days, the smart thoroughfares of Central Park were crowded with shining hansom cabs and horse-drawn buses. Traffic jams were frequent. The police arrested bicycle riders for speeding dangerously at 15 miles an hour.

Fortunately, Gertrude avoided all the potential mishaps, and early the next morning went to Fifty-seventh Street, having every intention of posing while the red-white-and-blue ring was painted into her portrait. August greeted her warmly, but added, "Mademoiselle, that ring means nothing." He dismissed the subject with a shrug. "It's you that I'm interested in." With that, the artist stepped forward impulsively, swept the astonished Gertrude Lytton into his arms and kissed her with fervor. That day there was no sitting. The ring was never to be painted; her beautiful hand in its pristine simplicity was enough. The two walked out of the studio as though in a dream and wandered through the Seventh Avenue entrance to Central Park until they reached the Metropolitan Museum. What they had viewed in the galleries became a haze. Later neither could recall anything. The two walked happily side by side, commenting animatedly in hushed tones as they strolled from one room to the next until they found themselves seated close together on one of the red plush settees. It was a moment of intimacy, of awakening, as each regarded the other with newly-discovered wonder.

A week before, by a puzzling sort of coincidence, a Mrs. Bundesen, the Lytton's French teacher, had come from Chicago and visited August's studio. He had, since that time, been haunted by the memory of her strange comments and could not quite erase the incident from his mind. Why had she come to call on him at all? Why had she broached the astonishing subject of his marrying Miss Lytton?

After looking at his exhibition, and especially at the portrait of Gertrude, the woman had turned to the artist quite unexpectedly and remarked bluntly: "What are you waiting for? Why don't you marry Miss Lytton? You're cut out for each other." Utterly taken aback, August had retorted: "Why! Miss Lytton is positively the last person in America whom I would ever consider marrying. She's the spoiled daughter of a rich American. Besides, she is an Episcopalian and I am a Catholic. Furthermore, I would never marry any woman who could not assist me in achieving an artistic career." Petite Mrs. Bundesen had laughed and shaken a finger in August's face. "Fate has decreed that you will marry. Wait and see if I'm not right. You two are destined for each other." The artist's bushy eyebrows knitted in rage at the fact that anyone should dare to attempt to force his hand in marriage. "Has anyone asked you to be a go-between?" he demanded curtly. "God forbid!" she said solemnly, adding that this was merely a case of a woman's intuition. If he wanted her honest opinion, she very much doubted that Miss Lytton would ever give him a thought. She has flocks of suitors, but you two complement each other to such a marked degree that it was impossible not to speak freely; in fact, she felt that he needed Miss Lytton almost more than she needed him. Mrs. Bundesen's voice grew soft in apology; "If I have seemed rash, believe me, it's only because I admire the two of you tremendously. You possess so much of the Old World gallantry and its high standards that I have come to take almost as much interest in your welfare as I have in that of my charming pupil."

As August now sat beside Gertrude Lytton in the museum, Mrs. Bundesen's prophetic words echoed in his memory. An inexplicable, almost hypnotic feeling engulfed him. For her part, Gertrude had respected, even been slightly in awe of, the talented artist. His brilliant personality was, of course, an asset, yet she felt he was a bit too self-confident and, besides, she disliked the fact that some of her women friends had seemed to fall madly in love with him while he, for his part, did nothing either to encourage or put a stop to the adulation. There was no earthly reason for Gertrude to contemplate marriage in order to seek escape. Life had been most kind to her. Whatever she wanted or needed had always been hers for the asking; her lovable qualities endeared her to all the family and, as an only girl, she was idolized by her brothers.

Only once had she ever been in love—that time when she felt deep and sincere affection for Herman Baruch who bore the nickname "Tot." On her first trip to New York, he had chaperoned her at her first play, escorted her to the opera, sent her small corsages and bought her her first beautiful brooch, an enameled four-leafed clover. Tot had loved Gertrude, and she had reciprocated his devotion from her earliest childhood years when they had first met at their Grandmother Wolfe's plantation in Winsboro, South Carolina; but the idyll had ended when Gertrude's father had flatly refused to give his consent to any possible marriage. Tot, he emphasized was her first cousin. Such near relations could not, must not marry. Gertrude, who never had to be told anything twice, silently acquiesced, her young heart breaking.

Thus Gertrude Lytton and August Benziger, two widely divergent human beings, representing opposite points of view, of varying faiths, upbringing and background, sat beside each other and pondered what the future might hold for them. For the first time, they had a heart-to-heart talk. The walls of the Metropolitan Museum would keep their conversation secret forever.

CHAPTER 10

Love and Marriage
(1898)

As good artists were a rarity in America at this time, portrait painters could be counted on the first three fingers, and so August's studio was bombarded by prospective clients to the point at which he now felt himself obliged to turn down commissions as all he could cope with were eight to ten orders in one year.

He could not bear the sight of art dealers whom he classified as "crooks." He had seen dealers ruin fine artists, and knew that the Paris art critics in particular had turned down first class pictures because the artist had not offered them a handsome bribe or given a painting as a gift to their salons. Had the artists done so, they would have had their work exhibited and, in all probability, won prizes. Fearlessly, before the Art Club of Paris, he revealed that dealers were dickering with artists in order to bring about false inflation, and described an incident in which two men had come to his studio, one a New York art dealer and the other a man named Duveen. Neither knew that the other had been to see him, yet both had gambled with him about prices, offering him tempting suggestions about how he could come to America and become rich overnight if only he would sign contracts with them. Both wanted him to confine himself to the painting of miniatures, explaining that the life-sized portrait was out and that the "in" thing was the miniature not more than 12 or 14 inches in height. August had always enjoyed doing these small portraits but felt that his real talent lay in the life-sized canvas and refused to have outsiders curb his style or dictate to him. As to the possible financial advantages being proffered, he felt them to be shady at best and would have nothing to do with the dealers who offered them to him.

Another of his recent Carnegie Hall visitors was Vice-President Hobart, who had been instrumental in August's returning to

America and who feared that he might delay painting the second portrait of President McKinley. To hasten the process, Mr. Hobart arranged that the sittings should be resumed in Washington by the beginning of February. Thus, before he had expected to do so, August was again commuting between Washington and New York. He found Mr. McKinley just as genial, kind and understanding as in the past, yet he sensed a strange unrest in him. In the first portrait of the President, he had been able to capture something of the genial warmth, dignity and quiet strength of this man of action. Now as he sketched, he was convinced that something had changed. Eventually, the President spoke openly.

From snatches of conversation and the dictation of letters to presidential secretaries, members of the Cabinet and army officials, August learned how strained Spanish-American relations had become and he knew that a number of high-ranking officials were openly advocating war with Spain. They declared that Cuba had become a hotbed of revolutionaries and that arms and ammunition were being smuggled to the island. The Spanish were working the Cubans into a frenzy and Spain, it seemed, which had once dominated the world, was now biding her time in the hope of regaining some of her lost power.

All of these problems were visible on the face of the man August was painting. The most unforgettable day for both was the morning of February 16th. By eight in the morning, the sittings were under way and the President was watching August as he picked out the colors on his palate when suddenly General Corbin, quite unannounced, rushed into the room. He handed the President a telegram and shouted: "The Spaniards have blown up the *Maine!*" President McKinley grew very white, shook his head and said, "I don't believe they have done this, I don't. It must have been an accident!" The sitting broke up and a Cabinet meeting was convened immediately.

During the time of the waging of this war, the second portrait was completed. Into it August painted the change of expression of the man who had struggled to maintain peace, who had been a firm believer that diplomacy could avert bloodshed and convinced that the independence of Cuba could be secured by amicable agreement. With the blowing up of the *Maine*, the deaths of two officers and 264 sailors, few were left who could be persuaded of his views. War boiled.

Forty-eight hours later, during another sitting, two prominent Americans came for an interview. August had met Theodore Roosevelt in New York before the latter had become Assistant Secretary of the Navy. Now he had brought with him his friend, John Jacob Astor. The artist continued to paint. He heard Roosevelt ask to resign his post in the Navy in order to be free to enlist against the Spaniards. Mr. Astor offered to equip an entire regiment at his own expense if "Teddy," as he called Mr. Roosevelt, would be permitted to organize a regiment of mounted riflemen. (Throughout the years, August was to see much of Mr. Astor, either in Florida or while crossing the Atlantic. It was during the maiden voyage of the *S.S. Titanic* that he lost his life by giving his seat in a lifeboat to a woman passenger.)

When General Miles requested the President to choose the new Army uniform, the sitting was again interrupted. August was invited to accompany the President, General Miles and Mr. Roosevelt when they spent several hours making a careful survey of colors and types of uniform. The traditional blue worn in the Civil War was discarded as impractical so the three men looked over the greens and browns. All agreed that the best for camouflage and fieldwork was khaki. A stout twilled cloth in cotton and wool that most resembled earth colors would best protect the men on the battlefield. August had always liked General Miles and was not surprised when the President made him Commander of the American Army. He was a man with great military experience who had fought in the Civil War and had used tact and understanding in breaking up the rebellion, and also avoided bloodshed in dealing with the Plains Indians. War fever continued to mount among shouts of "Remember the *Maine*" and the rhythms of John Philip Sousa's marches played on Fifth Avenue as men were paraded off to camps for military training. It was crisis time. When the President demanded that Spain withdraw from Cuba, Spain replied by declaring war, and when Roosevelt resigned his Navy commission the men whom he would join were already training in Texas. Flocking to join them were cowboys from New Mexico, Arizona and Montana as well as the Texas Rangers. Southern horsemen and Eastern college men completed their numbers, forming the "Rough Riders." By April 21, America was officially at war; by May 1, news reached New York that a naval squadron under the command of Admiral Dewey had destroyed the Spanish Fleet in Manila Bay.

At this point, August returned to Chicago as Marshall Field had ordered another portrait of his wife, this time in a yellow dress. While there, he stopped over to visit Miss Lytton and they resumed the *tête-à-tête* begun in the Metropolitan Museum. He found it difficult to express what was on his mind. In America, people just married, but in the world in which he had been brought up, marriage was preceded by "settlements and dowry arrangements." He explained that an artist's life is uncertain; if he married, he wanted a family and, for his wife, security. He informed Gertrude, with a consummate lack of tact, that she had been spoiled, as the daughter of a millionaire, and had everything: luxuries, extravagances and entertainment on the grandest scale. Her family owned the fastest pacers and trotters in Chicago, their summer home was palatial, and Gertrude had her own yacht on Lake Geneva in Wisconsin. What he needed, however, was a wife who could help him in his artistic career. He needed a homemaker with tact, ability, perseverance and character. After making this rather lengthy speech, he handed her a tiny gold medal no larger than a pea. He then took a gold chain from his own neck; on it hung an identical medal. August explained: "I always wear this medal of Our Lady of Einsiedeln. She is the patroness of the Benziger family. I have three such medals. One I wear: the second I gave to a New York lady whom I greatly admire. I cannot quite make up my mind which of the two of you I like best. One of you I am going to marry." He kissed her—then fled. How oddly this speech must have struck the ears of the handsome, young, sought-after American woman, even in 1898!

That evening, as she was about to go out, she missed the medal, but the chain had not been broken. Understandably upset, she called Tom, the butler, and promised that if he found the tiny medal, she would give him a $10 reward.

Upon her return that evening, she fell on her knees, knowing that a moment for decision had come, but she was not thinking so much about August as about the Catholic faith. She had learned a great deal about Catholics; she knew quite a few. Her mother's personal maid, Ellen, had been in the family since Gertrude was a child, had given her her first prayer book, had taught her to pray, had taken her to Sunday Mass. Later, one of Gertrude's best friends, Claire Williams, had chosen to become a Catholic and the two girls had spent an evening together discussing prayer and religion. That all-night meeting seemed to have lasted only minutes.

She knew then that she would become a Roman Catholic. Even should August Benziger change his mind, should something come between them, she would still persevere in her resolution to seek instruction and be baptized. Then, suddenly, she wondered if, perhaps, she had not been too presumptuous to make such a step without a sign from heaven. She settled on this signal: if God wanted her to become a Catholic, he would see that she found her medal by noon of the next day. That morning she went to the usual family breakfast and was greeted by Tom with, "See what I found!" There was the medal. That was all that Gertrude needed. Her decision became irrevocable.

Soon afterward, her father invited her to accompany him to New York as he had to go there on business. While he attended to his affairs, she could visit her grandmother Levie, a woman of 90 who lived in Highland Park, New Jersey. Gertrude was glad to go, and also took advantage of the opportunity to visit her favorite aunt and uncle, Dr. and Mrs. Simon Baruch and their sons who lived in New York City. Mrs. Baruch, Aunt Belle, noticed that a great change had come over her niece, who was noted for her cheerfulness and spirit of fun. Not so now. Worried, Aunt Belle asked her if she were in love; a moment of silence was followed by a cascade of tears. Aunt Belle went straight to her brother-in-law, fearful that perhaps the girl was in love with her son Herman whom they all called "Tot." That evening her father put the question to her squarely: "Are you in love with Tot?" "No," she replied, "I'm extremely fond of all the Baruch boys. Tot is the closest, since we've spent so much time together, yet you have always said that first cousins should not marry." There was a pause. "I'm in love with the artist. Only August says that he can't afford to marry me because artists are too uncertain security risks."

Her father promised to talk to August but warned her to make sure what she was doing if she married this artist. Marrying a man with an artistic temperament, he said, is like living with a keg of dynamite. Then, too, he observed, Benziger has the European approach to married life; while courting, these men make glamorous lovers but afterwards the woman is often discarded like an old bushy glove. "Look at his bushy eyebrows! He's a man of grim determination. The two of you are as different as night is from day." Yet, he added, if money was the only obstacle, he would see Benziger and talk things over, as he was greatly concerned about his daughter's happiness.

Late that evening, he returned to the hotel, mission accomplished, and remarked in a tired tone but with finality, "Benziger will only marry a Catholic. His faith is an insurmountable barrier." Her response was simple; she told him that for a long time she had been thinking of becoming a Catholic and knew that her parents had always been tolerant about religion. In that case, he assured her, he would not be one to stand in the way. He thought highly of Benziger of whose talents he was aware, but warned her that a genius seldom makes a good husband. Furthermore, "He has an abominable temper. For the rest of your life, you'll have to do exactly as he wants." He also reminded her that he didn't believe in divorce or separation. If she married August, she would marry for better or for worse; she should never come back to him with a sob story, never say that she had made a horrible mistake. He warned her that "marriage is not a speculative thing made in brokerage firms. Your future happiness depends on this decision."

Gertrude realized the seriousness of the moment, yet she was very much in love. "Father, did you tell him everything?" she asked anxiously.

Yes, he had told August about their Jewish ancestry and about her mother's family—that, as Portuguese Jews, they had fled to Holland, then settled in the New World; that in 1692, one of her great-grandfathers had become a Burgher of New York and that these facts are still on record in the City Hall; that one of her ancestors was a colonel in the Revolutionary War; that for seven generations, her mother's family had lived in South Carolina. Then he had told August about his own parents who had come to New York from London in the early 80s, that his father had died, leaving his mother a widow with six children and that she had struggled to raise her family alone. He explained that he had seen Gertrude's mother in New York and had gone to South Carolina to meet her relatives, that he eventually had become a millionaire and that his parents were proud of their name of Levie. He explained that all had gone well until he moved to Grand Rapids in Michigan.

Gertrude's brother, George, a tall, handsome boy, had come back from school one day with a bloody nose and a black eye— terribly upset. He told his parents that he had been beaten up by a gang of Irish toughs because he was a Jew. They said they hated Jews and did not want him back in school. While George had always had many friends, these suddenly stopped going with him.

His parents had spent sleepless nights, the father feeling that they should move away and change their name, and the mother, having come from the South where the people looked upon the Jews who had settled there as genuine Americans, disagreed. She *knew* that the family was endowed with both culture and refinement, and that they should, therefore, hold their heads high and continue to be proud of their ancestry. In the end, the anti-Semitism had become so marked that the family did move to Chicago to establish another home and business. "I was 40 then," he told August. He and his wife had gone to court and changed their name. Henry C. Levie became Henry C. Lytton. Although he had wanted to demonstrate through his own integrity that Jews could be just as honest, as good, as decent as anyone else, the forces of prejudice had become too strong and threatened to damage his family.

This all having been said, he had pointed out to Benziger that if he felt any doubts whatever about Gertrude's background, this was the time to withdraw, not later. He hoped that his daughter would never have to suffer from discrimination, as prejudice "is completely un-American, is not in the least typical of the American spirit." Finally, he told his future son-in-law that Gertrude had lived in Chicago since she was 12, had been raised a Christian, had made her début to society and assisted her mother in many philanthropic ventures. He added that she was also a Daughter of the American Revolution. Gertrude could hardly voice the vital question, "Father, what did August say to all this?" She was exquisitely relieved to hear that he had no objections, and that his father, Governor Adelrich Benziger, had been a broad-minded, tolerant man who hated prejudice, and that many of his best friends were Jewish or Protestant. There remained only a few more words of advice from Mr. Lytton to Gertrude: "Remember, the only way you'll ever hold Benziger is by giving him a great deal of love and understanding. You'll have to rule him, but without his knowing it. That's the secret of your mother's successful marriage to me." August, for his part, did not wait to talk things over with Gertrude. Early next morning, he rushed to St. Patrick's Cathedral, knowing that the Archbishop would be saying the 7:00 Mass. After the liturgy, he went to the archepiscopal residence on Madison Avenue. In his gloved hand he held his visiting card and explained that his was a matter of great urgency; he needed only a short interview. In a few minutes, he was cordially received by Archbishop Corrigan, who took him to task for not having visited sooner.

In a paternal manner, the prelate spoke of his own rejoicing at the success Benziger had achieved in a very short time. He had become, he said, the most outstanding portrait painter in America. Yet he did have words of warning for the young man: he had become too popular, what with his talent, his culture, his career. "Americans go wild about these things. Watch your step lest some silly woman lay a trap and corner you before you are ready to marry." August felt that the words had been taken out of his mouth. In Europe, he knew, he could carry on mindless flirtations without serious consequences; here, attentions could easily be construed as commitments. "I need a stable woman to be my wife." He spoke of Gertrude, "a Jewess from Chicago" whose portrait he had just completed. Perhaps the Archbishop would be interested in seeing what she looks like.

The prelate's reply was straightforward: the young lady was indeed beautiful and distinguished yet, "not being of our faith, you will surely not consider marrying her." August declared: "Miss Lytton is the one to whom I am going to propose today!" The archbishop, taken aback, queried: "Have you taken into consideration the consequences of a mixed marriage? What a scandal it would be?" He rose, looked at his watch and said that he was already late for an appointment, but he asked August to return the next day, bringing Miss Lytton with him, as he was anxious to meet her. Obviously, he wanted to discourage the marriage.

The next day was June 7th and, as Gertrude and August mounted the steps of the rectory, she turned and smiled. "Oh, I forgot to ask you. Does the Archbishop approve?" The answer would come in time. After introductions and niceties, August surprised the Archbishop by suddenly stating: "I have brought my fiancée. I feel that it is best for you to talk to her alone." Then he fled the room.

Gertrude felt surprisingly at ease in the presence of this Church dignitary; thanks to the training by Ellen, her maid, there was not much about the Catholic Church she did not know.

That first visit was only the beginning of many more. It lasted over an hour. At its end, Gertrude carried Cardinal Gibbons' *Faith of Our Fathers* in her hand; she had promised to read it and then to return to discuss any points that were not clear. She had told the Archbishop that whether she married August or not, she fully intended to become a Catholic and that, although she was of a Semitic family, she had never practiced the Jewish religion but had, rather, attended the Episcopal Church. She stated that she really had no theological problems, yet she had just one objection: she could not understand why it was said that no one outside the Catholic Church could be saved. She pointed out that her father and mother were deeply religious and that, as far back as she could remember, she had never heard either of her parents be cross, unkind or uncharitable. They were generous, wonderful parents and devoted to the poor. Her mother regularly made the rounds of Chicago's slums and brought bedding and clothing to prostitutes about to have babies. She saw to it that they had medical care and gave them a chance to start life over again. She affirmed that her parents lived, not for themselves, but for their children and others, and that she simply could not believe that they would be damned for eternity merely because they had not been baptized. "Surely," she said, "God is merciful!" Archbishop Corrigan explained that a small number of people had misinterpreted the teaching of the Church to suit their own narrow concepts and that their Jansenistic assertions must be disregarded. The crux of the matter was that those who had been given the faith and *who abused it* would not be saved.

Then he sent for August that same afternoon, as he wanted him to know that he had changed his mind. He congratulated him on his excellent choice and said that he was extremely fortunate to have found such an exceptional woman. He wanted to start her formal religious instruction at once and would personally answer any questions she might have. He had found her remarkably well-prepared, and, once the course was completed, he would christen her himself. "I trust you will permit me to perform the marriage ceremony here in St. Patrick's Cathedral when the moment comes." He shook August's hand cordially. "Your father, were he alive, would be very proud of you both!" The next day Gertrude began her instructions. She was baptized quietly in St. Patrick's with a friend of the Archbishop as godmother, and then she returned to Chicago. The press carried long articles about the forthcoming marriage. Since in Europe an engagement was considered a contract, after it had been formalized the had-beens, the hopefuls and the husband-hunters began searching elsewhere. Not so in New York. A Swiss columnist residing there sent a sarcastic society gossip item to the *Town Topic*: "Benziger Marrying a Jewess." The ugly insinuation was intended directly for August, and outsiders could not have guessed what it really implied: As a Swiss he would be ostracized. However, he told Gertrude nothing about such remarks and their implications; that would have to be his personal battleground.

Not long afterwards, he produced tickets for the *S.S. Bourgoyne* which was to sail on July 2, as he wanted to hurry the wedding. In a matter of weeks they would be off to Switzerland. All of this came as a shock to Mrs. Lytton, as she had expected a much later date for the ceremony and never doubted that the marriage would take place in Chicago. August pleaded that he hated ostentation and infinitely preferred that he and Gertrude be married in New York in an early morning ceremony, 8:00 in the morning, at St. Patrick's Cathedral. There would be no bridesmaids, no maid of honor, no reception. Everything would be simplicity personified. He loathed bridal gowns, he said, and *froufrou* wedding veils. Again he produced the tickets for July 2. Mrs. Lytton paled and began to weep, feeling that he did not know what it meant for a mother to lose an only daughter—and to have her go in stark simplicity. August only grew more determined. He must, he said, leave for Europe at once, and refused to go without Gertrude. Besides, he asked her, had she considered the risk she and her daughter would run by crossing the Atlantic just to buy a trousseau during this time of war? Mr. Lytton suddenly walked in and asked whether he and Gertrude would not also be at risk on the high seas at this time. August made a strong point; he traveled on a Swiss passport and Gertrude, in marrying him, would also become Swiss. "We are not at war with Spain. Furthermore, I know the inside story from Washington. This war is serious business. Why should we be splurging at a moment when Americans are mourning the deaths of their sons in Cuba? Mr. Lytton accepted August's thinking and grew quiet; he had waved off his own brother to the Civil War and knew the tension and sorrow of such times. Finally he spoke: "You are right. If Gertrude has no objections and you two can agree, I feel sure my wife will dry her tears." Gertrude consoled her mother, reminding her that right in Chicago there was a wonderful dressmaker who would be delighted to get her all fixed up in no time. "What I don't get now, I can stop over in Paris and order on my way to Switzerland."

August had met several Swiss in Chicago at this time and one of them became engaged to a Bostonian. The prospective bridegroom, Klaus, begged that his prominent artist friend become his best man, and August agreed to arrive in time for the wedding. As he had previous commitments, he managed to do so only the evening before the ceremony. Klaus took this occasion to harp on August's coming marriage. Was he a fool to give up everything in marrying Miss Lytton? Did he not know that the Swiss colony would ostracize him? If he took his bride back to Europe, neither she nor he nor their offspring would be accepted by the Swiss. No Jew held public office. No Jew was accepted in business. There was an unwritten law that made it impossible for them to earn a living in Switzerland. After all, Miss Lytton could be replaced. He felt certain that pretty Jane, the bride's sister, would marry him. All he had to do was ask her. The family approved. He, Klaus, had arranged everything.

August was adamant. He was engaged and had no intention of breaking his word. Klaus gave a final warning to his best man: "Well, you are wise to marry outside the Catholic Church. By doing so, you can divorce Miss Lytton any time it is convenient to do so. Besides, you will find what I've told you will come to pass and become unbearable. It will ruin your career."

The morning of the wedding, August, after a sleepless night, wrote his fiancée a letter, then rushed to the nearest post office and mailed it. Never had he been so despondent; never had life seemed so black. He packed his bag. No sooner had the short wedding ceremony been performed than he took the first train back to New York where he nursed his anguish. Blinded by so-called friends who came with gossip, he did not know what to believe. Was what he thought to be a true romance to end tragically? However, his engagement to Gertrude had resulted not only in negative comments but also in a deluge of congratulatory letters and telegrams. Who was right? Perhaps it would be better if he broke off the engagement. He had suggested this to Gertrude in his letter, and she would have the final word; if she accepted him conclusively, his fate would be God's will for him.

Gertrude received the letter, read it and reread it, wondering if she were in her right mind. Deeply hurt, yet sensing that there was something oppressive behind the strange episode, she did as she always had: she called for the family coachman, Olif, and rode in the family victoria to the Hub.

When she arrived, her father was dictating several important letters that had to be sent out. Looking up and seeing his distressed daughter, he put his arm around her and asked, "Shall we walk to luncheon?" He sensed at once that something had happened. The dapper, talkative father headed for Michigan Boulevard. Gertrude handed him the letter and asked him to tell her what to do. Henry Lytton was a mind-reader and knew his daughter well, but still the letter amazed him. When he was seated, he reread it slowly, aloud:

> Dearest Gerty,
>
> This is to tell you that if you have any doubts in your mind about wanting to marry me, now is the time to take that step. I beg of you, dear Gerty, to realize I will release you from any binding obligation. I admire you. I still love you, yet it is up to you. You have the final say-so. It is better now instead of later, for you to decide you have made a serious mistake in marrying me.

The father looked at his daughter, "You really love him, don't you, Gerty?" She nodded as emotion prevented a verbal reply. "Pay no attention. There is some dirty work going on. Let's send a telegram. That will settle the matter once and for all." Gertrude, who until then had been frantic, relaxed into relief. She had known that her father would have the right answer. The telegram, sent to the New York studio, assured August of her unchanging affection. The affair was never referred to again.

Barely 10 days before her wedding, Gertrude was once again in New York with her parents. She received further religious instruction and attended to final preparations. One morning father, mother and daughter were having an early breakfast at the Plaza when she suddenly began to weep. "What has happened?" her mother asked. "Nothing has happened," the young woman replied. "Only I have had the most horrible nightmare. I don't want to sail on the *Bourgoyne*, yet if I tell that to August, he will be furious. As it is, he has enough misgivings about marrying an American, and a rich, spoiled one at that." Her parents laughed, relieved that it was only a passing fancy that troubled her. Still, Mr. Lytton knew his daughter and was aware that she was not prone to emotional outbursts. He asked about the dream that had so upset her. He had a strange feeling that perhaps Gertrude was psychic—his wife certainly was—and he had learned that it was unwise to disregard her premonitions. Until then, though, his daughter had always been very matter-of-fact, almost as practical as he was.

Shuddering, as if to wipe a horrible image from her mind, she repeated that she had had a terrifying dream, but that everything in it was so very real that she felt that she and August *must* delay their plans for sailing on the *Bourgoyne*. "I saw how she crashed into a sailing vessel in dense fog, split in two and sank." The worst of it was that a horrible scene remained with her. She could hear voices and screams, and see the most brutal mass murder perpetrated by the crew. None of the passengers was saved. On the passenger list there were many women and children! "I just know that we must not, under any circumstances, sail on the 2nd of July." Her father offered to explain the matter to August and to change the departure date to the following week, and he was successful in doing so. The new reservations were for the *S.S. Touraine*, scheduled to sail from New York on July 9th, four days after the wedding.

Since it was customary in America for the bride's parents to arrange the wedding reception, the Lyttons took things into their own hands. There would be a family breakfast of some 100 closest relatives and friends at Delmonico's. August, although he had insisted on the utmost simplicity in most details, had no objection to this arrangement. After all, he did not want to hurt his future mother-in-law any more than he already had. Everything was arranged smoothly when, like a tornado, a letter swept him off his feet; it was a letter that was to affect his future, to haunt and trouble him for 50 years.

August had always gone his own way and never bothered any of his relatives or asked them for assistance in any way. However, out of deference to his parents, he now felt it only polite to include a list of Swiss relatives residing in or near New York to be invited to attend his wedding. The letter which arrived was written in the name of all his Swiss-American kin and was in familiar handwriting. He was informed that they were delighted to attend his church wedding, they held no compunction on that score, yet they would be unable to be at the wedding breakfast. Since the ceremony would be held in St. Patrick's cathedral, they would come there, but dining at Delmonico's was an entirely different matter. Perhaps he had forgotten that Jews and Catholics did not mix? Then he was told that they would look upon it as a direct insult if he seated Catholics and Jews side by side. Should he do so, they would see to it that he would have cause to regret this insult!

August was frantic. How could he avoid an open clash? He knew that the Lyttons had misgivings enough about their daughter marrying a Catholic and becoming a Catholic herself. What could he do to remedy this awful situation? He had the highest respect for the Lyttons, the Baruchs and Levies. He also knew that Gertrude herself had been criticized by her own people for becoming a Christian and moving to New York. Her family had social standing. Her relatives had fought in the Revolutionary War and were more American than most of her critics. Her family had served as outstanding leaders. Gertrude had accepted him, his religion, his people. Tormented, he worried about how he could avert a crisis. What explanation could he give for bigotry? Archbishop Corrigan had complimented him on choosing such a remarkable woman as Gertrude as his future wife. He was very much in love with her and had found in her the type of person he had always wanted to marry. His thoughts and emotions were a jumble. Totally bewildered, he sought the help of his fiancée, telling her that he was forced to change the wedding plans yet again.

Gertrude listened in amazement to his plan. There could be no gathering of any kind. The wedding would be performed by the Archbishop at 8:00 in the morning and the Nuptial Mass would be said at the altar of the Lady Chapel. No one except the most intimate members of her family could be present. The wedding breakfast would take place at Delmonico's, but instead of any large gathering, it would be most informal; the parents of the bride and only two or three of his Swiss-American relatives would be guests. The Archbishop had consented to come to the breakfast. Later that day, at just as informal a luncheon at Delmonico's, the Lyttons were free to invite six or seven of their closest relatives. The Lyttons were not only shocked at this change of attitude, and August's dictatorial manner, but also at the future that lay before them. It certainly looked as though the prospective bridegroom was already taking advantage of Gertrude's complacent disposition. They had heard many rumors of foreigners marrying American girls, then abusing them after they had taken all their money. Did August belong in this category? His manners seemed so pleasing yet, on this occasion, he was acting in a barbarous fashion. And why the early hour of the wedding? Mrs. Lytton protested. She felt it an imposition for the Archbishop to be asked to officiate at such an hour. August informed her that the prelate usually said his private Mass at seven and that the Lyttons always assembled for family breakfast at seven, thus he was imposing no hardship on anyone. Things could have grown tragic had it not been for Gertrude's *savoir faire*. She tactfully informed her parents that August really did have an excellent reason for his requirements, though deep in her own mind and heart she began to wonder what all the commotion was about. August had told her nothing substantive, yet his faithful valet had made several insinuations when the master was not around that it was a pity that there were so many meddlers trying to interfere. The Lyttons, seeing that Gertrude agreed in everything, decided it was wisest not to interfere themselves, but they mourned the fact that their daughter was so blinded by love that she could not see the handwriting on the wall. From this point forward, they observed only from a distance, although with a numbing feeling that this alliance might mark the end of all Gertrude's high aspirations and dreams.

The Archbishop's feelings were sympathetic to those of the Lyttons, but August was adamant; his wedding was not meant to be a function; he wanted no onlookers who would come to gape and criticize. This was his marriage; to him it was a sacrament, and at so solemn a function he wished no distractions. Those who really cared for him or his bride would be there; the others could be dispensed with—he did not need them. August awaited the wedding day with dread. He had managed to keep publicity to a minimum. There had been only one brief reference to a quiet, private ceremony to be celebrated in July.

July 5th was a sultry, humid morning. Inside Carnegie Hall, a nervous groom was being assisted into his Prince Albert. His valet, Tom, was visibly moved and depressed since their bachelor days had come to an end, and he was losing a wonderful master to a mere slip of a girl. Meanwhile, in the Lytton suite in the Plaza, there was buzzing excitement. Beaumont, the youngest son, was protesting being incarcerated in an Eton jacket by his formidable governess. She knew what was right, she averred; had she not just left the employ of the Prince of Wales to tutor this incalcitrant son in English? In another room Ellen, who had now been employed by the Lyttons for 30 years, was overflowing with happiness. She had been present when her beautiful young lady had been christened and confirmed; now she was to assist at her wedding. But Ellen also shed a few hidden tears. Although she had always liked the Swiss artist, she now felt that he had done a grave injustice to the Lyttons by ruthlessly upsetting all their plans. He had refused to have even one bridesmaid in attendance; yet he, for sure, had as best man his closest friend, Robert Schwarzenbach. When Mrs. Lytton had asked why he made an exception for himself, he had replied that Gertrude had her family; he had only his best friend, the man whose father had been instrumental in bringing him to America. Robert would take the place of his relatives.

Ellen was further estranged by the fact that August had told Miss Gertrude that he would wear a black Prince Albert and that it would be nice if she had a long, grey, double-breasted suit made to match his frock coat. This was too much for Ellen and for the Lyttons. In the end, Gertrude was married in a light pinkish suit with an elegant white blouse embroidered with violets and a large hat topped with ostrich plumes. This was a tiny battle won. She received her First Communion at her Nuptial Mass. During the ceremony, Archbishop Corrigan read a cable from Pope Leo XIII imparting the Apostolic Blessing. After the gospel, he said to the newlyweds, "I have no intention of preaching to you, yet I cannot help congratulating you both. Let me remind you of the words of today's *Introit*: *Deus Israel*; the God of Israel has joined you together. May he be with you all the days of your life. . . ." As they left the cathedral, the handsome diamond and ruby lavalière which August had given his bride the previous night shone in splendor, as did the simple solitaire engagement ring so set that it would last in perpetuity.

Thanks to August's untiring efforts, all went off better than he could have anticipated. The wedding breakfast was a harmonious family gathering, with no more than two Swiss relatives to mar the happiness of the moment. (If luncheon was a bit stiffer, that was because most of the Lytton relatives were strangers to August.) After breakfast, in accordance with a delightful Swiss custom, the bride joined her new husband for a carriage ride—this time in a hansom cab whose terrain was Central Park. When, after a few minutes, it was discovered that the cab's wheel had broken, August sheepishly asked if this were an omen of bad luck. He found another cab and they continued their journey through the Park, not feeling in the least like a bride and groom on their wedding day.

Having said good-bye to her parents and three brothers, George, Walter and Beaumont, and to the Simon Baruch's with their sons, Bernard and Tot, the bride returned with her husband to Carnegie Hall where they intended to pick up their mail. In the elevator, they were greeted by an American artist, Alexander Harrison, who observed to her: "I am very pleased to meet you, yet I am in grave doubt as to whether you should be congratulated, or I should express to you my condolence for being married to an artist! The wife of one of our profession must possess the patience of a saint, and must have the virtues of an angel." Gertrude was often to reflect on these words as she shared the restless life of a man who made his home on two continents.

Since they had been unable to sail on the *S.S. Bourgoyne* as originally planned, August had reserved the bridal suite at the new Waldorf. As he and Gertrude were walking through the hotel's renowned "Peacock Alley," they heard the excited cries of newsboys in the street shouting "Extra! Extra!" The glaring headlines of the *New York Herald* for July 5 stopped them short. They read:

THE BOURGOYNE SINKS AT SEA! 535 SOULS PERISH! AWFUL SCENES ON THE GREAT FRENCH LINER AFTER SHE MEETS THE BRITISH SHIP CROMARTHYSHIRE IN COLLISION 60 MILES OFF SABLE ISLAND. PASSENGERS AND CREW FIGHT LIKE MADMEN. WOMEN ARE STABBED AND DROWNED BY INHUMAN SAILORS WHO FORGET ALL BUT SELF IN STRUGGLE FOR LIFE. MOURNING IN MANY HOMES IN THIS AND OTHER CITIES.

August was choked by emotion. He could only look at his wife and seize her hand. Neither was able to speak. The warning received in Gertrude's nightmare had come true. Gradually the harrowing details had come to light: the *Bourgoyne* had struck the *Cromarthyshire* at five in the morning in a dense fog. Within 10 minutes she had plunged to the bottom of the sea, dragging with her hundreds of unsuspecting sleepers. Of the 734 passengers and crew, 535 were drowned. All of the first-class passengers were lost. Of the 300 women aboard, 80 were nuns; not one woman was saved! The French crew had been guilty of hideous atrocities. They had shoved helpless women and babies from lifeboats with oars and boat hooks. The few women who managed to cling to lifeboats or rafts were stabbed or drowned by sailors. Terrified Italians in steerage were insane with fear, and ran wielding stilettos and slashing down all who stood in their paths. Ship's officers had tried to stop the bloodshed but they were powerless; they were trampled by passengers or by their own sailors. The captain and his staff, to the last man, had gone down with the ship.

That first evening, as they dined alone in their suite, August unlocked his mind and heart to Gertrude. He minced no words in telling her about himself, warning her that she would have many difficulties to face because of his fiendish temper. Would she promise him that she would always forgive the things he said during these temper tantrums? He explained that she must never expect him to apologize verbally or ask forgiveness for these sudden outbursts. Later on, after having sufficient time to think things over, he would, in all probability, regret his action and be truly penitent. In Europe this sort of action was the man's prerogative, and women accepted it as such. It would be best for Gertrude, as his American wife, if she understood this custom beforehand, since so doing would greatly simplify their relationship. In all likelihood she would never know how many times he was genuinely sorry for his acts nor how much he regretted the incompatibility they caused, for, in the eyes of the European male, to apologize was considered a display of weakness. It just wasn't done. Later, August had spoken so beautifully about his mother, of the deep affection and respect he felt for her, that Gertrude felt consoled. Surely a man of moods who loved his mother as much as he did had kindness in his heart.

On Saturday, July 9, the temperature in their bedroom at four a.m. registered 84 degrees. By noon it was 103. With a sigh of relief, the bride and groom boarded the *S.S. Touraine*. Gertrude had lost sight of her parents until she finally caught a glimpse of her father standing on top of one of the piles where he was waving his silver-headed cane, his bowler hat atop it for identification. She suddenly burst into uncontrollable tears. August, with his arm around her waist, realized how she felt; she was leaving all she loved to give herself to him.

Strangely enough, aboard the *Touraine* were the survivors of the ill-fated *Bourgoyne*, and August had ample time to question some of them and validate the tales about its horrible demise and that of its passengers. It was then that he truly realized what he had been spared through Gertrude's intervention and the help of God.

Once out at sea, Gertrude went below deck to unpack. Beyond Nantucket, swells began to rock the boat. When August joined her, she noticed how impatient, even gruff he had become—like an irritable child. Suddenly her husband turned pea-green, a victim of the sea-sickness which very often assaulted him. She began to busy herself about his unpacking and attending to the thousand and one demands made upon a European housewife by every European husband. Her new life had begun.

As they docked at Le Havre, they were met by the agent of René Lorilleux and taken to the Gare Saint-Lazare in Paris where they were met by the Lorilleux car and had their first ride in an automobile. The entire clan of August's old friends assembled to celebrate the homecoming of one who was like a son to them. At dinner, pretty Gabrielle, now a handsome young woman, remarked to August within the hearing of Gertrude, not realizing that the bride understood French perfectly: "For the past two years, I have slept with your photograph under my pillow. Though you found me an excellent husband, I am still as much in love with you as when I was a child." Gertrude was puzzled; was this prophetic of things to come? Was their marriage sacred to no woman?

August had prepared his wife for Brunnen, and had also begged his widowed mother to spend the summer at *Villa Gutenberg* as she always had. He wished to be as diplomatic as possible. From the moment of their meeting, shy, retiring Mrs. Adelrich Benziger loved her vivacious daughter-in-law, although no greater contrast could have existed between any two women—the elderly lady, with her white hair pulled tightly back, wearing her inevitable dress of severe black—and Gertrude, smart, chic, the couturière's darling with trunksful of the latest Paris creations.

Gertrude was immediately enthralled by Brunnen. Hour after hour she would look out her window at the ever-changing scenery of the Lake of the Four Cantons, or go to the veranda to watch the mountains, tinged with pink, turn into fiery red at sunset. From every direction she could hear the tinkle of cowbells sounding gently on the terraced slopes. During those first weeks, August made an effort to familiarize her with the countryside, and with Lucerne and Zurich. Since Gertrude spoke no German, she at once arranged to take daily lessons at a nearby convent, hoping thereby to be able to share in the conversation as well as in the daily life of the household.

What an eye-catching figure the Benziger bride made, wasp-waisted and elegant, her bouffant skirt trailing along the wooded path. She was the center of attraction for some as she shopped for groceries, the villagers gaping in astonishment at this exquisite creature straight from the pages of a picture book. But other heads shook in disapproval, and local tongues wagged when they saw the gaily-colored parasol she was carrying. Gertrude had not realized that she had shocked the conservative residents by her bold display. Proper Swiss women carried black umbrellas, wore black clothes.

Color was not a part of their lives. Even visitors presented a problem. There was nothing August enjoyed more than entertaining a
houseful of guests, so he invited his sister, Mrs. Sonntag, who arrived on a visit from Freibourg. One of the first things this woman
did was see to it that her new sister-in-law's bright, lace-trimmed
sunshades were put aside, and that the handsome *aigrettes* which
adorned her hats were stripped from them. It was scarcely becoming for a Swiss woman to look as though she had just stepped from
a fashion plate. Once married, a wife's endeavor should be directed toward appealing to her mate alone, and to no other male!
Also, her stylish coiffure had to be changed at once. Her hair
should be dressed more simply—braided in the Swiss fashion, then
twisted in a high knot at the back of her head. This was a fitting
gesture signifying propriety and restraint.

August loved to see well-dressed women arrayed in finery, but
soon heard so many adverse comments about his wife's trousseau
that he finally capitulated to the pressures brought to bear upon
him. He agreed reluctantly that all the frills of Gertrude's wardrobe must be discarded, and even the use of face powder had to
cease. On marrying August, she, too, had become Swiss; in a
Swiss woman, none of this ostentatious display could or would be
tolerated. Cut to the quick by all this narrow-minded, provincial
gossip, her husband felt that it would be the wisest course of action
to close the many trunks full of finery, and forget them forever.

As that first summer drew to an end—those strange, lonely
weeks during which she had virtually been a guest in her husband's
home—Gertrude was sincerely grateful to August's mother for having taught her many aspects of Swiss living. By the time they
parted, the senior Mrs. Benziger to return to her Einsiedeln home,
and August and Gertrude to their Carnegie Hall studio, a deep
friendship had been cemented between them, one based on mutual
respect.

But once again storm clouds gathered over the lives of the
newlyweds. August received mail addressed to "August Benziger,
Judenberg, Brunnen" and to "August Benziger, [Jew Mountain]."
While he tried to ignore this cruelty, inwardly he shook with rage.
The worst of it was that it was such a sensitive matter that he
could discuss it with no one.

On their return to New York, Gertrude unburdened *her* heart.
Certain relatives, close in-laws who spoke both French and English, had whispered in her ear that she was living in a fool's para-

dise if she believed in her husband's future fidelity. Knowing August as they did as a lively, uninhibited artist, they doubted that her marriage had any chance of survival.

Through all this sea of misunderstanding, Gertrude had been gentle, patient, humble, and she had yielded to the many demands made upon her. She loved August; he loved her; that was all that mattered. For his part, August told himself that he had no cause to nurse any grievances, real though they might be. All disharmony was purely external to their union. Nonetheless, he was deeply hurt, and the grim realization gripped him that anyone could break up a marriage if that person worked hard enough at lying and destroying. The years ahead would be marked by fidelity, but they would not be easy.

CHAPTER 11

An American Woman Becomes Swiss (1899-1905)

August was determined that his marriage should last, but others gave it small chance of doing so. Negative views and comments came almost exclusively from the Swiss, both at home and in America, but more devious approaches were utilized to sow discord in Gertrude's mind. She possessed wealth, fame, beauty; the best things in life could be hers were she only to find a setting in which she belonged. In Switzerland, she could not expect to remain other than an outsider forever; her marriage would inevitably fail. So spoke her self-styled mentors.

Fortunately she took these proffered opinions straight to her husband. Being of granite tenacity, he vowed to show his critics, one and all, that they were mistaken. At first, he thought he would return to France and stay there, but Gertrude was expecting a baby and, being Swiss to the core, he naturally wanted his children to be born on Swiss soil. This child was expected within three weeks, scarcely enough time to make any major domestic adjustments. During these days his wife carried herself soberly and serenely. As a married woman, she was expected to conform to the custom of wearing only black clothing, like everyone else; bright colors were not only to be frowned upon but were presumed to be adopted for the very dubious and sole purpose of attracting men. She said little, but watched herself with caution in order to avoid any deviation from this dull, dead, depressing pattern. During the past year, she had had to renounce her favorite sport of riding. August had explained that since the duty of a Swiss wife was to bear children, it was scarcely becoming for her to be seen riding about the countryside in a lively, lighthearted manner. The peasants had been gossiping; indeed, they felt, none of them had time to waste during a busy day sitting on a horse, garbed in a fancy costume. What

kind of person was this Frau Benziger anyway, flaunting her out-
landish American fashions in such a prominent manner?

While the pleasures and companionship of riding had been
sacrificed by Gertrude, August, more than ever, had resorted to the
use of horses, albeit in a solitary manner. He was consumed by
anxiety and fear, not only on the subject of the stability of his marriage, but also because there was no doctor in Brunnen, and
Gertrude's time of delivery was fast approaching. Getting a physician from Zürich would be speedier than going to Einsiedeln which
was off the beaten path, but his efforts to secure the ministrations
of two Zürich doctors failed, although both were friends and clients. They scoffed at his fears. Since both were on the staff of
the Theodosianum, they insisted that August's wife should come to
that Zürich hospital if he wanted their help. Moreover, they felt it
to be entirely beneath their dignity to assist at a birth. Was not the
village midwife competent enough to delivery a Swiss woman?
Then why should his American wife receive special attention?

After having seen what went on inside the hospitals of Vienna, Munich and Paris, August had been left with a pervading
horror of these dens of disease. He personally knew of agonizing
deaths that could have been prevented by means of proper hygiene.
One thing was definite; as long as he lived, he would never permit
the woman he loved to enter any hospital.

At this most critical of moments, he suffered another disturbing setback. In the Benziger family it had been customary to hold
festivities at the time of christening. August now discovered that
none of his relatives would consent to serve as godparents to his
expected heir. When they were pressed for their reasons for declining, he was told that they strongly disapproved of the marriage
of a Christian and a Jewess, as the future progeny would have Semitic blood in their veins; it would certainly be wiser to look elsewhere and not attempt to involve them in this controversial issue.
At the last moment, an unexpected solution was achieved. Without
fanfare, two total strangers were invited to serve as godparents to
his first-born.

Mentally dejected by the needless cruelty he had just endured
from clients and relatives alike, August began his return journey
from Zürich filled with a heavy sense of defeat. In Schwyz, he
stopped to refresh his horse and take supper at the local inn. He
knew most of the judges and village scribes who habitually
dropped in at this place to gossip over their beer or *Kirsch*. When

he arrived, they happened to be discussing the latest newcomer in town who planned to stay and tend to their needs—the village doctor, a phenomenal man who had already saved the lives of several villagers that very week. The famed Zürich specialists had not been at all interested in coming to the rescue of simple country people, but favored city patients with laden pocketbooks. Dr. Paul Bommer, on the other hand, seemed sincere and dedicated to his profession. He was young, and newly embarked on his life's work; if he continued along the lines of his present record, all augured well for his soon becoming the outstanding medical figure in the Canton.

August needed to hear no more. He learned that Dr. Bommer had just bought a large house around the corner, and so he clattered past the courthouse and up the narrow street where, even at that late hour, a row of people stood in line waiting to be seen in his office. Never being a man to wait for anything or anyone, August strode past the patients, rang the bell and gave his card to the maid. As he was led in, he carefully studied the extremely thin man with the scrawny neck and protruding Adam's apple. The eagle-eyed physician returned his gaze. As the father-to-be told his story, Dr. Bommer bent his head and stared at the man before him. He admitted that midwives were still essential in areas where doctors could not reach patients, and were often excellent assistants at time of birth; still, August was perfectly within his rights to require a physician to attend his wife. He would examine her the next day when he came to Brunnen. He advised further that August take the next train to Frankfurt where there was a fine school of nursing. There he could choose an experienced baby nurse and bring her back with him. This done, he should be back just in time for the delivery.

May 20th found August pacing the walks of his flower-strewn estate. When Dr. Bommer finally called him, it was to place a lovely little girl in his arms. As the father looked proudly at the infant, he was seized with the overwhelming knowledge that nothing, now, could ever separate him from the extraordinary woman who had given him this child. He was delighted that his first child had been a girl. Girls would certainly be easier to raise than boys, and he hoped that he would have not just one, but a dozen. He proposed a name for her; she was to be christened Gertrude Marieli Rose on the following day—Gertrude, in honor of his wife; Marieli, in honor of his mother; Rose in honor of Mrs. Lytton. By her family, the baby was to be called Marieli, meaning "little Mary" in Swiss.

She would spend a considerable part of her growing years at the Brunnen villa, which was certainly in strange contrast with the luxurious mode of living in New York and Chicago. Spartan simplicity marked everything in the villa where all was of fine quality but of plain design, from the parquet floors to the polished birch banisters. There was no electricity, and the kerosene lamps and fitful candles gave the maids much cause for worry. If they were careless or neglected to clean the wicks, the tablecloth and dinner plates could be blackened by soot. Gertrude very much missed the electricity of Chicago and New York. She and August went to bed holding candles, and the last thing they did each night was to reach for the copper snuffer on their night table. Bathroom facilities were primitive in comparison with those to which Gertrude was accustomed in the States. In the Lytton home, each of the children had his or her own bathroom complete with porcelain tub and toilet. However, *Villa Gutenberg* did boast an ancestral iron bathtub which was the talk of all the neighbors, as no one else had such a modern convenience.

Guests flocked to Brunnen, especially the Americans and French, many of whom came to sit for portraits. Some even found gracious hospitality under the artist's own roof. For this reason, the charming hostess soon learned the many intricacies of running a turn-of-the-century Swiss home. The contents of the well-stocked cellar, including the choice wines left by King Ludwig II of Bavaria, were at long last to be served. During those first weeks, Gertrude made many an error in the arts of housewifery in this singular establishment. The worst had to do with the precious wines. Having been entrusted with the keys, she descended to the dark, damp, musty-smelling cave-like wine cellar. To her dismay, she found that every last bottle was covered with a heavy layer of mould and even more repellent films of cobwebs. In all innocence, she undertook to rid the bottles of their aged and hoary appearance by washing them in hot soapy water and rinsing them until they sparkled with cleanliness. August, finding her in the final stages of this activity, shouted in alarm: "Gerty! What in heaven's name are you doing? You've ruined this irreplaceable old bottle. See how you've thrown the sediment straight to the top. What was a most valuable wine has been completely fouled and isn't fit for human consumption!" What had happened to the cobwebs and the mould? No one would believe him at this moment if he told him that this bottle was 25 years old. Gertrude's eyes instantly sprang tears; she was always doing the wrong thing. Would she never acquire the sophisticated flourishes that were an essential part of her Continental husband's make-up? Knowing that August disliked any display of emotion, she gulped hard and succeeded in quelling her hurt feelings.

To most of August's many rules and regulations she agreeably conformed. Only once did she rise up in protest, even outright rebellion, and this incident had to do, of all things, with the laundry. It was the local custom for the village laundress to take over *Villa Gutenberg* twice yearly for a week or ten days. Between these visits, soiled laundry piled up in mountainous accumulation in an upper room which, understandably, became rank with its presence. At the time of the laundress's semi-annual visit, the accumulated laundry was borne in huge hampers to the wash-house where all items were sorted and then boiled in enormous open-air vats, over a fire stoked with bundles of sticks. Gertrude was horrified; she saw no purpose whatsoever to be served by delaying a task that could be easily performed weekly. Monday washday at the villa was soon inaugurated. The washerwomen protested that they would soon be out of work if these newfangled notions were taken up by others, but young Mrs. Benziger was adamant. Little did she think anyone, let alone the Swiss, would ever follow her independent, New World pattern; but strangely enough, the American idea of a weekly washday soon took hold on Brunnen. Other housewives dared to follow suit; a tiny victory had been won.

In the midst of these domestic frays, on December 14, 1899, August sat down to write a letter of truly tragic import to his in-laws in Chicago. He told of the sudden passing of his beloved mother who had been buried only the preceding day.

> I have just laid beneath the ground one who, until I met your dear Gertrude, meant more to me than life itself. I dare say, I was her favorite child. All the success I have had in life I attribute to her remarkable influence. She was the most perfect, the most unselfish, the humblest of all women. Her beautiful memory will remain with me every day of my life. Now, neither love nor ambition will be divided. Both center solely on my dearly beloved wife and on the sweet little daughter she has given me. We plan to leave for Paris in

January, as soon as the necessary details of settling the estate
have been terminated.

Brunnen, in December, was like Einsiedeln, cold, bleak, bare;
and August, who had worked energetically to obtain his commissions, now felt both inclined and bound to move to Paris. His
French and American clients were clamoring for portraits. Those
first weeks in the metropolis with his wife and new baby were, at
best, difficult. The couple had combed the city in a futile effort to
locate a suitable home, and August now needed a much larger studio than the one on Rue Washington. Thanks to the united efforts
of friends, a place was eventually found which could meet his
needs. Tucked away in a fine section of Paris was a vacant house
which had never been occupied. An artist had built it for his own
use but had been forced to abandon it. In the residence next door
lived Edmond Rostand, the distinguished French dramatic poet.
August and Gertrude rushed to see it, and found it to be everything
for which they had hoped. It had space for the future desired children, was in a tranquil and secluded setting and contained a near
perfect studio. Built of handsome grey stone, it was enhanced by
an iron grille of intricate latticework which protected the *porte
cochère*. Four marble steps led to a white marble foyer flanked by
marble benches. The austere dignity of the entrance, with its great
bronze lantern, conveyed a deep and satisfying sense of security.

The interior of the house seemed to have been made to order
for them. All they needed was to acquire furniture in order to take
immediate possession. The walls of the dining room were covered
with panels of olive-green Cordovan leather embossed with golden
cat-o'-nine-tails; adjacent to it was a cream-colored reception room
with Gothic wainscoting and fluted columns. But the real *pièce de
résistance* was the tremendous studio which formed an annex to
the rear of the house and which boasted a marvelous glass roof; it
was an artist's dream come true, set as it was amid ivy-covered
walls and a private enclosed garden. On the second story was an
additional studio, almost as spacious as the first. At once, August
began to plan where to set his easels, his dais. As his studio was
his sole and immediate concern, he instructed Gertrude to continue
her round of inspection and to determine whether there were suitable servants' quarters. She was beside herself with delight when
her husband delegated to her full authority for furnishing their new
abode. The moment they left the premises, August went to complete arrangements for purchasing this house at 8 Rue Eugène

Flachat. It was purchased in his wife's name, since it was actually a wedding present from her parents, who had hoped that the money would be spent in buying a New York or Chicago home. The Benzigers moved in with great speed to the loud accompaniment of carpenters' hammers and the deep thuds and scrapes of furniture movers. The memory of the austere days in Brunnen faded in the light of this bright and entirely new world to be enjoyed, a world of graciousness, friendship and charm.

August's French friends liked his bride and immediately vied to be of assistance in countless, cordial ways. As a rule, the French were prejudiced against Americans, but Gertrude's gentle and genuine sincerity captivated them. When the salon had been equipped with its Aubusson tapestries and brocaded armchairs, a whirlwind of parties began as August wished to reciprocate the accumulated kindnesses which had been showered upon him during his long and busy bachelor years. In no time, with the help of her friends, Gertrude found herself shopping expertly at the *Magasin du Printemps* or the *Bon Marché* like an experienced French matron. Even in this capital of gastronomy, the Benzigers' dinner parties became the talk of the town; so frequently did he give eight- or ten-course dinners that the simple family cook eventually came to be replaced by a chef with *Cordon Bleu* credentials.

August not only received countless guests but also, proudly, took Gertrude calling. He had eagerly looked forward to the day when she would meet his art masters. Bonnat was captivated by her at once. Being a tiny man, he impulsively jumped onto his six-foot stool, then peered down at her with an appraising eye. After remarking on her beauty, he leaned over and quite unexpectedly planted a resounding kiss on the center of each cheek.

Her introduction to William Bougereau's studio brought blushes of embarrassment. A butler opened the door and led them to the artist's studio. There was a warm and joyful welcome as the artist embraced Gertrude enthusiastically. But the eyes of the demure American suddenly sprang wide open. If the floor would only open and let her drop through! There, standing before them, was an angel—in the nude. Bouguereaus's model was clad solely in a pair of great white wings. At a word of dismissal from the artist, the earth-bound angel took her silk scarf, threw it casually about her shapely shoulders and strolled idly into the next room. From that time onward, Gertrude always stood timidly on the threshold of this man's studio before summoning the courage to enter into it.

Ever anxious that his wife should come to know his Parisian friends, August took her to the weekly salon of Princess Matilde Bonaparte. (This was the same lady who had taken a decided fancy to him some years ago in Saint Moritz.) One of these soirées, although deemed a brilliant success, had required all of Gertrude's tact and *savoir-faire*. Apparently the hostess and her friends believed young Mrs. Benziger to be Swiss, as her French was perfect, and they began verbal attacks on "these terrible Americans."

Anna Gould, who had just become the Countess Boni de Castellane, was one of those being ripped apart verbally at the table, her critics having chosen to overlook the fact that this New Yorker had been badly exploited by a French nobleman. As the tirade had lasted throughout the meal, Gertrude had been forced to listen to complaints that her countrymen were endangering the French monetary system, monopolizing and ruining the best couturières and causing the wages of domestics to skyrocket. She was glad when the moment came to excuse herself and flee to the sanctuary of her own home—knowing better that no country is without its own prejudiced denigrators.

Soon, a second daughter arrived in the Benziger household, and she was baptized Hélène. In contrast to the situation which had arisen at the time of Marieli's birth, there was no problem about finding godparents: the Marquise de Toulongeon had been delighted to serve as the child's godmother. Life became reasonably calm and serene, although filled to overflowing with visits made and received.

The ever-increasing number of guests at 8 Rue Eugène Flachat came from every walk of life and represented the poor and the wealthy, the mighty and the prepossessing, the humble and the artistic. Memorable guests were Her Highness, the Maharanee of Lahore, the Count de Gareta and the Princess Ratazzi but, without question, the visitor who caused the greatest consternation *chez* Benziger was a lady daring to wear men's pants! Wherever they went, Professor and Madame Dieulafoy were clothed in identical trousers and jackets. The professor was a noted research worker and instructor at the Sorbonne, while his wife was a doctor in her own right. She had accomplished a man's work in the world and had also been a valued member of countless African exploratory expeditions. In view of these unusual circumstances, the French government had issued a special permit granting Mme. Dieulafoy and Rosa Bonheur, the renowned painter of horses, permission to wear their highly-shocking trousers.

Life was lively and interesting in Paris but by no means thornless for the Swiss husband and his American wife. While for the most part extremely busy in his studio, August still managed somehow to find opportunities to open Gertrude's personal mail, even when it was clearly addressed to her alone. It was, she learned, his prerogative to do so since women had no legal rights of any kind in France. When, on one occasion, it became necessary to remove the family silverware from the bank, Gertrude was outraged to learn that her signature was insufficient to do so. By law, everything she had formerly owned was now the property of her husband. She followed him to the railroad station with anger in her eyes, and demanded that if he expected to have a knife and fork with which to eat dinner that night, he must alter his plans and return to the bank with her. Her irate mind focused itself on the fact that even her necklaces and rings were legally his! He returned to the bank with her.

Calm was restored in this domestic area, but was shattered in another. August had always displayed great fondness for his eldest child until one day when that unfortunate little girl took a too-realistic view of his work. Over a period of a month he had been engrossed in painting a portrait of Mrs. Fritz Achilles whose beauty and red roses intrigued the child. Each day she came to the studio and Mrs. Achilles gave her one of the flowers, which the little girl promptly carried off to present to her mother. One day Marieli tiptoed into the studio and swiftly glanced at Mrs. Achilles. She ran forward eagerly, holding out her arms to the beautiful, smiling lady. As her chubby hands touched the benefactress, or what she *thought* was the benefactress, there came a horrible, sickening crash and a terrifying ripping sound as the child tripped over the easel and plunged to the floor. On top of her lay the heavy life-sized portrait which had just been completed and was awaiting delivery to the client. When Marieli's parents were alerted by the cries, they rushed to the studio in alarm and extricated the child from the mass of torn canvas. There had been no Mrs. Achilles in the room, but the portrait had been so amazingly life-like that Marieli had paid her father the unwanted compliment of seeing its subject there in the flesh. Stung to fury by the destruction of his long weeks of work, the artist seized his small daughter and spanked her resoundingly there and then. Gertrude, mute with anguish for both her child and her husband, took the sobbing heap of humanity in her arms and carried her gently to the nursery.

Fortunately, the gaping hole which had been torn in the canvas was, in time, successfully repaired by means of a process which August learned from the curator of the Louvre, but one sort of damage could not be healed: Marieli was told that she could never again cross the threshold of her father's studio uninvited. For all of her childhood's long years, she was banished from those quarters or, at least, from the wonderful impromptu visits to the magical world of adult creativity.

At this time, Gertrude once again became pregnant, and August arranged with great determination that she was to be attended by Madame Lachapelle, who owned her own *Maison de Santé d'Accouchement,* a private lying-in hospital. To be a *sage-femme,* or midwife, in France was to be a member of a highly-regarded profession, and doctors were powerless to move a finger against anything these professional women might do.

On the 2nd of November, the Feast of All Souls, 1901, August had insisted that his wife join him in the city's traditional promenade to the cemetery to visit the graves of friends or relatives. The long walk had proven quite strenuous for the mother-to-be. Upon returning home, she excused herself and immediately went to bed, while August settled down to spend a congenial evening with his priest friend, Canon Faralicq, who had come to dine. Suddenly the children's nanny hurried downstairs, much perturbed, to ask that the *sage-femme* be brought at once. "Madame is in labor!"

August leaped to his feet and ran for a carriage. Within minutes, he returned with Mme. Lachapelle, mounting three stairs at a time in his anxiety. She took charge instantly, and urged him to return to his dinner, and before the meal was ended, the glad news was brought that he was the father of a third little daughter. He again rushed to his wife's bedside to embrace her. Fearing that something had gone amiss, Canon Faralicq had followed closely on August's heels. As he peered down at the puny eight-month infant, fear gripped his heart. How could this fragile wisp of humanity possibly survive? Dipping his hand in the warm bath water, he made the sign of the cross over her and inquired: "What have you decided to name her?" Gertrude whispered weakly: "Marguerite-

Marie—for my husband's sister who is a Carmelite nun." And so it was done; the priest gave the infant conditional baptism, and she was launched into life.

From that time on, Denise, the nanny, devoted all of her time to the two older Benziger children—Hélène, barely one year old, and Marieli, two. Mme. Lachapelle fetched a wet-nurse for the new infant, who was to feed her, hover over her and tend to her special needs. Whenever Denise went out with the children for an airing, she would remove the simple headdress worn inside and re-place it with a frilly coronet which boasted two long ribbons which touched the ground at her back; these were the respected badges of her profession. Life in the Benziger household was clearly grow-ing in complexity.

It soon took an unexpected turn. In 1901, the president of France gave a dinner in honor of the Swiss artist who had won every prize in the field of art, and members of the foreign colony, as well as prominent Frenchmen, were invited. One of the guests was a German from Frankfurt, Herr Ganz, who was considered to be the second-wealthiest man in Germany. His wife, a former Hungarian baroness, and a real beauty, was also present. The French Prime Minister, M. Rouvier, told August that he himself had given Herr Ganz much valuable stock market information, and that the man not only had a fortune in Germany, but also had ac-quired enormous sums in France. Accordingly, when Herr Ganz approached and asked him to paint a portrait of his wife, August acquiesced. The man, he felt, would surely be reliable financially. Further, Ganz had insisted on signing a statement that, upon deliv-ery of the painting, he would pay the full price at once.

The portrait presented a handsome woman in a white dress of intricate net design and low décolletage, a black fox fur in her lap, and black hair accented by sprigs of holly. Hers was a studious, pensive mein. One day, in the midst of the sittings, genial Herr Ganz asked the artist lightly if he would mind letting him borrow a large specified amount of money as he needed immediate cash to conclude an important deal and had failed to get to the bank that morning. August advanced the full amount to his client after giv-ing the matter only a passing thought. After all, here was a man who had dined at the presidential residence and was a friend of the prime minister.

Shortly after this incident, the portrait was completed and, in honor of the occasion, August held a reception to which many notables were invited. Expressions of sincere and lavish praise emanated from all sides but, to the astonishment of all present, Herr Ganz stood before the exquisite image of his wife in sullen silence. His fingers twisted ominously, knotted and unknotted. Seizing his hat, he left the gathering speedily and abruptly. Frau Ganz was at a loss for an explanation—then came ugly rumors. Herr Ganz refused to accept the painting; it was not, he said, a true likeness of his wife. He intended to press suit in court and fight the matter to the finish. Certainly no one could ever force him to take possession of the painting, much less pay for it.

French litigations were maddeningly slow. It was often years before a case came to trial and judgment rendered. Ganz hired an excellent lawyer and saw to it that his case was given wide publicity.

August was stung to the quick. Sensitive about his work, and aware that he had reached the height of his career in France, he saw no alternative to accepting this challenge, gross and unfair as it was. The French courts would have to judge whether he had succeeded in producing a faithful likeness, and whether or not his portraits were worth the fee he asked for them. Extremely upset by being placed in this position, he vowed fiercely that he would never again touch brush to canvas until he had been publicly exonerated from this insidious charge. With bitterness in his heart, he laid aside his palette, brushes, paints. His unfinished portraits were turned with their faces to the wall, and thus would they remain until the reception of a final judgment. It was not until four years later that the case was finally heard. In the interim, August became the victim of abysmal restlessness and dissatisfaction. Inactivity and tension wore his nerves to shreds. The best thing for him to do, he felt, was to seek another career in order to bridge the gap until justice could be achieved.

Shortly after his father's death, August had been approached by a M. Ritz of the Paris *Ritz Hotel* and by Baron Pfeifer of Lucerne, requesting permission for them to build a hotel on his Brunnen property. Many years before, Richard Wagner had also wanted to buy a plot of land there for the purpose of constructing a villa for himself, a plan which had eventually come to nothing. However, now, when August discussed this latest request with M. Firmin-Didot and his father-in-law, Henry C. Lytton, these men strongly advised him to erect his own hotel, one to be operated on the American plan of including both room and board in a stipulated rate; this approach was then unheard-of in Europe. As his mind leaped forward in anticipation of the future, August decided overnight that he would indeed build this, the establishment of his dreams, which would challenge existing precedents by incorporating many New World innovations. It was his conviction that if Europeans wanted to cater to wealthy Americans, they would have to make radical departures from the current standards of hotel design. All Americans took their private bath facilities for granted, and expected other conveniences built into their accommodations. The man who had temporarily rebelled against paint and art and put his artistic career on hold now became immersed in floor plans and architectural blueprints.

Gertrude was frantic, abhorring the very thought of building or owning a hotel. In vain, she attempted to dissuade her husband, pointing out sternly that artists were proverbially poor mathematicians. How could he possibly embark upon a highly-competitive enterprise when he was neither shrewd nor calculating? Most conspicuous of all was his lack of the stoic, controlled temperament required of a hotel proprietor. He too readily displayed his likes and antipathies to individuals; as a hotel manager, he would have to hold his reactions in check. It would be necessary to discipline himself severely in order for him to be seen as both unbiased and impartial under the most trying circumstances. Iron-willed, he turned a deaf ear to her remonstrances.

He drew endless plans and turned out vast numbers of blueprints, insisted that his guest palace be constructed of the finest materials, and planned to cater solely to the most discriminating and aristocratic visitors. When he had assembled all the new ideas he wished embodied in his hotel, he called in Herr Vogt who was later to use these same blueprints in constructing his Grand National Hotel in Lucerne and the Excelsior in Rome. The startling new style designed by Benziger of Brunnen was also to be copied in Saint Moritz, the Miramar in Genoa and Shepherd's in Cairo.

The property on which the edifice was to rise lay on the outskirts of the village of Brunnen right at the bend of Lake Lucerne. From this scenic spot, it was easy to cross over into Italy through the Saint Gotthard Pass; the newly-built railway tunnel from this Pass ran right through the Benziger estate and by means of it Paris, Rome, Vienna, Berlin and Amsterdam could be reached in only nine or ten hours. Nothing in Switzerland was far away, even the Matterhorn or Jungfrau. The location was ideal for families; bringing their children, they could leave them in Brunnen with their nurses and tour almost any part of the Continent with peace of mind and a sense of security.

In 1903 ground was broken. Over a thousand workmen hewed away part of a mountain to form a plateau 170 feet above the lake. There foundations were laid for a narrow, semi-circular building of solid granite brought from the Saint Gotthard Mountains. Every room on the south side of the nine-story building faced the incomparable beauty of the turquoise water and provided a balcony for comfort and viewing. Each suite had double doors to insure privacy and insulation against noise. Luxurious private bathrooms provided an abundance of hot running water, heated towel racks and "all the amenities." The drawing and dining rooms on the ground floor were two stories in height and faced with tremendous plate-glass windows, creating a panorama of the mountains. Elevators were installed, dishwashing equipment, the latest laundry devices, and even Singer sewing machines imported from America. Nothing was lacking.

By now, the Swiss countryside was buzzing. Benziger was openly ridiculed for his peculiar and exaggerated ideas. First, this fool of an artist had imported blue-blooded Kentucky horses for his stable and then had acquired for himself a millionaire wife. Now his latest trick was to install bathtubs and a full set of plumbing in every single room in his Grand Hotel! What in the name of heaven would come next?

He also succeeded in setting a record for the speed with which the building was erected. The entire project was completed in only 14 months. August had employed two shifts of workmen during the months when the weather was favorable, and had remained with the working crews throughout the construction time, blueprint in hand, inspecting, clambering over scaffolding, supervising.

The lawsuit that had been hanging fire for the past three years was finally to be heard, so the Benzigers moved back to Paris to be near the scene of action, to fight the case personally and learn the verdict—but still more infuriating delays were encountered. August's brother, the Carmelite bishop stationed in India, sent word that he had just arrived in Brussels, and hoped very much to meet his sister-in-law and bless his small nieces. Gertrude had heard much of his outstanding work in Quilon in the state of Kerala, along the western coast of the sub-continent. While still in his teens, he had entered the Carmelite Order at Bruges in Belgium. Always one to shun honors, on learning indirectly that he would be named Master of Novices upon his ordination to the priesthood, he volunteered immediately for service in foreign lands. In the end, as Brother Aloysius, he chose to go to India in the conviction that there he would be able to live a quiet, hidden life ministering to the people. Great was his surprise when, after only a few years of service, he was consecrated one of the youngest bishops ever to be elevated to episcopal rank. His diocese, although desperately poor, embraced some two million persons, most of whom were not Catholics or even Christians.

August went to the train station that January 17, 1901, to greet his brother as he stepped off the Brussels Express, and saw at once that he was deeply disturbed by some matter and was quite emaciated and drawn. He was clothed in a shabby brown habit and his bare feet were encased in simple sandals. At once he handed August his overnight bag, explaining hurriedly that he was very sorry, but that it was necessary for him to be detained for several hours on urgent business. August returned home, visibly annoyed by what he viewed as his brother's lack of appreciation of the welcome which had been prepared for him. Gertrude saw her husband's anger mount when the bishop failed to arrive in time for luncheon. August threatened to evict his houseguest if he could not display better manners than this. When he finally did arrive late in the afternoon, the poor man looked feebler and more depleted than ever. He had not eaten anything since the previous day and was in a state of near-exhaustion. In time they were to hear the incredible story hinging on his arrival and began to suspect that here was a man who possessed great and mystifying supernatural powers. From that moment on, they never questioned anything he might say or do.

Upon reaching Paris, Bishop Benziger had felt strongly impelled to rush to the home of his greatest benefactress. Throughout many years, she had maintained close contact with him and his work, and contributed her entire fortune to his missions. Arriving at her home, he had been informed that she was far too ill to see anyone. "Yes, I know," he replied, "in fact, she is dying." He asked that she be told that he was her friend, the missionary, that he had come to be with her during her last agony. The woman's daughter rushed down to greet him and told him that her mother had affirmed that all was well, and that she would not die until Bishop Benziger had come to be with her; she was certain that he was on his way. The daughter became steeped in anguish, since she knew that the prelate could not possibly have heard of her mother's imminent death. The bishop nodded his head quietly; he had known all of this through some inner power, without having been told by anyone. Having obtained permission to administer the Last Sacraments, he did so and said a Mass for the dying woman in her own room. It was not until some days later that he learned that the entire family had reproached this elderly lady for assisting a strange missionary in a far-off land with vast generosity. Had she seen fit to aid the local clergy, they would, at least, have attended her final hours; under the circumstances, none of them had been willing to respond to her need to have Viaticum brought to her. As the bishop intoned the prayers for the dying, this kindly woman expired, a contented smile on her lips.

During his brother's stay at 8 Rue Eugène Flachat, August brought together a group of outstanding members of the local clergy to meet him. Times were most serious for the Church in France. Religious persecution was increasing in intensity. Priests and nuns had been driven out of monasteries and convents, the latter being forced to live as seculars. Later, in 1901, the French Republic refused to allow any religious orders to exist in France without permission, thereby expelling all but a very few, and their works with them. In that year Waldeck-Rousseau, the powerful French statesman, had given his support to the socialists and radicals who abolished all religious authority. Among those whom Bishop Benziger met was the head of the French Dominicans, Père La Vigoureux. As they conversed, he asked his acquaintance why he had made no preparations to evacuate the religious under his charge. He should salvage as much as possible while he could still do so. The priest replied that he did not believe conditions to be as serious as reported; besides, he was a close personal friend of Waldeck-Rousseau. It was nonsense to think that France could ever become anti-religious. Bishop Benziger remonstrated with him, but to no avail. In 1905, when August and Gertrude were in Brunnen, they received an unexpected telegram from this priest, begging them to grant him temporary asylum. He had arrived in Switzerland as a refugee, having lost everything he and his Order owned. The government which seemed to him to have guaranteed him protection, under the direction of Waldeck-Rousseau, had been successful in driving the Catholic Church from France.

While Gertrude did all in her power to make Bishop Benziger comfortable while he was a guest of the family, she found little scope for niceties. He adhered closely to his diet of meatless soup, and his only indulgence was the smoking of tremendously-strong cigars. By five o'clock in the morning, he would be off to say his Mass in the church and meditate for two hours kneeling on the cold marble floors. Visiting his room one day before he returned, she discovered that he never slept in his bed but lay directly on the wooden floor with his cloak wrapped about him. He and his brother were cut from two very different bolts of cloth.

On leaving Paris, Bishop Benziger took the train to Venice for the purpose of visiting Cardinal Sarto, who was at the time Patriarch of that city and who had shown great interest in the missions of India. Upon reaching his residence, the bishop inquired of the simple, unassuming and shabbily-dressed brother porter if he might see His Eminence. He was then ushered into the parlor. The man wearing the threadbare soutane continued to converse pleasantly, and then sat down opposite him. Bishop Benziger stirred in his chair, disturbed that the message had not been delivered promptly. He repeated his request: "I would very much like to see His Eminence." The little man smiled and replied, "But I am he." This incident surfaced in later years to illustrate the humility and simplicity of the man who soon was to become Pope Pius X, succeeding Leo XIII who had died in July.

December 7th was the long-postponed and painfully-awaited day on which the French court was finally to meet to decide August's case. The presiding judge called in two art experts who were to examine the portrait of Frau Ganz, and give their decision in the matter. In the courtroom, August was initially seated opposite the much-saddened subject of the painting, but then she was asked by the judge to sit beside the work of art as the attorney for defiant Herr Ganz stoutly claimed that there was no likeness. Jules Le Fevre and Gabriel Ferrier, both celebrated portrait painters, soon rendered their verdict. All the newspapers of Paris, including *Figaro*, carried headlines on December 8th revealing the outcome of the litigation:

> The great masters pronounce Benziger's portrait to be a conscientious resemblance. The painting of Mme. Ganz is not only an excellent likeness—but the personal interpretation of her beautiful physiognomy is most outstanding.

The notoriety resulting from the trial, which August had feared might ruin his artistic career, served rather to enhance it. Herr Ganz was required to pay the full price agreed upon for the portrait. He was also to defray all court costs and attorneys' fees in connection with the proceedings. Ganz withdrew so cleverly and swiftly from France that he left no trail behind. Soon rumors circulated that Frau Ganz had applied for a divorce and married a far more worthy successor. The much-disputed portrait was hung in August's studio as a permanent memento of those wasted days of needless suffering.

The Benzigers returned to Switzerland. August hired a competent manager for the Grand Hotel and then invited his close friend, Abbott Gasquet, from Downside Abbey in England to bless it. By mid-June, the hotel was crammed with visitors, among them the Hinkles of Cincinnati, the Thaws from Pittsburgh and Princess Pauline Duleep-Singh, the youngest daughter of the Maharajah of Lahore, who sat for her portrait. Her father, the owner of one of the world's finest diamond mines, had been invited to London to visit Queen Victoria. While there, he had been politely but firmly advised that he would never be allowed to return to his native land. Although he was subsequently permitted a certain amount of political freedom, the blow, nevertheless, had been a swift and cruel one. Later, it was also pointedly suggested that since the Koh-i-noor diamond was in his immediate possession, he would be expected to surrender it personally to Her Majesty, Queen Victoria.

As the dark-eyed princess sat for the portraitist, tears often appeared. Intrigue and politics had denied her family both their home and their country; through an enormous injustice, they had become virtual exiles from India.

August always enjoyed the company of wonderful and loyal friends. One of these in Brunnen that summer was M.V. Deslandes, a member of the Portuguese government and director of the Royal Printing Establishments in Lisbon. It was through his good offices that August came to the attention of Don Carlos, King of Portugal. This ruler, during one of his frequent incognito visits to Paris, had been impressed by the Swiss artist's work, and requested him to paint portraits of himself and his consort but, tragically, the royal couple was assassinated before the commission could be carried out. A sympathetic friendship had earlier developed between August and Don Carlos who was, himself, a painter and lover of art, especially interested in the development of new techniques. He had sent a collection of his own paintings of Portuguese birds and flowers to be corrected by August. Out of gratitude for the artist's care, and in recognition of his talent, the king knighted his artist friend in 1895 with the Order of Christ, and shortly thereafter bestowed upon him the same honors once given to Velásquez, those of an officer of the Order of Saint Jacques. Finally he awarded him the advancement from being a simple Knight to becoming a Commander of the Order of Christ, a decoration initiated by King Denis I in 1319.

Renewed pressure was now brought to bear upon August to return to America, and to bring many of his portraits with him, especially the one of President McKinley, who had been felled by an assassin's bullet. His friends would mount a major exhibition of his work and see that his career prospered. He agreed to come for the winter months, but only on condition that his wife and three children accompany him. As Gertrude eagerly anticipated visiting her parents, August put his foot down at once, flatly refusing to consider any such possibility; his family was to remain at his side as he felt that should his small daughters spend any length of time with their grandparents in Chicago or at their summer home in Lake Geneva, Wisconsin, there was danger that they might become spoiled Americans! His ideal was prim, Old-World children of modest demeanor. Other than the opportunity of being again with her mother and father, Gertrude had no desire whatever to roam North America with three young children in tow, and would have preferred, under the circumstances, to remain at *Villa Gutenberg*. However, August's wishes were always respected, and so the journey was prepared.

As they boarded the steamer, *Lorraine,* the town of Le Havre was shrouded in heavy fog. Elise, the children's nursemaid, a young mountain woman herself, became violently seasick immediately, and so, too, did August, who had only to smell a ship in order to become a victim of nausea. Although unable to do anything to relieve August's apparently incurable affliction, Gertrude could certainly employ different tactics with the young nursemaid. She scolded her roundly and ordered her to sit up at once, making clear that the ship was not in the least pitching or rolling, nor was the sea even rough; in fact, it was still in dock and had not yet moved an inch. If Elise wished to do so, she could go ashore immediately and take the first train home to Switzerland. This was the first time Gertrude had ever spoken severely to Elise, who eventually became a model sailor. The journey was on; new doors would open. What would they all find on the other side?

CHAPTER 12

Commuting Between Two Continents (1905-1906)

The joyful Lyttons rushed to New York. Since it was the beginning of August and the east coast was sweltering, they suggested that they all escape to the more merciful climate of their Wisconsin summer home, but August was adamant: his wife and children must remain at his side at the Murray Hill Hotel. After a few days, Gertrude's parents returned to Lake Geneva with the hope-filled suggestion that, if August should change his mind at any time, they would be delighted to receive a visit from their son-in-law and his family.

August himself soon left his brood in order to take his portraits to Cincinnati and complete arrangements for the forthcoming exhibit. When he returned to New York after two weeks, he was shocked to find his three small daughters sickly and pale; they could not stand the enervating humidity combined with soaring temperatures. A doctor was called in and immediately ordered country air for these European youngsters accustomed to open spaces and Alpine breezes. August's hand was now forced. He put his wife and children on the first train headed in the general direction of Lake Geneva.

In the dining car, Elise was left in charge of the three little girls as her mistress was far too fatigued to eat but, wakeful and vigilant, Gertrude was suddenly seized with a feeling of restlessness. Perhaps Elise had more responsibility than she could handle; maybe she should look in on the four of them and help to bring back Marguerite, the youngest. As Mrs. Benziger entered the diner, her attention was immediately drawn to the waiters, all of whom were chuckling away, and to the diners who were looking in the direction of the three animated little girls chattering away in German. There sat poor Elise, with all eyes pinned on her, munching determinedly on the tough yellow skin of a banana and politely sipping water from her silver finger bowl. As her mistress approached, the girl could tell at once that she was doing something wrong. Marieli and Hélène, caught playing their pranks, lapsed into wide-eyed silence and hung their heads. Only then did Gertrude realize that Elise had never eaten a banana before, nor even seen one, still less could she have had any way of knowing what one did with a finger bowl. August's small daughters had apparently inherited his penchant for childhood mischief.

After a long day spent on the train, Gertrude noticed that Marieli and Elise looked pitifully woebegone; searching for mountains which were nowhere to be seen, both were acutely homesick for the Alps, and Marieli lapsed into a deluge of uncontrollable tears. In Chicago, the group transferred to the local train for Wisconsin. As they reached Lake Geneva, Gertrude began to bubble with enthusiasm. Every aspect of the countryside was now familiar to her. "There they are! Marieli, Hélène! Everybody's here to meet us." Forgetting all the rest of the world for one long moment, Gertrude flung herself into her mother's arms with a sobbing release of her pent-up emotions. The coachmen, grooms and the head farmer were all standing by in readiness to help. The children were snatched up and embraced by Mr. Lytton, while they squirmed and shied away from his bristling salt-and-pepper mustache. Gertrude gathered up her ankle-length skirt as she stepped into the family's *barouche* with its cream-colored upholstery and natty fringed top. Mr. Lytton and his eldest son led the way in a light phaeton, while the younger boys followed in a two-wheeled pony-cart. The children wriggled in joyous anticipation. At long last, they were out in the country. The winding road over which their carriage clattered took them uphill and downhill through grape-entwined trees until they entered a pebbled drive which passed among cool green oak and birch woods along a wandering stream emptying into the lake.

Everything was new. Until this magical autumn when the frosts had come early, the Swiss youngsters had never seen the rich, startling hues of an Indian Summer—the vivid clusters of red and gold maple leaves forming a tapestry hung on the sky.

The children's Uncle Beaumont, being only a few years older than they, enjoyed taking his small guests in his pony-cart on exploratory jaunts to the farm where they delighted in playing with the curly-tailed, squealing piglets, or watching the milking, or seeing how the russet apples were ground to cider. But best of all were the lively games of hide-and-seek held in the corn shed. One day, they had followed Beaumont to the fields to sample their first sweet corn. This new taste treat proved so delectable that they had sneaked back later to fill their middy blouses with a fresh supply; no one had told them that corn was never to be eaten raw.

By this time, their mother had left Lake Geneva to join her husband in Cincinnati. When the three of them were taken violently ill on the following day, the country doctor came at a fast clip in his horse-and-buggy to see what could be done to check their high temperatures. Nothing proved effective. Gertrude returned to learn that they were suffering, not from some strange children's malady, but merely from an overdose of uncooked sweet corn.

In the meantime, Mrs. Thaw had been exceedingly busy in Pittsburgh on August's behalf. Numerous orders for portraits poured in, and new clients requested interviews. One of these new acquaintances, Mr. William P. Snyder, an iron ore magnate, asked the artist to be his guest at *The Breakers* in Palm Beach, Florida, during the sittings for his portrait. George Oliver wanted three portraits painted, one of himself, one of his wife, and a third of his somewhat plain, retiring daughter, Amelia. The child had recently fallen into a state of severe depression, worrying about her homely appearance. August painted Amelia as he saw her, employing a background of cool trees and a charming stream; her arms were clasped affectionately around her favorite collie. Her deep, melancholy, dark eyes looked out on the world in such a way as to reveal her refreshing lack of sophistication and her lovely disposition. The portrait was widely praised. Through his kindly professional patience, the artist had brought about a remarkable change in his subject. By having been depicted in a favorable light, the unhappy young woman was at last able to overcome her inferiority complex. No longer fearing cruel comparisons, she began to show a pronounced interest in living. She began to travel and to enjoy the companionship of people her own age. As a result of August's painting, Amelia's world suddenly became joyful, colorful and worthwhile.

During a stay in a Pittsburgh suburb, August left the Thaw's home one afternoon following an all-day sitting. He had registered at a small, unpretentious hotel in town where he could enjoy quiet and privacy. So as not to be dependent on his hosts for transportation, he rented a horse and buggy by the month. While driving his horse down the mountainside, he unexpectedly encountered one of the first automobiles run by steam. On seeing it and hearing its frightening noise, the horse shied. Taking the bit in its mouth, the beast turned the buggy over with a crash and ran away, tossing the artist down a steep, rocky slope. Although he was the culprit who had caused the accident, the driver of the automobile did not even bother to stop to investigate the victim's plight. August lay unconscious and bleeding for more than twelve hours. When he was found at last and taken back to his hotel room, he appeared to be dying. Twenty-four hours later, the doctor held a candle close to his eyelids. They flickered slightly. Then those surrounding him heard the artist's anxious voice. The first thing he asked was, "Can I move my fingers?" His hands were held before him so that he might see. Only the thumb and forefinger of his right hand stirred. August smiled gratefully, and sank back in relief. "Thank God . . . I can still paint." To be able to hold his brush with two fingers was enough.

Gertrude came at once, packed his belongings and moved the convalescent to the Lytton home on the south side of Chicago. As soon as he had gained sufficient strength, he started on a portrait of Mr. Lytton. When that was completed, 10 more commissions followed in swift succession in Pittsburgh and Cincinnati, and, by June of 1906, the Benzigers were again headed for Switzerland. It had now become clear that, for the foreseeable future, they were destined for considerable commuting between Europe and America. After a short stay in Paris, the family returned to Switzerland where August again became immersed in the problems of operating the Grand Hotel, but the fall found them again in Chicago.

The children loved to go to their grandparents' home where there were always new and unexpected adventures. Among these was the fact that Grandmother Lytton was now riding about town in an electric horseless carriage, one of the first ones made. Proudly driving the astonishing, self-propelled contraption was Olaf, the coachman, aided by Arvid, the groom, meticulously dressed as footmen. Always a pioneer where change and swift progress were taking place, Grandfather Lytton had bought the Model H Studebaker which boasted curtained windows and even elegant silver vases for cut flowers. Although Lake Geneva was heaven on earth for the children because there they could roam in the gardens, visit the greenhouses and ride in the family yacht,

Gertrude, named in honor of their mother, nevertheless, Chicago had its own compensations. Here they could accompany their grandparents to the Hub store and beam at their handsomely-gowned grandmother, the most beautiful lady in sight with her fine lace petticoats, her billowing feather boas and her incredibly high-heeled shoes. Marieli, Hélène and Marguerite were terribly embarrassed at being taken to a store for boys and men, but their dismay turned to squeals of delight when they put on tailored middies, sailor hats and heavy navy blue overcoats which had been especially made to their measurements.

Now and again, Gertrude would leave Chicago to join her husband. Her absences from the Lytton home were gradually more and more frequent and of longer duration; then one day a telegram arrived which changed everything. August felt that the children were going to be spoiled if they remained with their grandparents any longer; he wanted them to come and join him—now. Gertrude had no choice. She and the governess began to pack frantically while her parents expostulated that this was no way to act, snatching the youngsters from their secure environment at a moment's notice—without a warning—on a man's mere whim. Gertrude just shook her head: "August wants it; he believes it is necessary." She, Elise and the three children reluctantly boarded the train for Cincinnati and, upon arrival, were met by a coachman who conveyed them to the Rogers Farm, some seven miles out in the country. August had learned of this rustic spot from some of his friends who used to enjoy dropping in on occasion for chicken dinners, but never to stay. August had concluded that this simple rustic setting would prove beneficial to his daughters. The food was good, especially the chicken and spring asparagus. He had never investigated what proved to be the quite primitive accommodations. Gertrude and her retinue discovered to their dismay that such a thing as a bathroom was nonexistent. An outside privy stood, remote and formidable, at half-a-block's distance from the house. Skunks and opossums roamed the premises freely by night and no one dared stir from her bedroom. She had learned to say little and never complained of any unfortunate situation in which August may have placed her, but she bided her time until her husband arrived for his first visit. Being a man accustomed to every comfort, he was the first to recoil from the primitive conditions in which he found himself. He immediately made plans to move his brood to Cincinnati. The Hotel Altamont on the outskirts of the city was large and well-equipped; it also offered a vivid view of the Ohio River whose frightening spring floods had raised the waters to overflowing levels. From their safe perch on a high promontory overlooking its rampaging gyrations, Gertrude and her children stared in horror at the sight below crashing and swirling, and were overcome with pity as they watched chicken coops, farmhouses and helpless cattle swept down the swollen torrent. The cruel ravages of this flood could never be forgotten.

Excitement of a different kind was provided by the strike of the hotel's waiters; one evening, as the guests were arriving for dinner, they all walked out of the dining room in a body. Instead of considering this a calamity, the mothers and the children's nurses stepped in at once and actually operated the hotel themselves for several days. This lively turn of events appealed mightily to the small fry.

Life here was cheerful as officers and their wives often came to dine and dance. As music and dancing were among Gertrude's greatest pleasures, she missed the mature companionship of her husband, who was forced to spend much of his time at great distances. One evening, the Commanding General of nearby Fort Thomas asked the charming Mrs. Benziger, who was always alone, to give him the honor of the next waltz. As the pair glided smoothly about the ballroom floor, Gertrude's eyes drifted casually to the side of the room. She was astonished to see her husband standing at the edge of the dance floor, regarding her motionlessly, his face suffused with rage. He had returned unexpectedly from a two-weeks' absence. Gertrude at once excused herself from her partner. As she approached her husband, August abruptly turned away and stalked up two flights of stairs, leaving her to take the elevator by herself. When they met in their suite, he refused to greet her or acknowledge her presence. An ominous silence fell between them. "August, what on earth is the matter?" asked Gertrude. "One would think you had caught me in an act of adultery, the way you're carrying on." With that he exploded in an angry tirade and curtly demanded to know why the mother of his three children chose to make such a spectacle of herself in public, as well as to disgrace the family name. Gertrude stared mutely. What a strange way for a man to speak to his wife! What could she possibly have done that was so shameful, so ruinous to the Benziger reputation? Her husband forbade her ever again to dance. She never did.

But life did go on. In honor of the unveiling of his portrait by Benziger, A. Howard Hinkle gave a huge stag dinner to fête the Swiss artist; 65 guests were invited. August approached the dreaded occasion with great inner quaking and many doubts. For days he had been unable to retain food, as his old childhood fear of being forced to stand and recite in class while all eyes centered on him had returned. After many toasts to his skill as an artist came to an end, the inescapable moment arrived when he was to give his reply. His knees trembled and the all-too-familiar nausea and cold sweat assailed him, but outwardly he appeared to be in perfect command of his audience. He had prepared his speech carefully, and this was its gist:

> Art is born. It is not made. May the deep vision and faith of men like your late President McKinley, whom it was my privilege to paint, live on. William McKinley's aim was to lay solid foundations to insure a long period of national prosperity. Likewise may the indomitable spirit and courage of your President Theodore Roosevelt remain alive forever in the capable leaders of America. Then, if you Americans have an excess of these great men whom you can spare, by all means, please rush them to Europe, where we require their services badly. Especially see that they are sent to Russia, where they're needed most urgently of all.

As the artist took his seat, there was laughter mingled with full applause. Already it was well-known by people in high office that Russia was arming and plotting world domination.

But for ordinary people this was not an immediate concern. The citizens of Winterthur, Switzerland, focused on the fact that they wanted a painting of their much-loved President Ludwig Forrer to be displayed eventually in the county courthouse. President Forrer had persistently denied their request, but recently yielded to it on the condition that August Benziger be the artist appointed to the task. Everyone who knew him admired the Lion of Winterthur, as he was affectionately called, having gained this appellation because of his enormous shock of snow-white hair and his great snowy beard. Although technically a Socialist, he was first and foremost a Swiss democrat. When the Socialists who had nominated him for office sought special favors once he held the reins of government, he replied that they had elected him President of Switzerland and, as such, he was no longer in a position to give special consideration to the wishes of particular parties; he had at heart only the interest and welfare of his entire country.

He had a remarkable success story behind him. Though the son of a Zürich day laborer, he had managed to work his way through the university, had studied law and become well-versed in both Latin and Greek. Unquestionably, he was one of the most brilliant and astute statesmen ever to rise in the Swiss political field. While he numbered among his friends the moguls, the tycoons, the rulers of the world, nothing was ever to change his limpid simplicity. His greatest relaxation from the pressure of official duties was to climb to his distant chalet in the high Alps. On one occasion, a mother, accompanied by numerous small children, had alighted from the train only to find that there was no porter in sight to assist her with her luggage. When her eyes lit on the bushy-bearded peasant standing on the platform, she quickly asked him to carry her heavy trunk to the hotel. Without a word, the white-headed president of Switzerland heaved the back-straining burden onto his shoulders and patiently followed the lady up the steep mountainside. Great was her consternation when, on turning to tip the sturdy mountaineer, she discovered who he really was. By then, the good man had gone quietly on his way.

President Forrer was frightfully sensitive about the loss of one eye. During the first sitting for his portrait he remarked that he had insisted on August's painting him, as he felt he could trust him to produce a decent likeness which wouldn't make him look like an idiot. At a later sitting, he grew somewhat perturbed over an ear which seemed inordinately large and red. He commented that he did not believe that his ears were either so huge or so highly colored as those in the painting. August insisted that he had not exaggerated. In order to pacify his sitter, the artist finally sent to the villa for his daughter, Hélène who, although only a seven-year-old, had a most uncanny way of discovering exactly what needed to be remedied. Because of her unusual artistic sense and acute perception, she was the only member of the family permitted to pass judgment on the artist's work. On this occasion, asked to study both the portrait and the sitter, she turned to her father and said: "Papa, the ears are too red." Forrer roared: "Child, don't you think my ears are also too big?" As the president and Hélène carried on a brisk conversation, August repaired the objectionable ear; the child finally looked up, nodded, beamed. Everything now met with approval. To reward her for her helpfulness, the president took all three Benziger girls on an outing in the woods. As they strolled along the mountain paths, he told them wonderful things about the wildflowers which blossomed in profusion on all sides. He was the first in his country to encourage the establishment of national parks for the conservation of wild plants, game and fowl.

As a keen student of human nature, August prided himself on always having on hand the comforts and amenities to which his sitters were accustomed. He offered this sitter one of his finest Havana cigars. President Forrer shook his head. "They are too fine and too expensive for my taste. I like the simplest and cheapest that money can buy. The plain, ordinary *Stumpen* will do for me."

There was another unusual side to this president; no one in Switzerland new more about railroads than he. He had centered his energies on the development of railway lines and the construction of dramatic new tunnels connecting his country with Italy and France. He also fought to bring about the electrification of the Swiss railroads, a remarkable accomplishment which made them the finest the world had known up to that time.

Only once was the president late for his 10:00 sitting, and when he arrived he was irate and so disgruntled that the artist soon laid down his brush in exasperation. "Mr. President," he said, "if you're going to be in such a bad humor today, there's really no use in my attempting to paint your portrait. Nobody would ever want to look at such a sour face." Forrer burst into laughter at this honest rebuff. "I guess you're right at that. I'll tell you what has happened." He sputtered out the details. Not until after he had boarded his train in Bern in the wee hours of the morning did he discover that the trainmen had forgotten to attach the passenger car. For over eight hours, he had ridden on a freight train which was transporting a large consignment of cows destined for the County Fair in Schwyz. Wedged like sardines, the cows, herdsmen and president were traveling companions. Was it any wonder he was in a bad mood?

Seeing the president's face light up as he told his story, August encouraged him to talk. When the children crowded into the studio to wish him a good morning, their father noticed that their eyes were glued to his client's footwear. As he shooed the girls away, he chuckled at the secret they shared. "Herr Präsident, you simply can't review the troops today in those dreadful shoes!" Both men studied the strange footwear that loomed conspicuously on Ludwig Forrer's feet, shoes badly torn, heavily caked with mud and displaying gaping holes which had been cut out for the relief of his bunions. The president drew in his breath sharply. "Goodness! My feet are a disgrace, aren't they? In my hurry to catch the train in the middle of the night, I must accidently have seized my gardening shoes. Now . . . what am I going to do?" A search was begun; none of August's footwear fit, nor did the gardener's nor the coachman's, nor any pair in the shops—all were too small. At last the Brunnen stationmaster arrived beaming. His shoes were incredible, outsized monstrosities which had to be seen to be believed. They went onto Forrer's feet with the ease of Cinderella's glass slipper, and so clad, he stepped off with vigor to go to review the troops.

On the day scheduled for the last sitting, Forrer was late a second time. He arrived in a state of high excitement after members of the Secret Service had delayed him. Word had just come that Japan was ready to wage war against America. Conditions were extremely grave; war might be declared at any moment. August's reaction was one of disbelief. "Such a step is hardly possible. The Japanese do not have the money to start a war." The reply was firm. "That's where you are wrong, August. While the Japanese may lack sufficient funds, mark my words, eventually they will be the aggressors. You see, they are backed by two great world powers, both of which are quite willing and able to finance Japan in her acts of hostility." A few days later, the Paris *Herald* ran the headlines: *President Roosevelt Orders American Fleet To Make Cruise Around the World.* Not much later came the news: *Roosevelt Sends Taft, Secretary of War, on Friendly Visit to China, Japan and Russia.* After having heard the confidential report of the Swiss Secret Service, August was keenly interested in these significant developments which would come to a head some 30-plus years later under the presidency of another Roosevelt.

Once back in America, August's first stopping place was the White House. Henry C. Lytton had commissioned his son-in-law to paint a portrait of Theodore Roosevelt to be given to the Chicago Historical Society, and the president consented on condition that it be used for that purpose alone. Early one morning, August arrived in the Blue Room and began to squeeze the tubes of paint onto his palette and lay out his brushes in readiness for his sitter's arrival. The president brought his children into the room with him. After greeting the artist, he turned to his sons and remarked, "I want you boys to see for yourselves what an artist does to achieve a living likeness." They remained a long while, fascinated.

At the conclusion of his daily sittings, August usually left the executive mansion to go to lunch, returning later in the day to work on the portrait. One day he was outraged to find that both easel and portrait had vanished. Nothing infuriated him more than having an outsider tamper with any of the tools of his craft. Bristling with anger, he rushed into the hallway to inquire of the Secret Service men who it was who had dared to touch his painting. Down the corridor, in the Yellow Room, were some 40 government officials and Cabinet members who seemed spellbound by the voice of the president, who was delivering an informal talk. Neither Roosevelt nor any of those in his entourage noticed the artist. As August stood on tiptoe to see what was going on, his heart stood still. There were his missing easel and painting. Hanging next to the painting, on the wall, was a Roosevelt portrait by John Singer Sargent. Between the two works stood the president himself, who was holding the floor in his loud, sonorous voice:

> Gentlemen, you see before you two portraits, both of myself. First I want you to study Sargent's painting. He has put all his genius into this canvas. Look at it well, for Sargent is a very great man. But, to be honest, there is nothing of me here. Sargent has not even got my hair, my nose, or the expression that is most characteristic of me. Now take this other portrait by Benziger. Regard it thoroughly. Though it's still unfinished, he's caught me, all right. It's a fighting image of what I am and the way I like people to think of me. That man Benziger is a real genius.

August hurried away, a strange shyness stealing over him. Fortunately, he had been seen by no one, but a warm feeling suffused his being. This had been the most gratifying of tributes, for the president was famous for his directness and honesty. In the future, when August's artistic career encountered difficulties, the words of Teddy Roosevelt were to echo in his mind, bringing him renewed faith and confidence in himself.

At this point, the artist decided that he would like to include part of the Capitol building in the background of this portrait, thereby providing an interesting historical touch. On the following day, he sketched it in. Later, when the president came into the room and saw the unexpected addition, he protested with vigor: "Professor Benziger, you have an infallible reputation for painting only true and authentic portraits. Now, please don't put into my portrait anything which you cannot see from this window; better not use any poetic license." August now studied the scenery from the window. As he appreciated the man's straightforward remark, the next day he obliterated the newly-introduced panoramic background and replaced it with the very visible fountain and obelisk.

Each day during his sittings, Roosevelt interviewed certain American citizens; thus it was that August was privileged to meet many of the country's industrialists, bankers and railroad barons. A vigorous running conversation flowed, and the president was never at a loss for replies to any question. He had a unique manner. While McKinley had been the pacifist and the gentleman, Roosevelt was the erect, alert, intense fighter. He was the man of action, the leader ready to spring into the thick of any battle. Even in repose, he was the very personification of bottled-up, dynamic energy.

Senator Simon Guggenheim, whose family had made a fortune in smelting and refining, had been elected to office by Colorado recently. As one would expect, he was well-informed on the subject of the intricacies of working mines and enjoyed visiting the president as he sat for his portrait, animatedly discussing business all the while. At such times, August became privy to confidential information on gold, silver, copper, lead, nickel and other mining operations and their prosperity, as well as the progress being made by the enormous smelting plants. The artist became initiated into the fact that vast wealth could be accumulated by deft manipulation of the stock market and, further, gleaned valuable market tips.

Edward H. Harriman, the railroad wizard who had successfully amalgamated several railway lines into the powerful Union Pacific, also made a strong impression on August, as the president had held many conversations with this man. On one memorable occasion, the sitting was interrupted by a hasty and urgent conference. When Roosevelt returned, he was so infuriated that he stomped about like a bull elephant, clenching his fists and shouting in indignation. "Senator Cullom has delved into the Harriman records and found many shocking irregularities," he announced. Cullom had openly declared in the Senate that Harriman should be sent to the penitentiary for some of his crooked deals. Roosevelt himself had just delivered a diatribe to Harriman, telling him plainly that he would not stop until he had landed him in jail, convinced that he had not been straight in some of those big railroad deals which had been completed. Beside himself with rage, he paced up and down his room, his brows knitted into deep furrows, his stance one of defiance. Forgetful of everyone, he came to the desk, pounding it with his substantial fists. August's eyes were glued to this man whose gestures and fury fascinated him. He had never seen such anger, such physical stamina, such brute force. All the while that August had been watching, his hand had been drawing; seeing the president's wrath inspired him but suddenly the president noticed that he was being watched intently. He came to look at the sketch and burst into laughter. "Professor, what are you doing?" August's reply: "I am going to call this portrait Teddy Roosevelt in Fighting Mood; it is a revelation of the strength of a man." Roosevelt's rejoinder was simple and direct: "I love a good scrap as long as there's a worthy cause back of it. If in any way I can benefit my country or my people, you can count on me to fight any time." He then took out his huge handkerchief and mopped his brow. "Come, let us forget about these scoundrels and crooks, Professor, and resume our pleasant relations."

August soon appeared with a sketch of this second portrait. The president liked it at first glance, but its creator asserted firmly, "I'm keeping this one for myself; I plan to call it the Harriman portrait because it depicts you standing up for what you believe is right." Everyone who saw this second portrait took to it at once as it revealed not only the restlessness that springs from deep conviction, but also a leader's determination to fight to the finish, regardless of the odds.

One morning August happened to turn aside the mirror he always used for the purpose of checking the perspective of both portrait and sitter at the same time. Soon the president came into the room. On looking into what he thought was the mirror, he was under the impression that he had glimpsed his own likeness, but what he couldn't fathom was how it was that whenever he moved, the image he was looking at remained stubbornly motionless. When August explained that he was looking at the portrait rather than the mirror, the president exhaled with relief. "For a moment there," he exclaimed, "I actually doubted my own sanity. I was positive I'd gone clear out of my mind. How was I to know that I was looking at my painting in that damn mirror, instead of seeing myself!" After some thought, he added, "When I'm gone, people aren't going to bother to read my books. Your painting will be the great pictorial document. Everyone will know me well by this record you have made."

One day he surprised the artist by querying out of the blue, "Who is the most prominent man you've ever painted?" Without a moment's hesitation, August replied: "Richard Croker, the Tammany Hall 'Boss'." Roosevelt's face flushed in swift anger, "But he's a man of very bad principles!" "Perhaps so," retorted the artist, "yet had he been endowed with your fine education and family background, Mr. President, I dare say his principles would have been entirely correct, too." There was dead silence for quite some time while August continued to paint, then Roosevelt unexpectedly and tersely conceded defeat. "Professor, you're absolutely right."

One of the president's favorite topics of conversation with August was that of the Swiss compulsory military service. The Chief Executive considered this to be the most successful military system in the world. It was his firm conviction that if America were to embrace such a plan for national conscription, it would be the making of her youth. Not only would it prove a great character builder, but it would also provide a great safeguard against invasion. Mr. Taft, his Secretary of War, strongly shared these beliefs. August then told the president of his sitting with Ludwig Forrer of Switzerland, and how the *Bundespräsident* had been roused in the middle of the night by his nation's Secret Service, alerting him to Japan's militaristic gestures. After August related the entire episode, Roosevelt remarked thoughtfully, "Every word of what you say, Professor, is the gospel truth, is absolutely correct." August persisted, "But it's impossible for Japan to wage war. How could she? The Japanese people don't have the funds; and we both know that wars are fought with cold, hard cash." Roosevelt's face grew grave. "In that you're right, Professor. The Japanese haven't the money, but there are two world powers that do. Not long ago, these nations were on the verge of making huge loans to Japan so that she might be the one to start the conflict. It was nip and tuck for awhile. War was as close as the snap of your finger." Then August observed, "My client, President Forrer, claimed that America was totally unprepared and that Japan could attack easily." "Granted, I'll admit that that is true. Yet, don't forget that once this country is roused, it takes very little time to organize our vast national resources in our own defense."

Another notable person August met at the White House was A.E. Stilwell, president of the Kansas City, Mexico and Orient

Railroads. Stilwell had been so impressed by the forceful portrait of President Roosevelt that he placed an order for a painting of Porfirio Diaz, the President of Mexico, whom he knew well, having at his request constructed a railway spur from the Mexican border into the heart of that country; he met with him often and considered Diaz to be one of the finest living leaders. In 1908, Stilwell planned a trip to Mexico and invited August to join him. As he had promised, he made arrangements for the portraitist to visit the Presidential Palace, where he was greeted graciously by Porfirio Diaz himself.

Although he had been born in 1830 of the poorest and humblest parentage, Diaz had proven to his countrymen that it was possible to rise above poverty and privation. His father had been a Spanish miner who died of cholera when Porfirio was only three; his Indain mother had, by means of her weaving, managed to provide food and shelter for her son and herself. With grim determination, the young man had studied law, then spent 30 years as a Mexican soldier fighting the French and, more specifically, Emperor Maximilian. When the Mexican Republic, bankrupt, had failed to make payment on its debt, Napoleon III of France had dispatched Emperor Maximilian, brother of Emperor Franz Josef, and 30,000 French troops to seize control of the country. The choice of Maximilian for this precarious assignment resulted from a desire to placate him and keep him at a safe distance from any possible European ambitions.

Porfirio Diaz had suffered a plethora of miseries at the hands of the French and, when he finally escaped from their hands, Maximilian, an opportunist, offered him many bribes to abandon the side of the Mexican Republic and take up his own weakening cause. No one knew better than the Emperor that Diaz was the key to the conquest of Mexico, and the most persistent and dangerous of all his opponents. Faithful to Mexico's guerrilla bands, Diaz refused the offer, and personally led his own troops to victory. Although he had proven himself a hero in more than 50 battles, when he became head of the Republic he turned his face against war; no one loathed it more than he.

As president, he assumed the tremendous burden of reconstruction, but conditions grew chaotic. Kidnapping, molestation and robbery were daily occurrences. National securities became worthless overnight. Mexico had no credit, and in London the silver Mexican dollar sold for ten cents. Maximilian had all but destroyed the nation, draining the last vestige of wealth from its soil and leaving it a despoiled and plundered country.

On learning of August's forthcoming visit to Mexico, Roosevelt had remarked that "Diaz is the greatest statesman alive," and added that, although many faulted him for ruling like an autocrat, such strength had been necessary if anyone was going to be able to take firm and complete control. This benign dictator had succeeded in bringing order out of chaos, and had no ambitions other than to rehabilitate his land. With the common man's welfare at heart, he built hospitals, orphanages and schools. Fifteen thousand miles of railroad track were laid, roads leveled, bridges constructed and systems of sanitation installed; shipping was encouraged and factories burgeoned.

When the matter of posing for a portrait had been broached by Mr. Stilwell, Diaz gave his consent. Eight sittings at the very most were agreed upon. Diaz did speak a smattering of English, but no French at all, so his lovely wife, Madame Carmelita, or his 25-year-old son acted as interpreters, and animated conversations ensued. On one occasion August broached a rather delicate subject. A death sentence had just been imposed by the president involving a prominent man who was to be executed by firing squad. Could he not, somehow, be acquitted? Diza shook his head sadly: "It is better to spill the blood of one guilty man than to precipitate a revolution and thereby shed the blood of innocent thousands."

As August wished to portray this man in full military regalia, he asked to examine his many colorful decorations; in preparation for the next sitting these were set out and covered several large tables. When asked which were the most important among them, Diaz merely shook his head and shrugged; he had paid very little attention to any of them and could hardly recall the occasion of their origin. To him, he said, the bits of bright ribbon were as transitory as was the loyalty of man. Once the selection of military decorations was completed with the help of Madam Diaz, the president ordered that both the decorations and his uniform be transported to August's hotel so that he could study and draw them in his leisure time. In order to know the correct position in which each medal should hang, the artist donned the dramatic collection and photographed himself while wearing it.

Diaz, learning that August admired opals, saw to it that he was presented with six flawless ones of varying sizes and colors as a gift from himself. These the artist always carried in an inside vest pocket, dropping them on a table from time to time to admire their iridescent beauty.

Before his final leavetaking from Mexico, August asked the president a pointed question. The American press had published disturbing articles relating the supposed fact that Diaz had given the Japanese nation certain coaling stations which were located at America's back door. Word had leaked out that Japan was arming for war with the full intent of attacking the United States. President Diaz became indignant.

> Indeed, I have not given any coaling stations to the Japs. Furthermore, I have no intention of letting them have so much as one single inch of our land. All America is shouting that we Mexicans have done this thing; but it's not true. The United States had better watch them carefully. They are anxious to throw their strength against the States. They're going to do so when the Americans least expect it. This war between Japan and America may come sooner than you think.

President Diaz shrugged his shoulders impatiently.

> Or, again, it may be to the advantage of the Japanese to let all this excitement die down and then strike when the Americans think the danger has subsided. This war between Japan and the States is bound to come. It is not far off, either.

In order to complete the Diaz portrait in his own studio, August brought it back to the States. In the high, wide forehead he had placed strength. The deep, dark eyes were magnetic, kindly, yet formidable, the nose strong and broad. The massive square jaws were cleft by an expressive mouth surmounted by a full, white mustache. Within the span of a few months, the portraitist had been privileged to paint two most powerful men, Porfirio Diaz and Theodore Roosevelt. They were alike in many respects; Diaz' task, however, was the more difficult as he was handicapped by a nation that had yet to be freed from despoliation and tyrannical enemies. Only three years following the completion of the portrait, he was forced to yield to his opponents in government and go into retirement. Like their volcanoes, the Mexicans were unpredictable in their loyalties.

Almost 10 years later, in June of 1914, the Benziger family arrived in Paris and were having dinner at the Grand Hotel when Mrs. Benziger looked up and saw former President Diaz enter the room, but no longer in uniform. "Look! There comes President Diaz," she exclaimed. August was mystified, "How do you know?" he queried, "You have never seen him." Her answer was instantaneous and simple, "But it's your portrait walking in the door." August turned quickly, leapt to his feet and strode across the space dividing them. The two men embraced. In a few moments, President and Sra. Diaz joined the Benziger table. As they talked earnestly, Diaz was asked why he had not fought to remain in Mexico. He seemed overcome with grief. Quite unashamed, he pulled out a large linen handkerchief, blew his nose and wiped away the tears that erupted onto his tired, lined face. Sra. Diaz related the manner in which they had fled their country, and added that the President had refused to remain in office if doing so would mean bloodshed for his people and dissipation of their meager resources. When August asked tactfully if there was anything he might do to alleviate their troubles, Sra. Diaz shook her head. While not wealthy, they were in comfortable circumstances; that was enough. Nobility marked their characters to the end. August felt enriched by their presence.

CHAPTER 13

U.S.A. and Switzerland
(1906-1907)

The Paris house was finally to be closed, as shuttling between New York and Switzerland had become a semiannual feat. The Brunnen summers loomed with great importance since at that time August would shift his attention from his winter of portrait painting to the operating of his Grand Hotel, which left him little time for anything else. Gertrude's role in this dual existence gradually grew in significance as the full responsibility for travel preparations depended upon her alone. The many factors involved in traveling with an artist husband and three small children she took in stride, proving herself both a competent manager and the most seasoned and mellowed of trans-Atlantic journeyers.

Gertrude was a practical woman. She wasted no time on useless details, and everyone was required to lend a hand with the unpacking while the ship was still in port, since she well knew that once it was put into motion, most of her band would succumb to seasickness. Many months of the next 11 years were to be spent sailing back and forth across the Atlantic. Great was the joy of the young Benzigers at the prospect of each of the voyages, as the French Line was a second home to them. They had made so many crossings that by this time they knew most of the members of the crew, and even some of the captains became their trusted friends. Each of their succession of French governesses conveniently fell victim to *mal de mer,* so no persnickety mademoiselle who was wont to watch how curtsies were made, noses blown and hair ribbons tied cared one whit about what went on once she boarded ship—and, further, their strict father was invariably *hors de combat.*

Never did this trio of youngsters enjoy more freedom than they did aboard these ships. They blithely played pirates in the lifeboats which swung perilously on davits, quite oblivious to the fact that they might be precipitated into the sea at any moment. Even more fun was fishing for hours from their stateroom portholes with tackle improvised from twine and hairpins. Loud were their squeals of delight when they "caught" strong-smelling salted herring which the kitchen staff, far below, playfully attached to their lines. Sometimes there was great excitement aboard as when the hold of one steamer caught fire and wild commotion ensued until the deck hands succeeded in extinguishing the conflagration.

On another crossing, three days out of Le Havre, their liner passed a listless fishing schooner flying the French flag upside down as a signal of distress. Efforts at communication brought no response. Aboard no sign of life could be detected. A call went out for volunteers to board the stricken vessel, now identified as one from the Normandy coast. Two lifeboats were lowered. A few minutes later, the splashing of oars could be heard as the ship's boats approached the schooner in the hot sunshine. There was a tense, interminable wait while passengers hung over the promenade deck awaiting the fearsome outcome. Soon the courageous rescue crew returned alongside. Shouting through his megaphone, the First Officer called to the Captain for advice: all adults aboard the schooner lay dead from yellow fever, the same plague which had quarantined hundreds of ships all over the world. None of the rescue party could now return aboard for fear of imperiling passengers and ship's company alike. Two children remained alive on the ill-fated vessel; otherwise it would have been blown up at once.

Volunteers were needed to sail the schooner back to Normandy. A physician, accompanied by vital medical supplies, slowly descended the hempen ladder and dropped into one of the two rowboats. As the doctor and some seamen vanished into the distance, cheers and applause from all sides bade them success on their heroic mission of mercy. The following night, a ship's benefit was held for the purpose of raising funds for the orphaned children; it was a muted and somber affair.

Once in America, August always traveled by train, but when in Europe, he avoided the dirty, smoky, slow, unpunctual railroad cars which crisscrossed the Continent, and sought an alternative. On his most recent trip, he lost no time in heading for Turin where he ordered a custom-built *Italia,* the forerunner of the now famous *Lancia.* He only returned to Switzerland after he had become the proud possessor of a formidable navy blue car sporting red leather upholstery, spare tires which adorned both running boards and a capacious luggage trunk attached to the rear. The audacious mechanic and chauffeur, Cesare Cavallo, had been sent by the automotive factory to deliver the car to Switzerland. Cesare was not only an ingenious mechanic but the possessor of almost every prize awarded to automobile racers. Fearing for the ultimate safety of his neck if he continued his dangerous stunt driving, he succumbed to the offers made by August to reward him amply if he became part and parcel of his Swiss household. Although he was diminutive, he was as agile as a jockey, and there was nothing about a car that he did not know. During all the years he served the Benzigers, never once was it necessary for their cars to be taken to any garage for repairs.

At this time the Swiss farmers had developed a particularly violent hatred of motor cars. As the dust of highways began to cover crops, they soon translated anger into action. At night they laid dangerous barricades of hayracks, pitchforks and scythes across the roads, and these were so carefully hidden that drivers could not see the danger ahead in the car's flickering headlights. Often August, Gertrude and their guests ran afoul of the traps. With their gas tank punctured, they would be forced to get out and push their vehicle uphill until it could coast down the next mountainside where gasoline might be bought and repairs made. As long as Cesare remained with the Benzigers, they never found themselves totally defeated, no matter how unexpected the assault. He realized that when a tank was punctured, he could leap out of the car and rescue the gasoline, catching it in a bottle, and then feed it drop by drop to the sputtering, resentful carburetor. After several such emergencies, a baby's bottle became part of the tool kit's valued items. No one ever found Cesare unprepared for a second attack; he was more than capable of outwitting his enemies.

Yet nothing would stop August. He had made up his mind that if automobiles were in accepted and popular use in the States, they could also serve to bring motorists to Switzerland. Never hesitating to schedule a trip on the grounds of looming possible obstacles, he once drove to distant Chur to pick up his friend, Bishop Schmidt von Grüneck. This time peasants, driving Gülla carts to fertilize their fields, opened the tanks, so August and His Excellency reached their destination soaked to the bone with the vile and stinking manure that had spattered their car.

There were times when it was not manure but rocks. Mrs. George Gould was severely injured by sharp stones thrown directly at her face. Since August's was the first motor car to appear in Canton Schwyz, and among the first seven or eight in the country, when he passed by, peasants would stand along the road, shouting and shaking their fists at the "Devil on Wheels." The speed limit had been reduced to a four-mile-an-hour crawl along country roads in the area, and in some villages it was only three. Later the speed along the Axenstrasse was increased to seven. All excesses were punishable by at least a $50 fine and some went as high as $70. The Carpenters of Philadelphia, J. Pierpont Morgan of New York, Herr Abegg of Zürich and M. Firmin-Didot of Paris were all fined $50 within a few hours of each other as they headed for the Grand Hotel en route from Italy. August was outraged. He acted. "Governor," he expostulated, "your police are ruining our hotel industry. I do all within my power to attract foreigners to our part of Switzerland, then your police do all they can to fine innocent people and drive them away. You will have to put a stop at once to these ridiculous fines!" The Governor seemed perplexed. He asserted that, in two month's time, his police had punished only one man, whereupon he drew out a notebook from his pocket in which was recorded the single violator's name and the date of his penalty. August just as promptly as he extracted from his own pocket receipts for 11 separate $50 fines that had been imposed upon himself and his friends within only the past week. August had paid all of them. The governor at once summoned the Chief of Police who, confronted by the irrefutable evidence, immediately confessed and was soon placed behind bars. Word spread speedily through Switzerland that motorists and foreigners were now treated with respect and consideration.

That matter having been settled, others managed to arise. One was the arrival of the latest governess who had bowed and cooed and fawned over the head of the house in a particularly unpleasant manner. August exploded. "Gerty! Why in God's name did you pick out that ugly-looking monkey?" His wife looked at him sternly. "It shocks me to have to admit it, August, but I simply couldn't trust you with a handsome, eye-catching governess around all the time." Sheepishly, August managed to change the subject.

After the May landings, he usually allowed himself three full weeks in which to track down and buy the superb wines which would stock his cellars at the Grand Hotel. During this interlude, he was often accompanied by his wife and daughters. A born wine connoisseur, he could sniff, twist the glass, taste, then immediately name the year and vintage of any noted wine. He often ordered the outstanding vintages to be shipped by cask so as to have them bottled later in Switzerland. With no speed limits to be observed in France, Cesare opened the throttle wide as they raced to Bordeaux. Here August would test and taste the Sauternes, the golden Graves or straw-colored Châteaux wines. To acquire his best Bordeaux, he went directly to Médoc. While he busied himself with sampling and ordering, Cesare would drive Gertrude and the children along the rolling vineyards overlooking the Bay of Biscay.

The Loire River with its historic castles meant little to August who was preoccupied by the present, but while he was immersed in the bouquet of white Anjou and sparkling Champagne, his family roamed the romantic Châteaux country to their hearts' content. Burgundy, known afar for its precious vintages, proved exciting only to the family's wine expert, but the other family members were aware that from here, the distinguished growths had been shipped by the kings of France and used in their coronation ceremonies for countless centuries. Beaune, while not an exciting tourist attraction, nevertheless produced the crimson Beaujolais, the delicately-flavored Pommard and fine white Chablis. From here it was just an overnight stop until the Lake of Geneva came into sight. Swiss wines were acquired and then the family returned home.

Once back in Switzerland, no one could restrain the small folks' exuberant joy. They had longed for their Villa where, for one wonderful week, they were permitted to run in complete freedom until mademoiselle returned from her vacation and austerity set in anew. "Austerity" meant study beginning at eight each morning and ending at five in the afternoon. Later there might be trips to Holland and Germany, too, in pursuit of excellent wines. There again, with map in hand, a veil over her hat and the inevitable goggles to keep the dust out of her eyes, Gertrude presented a picture of the indefatigable traveler. She it was who plotted the itinerary and kept her flock to their day's schedule. Furthermore, it was due to her determined pleas that history and art came to be woven into each journey, supplementing the economic necessity which lay behind many trips. Left to his own resources, August would have been so preoccupied with his concerns as a hotelier that he would have spared no moment for small enjoyments to be savored along the way; all the same, the Benzigers managed to derive an enormous amount of fun from their travels. Once the artist had been induced to pause long enough to pay a fleeting visit to a museum, he became absolutely fascinating. Never one to waste a moment, he knew how to race through a cathedral or museum, selecting the choicest objects for study and contemplation. Racing after their father's coattails, the three children were ecstatic at being able to see rare and beautiful masterpieces as their artist-father briskly outlined the best in still life, landscape and portraiture for his eager brood. Often they were literally running to maintain the pace of their long-legged Papa, and on many occasions they were almost trampled under foot as he impulsively wheeled about, without warning, for a closer view of something which had caught his fancy. His pale face aglow with pleasure, August would peer at a canvas, studying the brush strokes or a new color combination, then step backwards, eyes fixed on the work before him in order to gain a better perspective, and toss his admiring audience a barrage of acute comments. Then he was off and away again.

These moments of effusive enthusiasm and pleasure were, alas, counterbalanced by Gertrude's puritanical reactions; most unfortunately for an artist's wife, she sternly disapproved of nudes. Chills of horror shot down her spine when she found August pointing out a handsome Apollo, a provocative Pan or a lustful Bacchus to her innocent children. August and his wife could never reconcile their differences on this subject of modesty. As an artist, he believed there was nothing more beautiful than the human form. For her part, his wife felt that nudes should be confined to intimate places like a boudoir; certainly they should not be on open display in a museum which was as public as the railway station. The only one of the children who seemed to have profited from these discomforting moments was Marguerite, the youngest. Though no thought of disobeying her Mama entered her head, she nevertheless managed to hold her little hands over her face in such a way that she could still peek through her fingers. She commented to her sisters a bit later that Apollo did not look bad to her; in fact he looked quite good!

Perhaps Gertrude felt a sense of relief when June arrived and she learned that Cardinal Gibbons was going to visit the family at *Villa Gutenberg*. August had met him in Baltimore and been a houseguest at his North Charles Street residence. There he had been impressed by the fact that rich and poor, black men and white had stopped to pay their respects to the local head of the Catholic Church. In 1907, he had an opportunity to reciprocate the cardinal's hospitality when the prelate arrived in Europe to recuperate from illness. To do so, he urgently needed to find a place where he could enjoy peace and quiet. Great excitement was astir in the Benziger household as the family prepared to receive its distinguished guest. Questions arose from all sides as to how one went about entertaining a full-fledged cardinal. The *bon mot* "Be yourselves," seemed of dubious merit, yet that first evening when the churchman joined the Benziger clan, one and all found it to be a wise piece of advice. After the children had made their prim curtsies and bade His Eminence "good night," Cardinal Gibbons rose and followed them quietly to their third-floor nursery. As they lit their candles and prepared to hop into bed, he blessed each one and shouted a cheerful, "Sweet dreams!" to his "Three Graces," as he afterwards called them.

The next morning, mindful of their guest, the trio tiptoed past the cardinal's room to their parents' bedroom, there to await the prelate's departure to say Mass in the village chapel. A bold knock came at the door and a hearty voice called out: "Mrs. Benziger, these poor, old fingers have need of your help." Standing in his shirt sleeves, Roman collar in his helpless hand, was the 74-year-old cardinal. From that time forward, Gertrude daily and deftly assisted him into the unyielding clerical garment, and when it came time for him to leave, it was she who packed his ecclesiastical robes.

August had his car ready for his guest's use, as the village lay at the distance of a quarter-hour's walk, but His Eminence would not hear of driving to Mass in one of these new-fangled horseless monsters. In fact, he set so rapid a walking pace that he soon lost sight of the three children altogether. They trudged breathlessly behind, stopping along the way to rest under the pretext of picking cyclamens and chasing a few birds.

With watch in hand, the punctual guest waited at the breakfast table until the last straggler stood behind her plate, thus making an indelible mark on the minds of the Three Graces. Later in life, they still seemed to be able to hear his voice emphasizing, "Nice children never keep their elders waiting." A firm believer that youth should be allowed to share in all the happenings of the home, when the cardinal heard plans being made for the giving of a big tea, he asked if the children might decorate the table for the party as he had heard the little girls discussing the possibility among themselves. Since his oldest was only eight years old, August had grave misgivings about the results, but gave in to his guest's request. In no time, the girls had gathered great baskets of assorted flowers and arranged an imaginative centerpiece. From that moment on, they were entrusted with all floral arrangements for parties and special events. Their inherited talent for producing the beautiful was to be put to use.

When the family was alone, nothing pleased the cardinal more than an engrossing game of whist, with Gertrude as his partner. When she helped him to win, he would rise enthusiastically and shake her hand, but if her husband or his secretary, Father Donovan, were the winners, he merely shook his head and remarked: "The next time we will do better."

Sincere and very outspoken, the cardinal never hesitated to discuss any topic. In the Vatican, he was known as a courageous fighter, violent in his opposition to chauvinism, and as a man who fought all who wished to isolate themselves in America, cloaking their selfishness under the guise of patriotism. He chastised the Poles, Germans, Italians, and even the Irish for wanting their particular ethnic churches, sermons and pastors, and maintained that refugees had fled to America to escape from tyranny, not to build new ethnic ghettos. Accordingly, there could be no Spanish pastors, no German or Polish ones serving on demand of the parishioners. They must be first and foremost American, and for all the people. A Catholic was universal. The New World gave these people a chance to prove their intentions of becoming genuine Americans and unbiased Catholics. For this reason, among others, Theodore Roosevelt esteemed him as the most outstanding of Americans.

Cardinal Gibbons sought above all a real American clergy with no political axe to grind, and parochial schools without any nationalistic element. Sermons had to be preached in English, and classes taught in the same language. As America had become the melting-pot of the world, the peoples had to become united. The religion of the Catholics among them was to be an overall faith that eliminated partisanship.

For a man who was an outstanding fighter, one fearless in his beliefs, it was strange that he could, at the same time, be panic-stricken and timorous when it came to riding in an automobile.

Nothing at all had prevailed upon him to enter a horseless carriage. The children finally tried their luck at winning him over to the use of modern transportation, and one day the cardinal surprised all by announcing, "I will go to see your famous place of pilgrimage on one condition—that the children accompany me. If the car is safe for them, it will be safe for me, too." A memorable trip to Einsiedeln ensued. Decked in a gray duster and jaunty motoring cap, the cardinal sat on the edge of the back seat, flanked by the three youngsters. Each successive curve terrified him. He held his rosary in his hand, half-looking, half-praying, then would shout in alarm as the car careened around the mountain at the phenomenal speed of 15 kilometers, about 10 miles an hour! "Cesare . . . for the love of God . . . *piano* . . . *piano*! Our lives are in danger. *Piano* . . . *piano*!" Cesare would laugh as he slowed down. Then out would shoot an arm to enable His Eminence to tug at the chauffeur's ear. His "*piano*" tune was to echo for many years among sounds of the Benziger children's laughter. Nevertheless, the cardinal came to the point of secretly enjoying his rides in these up-to-date contraptions and, in later years, he was often to accompany August on his expeditions to Bern, Zürich or Lucerne.

Each time these quiet, happy visits ended, the children would weep, as they felt that they had lost a member of their family. Fortunately, their father had painted a portrait of their old friend which, for years, was to hang in their living room. Not an evening passed without a small procession wending its way to bid good-night to lovable Cardinal Gibbons.

Bishops flocked to the Grand Hotel where they knew they could be incognito and relax in an atmosphere that was congenial, among friends who respected and loved them. Some of the episcopal visitors were Bishop Denis O'Connell, rector of the Catholic University, Archbishop E.F. Prendergast of Philadelphia and Bishop Foley of Detroit. Among them, at the Grand Hotel, they found Philadelphian Dalgrens and Drexels, Atlee Burpee, Wideners, Lippincotts, Wanamakers and Biddles—as well as, from elsewhere, J. Pierpont Morgan, Robert Taft and King Gustav of Sweden—all creating an affable company wherein a spirit of fraternal democracy prevailed.

As is the way with many who are advancing in age, August grew cautious and conservative, so much so that he determined that all those little episodes and pitfalls which had been the joy and sorrow of his own youth should not be experienced by other people's children while they were at *his* hotel. He required that clients' daughters come to his studio for sittings properly chaperoned. Mrs. Horace Porter, whose husband was the American Ambassador in Paris, was told to be a little more particular about permitting her daughter to be escorted by foreigners! He was the first to be shocked when women smoked, and was horrified when, one day, he watched Mrs. Potter and Mrs. Marshall Field order a bottle of champagne. Knowing that both women were social leaders, he felt it quite out of place for them to imbibe in public; his suggestion that they desist was firmly dismissed by these two strongminded, before-their-time feminists who asserted their right to do as they saw fit.

Another very different kind of friend was John Pitcairn of Pittsburgh, whom nothing pleased more than driving with August through France and Italy. This serious-minded man was head of the Swedenborgian Church, at the same time as serving at the helm of the Pittsburgh Plate Glass Company. He loved to start out from the Grand Hotel with its proprietor and browse in antique shops, and that is how they came upon a beautiful madonna painted by Corregio: they stumbled upon it in a tiny shop in Turin. In this rare moment of discovery, both men stood in awed reverence, and then studied their treasure at leisure. Subsequently, they learned that an old and penniless village priest had been forced to sell the exquisite work, even though the painting had been a keepsake in his family for many generations. Originally it had been given to an ancestor in Vienna, a priest who had been confessor to Queen Maria Theresa. August bought it without further question.

In coming home via the Lake of Orta in Italy, he and his friend stopped at a small shop in another village where, as a young man in his early 30s, August had managed to pick up a genuine Titian. He had immediately spotted the wonderful treasure which sold for the incredible sum of a dollar. Offered here on this occasion were 14 Stations of the Cross by an unknown artist. Since their trip was nearing its end, August had little cash left; nevertheless, he quickly bought one of the works. When he returned later with sufficient money to buy the balance of the collection, he learned that the remaining 13 paintings had been sold.

Although he was positive that the single painting he had acquired was a real Titian, there was, of course, no actual proof that his hunch was correct. He knew that the master had been born in one of the neighboring villages in the Dolomites. The coloring, too, was definitely that used by the great draftsman. Years later, while his three children were playing hide-and-seek, they accidentally struck the fragile frame of this unauthenticated original. Down it came with a resounding crash. Frantic about the accident they had caused, the trio summoned their father. Infuriated as he always was by destruction, he immediately administered a severe spanking to the offenders. Then, picking up the frame, which happened to be none the worse for the tumble, he noticed that the canvas had parted from the stretcher. As he fetched hammer and picture tacks to restore his treasure, his astonishment was great as he discovered that he held TWO canvases, one lying on top of the other. Between the two was a piece of paper bearing sketches, and, in Titian's own handwriting, explanatory notes pertaining to the Stations of the Cross. A day of grief was transmuted into one of rejoicing for the Swiss family Benziger.

Mr. Pitcairn's innate love of children encompassed August's small daughters, and he was highly pleased when the lively procession of little girls joined him as he sat for his portrait. It was from him that they first heard of a man called John D. Rockefeller. Pitcairn had been one of the few who had faced and fought him: he had dared the railroads to break their contracts with the Rockefeller interests and had refused to be bribed by the Standard Oil monopolists. In the end, quiet little John Pitcairn won the fight to protect small landowners, and spoke of the struggle during long hours of conversation with Cardinal Gibbons and Archbishop Farley on the terrace of the Grand Hotel.

Among the many other visitors to the hotel was Albert Caldwell of Memphis, Tennessee, a man remarkably adept in the role of host, a man who had a special gift for attracting to himself the prominent writers of the day. On several occasions, his guests included Henry Wallace and Booth Tarkington, as well as Lew Wallace, the author of *Ben Hur*. Once, during an interlude between sittings, Caldwell grew bored with doing nothing and suggested to the artist that they both spend a few days in Venice. August went along in his Lancia. Having led the way up the Saint Gotthard Mountain, he turned to see how the Caldwell party was progressing, and was seized with horror at the sight which met his eyes. In order to make the grade on a hairpin curve below, Caldwell's chauffeur was banking the long car—but in a highly dangerous manner. Standing on the front seat of his Lancia and blowing his silver trumpet urgently, August shouted in alarm:

"Sam! Sam! For the love of God, jam on your brakes—and don't move!" Swiftly sensing the danger, Cesare stopped short. He and August tore down the mountainside, reaching the car just as Sam was about to faint from fright, having suddenly realized his proximity to death. Another inch and the heavy Pierce Arrow would have hurtled down thousands of feet into the chasm below. Thus ended Sam's mountain driving; Cesare took the wheel and brought the party to safety at the summit of the pass.

To a European like August, one of the most remarkable traits Americans possessed was their pioneering spirit, marked by adaptability, although it had taken him many years of personal contact with them to appreciate their ability to adjust to the social background of ancient Europe. On coming to America, he had often blushed at what he viewed as the *gaucherie* of some of his New World friends, but he was amazed to find how quickly they were able to conform to new ways and customs on the Continent. It soon required the most discerning eye to tell who, among his many guests, had been raised in a palace and who in a New World brownstone. Thus it was that when the Dowager Queen of Italy arrived in Brunnen, she became just another name on the hotel's roster of guests.

Queen Margherita had heard of August's success in portraiture. Being an artist herself, she looked forward to paying a visit to his studio to obtain instruction in the finer points of technique. Her Majesty was reputedly traveling incognito; however, a procession of three white Lancias pulled up to the hotel's doors. They were identical, with the exception that a specially-built armchair had been installed in the second one. This was occupied by the queen, escorted by Secret Service men disguised as footmen riding conspicuously on each side of the fenders, their smart livery bearing the royal coat of arms on their collars and buttons. A staff of 16 accompanied her. She had brought her own personal physician, ladies-in-waiting and even a male hairdresser. As soon as she reached her apartment, August brought his three daughters to welcome their honored guest. Curtsying, they presented Queen Margherita with enormous bunches of freshly-gathered daisies. Her favorite flowers were, of course, marguerites.

August personally planned each detail of her stay. He took her sightseeing and saw that her slightest wish was fulfilled. Because some trifling annoyance had aroused his artistic temper on that particular day, he managed to dispose of his wife by sending her on an errand to Lucerne. Two of the hotel's guests were suffering from toothaches and, there being no dentist in Brunnen, she had agreed to escort the patients. However, she reminded her husband sternly that the queen planned to visit the villa and the studio that same afternoon, and insisted that protocol demanded that a married man certainly could not receive Her Majesty alone. Her absence at such a time would prove both awkward and impolite.

The queen particularly wanted to see the room in the villa that had been occupied by King Ludwig of Bavaria, and she also displayed a keen interest in the studio and the portraits exhibited there. Turning to her companions, she remarked, as if having some strange premonition, "I can read the handwriting on the wall. These men—the presidents whom you see depicted before you— are the real heads of state. The kings and queens of today will soon become *passé*. They're all on their way out." Then, turning to her host, she questioned pointedly, "When am I to have the honor of meeting your charming wife, Monsieur Benziger?" August hastily proferred some lame excuse for the missing hostess. The queen was determined, nevertheless, that the proprieties be observed. With quiet dignity, she informed August, "I want you to bring Madame Benziger to me this very evening so that I may make her acquaintance. We will meet in my suite after dinner, and your wife and I shall enjoy a pleasant *tête-a-tête*."

Knowing that crowds congregated in the basilica during the holidays, August felt it wise to rush off to Einsiedeln early the next morning in order to make special arrangements for the queen to visit the miraculous chapel. Queen Margherita was delighted and also voiced a desire to see the ancient cloisters in order to know at first hand the nature of a monastery cloister and its austerities. As a queen, she might ask this favor which no other woman would dare to request.

The Prince Abbot was honored. He would be pleased to entertain Her Majesty. The guestmaster, for his part, reminded both his abbot and August that Cardinal Rampolla was staying at the abbey for the summer. Since he was the Cardinal Secretary of State of the Vatican, it would be a shocking breach of etiquette for the queen and the cardinal to be seated at the same table. August knitted his brow in dismay. "I don't understand. Why all this mysterious diplomacy? What sort of breach of etiquette do you mean?" The guestmaster, who had known him as a child, laughingly chided: "Have you forgotten your history so soon? Any other cardinal would be perfectly all right, but not this particular one.   Your dinner plan would constitute a very major and unpardonable *faux pas*."   He went on to explain that Her Majesty's late husband, King Umberto, had annexed the Papal States by force, defeated the Papal army and deprived His Holiness of all his possessions, leaving him only Rome.   The son of King Umberto had completed the despoliation, proceeding to seize Rome and designate it the capital of a united Italy, leaving the pope only the Vatican.   Naturally it was out of the question for the queen and the cardinal to meet.   Their encounter would provoke the utmost embarrassment.   The priest who served as kitchenmaster smoothly solved the dilemma.   "Tomorrow is a fast day," he announced cheerfully, "We can have no guests."   Finally, August planned to take Her Majesty to Pfauen Inn immediately following the Mass.   Here they would breakfast.   Cardinal Rampolla would be advised of the queen's arrival in ample time to absent himself for the day.   The remaining hours would be hers in which to explore the monastery to her heart's content.   So go the machinations of diplomacy!

About this time another woman arrived at Brunnen, traveling from America, and she was every bit as attractive and petite as the queen of Italy.   August was astonished to greet her, a 90-year-old Texan lady who had never before left her native land.   She was Mrs. H.J. Lutcher of Orange, Texas, and she had previously gone all the way to Cincinnati to see August.   He had been impressed by this wrinkled little woman with snow-cap hair and with youthful agility; however, he had explained that it was much too late for him to begin any new portraits as he was about to leave for Europe and would not return for many months.   Great then was his amazement and admiration for the courage displayed by her undertaking such an extensive trip in order to have her portrait painted.   She had brought along her exquisite needlepoint dress created for her in Belgium.   Her remarkable wardrobe had been planned especially for her and designed by a man from Texas named Nieman Marcus, a small-shop owner patronized solely by Texans.   Disappointed, she, nevertheless insisted that August and his wife come to her home for a visit, and finally they accepted the invitation.   On reaching the tiny station in Orange, they saw only a nag and a tumbledown buggy.   When they asked the driver for the Lutcher residence, the old man beamed.   He bade them "hop in," and he would show them where the "Queen of Texas" lived.

Having seen her charming clothes and observed the style in which she traveled, as well as the large sums she had spent on her hotel suite, the artist and his wife were astonished to find her "at home" in a simple wood-frame house. Their driver refused to accept any money for his services, announcing that it was an honor to take anyone to "that good soul." Without her, he explained, the town of Orange would have nothing—no school, no church, no library. "Why, she just plans everything, does everything, runs everything," he said proudly. August soon realized the truth of these words.

When the health of her husband had failed, he had left his Pennsylvania butcher shop and bought timberland in Texas, an investment which ultimately yielded a fortune. Although the lady of the house could read, she had not learned to write. When widowed, she had been cared for by a "Negro mammy and her niece," and soon took on the cares and concerns of all those who lived about her. Mamoose, as she was called, generated only goodness and kindness; they radiated from her being, but it was her mammy who ruled the house. One oppressively hot day, she noticed August's beard and mustache which had been allowed to grow longer than usual. "Shucks, Mistah," she exclaimed, "Youse bettah go'n some uh dat dere hair afore Mamoose sees yo'-all or youse shore gonna be vamoosed from heah, right quick!" August himself "vamoosed."

For diversion, Mamoose assembled her daughters and their husbands, and all went on a hunting expedition. In the back seat, flanked by her daughters, sat the elderly hostess, while the men sat forward with their guns in readiness to shoot. Never in his life had August seen so many pheasants and quail. In a very few hours the men had bagged hundreds. Protected by aprons, the women busily plucked the game in the back of the car while the hunt was in progress so that, when they all reached home, the feasting and celebration could begin at once.

Not everything was easy or untroubled at home. Mrs. Lutcher was constantly receiving blackmail letters. Some demanded $50,000, others threatened to kidnap her if she did not produce twice that much. Texas, at that time, was a wild and rugged pioneer state, full of daring individualists, and August was perturbed that nothing had been done to reduce the threat that dogged the footsteps of this kindly old woman. In no uncertain terms, he told genial, placid Mrs. Stark that if her mother-in-law could afford to pay his prices and give him orders to paint 14 portraits, then she most certainly could afford to hire private detectives to protect her. Mrs. Stark listened passively. Still worried about the threatening messages, August decided to take matters into his own hands if and when Mamoose ever came to Switzerland.

Soon after her arrival there, Gertrude and her husband prepared to take her on the ride of her life. Even though it was midsummer, they bundled themselves snugly into their warmest clothing and set out on the road leading to the Great Saint Bernard hospice. There the men and women parted company. Each group slept in dormitories with white walls and white-curtained alcoves. Seated in the refectory at long tables constructed of hand-hewn wooden planks, they partook of the famous bread which was baked only twice yearly. Almost as hard as cast iron, it had to be dunked in order to be eaten. They made the rounds of the ancient monastery founded by Bernard of Menthon, a northern Italian nobleman, as a hospice for pilgrims, many of whom perished of hunger and exposure before being able to reach their destination. Most had hoped to traverse the road that passed in front of the monastery as it was one of the shortest routes leading from France into Italy. Here, monks were schooled in rescue work, and these men in turn trained their huge Saint Bernard dogs for the arduous task of finding those buried by avalanches or caught in impassable snowdrifts.

When the Benzigers' visit to the hospice ended, a large crate was put into their car. From it popped up two shaggy heads. They were the puppies who would grow to enormous sizes and guard the life of Mamoose. Once they arrived in Texas, their protecting presence was felt immediately and the threats of the local terrorists ceased, although one wonders what terrors the dogs experienced in the transfer from the chill of the Alps to the heat and humidity of Texas.

These were still the days when motorists were impeded by an annoying assortment of rules and regulations, especially in this region. Not wishing to be delayed a further day in this mountain fastness, August's party proceeded at a crawl. A local regulation required that all cars have teams of horses hitched to the front, and no automobile was to climb or descend any mountain road at a speed faster than a horse could travel. August decided to risk the penalty, which would amount to 75 Swiss francs. When he reached Martigny, which lay at the base of the mountain, crowds of villagers were milling about, and a policeman stood in front of a barricade. "*Arrêtez*! *Arrêtez*!" he called out curtly. "You're under arrest. Pay me the penalty fee or I'll throw you in jail!" August retorted that the law was cruel and unjust to the motorists. The mob closed in and began to jeer, "Down with foreigners! Down with cars! Down with the motorists who ruin our roads." Anger heightened. Finally, August, who had bided his time, asserted calmly, "You cannot touch me until I telephone to Bern. The President of our Republic promised to send a permit allowing us free access to this mountain pass." The policeman backed off and the townspeople hushed as he pulled from his pocket the telegram authenticating his claim. The officer attempted conciliation. "Are you Benziger? How was I to know that this damn Italian car belonged to a Swiss? I took you for a foreigner." August's reply was tart: "That is all the more unfortunate. We Swiss happen to depend on foreigners for our bread and butter. If outsiders did not visit our land, stay in our hotels and do business with us, we'd soon go into bankruptcy." August offered to give the man a 20-franc tip. In a grandiose manner, the officer brushed it aside, then muttered under his breath, "Wait until we are on the outskirts of town!" Jumping onto the Lancia's running board, he accompanied the party until they were out of earshot of the others—then he gladly took the money.

This episode was to end the absurd laws which had impeded motorists from driving into Switzerland where they would suffer the embarrassment of touring in cars with horses attached to their bumpers. The incident was one of August's lesser but more humorous diplomatic coups.

CHAPTER 14

American Portraits and the Advent of War
(1908-1914)

The longer August remained in Brunnen, the more the desire for him to return to the States grew, and he realized that he had to establish a permanent residence in America. By 1908 the Benzigers had moved into 140 West Fifth-seventh Street, a 14-room apartment only a few houses away from August's first camping ground, Carnegie Hall; this was to be the Benziger home until 1919.

Here the artist painted slowly, methodically, systematically, and never took days off. He had schooled himself in self-discipline, so no painting ever became a mere flight of imagination. He bypassed art dealers with disdain as he felt they cheapened his trade and that his portraits were his own best recommendation. That he had found the key to individual character was demonstrated by the striking likenesses he produced as the ribbons of paint squeezed on to his palette became the means by which he molded the human form on blank white canvas. He never left lean or thinly-painted surfaces; the colors, thickly piled over each other, swirled and caught the light. A human physique that smiled, saw and lived had been created. The innermost being of his sitters radiated from their eyes because he had studied them intensely for their uniqueness. No matter how ugly the client might be, the portraitist would pick out the salient features and, by truthful frankness, enhance them instead of allowing them to detract from the sitter's personality. To him, every soul was beautiful. Details were painstakingly incorporated. Among some 78 portraits of men in frock coats, each coat was executed with the precision of a tailor. That of a Theodore Roosevelt differed from that of a scientist such as John Brashear or a banker such as Michael Jenkins or of Governor James Phinney Baxter of Maine.

August had started out on his artistic career enamored by the female figure. Nothing had pleased him more than toying with drapery, wisps of net or veiling or fine laces. Hats and furs and flowers were all incorporated into the ensemble but, gradually, he became irritated by what he felt to be the fickleness of women. To him, they were like Dresden china dolls, their dainty frailty and languid femininity definitely passé. To his way of thinking, strength and dependability could be found in males alone. John Singer Sargent, whom he considered to be on a par with Franz Hals, agreed with him on this subject. They came to admire each other's techniques. Often he watched Sargent during a sitting and once watched him transform simple Mary Leiter of Chicago into an image of lovely Lady Curzon. He had raved about that portrait which the genius of a Sargent alone could produce.

Once, when in Sargent's studio, he had noticed and commented upon a completed but unsigned painting. The master had replied bitterly: "Why should I sign my work of art? I have been given nothing for my pains or genius. I have needed over 100 sittings, yet the fair lady walked out on me. Now I am without a sou. Benziger, don't be a fool. Never sign anything until you have been paid. I am sick and tired of the female species. I am going to retire and devote my life to something more satisfying."

Many years later, August met him again in Boston, and they dined together. August reprimanded the American for giving up portraits for he felt he was wasting his precious talent on murals, but Sargent responded: "Benziger, there is no use arguing. I have finished painting shallow women, finished catering to their whims and caprices. They are too selfish, too particular. They know nothing about art. They do not appreciate what I give them. They cannot make up their minds as to what they really want. In painting murals, I do not have to deal with selfish human beings—who hurt my pride and even ruin my vanity." From that time on, while August could pick and choose from among his would-be clients, he clung chiefly to accepting commissions to paint portraits of men.

When in New York, August could never resist the fantastic pull of Wall Street. At heart a gambler, he often stopped to check on the progress of the stock market. Since his client and friend, Benjamin Douglas, had his office in the vicinity, he would stop to visit him, and sometimes be persuaded to go home with him. Together they would board the Hoboken Ferry for New Jersey and, while in West Orange, closet themselves in the laboratories of Thomas Edison.

This great scientist fascinated August. His energy reminded him very much of that of his own father. Edison locked himself up in his office and never went home, except on Saturdays. He would snatch a few hours of rest on his office couch, keeping three secretaries busy night and day. When not dictating notes, he supervised no less than 100 assistants laboring on the latest inventions.

August inquired how it was that, having invented the electric chair, he disapproved of electrocution. Edison explained that the chair had merely been a sort of by-product. Necessity had forced him at one point to do something about the alarming rat population in his Cincinnati offices, and he dealt with the problem by utilizing electricity. Later, by means of a more delicate system, he even executed thousands of cockroaches. The electric chair was a natural outgrowth of this type of invention.

August was present when Edison showed the first moving picture. Later he heard the first "talkie," only to return shaking his head. He told Gertrude that the noise had been horrible. He had been present again when Edison invited 40 friends to listen to a "gramophone" in which a little diamond replaced the steel needle. At this time, Edison had predicted that although he had invented the "talkies," they would never be popular, and added that airplanes would never be practical. August insisted that he had seen some wonderful demonstrations of planes by an inventor and developer of these machines, Glen H. Curtis. He had also talked to the Wright brothers; they all felt as he did, that the future of aviation would transform the continent of America.

August had been so impressed by the experiments he had seen tried out at the Edison laboratories that he was one of the first to advocate incandescent light. He left his wife no peace until he had had the bright, sputtering arc lights installed in his studio.

When he had to call in at Buffalo on a commission, he invariably stopped over in nearby Rochester. Having been a photographer, spending years in the study of this science and art, he had developed the greatest admiration for George Eastman and was an enthusiastic follower of the progress of Eastman Kodak Company, feeling convinced as he did that, in time, the Rochester industry would lead the world in photography. And so it came to pass.

Buffalo never held much attraction for him yet, as it was the home city of S.H. Knox, August had no alternative but to go there for sittings. Young Knox and young Woolworth were cousins and farmers who each put $800 in a ten-cent-store business. The venture failed. The cousins returned to farm work but when they made a little more money, they started up again. Having learned from their failures, they expanded their merchandise, and so succeeded in founding the first successful Five-and-Ten-Cent-Store business. One of the major moments of Knox's life was the day when Woolworth opened a store on Fifth Avenue. There had been opposition, yet everyone drove to the opening, at least to look if not to buy: the rich and poor—the ladies with Pierce Arrows and elegant Packards as well as officeworkers and chars.

When Mr. Knox came to 140 West Fifth-seventh Street for sittings, he often had luncheon with the family, and it was there that the children heard him talk about his beginnings, so it was a red-letter day when they were first permitted to go, escorted by a governess, to the Woolworth store. Their mother did not like the idea of this outing. She felt, as did many others, that it was unwise to permit young people to accumulate cheap or tawdry articles which might undermine their ideas of propriety. Once the children had been to the Five-and-Ten, however, they returned jubilant. For once in their lives they felt that every item was within reach of their limited resources; they had become millionaires in an hour. Everything, literally, cost five and ten cents.

August was to spend part of the winter of 1909 in Augusta, Georgia, at the Bon Air Hotel, completing while there the portraits of James Seer Kuhn and his wife. At this time, his next door neighbor happened to be none other than John D. Rockefeller. Although the artist was up-to-date in many things, he still clung to the Old World idea of dignity. He never could nor would condescend to clean his own shoes, which he invariably stuck outside his bedroom door. Great was his amazement one morning to find a guest in shirt-sleeves offering to let him borrow his shoe-shining kit. Sensing how he felt, Rockefeller gave him a practical example of just how the job was to be done. From then on, August polished his own shoes when away from home!

About this time, William Howard Taft had been chosen President-elect, and had come from Georgia to recuperate from his strenuous campaign. August knew him well, as this man and his Cincinnati family had taken great pains to be helpful to him when he first started out in America. Taft was an early riser, and each morning he and Rockefeller played golf. August would follow, using this opportunity to make sketches of them, unable to overcome the temptation to caricature such a strange pair of players as the rotund Taft and the lean, emaciated little Rockefeller; but what impressed him most was the fact that the wealthiest man on earth had no time to himself. Even when playing golf, he was hounded by an efficient Swiss secretary who had been in his employ for 17 years and kept the aged boss informed about the stock market at every hour of the day. When the game was over, the three men would breakfast together. While August had been asked by a friend to paint the portrait of the President-elect, Mr. Taft was not in the least enthusiastic about the idea. If Benziger was going to make of him a huge, voluptuous monstrosity, he'd prefer no painting at all. Zorn, an earlier artist acquainted with him, had made him anything but attractive and, consequently, he had a horror of sitting for anyone. The decision was left in abeyance: would he or would he not sit?

Meanwhile, August had engagements in Florida during this winter of 1910. Although his wife had an aversion to the balmy, sandy stretches where much time, it seemed to her, was wasted in idleness, August left her no peace until she agreed to join him, and assured her that the Sacred Heart nuns on Madison Avenue would take excellent care of their brood.

Florida always brought Gertrude memories of a certain railroad wreck. On one occasion, she and August had planned to leave New York when she had a horrible dream and canceled their reservations for the night express. Although they left a day later, their train was delayed for hours because of a frightful accident in which almost everyone aboard perished. The Benziger's train crawled at a snail's pace through the debris of one of the worst railroad disasters in the South. Gertrude shuddered as she saw the splintered cars, the twisted rails, and thanked God that she had listened to her inner promptings of the preceding day.

Meanwhile, August mused about far-sighted Henry Morrison Flagler, a Standard Oil heir, who had seen more in Florida than sandy, sun-beaten stretches. He believed that out of these dunes a winter playground for America could be made. His far-sightedness had been rewarded; he had been the first to inaugurate hotel chains. In St. Augustine, the Benzigers stayed as his guests at his Ponce de Leon Hotel, and in Palm Beach at his Royal Poinciana, the grounds of which covered 35 acres. The six-story structure accommodated 1,750 guests and in its dining room, 2000 were seated at the same time.

Mr. Flagler took great pride in showing where a cargo of coconuts had gone aground near Palm Beach. The few inhabitants at that time, not knowing what to do with the debris, had buried them in the sandy wasteland, and so arose the palm trees which have grown with abandon to cover the area and become, almost, its symbol. Once having developed a tropical paradise, he acquired a badly-managed railroad and reorganized it in order to bring tourists to this place.

Once the Benzigers had paid visits to their many friends, for everyone who could afford to do so was wintering there, August insisted upon seeing his taciturn client, Josiah Vankirt Thompson. Thompson was no easy man with whom to do business. Born on a farm, he had clung to the simple habits of the land. On several occasions, he had invited the artist to come to Uniontown, but Pennsylvania was a long way off; August really preferred to have his clients come to his New York studio.

As he never started any work without first looking into the sitter's background, on this occasion he had learned that Thompson was president of the First National Bank of Uniontown, and also one of the largest coal operators in America. It was known that he owned 50,000 acres of anthracite in Green County, and thousands more in Virginia and eastern Ohio.

On their way home, the Benzigers stopped off in the little village of Hot Springs, Virginia. Mr. Thompson, who never cared for society, went out of his way to fête the couple and made them his guests at the Homestead Hotel. Arrangements were then made for August to come as soon as possible to Uniontown, as Thompson had no intention of ever going to New York. There was nothing for it but to go, and August rushed off, taking with him all of his paraphernalia. The sittings with this self-made man were a huge success; they produced a compelling image of a man who had brought wealth to countless citizens, and was known to pay his workers the highest salaries for comparable work. An indefatigable worker, he, like Edison, never left his office during the week. On Saturdays he returned home, only to rush back again to be at his desk on Sundays.

Delighted with his portrait, he gladly paid August his fee, suggesting that he begin at once on two more paintings—one of each of his sons.

Back in New York, the large check was taken to the president of the National City Bank. The gentleman shook his head: Thompson was a security risk. August was incredulous. The Thompson files were sent for; the records showed that the client was really worth three hundred millions. He had, in fact, just completed a deal with Mr. Frick for coal property amounting to two million dollars. Then he had turned around and, with that money, bought more coal mines for fifty million dollars. Had there been a crash, Wall Street would have wiped him out! The bank refused to cash the check.

August spent much time visiting banks but all demurred, basing their refusal to cash the check on the same grounds. When he protested, he was reminded that of each hundred millionaires, only two or three at the very most ever kept their millions. Gambling was the besetting sin of the newly-rich. Fortunately for August, after a wait of six months, he was paid. In the meantime, the paintings intended for Mr. Thompson's sons were well under way. August returned to Uniontown where he thoroughly enjoyed being with a person of this rugged a temperament. Mr. Thompson picked out the frames he liked best and then parted sadly, for he had taken a great fancy to the Swiss painter.

When the frames were completed, the paintings varnished and thoroughly dry, they were shipped back to Uniontown. Three weeks later, the crated portraits were returned unopened. Receivers had taken over the Thompson bank; his client had gone bankrupt.

Though there were disappointments, painting did have its compensations. Yearly, Emil Winters, a Pittsburgh banker, moved into the Plaza Hotel in New York. His lavish entertainments always featured the finest talent. One winter it was Victor Herbert who brought his orchestra. August and Gertrude, both musically inclined, took an immediate fancy to the composer in whose home they often spent enjoyable evenings thereafter. This musical genius had had the top floor of his apartment padded so that it was soundproof, and here they listened as he tried out tunes for new operettas, playing sections from the *Babes in Toyland, Naughty Marietta, Princess Pat* and *Eileen*, the latter written for Judge Cohalan's daughter, the girl who later became a Religious of the Sacred Heart.

One thing was certain about Victor Herbert: he could never disguise his jovial Irish background. He recounted the fact that, as a destitute Dublin musician, he had gone to Austria in the hope of playing in the great Vienna Opera House. While in the orchestra, he had met and married Theresa Foester, the Austrian singer. On reaching America, the couple had been so poor that Herbert, who owned but one shirt, had to remain in bed while his wife washed and ironed it.

Genial, home-loving Mrs. Herbert could never master the English tongue, and always had to struggle with her German accent, yet her *hausfrau* qualities endeared her to all. Her *apfelstrudel*, her dumplings, her rich Austrian pastries kept her husband rotund, but their home was physically and psychologically beautiful and warm.

For the Benzigers, many a chance acquaintance made aboard ship matured into lasting friendship. George Allen, a widower from Philadelphia, was on the steamer, *Rotterdam*, with his little daughter, Inace. Seeing the happy Benziger trio, he asked if his little girl might join them. Playfully, they dubbed her Sister Number Four. Back in New York, Mr. Allen gave August a commission for two portraits. One was to be of Inace with her mother, who had died some time before. Photographs had to be substituted for the reality; yet, when the work was completed, Mr. Allen stood weeping before the realistic portrayal of the woman he had loved, holding in her arms the fair-haired child with somber eyes. The second portrait was of George Allen himself, depicted just as he was about to rush out to his office.

On the French liner, *La France*, was a middle-aged couple who seemed to be having a great deal of trouble coping with a little boy and tiny girl who had the vivacity of quicksilver, and whose governess had succumbed to seasickness. Quiet, austere Abraham Hatfield regarded his noisy brood with helpless dismay. Mrs. Hatfield was just the opposite of her extremely serious husband. She was filled with exuberance, and her flow of wit, humor and philosophy, animated by lively anecdotes, made her the center of every gathering. The Benziger girls, several years older than the Hatfield children, looked on them as if they were live dolls, and volunteered to keep an eye on George and minute Helen—and so they did. After an uneventful transatlantic crossing, grateful Mrs. Hatfield rushed up to thank and bid farewell to the Benzigers who lived just around the corner from them. She hoped to see much of both parents and children in the future. August immediately squelched such a thought. "Oh no! My children never go to the home of anyone. We will naturally be delighted to have your children call on us!" Quick as a flash, with her instinctive spirit of repartee, she replied, "Then, Mr. Benziger, it means plain good-bye. It is up to you to make up your mind. This is a 50-50 proposition. If our children go to your home, then your children also come to ours. Otherwise you will never see any of us."

Unaccustomed to having his authority questioned, August backed down. He was not quite sure whether he liked Mrs. Hatfield or not, although he had respect for her husband who, though retired, had devoted his fortune to restoring the Anglican Church of St. Mary the Virgin in New York. Hatfield was not only a great philanthropist but also a tolerant and broadminded man.

Every few months, tactful Mrs. Hatfield invited all the Benzigers to her home for dinner. She really felt sorry for the children brought up on such a Spartan regime. Strangely enough, Papa Benziger consented meekly. His daughters donned their Sunday best, and all went gleefully to the Hatfield apartment. The men immediately closeted themselves in the den. Astute and scholarly, Mr. Hatfield showed slides and turned to his stamp collection—next in value to that of King George V of England, the most priceless in the world.

The second home the Benziger children were permitted to visit on an occasional weekend was Briarcliff Lodge, the estate of Mr. and Mrs. U.T. Hungerford, who had taken a tremendous fancy to plump little Hélène. This quite elderly couple had seen her aboard the steamship *Rotterdam* and had watched how she tried to keep up with her tall, handsome father by clutching his coattails as he paced the deck. Although Mr. Hungerford owned the Hungerford Brass and Copper Company and was many times a millionaire, he and his wife were childless and longed to adopt little Hélène in order to complete their happiness. They approached August tactfully and made him a generous offer. Stunned, he explained that he had always wanted twelve girls, not just three. Adoption was out of the question, but year after year the Hungerfords came to Brunnen, always hoping. Annually, they showered Hélène with 100 American Beauty roses on her birthday. Another time, Mr. Hungerford learned from her sisters that she loved orchids best of all. Not long afterwards, a dinner party was given at the St. Regis Hotel just for the Benzigers. A private dining room was engaged for the evening as August had always flatly refused to permit his children to go to big hotel dinners, to the opera or the theater. All the greater was his consternation when he entered the small dining room to find the candle-lit table covered with hundreds of purple orchids, Mr. Hungerford's way of saying that he did not approve of the austere manner in which the girls were being raised. The children were thrilled by the beauty of the flowers, but their father was humiliated to think that any of them could long for anything so extravagant. Orchids were not for children!

A third home was permitted for periodic visits. How the children loved to go to the French Renaissance Château on Riverside Drive and 73rd Street! The Schwabs, who had no children, pleaded for their company, and so the girls attended the Sunday recitals given at this dream palace. Having visited the Loire valley with its castles, Mrs. Schwab had been deeply impressed by the granite Château of Chenonceaux; plans had been drawn for the New York mansion so that it would resemble its architecture, with identical turrets and spires covered with grey slate. Inside was an organ considered the finest in America; so that the acoustics would be absolutely perfect, gorgeous Gobelin tapestries had been hung and hid the pipes from view. When music was played, each of the 75 rooms was filled with sound.

The three little girls spent many happy Sunday afternoons watching from the great marble gallery on the second floor. There, amid the palms and beautiful flowers—sent from the Schwab greenhouses in Loretto, Pennsylvania—they peered at the exciting pageant below. Concealed from view, they saw the organist, whom they called "Gibby." Arthur Gibson was engaged by the year by men like Frick and Carnegie to play informal recitals. Sunday was his day with the Schwabs. Sometimes it was Fritz Kreisler who accompanied on the violin, or Madam Schuman-Heink or Marcella Sembrich who sang favorite arias. Opera singers and concert artists flocked to the Schwab home.

Charlie Schwab enjoyed nothing better than gambling. Weekly a stipulated sum was set aside to be wagered in the Sunday bridge games. Fabulous amounts used to change hands; in fact, the stakes were so high that August was shocked to see vast sums being tossed away in play. He would confide to his wife that in one evening more money had been lost by a single player than he himself had earned in five years. The most daring gambler he had ever met at the Schwab home was John W. Gates, whose passion was poker.

Gates had come from Chicago and started as a barbed wire salesman. Business had been slow because farmers were skeptical about this new-fangled invention, but Gates claimed that barbed wire was "as light as air, stronger than whiskey, cheaper than dirt." However, all the publicity in the world brought no substantial profits. In desperation, he went to the cattle country of Texas. There he rented a corral outside of San Antonio and issued a challenge to ranchers, insisting that his barbed wire fence would hold back the wildest longhorns. He invited them to bring 40 huge steers and guaranteed that his fence would hold them back. The cattle stampeded but the wire held. Single-handedly, John W. Gates had brought about a revolution in cattle ranching. Ultimately, the American Steel and Wire Company earned him millions of dollars before he was 30.

People of all types dropped in to call on the Schwabs. It was at their home that August met Judge Elbert E. Gary, who succeeded Schwab as president of United States Steel. Thomas Edison walked arm-in-arm with Schwab, talking about the future of American industry. Sometimes, quiet little Andrew Carnegie, Schwab's superior, dropped in quite alone, but he never came when there was a crowd. The devotion between these two men was touching, each insisting that he owed his good fortune to the other.

Years before, in Pittsburgh, August had met Schwab in the Carnegie home. During the winter of 1905, he had been asked to luncheon. Being a punctual person, he had arrived in plenty of time, only to learn that Mr. Schwab was closeted with Mr. Carnegie. Invited into the study, he sat and listened as the two men continued to discuss a business deal. The butler entered, announcing luncheon, and then, turning to Mr. Schwab, reminded him that the coachman had been waiting outside since ten in the morning. It was already past noon. Mr. Carnegie was visibly annoyed. His face darkened as he growled, "My boy, why will you be so wasteful? All morning I have been preaching economy to you. I waste my breath. You allow hard-earned money to be thrown away. Are you never going to learn?" Schwab, whose proverbial good humor could never be upset, merely chided the old man. Carnegie finally burst into laughter, "You see, Mr. Benziger, how much good my lecture has done? I might as well spare my breath. Even to this day, Charlie owns a Pullman car, while I cannot afford such a luxury."

During luncheon, the conversation turned to many things. Schwab reminded the philanthropist of his pig-headedness. Had he, Schwab, not tried in vain to get a new blast furnace for U.S.

Steel? Had M. Carnegie not persisted in his conviction that the furnaces were far too costly? Mr. Carnegie, with his dry Scottish wit, reminisced, "What did you do?" After many refusals from his superior, Schwab had gone straight ahead and built the blast furnaces while Carnegie was in Scotland. Carnegie's unexpected reaction? "What a blessing you did. Thanks to your far-sightedness, I made a fortune. You had the vision. I was too cautious." The conversation continued, Schwab saying to Carnegie, "You would never have trusted me had it not been for the English who offered to pay me a million dollars a year if I worked for them," and Carnegie replied: "Right you are, but don't forget what I told you. 'If you are worth a million to the English, you are worth a million to me.' Then and there I signed my first five-year contract with you. I kept you in America. We needed you right here."

Andrew Carnegie, who for years had been the key figure in the steel and iron industry in America, sought retirement. Having reached the pinnacle of success he, nevertheless, had frugal needs and longed to devote what was left of his life to full-time concern with philanthropy. He confided his secret aspiration to Charlie. As Carnegie's right-hand man, he seized an opportunity while at a dinner given by leaders of the steel industry. Seated next to him was Pierpont Morgan, with whom he had little in common, yet he envisioned a fabulous era ahead. Much could be achieved if the steel industries worked harmoniously together while, on the other hand, competition could wreck them. Each mill could produce better quality goods if specific products were assigned to each company and cutthroat methods avoided.

Once dinner was over, Pierpont Morgan cornered Schwab. He inquired confidentially whether Carnegie could be induced to sell his vast steel holdings. If so, what would be the price? This was Schwab's moment of triumph. He returned to his superior who was willing to talk, yet refused to write down any figures. Schwab had jotted down what Carnegie thought a fair price, then rushed back to Morgan the Magnificent. Schwab knew with whom he was dealing. He had managed to rouse the interest of one of the world's major bankers; he also knew how to hold it. On learning that he could, perhaps, buy out Carnegie, Morgan asked what the selling price was. For 26 years he had waited, dreaming of the day when he would be able to amalgamate the huge steel industry of America into one vast concern. Schwab informed him that the price was $400 million. The deal was agreed upon then and there.

Within a matter of days, Morgan named Schwab president and organizer of United States Steel.

Carnegie was finally free to devote his millions to his pet projects. He retired, and planned to contribute half the cost of 2,800 Carnegie libraries, as he was a firm believer that books would eradicate ignorance and felt strongly that they should be made available to everyone. The penniless bobbin-boy of Pittsburgh, who had once worked in a cotton mill for $1.20 a week, had worked hard and was finally able to make real his philanthropic dream.

In later years, when the Schwabs were going to travel to Pittsburgh in their Pullman car, Gertrude was invited to join them as August was already in that city. The train journey was memorable as it gave Gertrude a first-hand opportunity to study Andrew Carnegie, who was also a guest on his way to the unveiling of one of his libraries. The Schwabs and some of their friends were playing bridge, while Mrs. Benziger and Andrew Carnegie sat and reminisced. On reaching a country station, the train was halted in order to shunt the Pullman car to another track. As Gertrude and her escort paced the platform, Carnegie stopped to listen to the ticking of the telegraph. Turning, he asked, "Do you know the Morse Code?" Gertrude professed her ignorance and her surprise that her companion was so familiar with it. His reply opened vistas for her:

> Ah, Mrs. Benziger, it is a long time since I first came to this country from Dunfermline, Scotland. I was a poor, penniless lad, living with my simple mother. Our small cottage had no running water. When she washed clothes for a living, I used to carry the buckets of water. When she had finished her day's work, it was I who emptied the tubs. I got my first part-time job in a country station, running errands and sweeping floors. I had always wanted to study. Desirous of learning, I spent every available moment reading. Only I was handicapped; I had no books. How I longed for books! Books that I could read at night, so I would have a chance to make something of myself.

> I used to hang around the station envying the telegraph operator. During lunch hour when he was gone, I heard a message ticking away. I had picked up the Morse Code. There was no one at the station. The message was that a runaway train on the main line was heading toward our station. Within a matter of minutes the fast express was due to come from the opposite direction. Something had to be done, and

done at once, or there would be a frightful wreck. I telegraphed to the station ahead, "Hold express."

Mr. Carnegie smiled as he looked at Gertrude. "Mrs. Benziger, that was the turning point of my life. That was the very beginning of my break. I was given the opportunity to work up and up, yet I have never forgotten what the lack of books meant to me then. Books alone can enrich and change the life of all who wish to delve into their depths."

Back in New York, the Schwabs had come to dinner. Mr. Schwab, studying the latest portraits, remarked, "Benziger, why is it that you have never painted my portrait?" August quickly retorted, "You are a friend. I never paint friends or members of my family. You have never given me an order. Naturally, I would never broach the subject." Schwab answered, "Goodness, if that is all that is keeping you from painting me, then I beg of you to begin immediately." Then he leaned across the table to his wife, "What do you think, Old Lady?" (Mr. Schwab called his wife *Old Lady* and she, in turn called him *Laddie*.) She looked up at him with a smile of delight. "I've always wanted one of you by Benziger. I am so happy, Laddie, that you have decided to ask him."

Mr. Schwab went on. "Why don't you begin tomorrow? I will wait for you at the house. Bring along your paraphernalia and start at once." August shook his head. "No, Mr. Schwab, I do not want to paint you in your Riverside mansion. The you who lives there is not the real you. The you who runs the steel mills, who makes Bethlehem what it really is, is another you." Marieli, in later years, remembered her father's account of this conversation. "Here you are the wealthy playboy," she heard her father say:

> Here you relax and rest and plan. I want the you who is the
> greatest steel man of all times, the genius who dreams up
> great things. Your Bethlehem Steel has transformed the ho-
> rizons of this land; in time it will do the same for the whole
> world. You have revolutionized building techniques. Your
> pre-fabricated steel girders have become the skyscrapers of
> the future. Through them you have changed the skyline of
> our large cities. Your steel is about to perform the same
> miracle with trains and automobiles. You have never been
> afraid of endangering your health by hours of extra work.
> You have never been reluctant to put on overalls. I've not
> forgotten what you once told me—that bare hands grip suc-
> cess better than do kid gloves!

> I'd really like best of all to follow you about your steel mills
> for two or three days—watching, studying you and your
> men.

Two days later, August and his wife accompanied the
Schwabs to their simple home in Bethlehem. August left at dawn
to accompany Mr. Schwab on his tour of the factory. What most
amazed him was to find huge stock piles of shrapnel, explosives,
and shells weighing two tons each. There were heavy ordnance
guns 75 feet long. Tremendous plates for great battleships lay
stacked side by side. The two-mile-long Bethlehem plant was
working night and day. Its mammoth mills, its tremendous machine shops employed over 40,000 workers. A sense of fear, even
doom, gripped August's heart. That night, when he came back to
the house where the two wives were waiting, he remarked, "It
looks to me as though we are on the verge of some horrible war. I
had no notion that so much ammunition existed."

Mr. Schwab said little. He nodded. "The picture is mighty
grim. Yet if I did not step in, someone else would. We have just
acquired the Fore River Shipbuilding company at Quincy, Massachusetts." He elaborated the picture:

> Nine years ago, back in 1905, I told you that what Krupp
> was to Germany, Bethlehem Steel will be to America. At
> that time, Wall Street predicted that my Bethlehem would
> collapse. No one took me seriously. No one but my dear
> wife. Yet within these nine years my corporation has be-
> come the largest producer of steel and armaments on earth.
> Bethlehem is the greatest privately-owned factory in the
> Western Hemisphere. Wait, and time will prove that I can
> surpass the Krupp output. Preparedness is the keynote. Pre-
> paredness is my motto.

One evening, as the Bethlehem visit drew to a close and a last
dinner was being served, Stone, the gray-haired butler came quietly
to his master and handed him a telegram. Mr. Schwab studied it
carefully, then passed it on to his wife. "What do you think of this,
Old Lady?" Perturbed, she inquired, "What can it mean, Laddie?"
Taking the telegram back, he read it aloud, then commented, "The
Czar of Russia is making me a generous offer. He is willing to
pay twice as much as Argentina for two battleships we are building. He wants immediate delivery of *Rivadavia* and *Maruavia* for
$44 million."

A few weeks later, during a sitting, August asked, "By the way, what ever happened to that offer made to you by the Czar?" Schwab replied, "I turned the cable and entire matter over to the Argentine government. The ships belong to them. They prefer to keep them. They need a strong navy to protect their own coast and keep Brazil from becoming too greedy." And then he mused again: "I don't know what has come over Russia. The nation is preparing like crazy for war. My yards are filled with ammunition and guns destined for Russia. It looks to me as though the next war may not be started by the Kaiser. After centuries of waiting, Russia may finally make a dangerous bid for world domination. She has always wanted Austria and Poland. I really do not like the way things are going. Time alone will tell if our friend Carnegie is not right; he wants peace through mediation. Arbitration alone will save us from world conflagration."

On one of the yearly expeditions to Europe, the Benzigers stopped near Tours. They had been asked by a client, Mrs. Horace Brock of Philadelphia, to call on her sister and brother-in-law while they were in France. Professor Carvallo of the Sorbonne was a Spaniard. He had married a wealthy American, and together they had renovated dilapidated castles, and ended by living in a 16th-century château called Villandry, which resembled a huge fortress. Always one to keep a promise, August and his family stopped long enough at Château de Villandry for the head of the house to leave his visiting card, but Professor Carvallo insisted that the entire family spend the night. The hospitable host and hostess turned over the ancient tower suite to them. From the bedrooms, the enchanting view of the historic Loire winding through peaceful meadowlands was balm for the spirit. The children were delighted. They were not passing by on a tour, but were really living in an honest-to-goodness Renaissance castle with all the trimmings, including servants in livery and an enormous king-sized bed. Even a murder had been perpetrated here. An heir to the throne of France had been assassinated in that very room. They were excited to hear that the ghost of Henry II still haunted the tower.

Dinner was even more exciting. The servants, wearing white gloves, carried huge trays with mountains of food; a whole suckling pig was served in style, a bright red apple in its mouth. All the vegetables and fruit came from the house gardens, including the luscious white-stemmed, blue-tipped asparagus. Once the meal was over, the children were excused. They had had a long day; it was bedtime. Their father and mother remained in the living room, listening spellbound to Professor Carvallo. His gallery of Spanish paintings was one of the finest August had ever seen.

The children went off disappointed. They had hoped that their mother would at least escort them to their distant tower room. Things were terrifying by candlelight; the eerie sounds were frightening. Their father had suspected that they were afraid but refused to coddle them. No sooner had they undressed than all three hopped into the huge bed. Tired out, they immediately fell asleep, only to be awakened by the most ghoulish sounds—the creaking of boards, clanking of chains, even groans. They jumped to their feet. Hélène, with trembling hands, managed to light a candle and led the way as three barefooted runners tore down the winding spiral staircase into the cozy den below. Papa Benziger looked up, highly displeased by the disturbance caused by his off-spring, but Gertrude noticed at once that something was really wrong. She excused herself to join them on their trek back to their room. Once there, she and the three cuddled together in the bed. With mother there to guard them, they slept the sleep of the just, but at dawn awoke, glad to be alive and anxious to get away as fast as they could from a real haunted castle. Make-believe ones were henceforth more to their liking.

Before they left, Professor Carvallo remarked that since August had taken such a fancy to Spanish art, the two men should motor through Spain. August gladly accepted the offer and suggested that he might contact his St. Louis friend, Robert Brookings, who had expressed a desire to know more about Spain and its art. The trio would meet during the early summer of 1914.

Genial, handsome, brilliant Robert Brookings had come to Brunnen for several summers. He and August had met on the terrace of the Grand Hotel and had instantly taken a liking for each other. Both were tall, middle-aged and each wore identical beards and mustaches. Brookings, after having introduced himself as coming from St. Louis and being a bachelor, remarked that he had been staying across the lake, almost opposite to Brunnen. Intrigued, August heard the word Schöneck, and said, "Why, sir, you don't look sick to me." August, of course, knew that Schöneck was a sanitarium at Beckenried for persons with nervous ailments. Brookings laughed; Professor Bossart, the physician in charge, had cured him of insomnia. He had asked him how many hours of sleep he managed to get at night. Brookings had answered, "Two at the most." The doctor replied, "Fine, fine. You really don't need more. How fortunate for a man of your intelligence. You should be delighted. You have more time to improve your mind; you can work through the hours of the night!" Brookings shook his head. "Do you know what happened? I went to bed and for the first time in months, slept the whole night through, so now I plan to come to stay in your hotel. In fact, I stopped in to make reservations for next week."

Then he told the artist something about his personal life—how as a boy of 14 he had refused to continue with his studies. He knew his family was poor, and felt that he was just an added burden, so he set out on his own and earned his way by working in a factory that manufactured wooden handles for brooms and pots. He became a traveling salesman and eventually acquired ownership of that factory where he worked. Eventually he was able to turn over millions to establish Washington University in St. Louis and the Brookings Institute in Washington. Enamored of learning, he longed to make higher studies available for all who desired to take advantage of them. Dissatisfied with the little he knew, he planned his own life in such a way that every other year he spent 12 months improving his own mind. He took up the study of German in Germany, where he worked at the language until he could speak it as perfectly as a native. As he was anxious to learn to play the violin, he took up the study of it with the same élan with which he had approached German. It was his ambition to play as well as his master Joachim, although he never reached that goal.

Brookings was enthralled with the Benziger paintings. Remaining at heart a salesman, he came to New York with a proposition. He explained that although he had had no less than 10 portraits painted for Washington University, not one of them was a real likeness. Would the artist be willing to paint his image on his terms? Should the staff decide the portrait to be a poor likeness and refuse to hang the painting, August would keep the portrait and accept no pay. Nothing intrigued Benziger more than a challenge. "I am willing to risk my reputation. I doubt if there will be the slightest trouble about a likeness. I, too, have one requirement which you must promise to meet. Not a soul is to see that portrait until it is completed." The painting was started; Brookings showed great satisfaction. Yet, knowing that the requirements would be stiff, the artist decided to take his work to St. Louis and hang it in its final setting. There he could better perceive what the lighting effects would be. Once again he reminded Mr. Brookings of the original agreement: not a soul was to lay eyes on his portrait until it was completed. A good deal of work was still necessary, yet he crated his painting and shipped it to St. Louis with explicit instructions. No one was to open the crate when the portrait arrived in St. Louis.

When August reached that city, Mr. Brookings took him straight to the university. The huge auditorium was partly-filled. As his eyes turned toward the stage, he stood in agonized horror. Ten portraits of Mr. Brookings were hung in a row—ten stark memorials of failure. In their midst stood his painting, as big as life. Infuriated, he turned to Mr. Brookings. "How dare you? You've not kept your word. You are dishonest; you treat me more like an executioner walking me up this aisle to my doom than a friend." Brookings went up to the stage. August stepped from the aisle into a seat. He had barely taken his place when the room stirred with excitement. Into it came the director of the board of the university, William K. Bixby, who was also head of the St. Louis Museum of Art. Looking at the collection of paintings, he began to study the newest addition. Every eye in the room was fixed on the Benziger. After a few minutes of painstaking scrutiny, Bixby walked to the back of the canvas, then emerged and faced the audience: "I had to ascertain for myself that no artificial medium had been used. You are to be congratulated on your choice of Mr. Benziger as an artist. I know of no man alive who could have painted eyes as realistic as these. Not since the days of Rembrandt has any artist caught the soul of a sitter as he has that of Mr. Brookings." Bixby came down the aisle to shake hands with August, and then commissioned him to paint his own portrait. He was followed by Brookings, who approached with extended hand. "Will you forgive me? I knew this would be the verdict, but I was also sure you would never consent to this ordeal. Now that you have succeeded with one portrait, I would like a second of myself. When can you start?" Brookings agreed to meet August during the latter part of May in Paris; together they would join Professor Carvallo for a jaunt into Spain. At the last moment, Brookings had to telegraph to Brunnen that he could not come. Later, when he did stop over in Switzerland, he told his host quite confidentially what had happened.

Andrew Carnegie, who spoke no German, had pleaded that Brookings, a close friend, join his party. Besides his pet project of erecting libraries, the Scot had another: world peace. For years he had dreamed of the day when international quarrels would be settled by means of arbitration, wars banned and a world court sit in judgment on any aggressor. This had been his aim when, in 1898, he had given the Dutch government $1,500,000 to build an international court in The Hague. Carnegie had also visited the Czar of Russia, Nicholas II, who had agreed that the idea was perfect. Yet, he asked, what did the Kaiser say?

Knowing of Brookings' familiarity with German, Carnegie felt that he would be a valuable addition to the party going to Potsdam to speak with Kaiser Wilhelm II. During the interview, the Kaiser was enthusiastic and agreed to sign a treaty on condition that America and Russia did the same. Carnegie returned home at once and contacted President Taft, who assured him that he would bring the matter to the attention of Congress. He never did anything of the sort. When war finally broke out, a heartbroken Carnegie blamed the American president. He was convinced that Taft could have averted the world conflagration just begun. If mediation worked in business, it could also work in international politics.

While these world discussions were going on during the summer of 1914, the Benzigers were busier than ever in their Grand Hotel. One of the guests whom they most looked forward to welcoming was Cardinal Farley of New York, as he was an old friend and frequent visitor at their home in the States. After years of hesitation, he had finally decided on August as the artist who should paint his official portrait, and had determined that the time to begin was now. No one could have been more excited than the Benziger children. Until then, they had never had a close-up view of how a high church dignitary robed in all of his ceremonial vestments. They would peek, and then keep the secret to themselves as a private treasure.

Marguerite, the family mischief-maker, managed to leave a studio window unlocked. Early one morning the three girls, aged 12, 13 and 14, slipped through the window into their hiding place. The studio had a wooden balcony; the staircase leading up to it was never used. There, amid dusty, discarded, half-started canvases, they hid in excited security, for their father, also an early riser, was already on his way to the studio. Then Cardinal Farley, escorted by his two secretaries, soon climbed to this room which stood on a high hill. Monsignor Patrick Hayes and Monsignor Thomas Carroll unpacked the robes to be donned for the sitting. With quiet dignity and a remarkable sense of humor, the cardinal slipped into his cassock that buttoned down from the neck to the hem. Over this was placed a lacy garment called a rochet, which reached to the knees. Next, it required two men to lift the hugh *cappa magna,* the cloak of brilliant moiré silk which covered the whole person of the cardinal and from which his head alone emerged. Then, with a deft motion, he seized the front, holding it up with both hands so that the red cassock and white lace rochet were seen. The priests finally arranged the red train which was several yards long.

With the dexterity of an expert, August adjusted folds here, smoothed out an ugly wrinkle there. He scrutinized his model minutely, turning him from side to side, anxious to catch the most appropriate expression. He seized the *ferraiola,* a cape worn only at nonecclesiastical functions and draped it over the back of a chair. Carefully he laid upon it the red, broad-brimmed cardinal's hat. Stepping back, with half-closed eyes, he squinted into the mirror to get the full effect. Then he returned to his model, making sure the composition was perfect. He slipped the *zucchetta* into position on the cardinal's head. "It is necessary for me to see the skullcap. You will have to wear it a bit more forward; otherwise I will not have enough of a contrast." Not quite satisfied, feeling that something was missing in the composition, August looked around. "Ah, yes, I almost forgot the red *biretta.* Your Eminence must hold it— so—between your fingers."

August kept a stack of chopsticks just for measuring features. He put them to use. Next he took a huge magnifying glass and went up to his client—sketching on paper the blood vessels, the size of the pupils, the minute details that comprised the markings of the eyes, and commented, "There is nothing I like better than painting eyes." Then he lapsed into silence. After he had sketched at fever pitch for over two hours, he dismissed the sitter. Artist and client left together, chatting amiably as they headed for the hotel below.

The three girls had been afraid to move. Though they were well-concealed in their lofty perch, any sound on the rustic balcony would have given away their hiding place. Descending, they stared at the wonderful *cappa magna.* Not even their beautiful mother had ever had on anything quite so effective. The children smoothed the rich material with their fingers. Hélène sighed, "How I'd love to be a cardinal, if only to wear such gorgeous clothes!" Marguerite, with a glint in her eye, whispered, "There's nothing to stop you. Why don't you try? You are short, plump, just as small as the cardinal. He'll never know the difference. He's tiny for a man; his garments will fit you perfectly." She had already seized the *cappa magna,* aping the gestures used by the secretaries. Marguerite and Marieli held it high to help their sister wriggle her plump figure into it. Marguerite looked critically at her. "I guess, Hélène, you are bigger than the cardinal. Your feet stick out. Somehow it doesn't look as nice on you as it did on him." Again Marguerite laughed, "You have forgotten your skull-cap, your cross and ring. You'd make a very absent-minded cardinal!"

The blissfully-happy child was strutting around the studio, followed by her awed trainbearers, so none of them had heard how loudly the rusty door creaked. Marguerite was saying at the top of her voice, "It's really very wrong of cardinals to be men! You'd think, wouldn't you, that women would be allowed some place inside the Church. Clothes like these are hardly appropriate for men." Then, as the three girls looked up, they saw someone through the mirror. Paralyzed with fear, they realized that they had been detected.

They had expected to see their father; instead, Cardinal Farley stepped into the studio. He was laughing so hard that he had to pull out a handkerchief, wipe his eyes and blow his nose. Marguerite peered into the ruddy-complexioned face. "Are you going to tell Papa?" "If I did, what would happen?" She shrugged her shoulders nonchalantly, "Well, we all will get into trouble, all three of us." Still laughing, the cardinal confided, "This is my secret and yours. Just be careful, Hélène, how you get out of my *cappa magna.* We cardinals can only afford one in a lifetime. I will show you how to take off the robes." Then, looking at his watch, he warned, "You'd better hurry. I feel you will really get into trouble if you are late for luncheon. Don't keep mademoiselle waiting; she has been looking for you all morning." This incident was part of the fun of his visit, but his real purpose in coming to Europe had been his *ad limina* visit to Rome. Feeling his age, he had confided to Pope Pius X that he would appreciate the nomination of an assistant, and had advanced the name of his secretary to fill the position. His request had been kept a secret. When a large envelope bearing the papal seal reached the cardinal, he hurried to see August and confided to him the fact that Monsignor Hayes had been nominated his coadjutor, with right of succession.

A party was organized for July 13. Unsuspecting Monsignor Hayes found a colored streamer at his dinner place. Thinking it was merely a party favor, he pulled it from the floral centerpiece and discovered his nomination as bishop. He was given the title of Bishop of Tagaste, yet he never changed his quiet, humble, unassuming ways.

Cardinal Farley and his entourage were the life of all the parties. Their laughter was so hearty and contagious that everyone loved these American ecclesiastics. At heart Cardinal Farley was a boy who, at a moment's notice, was ready to go anywhere. He would slip on a grey duster, don a matching cap and dash off to Munich, Vienna or Zürich at the merest suggestion of his host. One expedition to Germany ended up with barrels of beer being loaded into and onto the Benziger car, since a picnic had been planned for the following week and only the needed Munich beer was missing from the store of provisions. As August's group had to pass close to Einsiedeln, he wanted to visit his cousin Franz. When he did so, he left the cardinal and the two secretaries at the shrine of Our Lady. Later, the Abbot invited the group to dinner and would not take no for an answer, so August informed the cardinal, who realized that there was no alternative to accepting. They would dine at the abbey, joining the numerous monks in the refectory where all partook of simple but hearty fare. When the meal was finished, the community came to the monastery door to bid farewell to their guests, and gathered around the car. Only then did the incongruity of the scene dawn upon August. Barrels of beer, tied to the running board, loaded on the trunk rack, piled as high as the windshield, almost hid the cardinal from view. There was no alternative to making little of the incident.

Generally neither August nor the cardinal would have given the matter a second thought, but in Europe cardinals were meant to be driven about in state with the same honors given to a prince or king. However, none of the monks so much as raised an eyebrow at the time. All the same, August later learned that they had had a good laugh at his expense as they felt that only a Benziger could or would have been so unconventional. Once they got a safe distance from the abbey, August turned apologetically to the cardinal. There was a cheerful twinkle in the latter's eyes as he asserted, "Benziger, that is just what makes you so unique. You are so unpredictable. Never any fuss, never any nonsense, never any ostentation. You are yourself, just plain naive, spontaneous and honest.

I have no objection to riding with beer barrels. You know and I know that I don't imbibe." Just as long as the New York dailies got no snapshot of him in this predicament, he had no objection. The prohibitionists would have loved to publicize the allegation that he had supposedly come to Europe for reasons of health but, in reality, his *ad limina* visit had been a beer-cure!

Each summer season was climaxed by one or two grand picnics which were planned months ahead. Sometimes there might be 20 or more cars following the leader into the High Alps. Since every inch of Swiss soil belonged to one or another farmer, arrangements had to be made well ahead of time. The spot was carefully looked over and the use of the ground paid for so that no irate peasant with pitchfork would charge into the guests. Grass was of more value than money, and hay meant fodder for cattle. Walking across a field was as unpardonable a sin as stealing grain.

Sometimes August tired of the higher altitudes. When a group of older people accompanied him, he enjoyed the quiet of lovely Lake Lucerne, fringed as it is by lovely coves. He especially loved the serene, unknown ones approachable only by boat. Hiring a huge stone-barge that could hold between fifty and a hundred people at a time, he would take along provisions for a feast. Local peasants yodeled and played their accordions. There was relaxation for guests in a setting that was unique. Once the barge grated along the sandy bottom, out jumped the eager guests. In a shady, secluded spot, they found an open fire and huge sides of beef secured on an enormous spit. On one occasion of this sort, Bishop-elect Hayes, Monsignor Carroll and Pat Lannon donned aprons and chef's caps and began to season and turn the roast, and later to carve it for the guests.

The younger male members rolled barrels of Munich beer into the icy mountain streams, cold with glacier water. Other guests melted cheese over the fire; when soft, it was scraped onto fresh bread—the *raclette* being a dish particular to the peasants of Switzerland. August and his wife were perfect hosts. Nothing had been forgotten.

Conversation turned to the fact that Cardinal Farley had been given a large benefaction to be used to beautify St. Patrick's Cathedral, and he hoped to use it to purchase new windows for the Lady Chapel. He had been awed by the luster of the ancient stained-glass of Chartres, and lamented the fact that the making of it had become an almost lost art, so he turned to his Swiss friend to help

him find what was best suited for his church. August, after much
hard work, managed to contact five places, requesting that they
send samples and submit designs. The specifications he outlined
were minute. All five studios replied. In the design chosen, the
many hues blended like faceted gems, creating translucent beauty.
Once the windows were installed, they enhanced not only the Lady
Chapel, but also formed a glorious background of color for the
main altar and sanctuary. With August's help, the cardinal had
been able to achieve an effect he could never have accomplished
alone.

But not all was beauty and serenity that summer of 1914; ominous grumblings among the nations grew louder as war clouds
lowered heavily over Europe. By June 28, peaceful Austria was
thrown into mourning. The heir to the throne of the Austro-
Hungarian Empire, Archduke Franz Ferdinand, and his pretty
young wife had been assassinated by a Serb in Sarajevo. Three
times earlier, Russia had prepared for war; now she was armed to
the teeth. For years, rumors had come and gone. Europe could
never forget that in February 1909, in December 1912 and again in
August 1913, word had leaked out that Russia was ready for war.
Each time Germany retaliated by ordering out her army for full
maneuvers. Europe quivered under this reverberating uncertainty,
this show of force and arms. Then, once again, peace seemed to
settle like a pall to hide the rising storm from sight. August felt
most uneasy; peace of mind was not to be had. He remembered
that for years Bethlehem Steel had shipped mountains of ammunition to Russia. Why should Russia be preparing frantically for
war?

Cardinal Farley talked things over with his host. Should he
return to New York immediately or not? Pope Pius X had urged
him to remain in Europe in order to include the July Eucharistic
Congress at Lourdes in his itinerary. Another month was a short
time; perhaps the danger was not imminent. If there should be a
war, it would certainly be localized in the Balkans, and not affect
the rest of Europe.

Although invited, the Benzigers were not free to accept Cardinal Farley's invitation to go to Lourdes, but August agreed that,
once the Eucharistic Congress was over, he would meet the cardinal in Turin. From Turin, he and the cardinal and the cardinal's
entourage would then drive on to Bobbio. Bobbio, unknown to
most tourists, had once been a prominent seat of learning; there,

one of the oldest and most priceless libraries in Europe had been housed within the confines of monastic walls. The Vatican Collection and the Ambrosian Library in Milan had been enriched by the treasures that its founders had brought there from Ireland; St. Columbanus, a scholar, was the wise monk who had converted not only large areas of Europe, but had also taught the farmers of this section of Italy how to till their arid soil and produce plentiful crops by means of irrigation and systematic planting. Bobbio was a bishopric to whose rehabilitation both Cardinals Farley and O'Connell of Boston had contributed generously. It was the one place in Europe that Cardinal Farley most wanted to see. It was his desire to offer Mass at the shrine of St. Columbanus.

Cardinal Farley, while resting and waiting for August in Turin, wrote Mrs. Benziger. He wanted his hostess to know he had really missed the family. The letter was dated July 30, 1914.

My Dear Mrs. Benziger:

. . . We have had a glorious celebration at Lourdes. The Eucharistic Congress surpassed anything I had anticipated. The evidence of such faith is rarely seen elsewhere. The impressions made will last a lifetime: the splendor of the ceremonial, the Pontifical Mass by the Legate of the pope, Cardinal Belmonte, at which assisted two Cardinals in *Cappa magna*, nearly two thousand archbishops and bishops, more than four thousand priests and eighty thousand of the laity. The Congress was the largest and most distinguished ever held. I only wish you, yourself, and Mr. Benziger could have been there. How the dear children would have enjoyed it!

When August left Brunnen for Turin, he embraced his wife and children, feeling quite sure that everything would go smoothly during his absence. He could count on his wife to keep an eye on everything, as she was far better suited to the hotel business than he, being quiet, calm and serene. Guests could come and could go; she was distant, but kindly and interested in all.

Among the latest arrivals had been the Bellamy Storers. As American Ambassador to the Austrian court and later Minister to Spain, he had served his country well. Unfortunately, his wife brought a brilliant career to a sad end when she unwittingly trod on the toes of Theodore Roosevelt and the papacy.

Maria Longworth Storer came from a prominent Cincinnati family and her list of friends in high places was long. Among

them was Theodore Roosevelt, who had met her when he was Secretary of the Navy. When he became president, he was naturally
eager to win over the support of Catholics through her influence
and activity. She corresponded freely with him, just as she did
with Archbishop John Ireland of St. Paul, Minnesota. Apparently
Roosevelt had hinted to her that he would like to see her episcopal
friend made a cardinal. Mrs. Storer, during a private audience with
Pope Pius X, referred to this desire. Then she unfortunately visited
a noted Roman tailor who made the expensive ecclesiastical robes
necessary for cardinals and hinted at future orders from Archbishop
Ireland. Word of her suggestion got into the press, and the Vatican, displeased at anything coming out before the official Consis-
tory announcement, contradicted the statement: no pronouncement
had been made! Roosevelt, for his part, denied stating any prefer-
ences and felt that he had been placed in an awkward position,
seemingly trying to meddle in ecclesiastical affairs. As a result of
the turmoil, capable, handsome and erudite Ambassador Storer
ended his diplomatic career, and Archbishop Ireland lost his red
hat!

Mrs. Storer was the mother of the Marquise de Chambrun.
For years, she and the Chambrun family had come over to
Brunnen. The Marquis Pierre de Chambrun was a member of the
French Chamber of Deputies and knew more about French politics
than most men in his country. Early one morning, shortly after
August's departure, the hotel manager knocked excitedly at Mrs.
Benziger's door. "The Marquis de Chambrun is most anxious to
speak to you. It is best that no one sees you together. He is wait-
ing for you in my office."

Surprised by the early hour of the interview, Gertrude rushed
downstairs. He told her he was leaving at once for Paris and that,
her husband being away, grave decisions would rest on her shoulders. Within a matter of days, perhaps hours, there would be war.
He begged her to tell no one, but to prepare herself for the worst.
She should lay in a supply of food, and provide herself with the
necessary money. In the event of war, stores would be closed,
banks would refuse to issue cash and railroads would no longer
function. Gertrude listened with growing alarm. He assured her
that a secret message in code had just arrived and he must leave at
once. In order to avoid arousing suspicion, the rest of his family
would follow later. France was on the verge of war. Russia was
mobilizing. Austria would be attacked. Gertrude, grateful for

these warnings, quietly and efficiently prepared for the emergency. She laid in the provisions and telegraphed her husband to return at once.

The first of August was the national Swiss holiday. That was the day when, in 1307, thirty valiant men from the Cantons of Uri, Schwyz and Unterwald formed a league to free themselves from the tyranny of the House of Hapsburg. At Rütil, a meadow almost opposite to Brunnen, with just the Lake of Lucerne separating them from spying soldiers, the men of Helvetia had sworn to become a nation of free men, to die rather than live in slavery.

On that particular first of August in 1914, preparations were on foot for the evening activities. It was customary to set huge bonfires to celebrate Independence Day. Fireworks would light up distant peaks and Lake Lucerne would glow with the color of tiny boats decked with lanterns and gliding across the waters. Then, with the suddenness of a thunderstorm, tolling bells were heard. They echoed and re-echoed from the mountain hamlet of Seelisberg across the lake; the sound clanged ominously. Although midafternoon was a time when no one celebrated, the bells of the village chapel in Brunnen, of the parish church in Ingenbohl and of the nuns' chapel and the orphanage all joined in the warning—clanging, clanging, never ceasing. Everyone became still. From the lips of each one came the dreaded phrase, "It is the *tocsin*."

The *tocsin* shrilled like a fire alarm as each able-bodied male dropped everything. Men and boys of more than 18 ran home. Those who were far away ran to the nearest train in order to join them. Those who lived near seized their guns. Within a few hours, all of Switzerland was a vast military camp. Armed men marched to the nearest town hall for orders.

The concierge at the Grand Hotel was an elderly man. Fortunately he could stay on and was able to pass on the word that Germany had declared war on France, and that Austria had been at war with Serbia for three days. Two hours later, all of France was mobilized. By then, capable Mr. Moser, the hotel manager, was wringing his hands as pandemonium on all sides culminated in a hurried exodus. The hotel staff had automatically disbanded. None seemed to care about money; whether they were paid or not mattered little.

The haughty Prussian *maitre d'hôtel* had assembled his corps of excellent Italian waiters. From under his Mephisthophelean black eyebrows peered tear-reddened eyes. He was no longer interested in jotting down reservations in his date book. What the clients wanted was of no importance, nor was he concerned about the bus boys whom he used to kick for slowness of action. Now, as they lined up before him, he tearfully embraced them, one and all, and he confessed his hatred of going to war. The very men who had worked for and with him, he would probably have to fight. Then, with the bearing of an officer, he right-about-faced, marched toward the swinging pantry door and headed for the kitchen. There he embraced his most hated enemies, among them the loathed French chefs! Now he bade them a fond farewell. They, in turn, dropped everything, tossed aside their tall white hats, yanked off their stained aprons and headed for the first trains that would bring them across the Alsatian border.

The foreigners managed to escape in one frantic rush, to cross frontiers before they became hermetically sealed. There remained at the hotel only the 100 forsaken Americans. These banded together and took counsel with Mrs. Benziger. By then she felt free to pass on the advice given by the Marquis de Chambrun. They sat tight and awaited developments.

Room-service was abolished. The exotic French cuisine was replaced by simple fare. Banks remained shut. Travel agents closed their shutters. Transatlantic transportation was canceled. Belgium and France had been invaded. The disquieting news grew worse from day to day. The hotel lacked a cook so Pat Lannon and Marieli, the 14-year-old daughter of the Benzigers, took turns in concocting plain American food. While lamb stew was a general favorite, boiled-beef, cabbage and plain boiled potatoes were consumed with relish by homesick Americans who had become stranded in the tempestuous heart of Europe. They were no longer particular; anything would do so long as they had food, a roof over their heads and the security of knowing that they would not be thrown out for inability to pay the bill! Brunnen became a haven of safety for those who had no other place to go. Europe now settled down to the routine of war. The fully-mobilized Swiss had manned their frontiers, ready to guard their neutrality with their lives.

Meanwhile, August had reached Turin, unconcerned about happenings elsewhere. He had met the cardinal and the three priests accompanying him, and together they had driven to Bobbio. There they spent the night in the village, tucked away in a mountain fastness which had once been a hermitage for the Irish scholar,

Columbanus. Mass was offered at the basilica, but August, fearing war, urged that there be no delay; it was imperative to reach Switzerland quickly.

As his favorite route lay across the rugged Dolomites, he scurried toward the northern border and Italy's largest lake, the Lake of Garda with its awe-inspiring mountains rising some 6,000 feet above the waters. If all went well, they would head for Cortina where he hoped to receive a telegram from his wife about the political situation. He hoped to make the mountain town before twilight; at dawn they would leave and climb the steep Brenner Pass. On reaching the Italian border, he asked the frontier guardsmen, "What news of war?" They shook their heads, "*Niente . . . niente.*" "Nothing . . . nothing." It really mattered little what went on with the rest of the world in this distant Italian outpost. Passports were not needed anywhere in Europe. Crossing from one country to another was merely a question of routine, so far as civilians were concerned. The car's *triptyque* was looked at, the engine number checked. Farewells were waved, and the Americans were off again on their race for the Brenner.

When the jovial Tyrolean customs officials were sighted, August halted and asked anxiously, "Are the Dolomites safe? I hear there is war between Austria and Serbia. Had we better go to Switzerland via Turin, and not Innsbruck?" The Austrian officials shook their heads, "*Ach*, merely rumor. We Austrians are at peace with the world. If there were a war, we would surely be the first to be notified. No need to worry. Go ahead; the road is clear."

As they ascended the steep hairpin turns of the gigantic Dolomites, the passengers drew the car rugs over their knees. While passing through some of the tiny villages, the cardinal asked, "Why is the Vesper bell ringing at this strange hour? Vespers have been said long ago." Strangely enough, in each hamlet peasants were congregating around the church. The village squares were black with milling people. Something was happening, not in one place but all along the road. August stopped at the nearest village, listened, then turned white. "That is the *tocsin*. There is war. This is the only means the outlying farmers have of knowing; they must arm and report at once."

August spoke to some of the natives. They informed him that the order for general mobilization had been issued. Austria was indeed at war. In no time, roads that had been empty and forsaken rumbled with the noise of horses and ox-drawn carts and carriages of every description, all headed in the same direction. The road to Cortina was jammed with hurrying humanity. There was nothing to do. Caught in this snail's pace, the party barely moved. Children were clinging to the menfolk; women were weeping. Cortina, the mountain town that should have been reached by twilight, was entered only after midnight. Exhausted, the men found beds in the deserted *Hotel de la Poste*. The only maid still present showed them to their rooms. Sleep was impossible; the village reverberated with cries and screams and excitement as trucks carried men off to war.

August roused the group at dawn and suggested that only the cardinal say Mass; it was imperative to move as quickly as possible. Cardinal Farley offered the liturgy for peace. There was no breakfast. Besides, the parish priest urged that they get out and get out fast; foreigners were to be interned. Cars were to be confiscated. There was no time to lose; things were very serious. At the hotel, no one was about to collect the bill. The town was deserted. Gasoline was urgently needed as without it the journey could not continue at all. Everywhere stores had been shut down, but finally they located a distant one where a tearful child told them that his daddy had gone to war and left him here alone. Gas? Oh, yes, there was gas in the basement. He led the way. By lighting a match, they were able to follow the tiny creature who was too small to lift the five-gallon cans of fuel. Soon a procession was formed, each of the priests, as well as the cardinal, hauled the vital liquid to the car. They filled the tank, and then every available place, even the running board was loaded with extra cans of gas. The cardinal, the priests, August all sat on containers of the volatile fluid which might mean the difference between getting home safely or being interned for the duration.

August had no intention of permitting the cardinal to fall into the hands of the Austrians. He wanted no international incident. A telegram from Gertrude had reached him that night at Cortina, telling him that Switzerland was mobilizing. He took his seat next to the chauffeur who, fortunately, was a Swiss, and gave orders that he was to stop for no one until they reached the Swiss frontier. In his hand he held his three-toned silver trumpet which was used on dangerous mountain passes to warn the postilion drivers of on-coming cars.

On their mad dash for the Swiss frontier, they began to see troops in marching formation. Soldiers, thousands of them with guns and supplies, were heading for Cortina. Louder and louder the trumpet sounded. More and more insistent was August that the speed be stepped up. The six men in gray dusters clung to their seats as the car sped over dangerous curves at 50 and 60 miles an hour. Heavy tires screeched. The tense, frayed nerves of every man waited, fearful of the false move which, fortunately, never came.

The military formation grew denser. By rights, the car should have stopped as marching armies certainly have the right of way, yet August knew that wave after wave of armed men would soon engulf them. As legions of artillery and cavalry moved on, he daringly blew his trumpet. As if by magic, the soldiers cleared the road. To the right, to the left, the men parted. August and his guests drove right down the center, heading for Innsbruck. Officers saluted. The salutes were returned with military precision by the erect, diminutive little cardinal and the four others. Cardinal Farley had been taken for a general *en route* to Innsbruck for a vital military staff meeting.

None of the passengers in that car knew how close they were to death. Orders had been given to shoot on sight six escaping spies. Dead or alive, they had to be caught. Only a roadblock right outside of Innsbruck stopped August's party. Instantly they were surrounded by infuriated soldiers. An Austrian general in person placed them under arrest, commanding that the prisoners and their car be taken to the Town Hall.

Inside the imposing building, situated in the heart of the city, an impressive array of generals had assembled, as the Defense Council for the Austrian Empire had held an all-night session. The huge courtroom was packed with the highest-ranking officials. Into this array of ornate uniforms were ushered the six dusty, bedraggled tourists. They had been roughly shoved, jostled like common criminals. The military guards held tightly to their prisoners. Sentries with flashing bayonets saw that no one came near. Fortunately the group was kept together. A court-martial was immediately begun. Without further questioning, they were condemned as spies.

August rose in the presence of the assembled council. He pleaded that they be given a chance to defend themselves. If these gentlemen were arrested, he asserted, dire consequences would ensue. He had only done his duty. He was responsible for the safety of these prominent American ecclesiastics. He did not want

Cardinal Farley and Bishop Hayes to be caught inside Austria, so they were heading for Switzerland. He had made a mad dash for the Swiss border since he had heard that the deadline for crossings was that very night; otherwise they would be interned, and the car confiscated.

The general who was the judge considered the cardinal an important spy. Although August, because of his car, had his *tryptyque,* there was no guarantee that the four men in gray had not hired him for espionage. Sneering, he pointed to the so-called priests from America. Why were they disguised? Where were their habits? Angrily, August pleaded. Since passports were not carried, would His Honor order the guards to search the vest pockets of these men? In America, it was customary for tailors to insert the names of their customers in their custom-made suits; thus they could verify that he had spoken the truth. The clergy were searched immediately. Even this evidence did not satisfy the highly-skeptical judge. Monsignor Hayes suddenly remembered his "faculties," which were papers signed and sealed by the bishop authorizing a priest to perform his priestly functions. Without this document, permission to offer Mass outside of one's diocese could be denied. He handed all four of the "faculties" cards to the guard, requesting in English that they be taken to the bench. The judge looked at each. As he came to the name of Cardinal Farley, the sneer slid from his lips. He looked up. Two soldiers had brought the diminutive prelate before him. Everything happened so quickly that it was only then that the cardinal realized that his identity had been doubted. He slipped off his gray duster and stood there in his clerical coat and Roman collar, with the little touch of cardinal red outlining the neck of the soutane. He adjusted his red skullcap. This gesture caught the general's eye, just as he was about to command that this man be thrown into jail. Instantly this official who had been so rude, so unbelieving, rose to his feet, and spontaneously every soldier and officer in the hall followed suit. Apologizing for his incredulity, he fell on his knees, as did all present, and asked for a blessing. As the cardinal looked about the room, he realized that this drama could only have been acted out in a Catholic country.

Outside on the streets below, crowds shouted, "Down with the spies. Kill the traitors." Fearing for their safety, the general detailed a military escort to protect them.

As Innsbruck was left behind, August told the chauffeur not to stop until they had reached the Swiss frontier. All night they rode through the Arlberg Mountain Pass, on to Feldkirch, and there they crossed into Switzerland. In Brunnen, Gertrude was keeping watch. She felt certain that if anyone could get back home, her husband would somehow manage the feat. Then, early one morning, from the hotel terrace there was heard the familiar silver trumpet as the car rounded the steep curve leading into the property. The Lancia suddenly sputtered, backfired and stopped and everyone rushed down the hill to greet the wanderers. Wild excitement prevailed as the chauffeur threw up his hands in horror, "Not another drop of gasoline!" "Thank God, we are home!" shouted the cardinal as he patted the chauffeur on the back, mindful that they all owed their lives to Rudi and to his courage and skill.

The men in the car were white with dust and ashen from fatigue. As they rose from what had been their potentially-explosive gasoline-tank seats, everyone laughed. When the cardinal tapped the tins, they resounded, hollow and empty. Bishop-elect Hayes approached the weary cardinal, took him by the arm and led him to the hotel. "Your Eminence, it was also Monsignor Edwards and not Rudi alone who brought us home safely. Not once since we left Innsbruck has he opened an eye. He sat on the edge of his seat, clutching his rosary, his lips never ceasing to move. These *Ave Marias* must have opened the way to home and safety." Monsignor Edwards, well on in his 80s, and always one to enjoy excitement, replied with calm dignity, "I've had the thrill of a lifetime. Enough excitement to last me forever. No need to make fun of me now. You know I've always wanted to see this part of Europe—though I hadn't planned to do so." Monsignor Carroll responded with his youthful laugh, "Oh, so? You've seen lots since we were arrested yesterday afternoon! You've seen nothing, since you had your eyes closed all the while. I'm positive you prayed us into safety." "Come, now," said the aged priest, shaking his head, "Let's be perfectly honest. You know we were not driving, we were fairly flying! I really do believe I prefer horses to automobiles!" In his joy to be back in Brunnen, he shook hands warmly with Mrs. Benziger and even embraced all three children.

As he reached the door, Cardinal Farley turned and went up to his host. "You've given me a perfectly wonderful ride. I never had one minute of doubt that you would manage everything for the best. Thank you for taking us to Bobbio—thank you also for bringing us home!" That afternoon the Lancia was turned over to the Swiss army for the use of the military authorities. Five years later, after having seen duty at the front, it came home.

It was a mistake to think that now calm would be settling in for Cardinal Farley. On August 20 he received a telegram from the Secretary of State at the Vatican. In it, Cardinal Merry del Val informed him that Pope Pius X had died. Heartbroken at the loss of a father and friend, both Cardinal Farley and Bishop-elect Hayes wept unashamedly. All that day, the former closeted himself in his room while Monsignor Hayes went to seek solace in the dense pine forest behind the hotel. The Benziger children had heard of the loss and had seen from their window how, bowed with grief, the Monsignor had headed for the hills where he remained for six hours. Knowing and revering him, they had slipped through the dense pine needles to watch, and to marvel that great men are also human, that they could suffer and weep like anyone else. The Cardinal and his party were prepared to leave within 24 hours for the rituals in Rome. Before the farewells and departure, a small ceremony was planned; the guests were assembled and each was asked to contribute a little something. Money was so scarce then that even a few dollars seemed much to the once-wealthy Americans. Bishop Hayes had written, then read, a tribute to Mr. and Mrs. Benziger:

> In this supremely critical hour of European history when, like a bolt from the blue, the destiny of races and nations has been cast in the balance of might and arms; when sunlit hills, smiling valleys and fertile plains that yesterday were havens of peace and rest are overnight transformed into martial camps and foreboding battlefields; when the channels of travel on the highways of sea and land have been menaced, and the agencies of communications with home are disrupted by armies in battle array:

> We, the American guests of the Grand Hotel, Brunnen, who find ourselves strangers under foreign flags and cut off from all we hold dear, recognize that we have been singularly blessed, under an All-Wise and Fatherly Providence, not only with safe sanctuary and generous hospitality, but more than all, with a hearth and home under the roof of Mr. and Mrs. August Benziger.

> We, therefore, take occasion, by this presentation, to express, in some slight measure, how profoundly appreciative and everlastingly grateful we are to our host and hostess; to our

host, for his wisdom in counsel, his strength in our anxiety, his sacrifice of self-interest and his large-minded nobility in providing for our comfort; to our hostess, for the prudence and courage manifested in the first days of the crisis, for the charming sweetness and delightful grace with which she has reigned so queenly over us all as one large family.

In the village they had bought a silver loving cup; the 80-some guests presented it and remained to express their thanks and gratitude for aid given at a most difficult time. That evening there were many tears. The Grand Hotel family had become cemented in friendship; war had brought them together even more closely than had peace. The next day there was a void. Cardinal Farley and his party had reached Rome from where he had written:

> We are now in the *Hotel de l'Europe*. I sent you a telegram informing you of our safe arrival. The train service in Italy has not been seriously interfered with. All is very quiet and [there is] no evidence of war.
>
> The only thing is the money trouble. The banks are very conservative and reluctant to let much money out. Americans, thanks to our government, can get money on letters of credit, etc.
>
> The Holy Father's funeral ceremonies continue, but the body was buried last Saturday in the crypt of St. Peter's.
>
> Cardinals O'Connor and Gibbons are on the sea, coming from New York to Naples. Cardinal Gasquet arrived last night from England.
>
> I hope that you are well. We were very lonesome leaving what had been a real home to us, with all the agreeable guests of the Hotel to make everything still more agreeable.

Back in Brunnen, things went on as usual. August tried his best to arrange for transportation. He who could wangle hotel accommodations and passage on sold-out ships now found his hands tied. One of the New York guests heard of a sailing vessel; passage could be had at a cost of $1,000 per person. Mrs. Loree and some 20 other Americans hurriedly signed up. August begged her to bide her time, as he felt this crossing could be made only at great risk. Nevertheless, the group departed, and eventually reached America, but not without much discomfort.

A few days later, Cardinal Farley sent a telegram from Rome, notifying August that he had passage for the five Benzigers on the

Santa Anna sailing from Rome on September 15. A letter soon followed, begging the family not to delay. Should Italy break the Triple Alliance and enter the war, there would be no telling when they would get out of Europe. August needed no second prompting. Already packed for an emergency, the family left Brunnen at once.

On reaching Rome, they were met by Monsignor Hayes who took them quickly to rooms he had reserved in their names at the *Hotel Royal*. The Eternal City was one of the few capitals left in Europe that was not plunged into military darkness. The Conclave had come to an end. Cardinal Giacomo Della Chiesa, the former archbishop of Bologna, had been made pope and taken the name Benedict XV.

Since the Benziger sisters had never been to Rome, Monsignor Hayes became their *cicerone* and took them everywhere, even to places where few travelers went. Meanwhile, Cardinal O'Connell of Boston had landed, bitterly disappointed at being too late for the Conclave. A friend of the Benzigers, he arrived at the hotel one day in a cab laden with all kinds and sizes of pictures. He wanted the candid opinion of the artist as to their value and authenticity. Another friend then in Rome was Cardinal Gasquet, whom August had known when he was a student at Downside in England. For many years this prelate had summered in Brunnen and come to know the children from their infancy upwards. At times he had shown marked annoyance at their Americanization of the English language, and even suggested that they be spanked for naughtiness. "Spare the rod and spoil the child," he had philosophized in their presence. If they all venerated, they also feared this English cardinal. Yet, after their visit to the old roman *Palazzo di San Callisto,* these fears vanished. In 1907, this renowned Benedictine historian had been assigned by the pope the duty of revising the Vulgate, so Cardinal Gasquet was well prepared to lead a conducted tour through rooms stacked from floor to ceiling with mellowed, priceless vellum and parchment sheets. He explained how, with the aid of X-ray, original texts had been unearthed hiding behind the current surfaces. Copyists of centuries ago, lacking parchment, had erased the original words and designs, and reused the priceless vellum. He also explained that St. Jerome, in the 4th century, had known no Hebrew. Having neither grammar nor dictionary, he had had to learn the language by heart. Naturally, he was bound to make mistakes in producing his translation of the

Bible; so, too, the men who transcribed his writings. The tedious but fascinating assignment of editing this important text would last beyond the Cardinal's lifespan. Others would have to assist in completing the revision of the Latin version of the Bible.

Only someone like Cardinal Farley could have arranged for an audience with the new pope. Mindful that their days in Europe were numbered, he asked Benedict XV as a personal favor to grant this privilege to the Benzigers. The highlight of their stay in Rome was their visit with the venerable pontiff upon whose shoulders would fall the burdens of war-torn Europe. The entire family had the joy of being present at the first public audience granted by the new pope. August was especially impressed by this man who was even smaller than Cardinal Farley, and whose mien was far from attractive—almost ugly, yet whose bearing was noble. His kindly face brightened as he spoke, gesticulating with his beautiful hands. His coal-black hair was slightly sprinkled with gray; he seemed neither old nor young. On making the rounds, his *Maestro di Camera* recognized August and whispered to the pontiff that he had just arrived from Switzerland.

Four days later, a far greater joy was in store for the family. On Saturday, September 12 at 11 a.m., August drove in state with his family to the *Portone di Bronzo*. Formal invitations were presented. The Swiss Guards saluted smartly and presented arms. Then an escort accompanied the Benzigers up the marble steps of the *Scala Regia* to the huge *Cortile del Belvedere*. All the pomp and pageantry were set in motion as though August were a member of a royal family. His children could hardly believe their eyes; they were dazzled by the bowing and saluting. Through one *antecamera* to another they were ushered until the *Sala del Tronetta* was reached.

The Throne Room was crowded. Each pilgrim was assigned a specific place by the *Maestro di Camera*, whose duty it was to know all persons present. This time, as the Holy Father walked around in a quiet, informal manner, he recognized August, stopped to converse with him in French and asked how long he proposed to remain in Rome; what were his plans? August explained that he would be leaving the next day for Naples; that Cardinal Farley had made it possible for him to sail on the same ship with him when he returned to America. Benedict XV smiled. "Ah, give the Cardinal our final good wishes. We will ask God to bless you and give you a *bon voyage*."

Marieli, Hélène and Marguerite could hardly contain their curiosity. Once outside the Vatican, they pestered their parents with questions. How was it that the Swiss Guards had formed an honor guard to escort their father? Why was it that the Noble Guard, the Palatine Guard and the Gendarmi each in turn had snapped to attention and saluted? August said nothing; he was reticent about honors. Their mother explained that it was because of the medals their father was wearing. For the first time they had seen him don a beautiful enameled cross and star and ribbons. These, they learned, were the honors he had received from the King of Portugal. Being a Swiss, and loyal to his country, he would only wear them within the precincts of the Vatican, for they were all Church honors. Not only was he really a Knight, but a Commander of the Order of Christ. Were he a citizen of a country other than Switzerland or the United States, he would be Sir August and she Lady Gertrude.

The excitement of leaving Europe, the final preparations for sailing, meant getting to Naples in time. The *Santa Anna* was a tiny freighter that had, at the most, carried a dozen passengers. She had now been converted into a passenger liner transporting 200 travelers. Cardinal Farley, escorted by Cardinal Logue of Ireland, was already on board. The tiny cabin assigned to the five Benzigers was so small that two would have had to sleep on the floor. Fortunately Cardinal Farley came to their rescue. He explained that he had inquired about acquiring more space, and the captain had offered to give up his own spacious stateroom, into which Cardinal Farley would move. The Benzigers could take over his cabin and so cross in comparative comfort. The stewards were sailors who had never waited on anyone. The tables were mere planks on trestles, set up with plates, spoons and knives. Forks were at a premium, yet everyone was so delighted to be escaping from Europe that no one really cared whether there was proper service, food or bedding.

The crossing on the *Santa Anna* was eventful. Fortunately, there was a remarkable captain whose clear head managed to steer the ship through mutiny on the Mediterranean and a hurricane on the Bay of Biscay. The Straits of Gibraltar should have been reached in moonlight. Instead, a dense fog shrouded them from view. The weary passengers had gone to bed, listening to the blowing of the fog horn every few seconds, and then the ship came to such a sudden halt that the reversing of the engines threw many out of their narrow bunks. Automatically the lights had been switched off. Expecting a disaster, August had called the children and rushed up on deck. Hand in hand, they groped up the gangway. In ghastly silence, the ship listed, as terrified passengers peered into the dense fog. Far below, a huge searchlight played on the side of the vessel. Someone said it was from a submarine—in all probability, a German one. Although the name *Santa Anna* had been painted over, this was a French ship sailing between Spanish and French ports and carrying cargoes of Malaga grapes.

Not once, but several times, that submarine slowly circled the *Santa Anna*; then, out of the dark, came a loud voice: "Who goes there?" From the bridge the captain shouted, "*Santa Anna* of the Fabre line, out of Naples, heading for New York." Again in English came the words, "We are going to board you." The passengers groaned. English was the universal language of the seas. Were the Germans going to search all papers, as had the Italians just out of Naples? The *Santa Anna* had barely left the Bay of Naples when an Italian patrol boat had halted the ship and soldiers came aboard. Every Italian-American male had been taken off forcibly. Although Cardinal Farley had protested, the weeping, angry passengers had, nevertheless, been taken ashore.

Now the ship was being boarded again. In darkness, the weary, tense passengers waited for what seemed endless moments. Finally, word came from the bridge—it was an English submarine!

Just as suddenly as they had been turned off, the lights came on. The passengers looked at each other in dismay and embarrassment. Everyone had rushed to the deck in a frantic effort to find out what was wrong. Cardinal Farley looked sheepishly at his white flannel nightgown, with slits up the sides. Portly Monsignor Carroll was in his striped pajamas. Kindly, tired Monsignor Edwards had on his flannel BVD's, and a hat on his head. The only man on board who was properly dressed was Bishop Hayes, who had on his trousers and a shirt, and in his hand he carried a briefcase filled with important papers pertaining to the archdiocese of New York. August was barefooted and in his nightshirt. The only other ones to be "modestly attired" were the women, most of whom wore coats or dressing-gowns. The pent-up emotions of the past half-hour were now broken. Everyone laughed hilariously as the men made hurried exits.

The English, knowing that the German submarines were waiting to sink the *Santa Anna*, had sent their ships in search of the vessel. They wished to give her advanced warning and feared that she might sneak out of the Straits before becoming aware of the danger awaiting her. All that night, the *Santa Anna* anchored safe under the protection of the British navy. Next morning at dawn, she was escorted by British submarines to make sure there would be no attack.

Before she reached New York, August's premonitions came true. Grand Duke Nicholas of Russia addressed the Austro-Hungarian population and invited them to throw off the Hapsburg yoke. The Romanians occupied Transylvania. The war, which everyone had hoped would be curbed, finally flared into fury instead. Germany, glad for an excuse to aggravate the Russians, marched into France and Belgium. The war that had been hovering on the horizon for years now engulfed all Europe. Europe was burning.

CHAPTER 15

Years of the War
(1914-1919)

Once back in New York, strangely enough, the terrors of the war were soon forgotten. America was so far away! Life was so very comfortable! The horrible conflict between Russia, Germany and others on the European continent seemed remote to the average American.

August's clients continued to show their gratitude by showering him with gifts, but he resented anything that might give his family a false sense of pride and encourage them to look upon frivolities as essentials. He had a strange way of disposing immediately of any gift that was sent, especially extravagant presents. When the huge, beautifully-wrapped candy boxes came, they never stayed long in his home. A regular routine was followed: the entire family was assembled to admire, to comment, to gaze at the expensive gift, then the boxes were sent right off to a family that might appreciate them far more than would his own. There were the O'Gormans with their seven children, or Mrs. Achenbach in distant Texas whose sweet tooth could never be satisfied.

Sometimes, instead of candies, there were baskets of luscious fruit. The Benziger chauffeur immediately picked them up to transfer them to their final destination. Potted plants and lovely floral arrangements were treated in the same manner; they were taken to a sick friend whom they could cheer or, perhaps, to ornament the private chapel of Cardinal Farley. Austerity was the hallmark of the Benziger home. Essentials were not lacking. The children were surrounded by exquisite and priceless works of art, yet August saw to it that none of them would be mistaken about the real values in life; otherwise, they might easily become spoiled or anesthetized into a false sense of security.

The humdrum routine of childhood lost its monotony because of the comings and goings of the many clients. All sorts of people flocked through the doors of that New York studio. Some left behind a deep impression of loveliness and friendliness. Others, with haughty mein, lorgnettes and mincing steps stared soullessly. After making a round of the studio in their supercilious manner, they stalked out as they had stalked in, leaving a nasty taste behind.

There were many distractions to be enjoyed from the girls' 10th-floor bedroom. Nightly there was the clattering of hooves as dozens of carriages drove in style to deposit the befurred and bejewelled concert goers at Carnegie Hall. Later, when automobiles replaced the horses, the tooting of horns broke the romance of prancing thoroughbreds, just as the pretty lawns, or brownstone houses were to be replaced by ugly skyscrapers and lofty apartment houses. The Fifty-seventh Street residential district quickly descended to the level of a typical business street, albeit one frequented by music lovers and art enthusiasts.

The children knew the day of the week by the sound of the ragpicker's call: he rang his melodious bell as his mangy horse ambled down the cobblestoned street. The advent of spring was heralded by the call of the flower peddler; his potted daffodils or bright geraniums carried their cheerful message all the way to the 10th floor. Sometimes the joyful strain of the organ-grinder had the children rushing to the windows. No one made them happier than the burly Italian whose organ melodies wafted to their heights. Marguerite, the youngest, regaled her sisters by tossing carefully-wrapped pennies to the street below. These she had hidden frugally for just such occasions. Nothing pleased her more than the pert little monkey with his red cap who picked up the coins for his master. The organ-grinder would go on cranking his hurdy-gurdy while, from the sidewalk below, people looked up to see from which window the rain of pennies came. Marguerite was often reprimanded for her extravagance, but she would reply, "Well, Bishop Hayes told me that an organ-grinder is every bit as useful as a doctor or a lawyer. He has the vocation of making people happy through music."

Daily, after classes at either Miss Spence's School, which was attended by the two older girls, or the Sacred Heart Convent on Madison Avenue, where Marguerite studied, the girls were chaperoned to Central Park where mademoiselle permitted them to roller-skate. Once in a while she could be induced to leave her park bench and walk as far as the Fifth Avenue zoo. All the same, the children loathed the park. Only when snow and ice shrouded the city and the Fifty-ninth Street pond froze over did they really feel happy, skating to their heart's content. Still, they longed for the freedom and beauty of the Swiss mountains; Central Park could not bear comparison with them!

There were times when rowdy boys would shout at the girls dressed in identical striped jackets: "Hello, Sing Sing!" or they would call and whistle: "Say! When did you get out of Sing Sing?" Mademoiselle was of no earthly help. She could not even tell them what "Sing Sing" meant, but they felt instinctively that the shouts were not complimentary ones.

When clients stayed for an informal family luncheon or dinner, the children were naturally present; however, they had been taught that they "should be seen but never heard." When alone though, orders were reversed, for nothing impressed August more than a good conversationalist. He insisted that his daughters should learn how to talk intelligently, for the art of conversation was as essential to him as were polished manners. One fatal day, Marieli, wishing to start a conversation, asked: "Mama, what does Sing Sing mean?" Startled, her father looked up: "What a stupid question! Besides, I thought you were all forbidden to read the horrible New York papers!" Anxious to avoid a scene, their mother, with her accustomed quiet dignity, replied: "Children, Sing Sing is a place that is never even spoken of. It is a horrible prison where hardened criminals are sent to atone for crimes." The sisters looked at each other wonderingly. Why should they have been asked if they came from Sing Sing? Hélène, who was always conscious of her clothing, suddenly realized the full implication. Hurriedly she asked, "What do they wear at Sing Sing?" Visibly annoyed, then, her father replied: "Why must we discuss something as trivial as prison clothing? Anyone with sense knows they wear stripes. . . ." Marguerite asked saucily, "Stripes? Papa, big green and white ones? Big broad ones?" Not caring to waste any more time on this subject, the exasperated head of the family commented: "Naturally, they have to be big and broad; besides, color is immaterial, whether they are green and white or black and white— anything, as long as they can be perceived miles away. The important thing is to have the wearer stand out from the crowd. I feel certain that if you girls kept your eyes glued on your text books instead of reading lurid headlines, none of you would be so concerned about what goes on in Sing Sing." The impact of that remark spoiled the girls' appetites. From then on, they flatly refused to wear their lovely, warm green-and-white-striped jackets, new only the year before, as they had become objects of horror to them.

Being an artist, August felt that he could indulge in idiosyncracies. He really abhorred plain, drab, neutral tones, and only long-sufferingly tolerated his wife's black and gray clothes because tradition demanded drab colors of a Swiss wife, but as to his children—that was a different matter. They were rarely in Switzerland long enough to upset the natives, and besides, they were young, so he insisted that they wear bright, cheerful plaids, checks or tweeds. He liked them in identical dresses, according to French custom. Strangely enough, in New York no two people wore the same clothes, so his three tall girls caused quite a sensation as they walked down the streets and avenues.

Much to everyone's chagrin, the eldest never conformed to man-made plans. She shot up like an asparagus plant; at eleven, she topped six feet. The taller she grew, the more difficult it became to keep her in clothing; her dresses cost a small fortune and the bills infuriated August. Furthermore, as the villagefolk of Einsiedeln were shocked by seeing such long legs covered only by socks, they muttered about these immoral Americans who indecently exposed too much flesh. From then on, Marieli was forbidden to wear socks and, although only a child, she had prudently to don long, black-ribbed stockings—summer and winter—and her pretty ankles were covered by ugly buttoned shoes!

The sisters dressed alike, even to lace corset covers and hand-embroidered petticoats, and all three were growing so rapidly that their father sent for a French seamstress, Madame Lazaro, and requested that she do something about adapting the outgrown dresses. His budget forbade further expenditure on clothing for them for a two-year period. During that time he permitted only the addition of plain borders of brown, blue or white at hem and wrists. The elongated wardrobe would be sufficient for them.

Fortunately, during this perplexing time, Mr. Lytton came to the rescue of his grandchildren. Being in the clothing business, he groaned aloud to his daughter, "Gertrude, the children look like freaks. You simply cannot let these sights walk about the streets. Put a stop to it, and tell your husband you refuse to tolerate this humiliation." Gertrude, who had never hesitated to carry out her father's wishes, only with difficulty restrained herself from weeping, and replied: "August has such strange notions. He feels we must economize. Besides, Marieli grows by leaps and bounds; it is nonsense. Every few months she needs an entire new wardrobe, which we simply cannot afford. In Switzerland, two suits of clothes last a lifetime. If we lived there, our children would be forced to wear black . . . ; anything, my dear father, is better than black. I do agree that these borders added to the hems look like patchwork, yet there is no alternative. August holds the purse strings."

Grandpa Lytton had other notions. Fortunately for all concerned, the head of the household was off on business; that meant that Grandpa had *carte blanche*. He hired a car, and the entire family went on a shopping spree which ended at Huylers, where they all excitedly ordered forbidden chocolate sodas.

Gertrude and her father left no stone unturned in the process of finding clothing suitable for three growing young women. They were so carefully conservative in their choices that the scrutinizing eye of August never detected the new outfits until months later. By the time he did, it was far too late to cause a scene.

On their way to Mass at St. Patrick's, he noted with pride how handsome his three girls looked. Startled, he stopped and commented, "Why, Gerty . . . when did you buy those new hats? How could you be so extravagant? The panama ones I bought three years ago in Mexico are as good as new . . . ." "Yes, dear," she murmured anxiously, "They are still very good. The girls wear them every day to school." Marguerite, whose ears were always primed to catch snatches of conversation, remarked, "Papa, it was Grandpa that gave us these Easter hats. We got them and our coats three months ago." Ashamed at having let such an important matter slip, August lapsed into silence, inwardly acquiescing that the new outfits were most becoming.

Not all of August's attention was concentrated upon painting and pragmatism; his spiritual life was important. Ever a practical man, he developed it by means of a definite pattern, attending Sunday Mass and liturgies on holy days with great regularity, but he seems never to have had spurts of fervor. He took his religion as a matter of fact. Sunday after Sunday, he followed the same routine until the day of his death. Five minutes before the time to leave for Mass, the girls lined up in anxious readiness as his hurried exit from his studio meant that everyone was to spring into action.

Marieli assisted him into his heavy overcoat. Hélène handed him his soft felt fedora with its crown well-creased lengthwise. Always meticulous about his appearance, he held the hat in his hand, studied it carefully to make sure it had been brushed, then rolled the brim high on both sides. Elegance personified, he took the gloves and prayer book which Marguerite held. Tardiness was never tolerated; anyone who kept Papa waiting felt his wrath. The procession of five left the elevator to march down the street to Fifth Avenue where they met with much bowing and hat doffing. No matter how angry August might be with his own brood, he was, perhaps, excessively polite to the outside world. People stopped to gape, to comment, to wonder at the extraordinarily handsome couple with their well-mannered children.

Every Saturday, the girls were escorted to the cathedral for confession by their mother herself. Unfortunately Gertrude never managed to have her husband join them. He had strange notions about the reception of this sacrament and would not tolerate the presence of his family when he furtively slipped into a confessional. Confession was something that concerned his soul and God alone. It was no one's business how often he went or to whom he confessed. No one except a Capuchin Father would do. In Europe he would drive great distances to visit these simple sons of St. Francis; in New York he had his chosen confessor at the Capuchin monastery where a German-speaking priest served to shrive him.

How his daughters dreaded the day when Papa went to confession. Though he never divulged the fact ahead of time, sooner or later they learned that they would have to share his lengthy penance. Sheepishly, after dinner he would startle the assembled household with: "Now, instead of playing dominoes, we will go to our bedroom to say the rosary." Meekly the girls followed their happy mother there. Nothing pleased Gertrude more than the knowledge that her husband would, on the following morning, join the rest of the family at the Communion rail. He was Jansenistic in his attitude toward frequent reception of the Eucharist, and felt that it was imperative to go to Confession far more often than was the general custom.

The entire family knelt around the huge king-size rosewood bed. Devoutly August began to pray the mysteries of the rosary in German. His daughters dreaded the elongated version which he used and could never fathom why he always received long penances when all they ever had were a few *Aves* or *Pater Nosters*.

He said not only the Joyful but also the Sorrowful and Glorious mysteries. Once in a while, he ended there; sometimes he continued and added fifteen more decades. Knees ached; encroaching sleep made it difficult to keep eyelids open, since each rosary took at least 20 minutes. August would not, under any circumstances, be hurried with prayer. Once the lengthy penance was completed, Papa would jump from his knees and seem in such a jovial mood that the girls forgot their tiredness. He kissed them, sighing contentedly. "I'm so glad you helped me say my penance; alone I would never have finished. We never know when we are going to die; this way, I will be quite ready."

Always austere, even severe with his own family, he constantly helped others in trouble. A friend, who later became a client, was in difficulty. John H. Patterson of Dayton, Ohio, was proprietor of the National Cash Register Company. Having been accustomed to breaking the Sherman Anti-Trust Law, he, with 26 of his colleagues, was prosecuted by the government. They lost their case, and were sentenced to short prison terms. Their cause would later come before the Supreme Court. August took the matter to heart, so he went to Washington to talk over the matter with President Theodore Roosevelt. He was aware that this president had clashed more than once with the masters of finance in his fight against Wall Street, and felt that he was right in not permitting a concentration of power in a few hands, yet this particular case seemed to have been treated unfairly. August told the president so in plain language. Why, he asked, was he trying to ruin big business? Roosevelt listened attentively, yet he could not be swayed. August then warned that he would advise Patterson to fight to save his honor.

Leaving Washington and returning to Dayton, he was commissioned to paint the Patterson portrait. During the course of the sittings, he asked his client why he had chosen a man of another political party as his defense lawyer, and one diametrically opposed to all of his own principles. "How can you expect that Mr. Maxwell will fight your cause? What made you do this when you should have had a great lawyer like John B. Stanchfield? He is a New Yorker with power." Patterson seemed worried, and confided that he had once asked Stanchfield to defend him, but that his price of $100,00 was far too steep for him to pay. August asked how much Maxwell had charged. "So far I have paid out $80,000." August smiled wryly: "$80,000 for a verdict of guilty and a jail sentence thrown in. Why, Mr. Patterson, how can you place so little value on your freedom? It is not too late; let me try to see what I can do with Mr. Stanchfield." Patterson doubted that much could be done at this late date; besides, he had no means of approaching such a powerful lawyer. "Leave it to me," replied August:

> Years ago when I first came to America, I went to him. Your case is much easier. I was in Pittsburgh painting the Thaw family. Mrs. William Thaw, Jr., had insisted on my coming to America. Just to prevent me from becoming too discouraged she had me paint half her family. I was lastingly grateful for her generosity and interest. Had she not insisted, I would never have come to this country.

> Now the Thaw family had a great tragedy befall them. One of their near relatives, Harry K. Thaw, killed New York's most noted architect, Stanford White, at the height of his career. He shot him in cold blood in Madison Square Garden.

> Fortunately, having lived as much in Paris as I had, I knew a good deal about this murderer. He had none too savory a reputation. His notorious conduct had led people on the Continent to classify him as that "crazy Thaw" or that "crazy American." I immediately visited his grief-stricken mother in New York and pleaded that she engage John B. Stanchfield to prove the insanity of her son. No one in his right mind would have carried on as he had in Europe.

Mr. Patterson listened attentively. When August had finished, he looked relieved: "If you think you can accomplish anything, try."

August planned a formal dinner. Stanchfield, only the preceding week, had asked him to arrange for him to meet Cardinal Farley. This would be a moment for introductions if the artist primed the Cardinal as well, reminding him that Patterson had previously taken trouble to show him through his factories. The dinner given shortly afterwards in honor of Cardinal Farley was a huge success. John Stanchfield would be delighted to plead for Patterson before the Supreme Court. When the case was finally heard, Mr. Patterson and his partners won out, thus enabling them to clear their names.

August had learned to place great value on dinner parties. Cosmopolitan in his point of view, he thoroughly enjoyed sharing his friends with others, for friends were God-given, so he used every opportunity to have them meet and profit from each other's company. Only August could have risked taking a list of names and shuffling them like a deck of cards. An expert in his knowledge of human nature, he could bring together a conglomeration of people, and bring about amazing results.

Gertrude was a tremendous asset; she knew how to carry out his slightest wish, and loved him enough to do so. Through 50 years of married life, she was to complement him, and supplement for what her husband lacked. What one did well, the other could appreciate. Without Gertrude, his life would have been barren; he would have lacked the stability necessary to cope with the requirements of his position. Her rare beauty, her exquisite manners, her tremendous tact won for both enduring friendships. August, so easily bored with the frivolities of society, leaned increasingly on Gertrude. His wife, in turn, thoroughly enjoyed these niceties of social encounter; she knew how to make the best and the most of them.

There were times when Gertrude, sometimes timid, would shudder at August's boldness. He had the self-assurance of a psychiatrist, and probed with the penetration of a physician, in order to bring together a covey of divergent characters. It was his firmly-held conviction that certain elements of society benefitted from rubbing elbows with people of opposite tastes and varying forms of education. He shuffled place cards as though preparing for a rubber of bridge. Aghast, one day his wife exclaimed: "Look, August, ungainly Elizabeth Marbury will rub prim and proper Abraham Hatfield the wrong way. . . . Put someone with his education who is a less ardent Catholic than Elizabeth next to him." August replied, "You've hit on the very reason I have them as table partners. Hatfield is too big a man to care what a person looks like; he is interested in essentials. He weighs values and spiritual realities. Miss Marbury is so bluntly outspoken, and he is so broad-minded and tolerant, that this is an interesting experiment. The Anglican and the Catholic can exchange spiritual aspirations."

Another unlikely pairing was arranged. Pretty Isabel Pereda, a Latin-American beauty with a cameo-like complexion which had fascinated August as he painted her portrait, was the niece of an admiral of the Argentine navy and the daughter of a man who owned vast estates in his native land. Her charming grace and personality would be a challenge to the stiff, self-conscious president of the Pittsburgh Steel and Wire Company. Wallace Rowe liked pretty girls; he was quite at home with all of his daughter's classmates at Miss Spence's School. Isabel Pereda would make him feel at ease at once. August would pit a smoothly-polished diplomat like General Stewart L. Woodford, who had previously been an ambassador, against a brilliant conversationalist like Anne Morgan. The daughter of Pierpont Morgan was probably one of the most sagacious women of her period. Her knowledge of France and of foreign affairs would keep the kindly old director of the Metropolitan Life Insurance Company interested and happy!

And then there was Mrs. Perry Belmont! Although she had taken a tremendous fancy to August the first time they met, he had brushed her aside with "Madame, I think you've made a mistake. I cannot be your dinner partner. As you are New York's leading suffragette, I disagree with all your views; I neither approve of divorce nor of votes for women." His manner, his blunt outspoken speech intrigued Mrs. Belmont and she burst into laughter. "Why, Mr. Benziger, at least you are fiercely honest, even if you show but little tact. To please you, I will keep off both subjects. We do have a lot of things that interest us mutually; we are both lovers of art. Come now, don't be too difficult." They became friends. She even invited him to her home, requesting him to bring his wife to dinner. There were also times when August invited her and a few of her friends to his home. Although he did not thoroughly approve of their mode of leading their private lives, their personalities charmed and fascinated him.

A stickler for etiquette, he insisted that it be observed by others while they were guests under his roof. These friends, instead of ridiculing him for his fastidiousness, admired him for the courage of his convictions. A rather delicate matter was that of the low-cut décolleté gowns. As an artist, August loved the beauty of the lovely women who frequented his studio. Nothing shocked him. Yet their low-necked dresses were taboo when he invited Church dignitaries to his banquets. In order to make sure that none of the guests forgot decorum, his wife included with the invitation "an appropriate note," a reminder that no décolletage was permitted when attending a dinner at which a cardinal or archbishop was present. Should a lady forget, the parlor maid presented her with a lacy scarf or silken fichu to cover her bare shoulders.

Once there had been a near incident, when August and Gertrude were first married. A Paris dinner had brought together the Papal Delegate and a prominent Parisienne. This portly lady, in a very low-cut gown, met the papal representative. According to custom, she stepped back to permit the Nuncio to enter the drawing room first. His excellency had removed his biretta. The lady, bowing low, with charm and grace, murmured: *"Couvrez-vous, Monseigneur."* ("Cover yourself, Monseigneur," or, more precisely, "Put your biretta back on.") The prelate, holding in his hand the biretta, or clerical hat, stared right through her. *"Après vous, Madame."* ("After you, Madame.")

When Cardinal Gasquet, the English historian, came to dinner one evening, August gave him a Bryn Mawr graduate as partner. Gertrude, on seeing the table chart, had protested; she felt that Margaret was far too immature for this great biblical scholar. August explained that, although Miss Haskell came from a small midwestern town in Nebraska, she had a brilliant mind. She intended to study law in London so as to become a British barrister. Cardinal Gasquet was just the man to give her useful information. Gertrude asked, "What will her father say? You know he is none too friendly towards Catholics." August held forth:

> Leave that to me. I know George Haskell far better than you do. He is no snob; besides, he had brains enough to corner the butter market by freezing all surplus stock he could lay his hands on. He did the same with eggs by keeping them in cold storage; that is something no one else had thought of doing with such vast quantities. Prices soared.

> He is too big a man to disdain anyone. Just wait; his creameries will one day change the face of the dairy industry in America.

> Besides, my dear, if Margaret Haskell tires of the sedate cardinal, I have selected as her other partner Colonel Hudson Poole. This fascinating and charming White House aide is full of fun. Only yesterday Margaret admired his portrait, asking me about the blueprints he was holding in his hands. I told her that he had lived in Manila constructing fortifications for the Philippines. With these two extremes, our Margaret won't have a dull moment.

On another occasion August had been asked to accomplish a rather delicate mission. Being a layman, he could, perhaps, intervene in a petty quarrel between two prelates better than an ecclesiastic! The Archbishop of Philadelphia, who was a good friend of his, said, "Benziger, the two cardinals are so annoyed with each other that they are not on speaking terms. You may be able to act

as intermediary. Invite both of them to one of your dinner parties." Unabashed, August promised Archbishop Prendergast that he
would see what he could do. Taking the first train to Boston, he
spoke at length to Cardinal O'Connell, then took the next train
back to New York where he visited Cardinal Farley. The latter was
much amused at the plot to bring him together with his *confrère*.
Fifty guests were invited. In order to observe strict protocol, the
cardinals of Boston and New York were seated at both ends of the
table. Conversation flowed. Peace was fully restored. The deni-
zens of the outside world would never suspect the role played in
this affair by their artist friend.

Only once was August trapped into giving a dinner that might
have had dire consequences. Franz von Papen, then Military
Attaché to the German Embassy, came in the name of the German
Ambassador. The Benzigers knew both men, for they had been to
Brunnen. Herr von Papen informed August that Count Johann
Heinrich Bernstorff was anxious that the artist do him a favor:
could he give one of his famous dinners so that the German Ambassador might meet Cardinal Farley? Then von Papen mentioned
a long list of people whose acquaintance might be valuable to
Bernstorff. Since America was neutral in the war, a dinner of this
sort could prove tremendously useful. August fell for the bait.
Cardinal Farley had no objections. Besides, von Papen was a
prominent Catholic. Yes, he would be glad to meet both Germans.

The guests invited to that dinner were carefully chosen so that
no one could take offense. Germany had already started her U-
boat warfare and feelings were running high, yet hundreds of citizens were taking advantage of American neutrality by selling arms
to both sides. In all, some 30 guests came to dinner, many of
them in the ammunition business. No speeches were ever made at
these dinners, for August loathed formal toasts. Great, then, was
his amazement when von Papen rose to propose one. There was
no chance to interrupt; when he had finished, suddenly, as by some
prearranged signal, the German Ambassador followed and took the
floor. Count Bernstorff began a lengthy dissertation. He warned
those present that they had a grim duty to perform. They were to
inform their friends and relations to keep off the high seas. The
U-boats had started to sink all ships carrying arms and ammunition.
Americans traveling on such ships risked being sunk without
further warning. Apart from the two Germans present, the host
was the only other foreigner. This placed him in a precarious posi-

tion, for had his friends not known him as well as they did, they could easily have taken him for a German accomplice.

Men like Charles Schwab of steel and munitions fame, and John Semple, inventor of the tracer bullet, congregated around their host once the meal was over. Dudley Field Malone, Port Collector of New York, who had seen the bills of lading, wondered why such an ultimatum would be given at a dinner party! Senator O'Gorman, whose sympathies until then had been for the Germans, was enraged by this breech of etiquette, to say nothing of the arrogance of the assertions. To make matters even worse, the next morning the New York papers carried the German ambassador's speech, as well as a list of the invited guests.

Now, although August did not mind publicity for his hotel business or his art, he abhorred it when it came into contact with his private life. What went on inside his home was his personal affair; it brooked no incursions.

Only a few days later, on May 3, 1915, the British liner *Lusitania* was sunk, with a frightful loss of lives. Many Americans went down, and all who had been present at that Bernstorff dinner shuddered at the implications. Plainclothesmen interrogated August the night of the sinking. Members of the Secret Service insisted that the eldest daughter be questioned. Awakened from sound sleep, she was closeted with four men who questioned her for an hour and made notes. They wished to know why the dinner had been given, who had been present and what had been said. Since none of the daughters ever attended any of the banquets, Marieli could give little information. She did remember that her father had been furious because he felt that the Germans had betrayed his trust in them. As she had seen none of the guests, nor even met any of the Germans, the Secret Service agents retired apologetically. For many years, the "von Papen incident" was to do much to upset the household. August never again gave a party for chance acquaintances!

Behind the scenes of these dinners, Gertrude was the genius; she used her Southern heritage to advantage. With equal aplomb and *savoir-faire* she could handle the most temperamental of chefs and plan amazing dishes, her motto being, "Anything that is edible and appetizing should be tried once." Cooks might come and cooks might go, yet Gertrude insisted on one quality—equanimity. Hot-headed chefs who had no command over their tempers never stayed. Her *cuisine* was run with the precision of a factory.

The prized family acquisition, excelling any Parisian *Cordon Bleu,* was none other than a black woman, a "mammy" who had once been a slave. Though Mary Strother could neither read nor write, she could certainly cook. From the moment she took over the Benziger household, there were no further culinary worries.

On one occasion when August rushed about in his nightgown and bare feet shouting that a fire had broken out in the next apartment, Mary ran in with wet kitchen towels that she had just soaked in water. She tied these over the mouths and noses of each of the family and shooed everyone out of the apartment, down the marble fire-escape. Only a little while later did Gertrude realize that her faithful servant had stayed behind.

The fire on the ninth and tenth floors which had wiped out the duplex apartment on the opposite side of the corridor from the Benzigers' proved to the entire family that their "first fireproof apartment house in the city" really was fireproof. On returning to their smoke-filled rooms, Gertrude anxiously inquired of Mary what had happened, where Mary had been. Mary shook her head wisely: "When yo' all was hurryin' t' git out, yo' lef' behime all yo' vallibles. Ah didn' trust dem fiahmen wid all dat jewlry in de house, so Ah jes stayed to see dat all dey opened was doors, an' not closets!"

Mary would never retire to rest until the girls' parents were home. Nightly they went to dinners and receptions; nightly Mary sat up in the kitchen awaiting their return, no matter how late they came. When reprimanded for not going to bed, she would protest: "Ah doan' trust dem French Ma'amselles. Ef'n de babies wants me, I'se hyuh, an dey kin holler fo' me."

Only once, after many years of faithful service, did Mary show signs of exasperation. August, who always had a hankering for soft-boiled eggs, had a habit of consuming several at once when he was very tired. On this occasion he had already indulged in a hearty meal, so Mary felt it was wrong for him to consume a dozen eggs. When the last two-minute eggs had been placed in a dish of hot water, she was unable to contain her curiosity and followed the server into the pantry. Mary's portly figure stood in the doorway as she quietly watched the master of the house swallow the fresh eggs whole. Pointing her finger, she exclaimed, "Ah! You'se should be 'shamed to look dem hens in de face!"

When banquets took place, no one knew better than Mary how to make herself scarce. Chefs ruled over the kitchen, yet it was she who scrubbed the barnacle-covered blue shells until the mussels sparkled with cleanliness—and there were many, many of them! Gertrude had learned how to find delicacies which were un-known to the average shopper in the New York fish markets. She would order 100-lb. sacks of mussels, which her Italian fishmonger often gave her gratis, so happy was he at the thought that one American at least knew the value of shellfish. Since her husband flatly refused to touch "rabbit food," she had to find a substitute for lettuce. Hearts of artichokes or white-tipped asparagus were preferred, so Gertrude catered to his extravagant tastes often. When alone with his family, August never touched wine, but when friends were invited, he treated them to the best vintages, served in rows of crystal glasses that stood six or eight deep at each place. His knowledge of cheese was equal to that of wine, and he dis-dained, with a shrug of the shoulder, the "huge-holed contraption" called "Swiss cheese" in America, a "rubbery, tasteless product on a par with chewing gum." He claimed that it had been concocted solely for export to the States, and would serve only the finest chunks of Emmenthaler or Gruyère, or sometimes a Tilsiter that had been especially ripened in Switzerland for his use.

Because of his understanding of good cheese, he and Profes-sor John Brashear of the Carnegie Institute of Technology in Pitts-burgh were drawn close together. Professor Brasher wrote, on February 16, 1915:

> Pray do not think I have forgotten your kindness in sending me that wonderful Swiss cheese. The package had been in my room for several days. I thought there was a strange sort of fragrance that permeated my room. When I started to open the package, which I first took to be a consignment of letter paper, I thought, "What the deuce makes this letter paper smell like that?" So when I came to the big Swiss cheese, the great mystery was solved.

> Let me thank you for your fragrant remembrance, for really it was very kind of you to remember what I had once said, that I was very fond of Swiss cheese, the kind which I once ate in Switzerland and which cannot be bought here, since it is not for export.

Professor Brashear liked to talk about his childhood days—about the time he met a traveling astronomer in his Pennsylvania village, who had permitted the little lad to look through a telescope into the heavens. John had wanted to see more than had the oth-

ers. He had become fascinated, and resolved then and there to become a student of the heavens.

Later, as an astronomer and optician, he produced the largest
prisms and lenses in the world. Observatories turned to him for
his inventions. The brother of Kaiser Wilhelm II came to Pittsburgh especially to visit him, as he himself was a lover of astronomy. In a listing of astronomical instruments in the Berlin museum, Prince Heinrich omitted several important items. Professor
Brashear named them. When the German prince wondered how an
American would know so much about what they had in Berlin,
Brashear informed him that he had made them right in his Pittsburgh laboratories.

Charles Schwab, an ardent admirer of Brashear, had given August the order to paint the noted astronomer. He was so delighted
over the likeness of his friend, who was shown holding a huge
prism in his hand and leaning over a globe, that he immediately
commissioned a second portrait. This one was to be given to the
Carnegie Institute of Technology.

August wished to know the honors which had been awarded
to his sitter so that he could list them as titles in a folder he was
preparing. Brashear wrote:

> . . . my dear fellow . . . what could you do with such a string
> of nonsense as the titles I have from America, England,
> France and Germany? Why, you would spoil your wonder-
> ful portrait with such an array of stuff. All I can say is that I
> would rather be counted as one of those who has at heart the
> interests of his fellow man, and trust that my labors are al-
> ways in the line of human uplift . . . this counts far more
> than all the degrees and honors that have been heaped on
> me.

One of Brashear's closest friends was Worcester Reed Warner
of Cleveland. After attending the ceremony for the unveiling of
the portrait, he wrote to the scientist:

> The picture of you is a splendid one. If I did not know you
> personally, that portrait would make me well-acquainted
> with you. . . . In fact I have never seen any painting which
> seemed to me to indicate the soul and nature of a man as
> well as this does. I heartily congratulate you and the Carne-
> gie Gallery, for I count this picture as one of its best acquisi-
> tions.

Worcester Reed Warner and a friend, Ambrose Swasey, were partners who established the firm of Warner and Swasey Company in Cleveland, and manufactured optical and astronomical instruments, as well as precision machinery. Mr. Warner was haunted by the Brashear portrait and determined to have one of himself; consequently, he left August no peace until he consented to paint him and his wife. Mr. Warner came to New York for the preliminary sittings; later, he sent photographs of the California Lick Observatory which he had been instrumental in building, hoping it would be used for background. He wrote:

Cleveland, April 19th, 1915

The photographs which I sent you represent the Lick Observatory erected on the top of a mountain over 4,000 feet high. One shows you a winter scene, the other was taken in summer. The Observatory is really the Supreme Court of Astronomy, one that gave Mr. Swasey a greater reputation than we ever earned either there or elsewhere. The great telescope in this Observatory was made by us 'way back in 1888, or 27 years ago.

Mr. Warner was delighted with his portrait. He proudly called in his friends to rejoice over the striking likeness yet, strangely enough, Mrs. Warner was far more difficult to please in the matter of her own portrait. August bitterly resented that some women put artists in the same category as their dressmakers. These, he felt, were clients who could never make up their minds; they expected constant alterations, a little here, a little there; the hair, the eyebrows, the rings. One day they wore one color, the next day another. Naturally all of these things affected the flesh tints and shading. In his view, to fritter away valuable time and talent on such trifles was exasperating. He was annoyed that Mrs. Warner could not make up her mind, so he wrote to her husband:

After Madam's unpleasant remarks, I begged of you to call off the whole portrait question. You would not hear of this . . . yet, you must know, we have a thousand expressions, that we change very considerably, two or three times daily. Look at yourself in the mirror in the morning after you get up, then after luncheon and before you go to bed! How much more, then, do we change in a year? It is at least three years since we started the portrait; one sitting in Cleveland, several in Tarrytown, and the rest in my stu-

> dio. Every time an entirely different light, not to speak of different expressions.
>
> Now you know that when I was painting your wife's portrait, Madam took my looking-glass and saw her portrait through the mirror; after studying it a long time, she said she saw herself in the portrait just as she knew herself, nor was I to change it any more.

Through tactful intervention, Mr. Warner excused his wife; she had not meant what she said. He requested that August continue the interrupted work.

During periods of indecision it was always Gertrude, the patient, long-suffering wife, who managed to steer her husband through trials. Some might have had dire consequences had it not been for her, although he was generally quite businesslike before embarking on any order. He inquired about the needs, the wants, the tastes of his new clients. These were meticulously honored, and there were few occasions of misunderstandings.

When he had been invited to come to Cincinnati to paint a life-size portrait of DeWitt Balch, he had, as was his custom, made notes of what was wanted. Then he returned home to make sketches and await his model, the tall, handsome golf champion of the States. Nothing could have shocked him more than the fact that, just before the completion of the project, he received a strange request demanding that the full-length portrait be changed to a bust: "We want more face—less length. Besides, are we buying a picture by the yard? You will have to change to a bust style." Infuriated, August rushed back to Cincinnati. What had happened? Who had countermanded the original order? An executor, peevish because he had not been consulted, had tried in this manner to halt the progress of the portrait.

Another painting in which August had taken much pride and pleasure met with an almost identical fate. Now, if a bust was wanted, a bust was painted. He never quibbled. When a full-length painting was what was required, that was what he produced. He had been highly successful with the order given for the Bixby painting. Among the most enthusiastic was the subject himself who was, after all, head of the St. Louis Museum of Fine Art and a person of discriminating taste and a mind of his own. A full year after that portrait had been hung in the Bixby home, August received a letter requesting that on his next visit to St. Louis, he alter it. "We have changed our mind. We no longer want a large portrait. Can it be cut down to something like our Raeburn to fit into a smaller place?"

With a heavy heart, August went to St. Louis, as he had really expected more from this art-conscious family than this type of request. He explained that had they wished a head and bust, it would have been far easier and cheaper to paint. He would have made it according to specific proportions. A bust could never be successfully snipped out of a three-quarter length canvas and be made to look like a Raeburn. This was not a matter of cutting out paper dolls; the resulting portrait would be neither one thing nor another. Fortunately he was able to prevail upon the head of the house to leave a good portrait alone.

Probably the bitterest disappointment came from Washington, D.C. August had met and asked Alexander Graham Bell to pose for sketches and sit for his portrait. The scientist had taken a liking to the Swiss, and had agreed, on condition that there would not be too much loss of time. Few people had ever fascinated the artist as had Professor Bell. August felt that he was the greatest man of his era, humbler, even more wonderful than Edison or Eastman. With solicitude he prepared, not a canvas, but a priceless piece of wood, especially prepared so as to mellow with age. He wished to immortalize the Alexander Bell who had brought telephonic communication within the reach of every man.

On the wooden panel, he laid the black and white and brown foundations. With heavy strokes, he molded the shaggy white head and beard, the bushy eyebrows, the piercing, pensive eyes of a dynamic personality. When it was completed, it seemed that the great-hearted genius was about to step into the room. Doctor Bell's arm rested on a cabinet that contained his priceless notes; clasped close to his head he held the instrument used for the first time in telephoning across the American continent—a span of three thousand miles from San Francisco to New York; a country was bridged as across it a human voice was heard! August was impressed by the importance of this new era; he was convinced that, within a short time, peoples at the opposite ends of the world would be afforded the joy of talking to each other.

In order to save time, he took some two dozen photographs of Bell, spending hours in getting the right pose and impression. With these, he was confident, he would be able to do great things.

Mrs. Bell did not care to have the telephone receiver in the painting and asked that it might be removed. August, who felt that the very purpose of the portrait had been to immortalize the historic occasion, had no intention of ruining his work by changing anything. He was hurt that there had been so little understanding. Instead of arguing, he took the Bell portrait from its easel to remain for all time among his unfinished works. When contradictions of this kind occurred, and fortunately they were very rare, he felt that, after all, he was not the loser but, as in this instance, the Bell family was, and so was posterity.

Though he was never again to touch that lovely panel, the massive sketch was so realistic that all who saw it were taken aback in amazement. Discriminating art collectors, like John G. Johnson of Philadelphia, who had founded his own art gallery, and Henry Walters of Baltimore, insisted that any artist who could mold with oils as August had was a living genius.

Mr. Walters was president and chief executive of the Atlantic Coast Line. He spent the fortune amassed from this business in establishing an outstanding art gallery in his Maryland city. Differing from many of his countrymen who depended on the whims of art dealers to fill their galleries with material collected in Europe, Henry Walters went in person to the continent, often escorted by his family. He did his own observing, his own studying, his own selecting. It was he who brought back paintings and priceless bibelots which placed his gallery on an exceedingly high level.

Walters was delighted to find a man of August's experience in portraiture right in the United States, and immediately placed an order for a portrait of his friend, Michael Jenkins. What he wanted to ascertain was whether or not Mr. Benziger would be able to paint as lifelike a portrait as he had of Bell, simply from photographs. Mr. Jenkins, a major philanthropist, banker and financier, had died; Walters wanted a portrait of him for his own gallery.

The budding artist, in his Vienna school days, had discovered that photography could and would become an important aid to portraiture. Through its use, he could cut the number of sittings in half and, furthermore, photography could keep details precise. Thus, when his clients departed to their affairs, he had on hand authentic and unchanging material from which to work. Photography also provided a side advantage by protecting him from the type of women sitters much given to changes of costume, hair-do or the surreptitious moving of beauty moles which, sometimes, mysteriously varied in number.

August, who had already created several successful portraits of dead persons, was delighted to make one of Mr. Jenkins. Once it had been completed, Mr. Walters insisted that it be hung opposite the portrait of his own father, which had been painted by the great Bonnat. No one could have paid Mr. Benziger a higher honor. At long last, he had been classified as being of the same distinguished school of portraiture as his master, Bonnat.

As far as August was concerned, he had met far too few Americans who could be placed in the same category with Mr. Walters. Here was a real gentleman of the old school, one whose polished manners, exquisite tact and self-forgetfulness placed him on a level above that of ordinary men.

Later on, through his painting, August was to make another friend with the same gentlemanly qualities, except that instead of coming from Baltimore, Henry Heide had been born in the Rhine-land and arrived in America as a young lad. The Heide estate had been built through the candy business. Having started at the bottom, Henry eventually owned his own factories where all who worked for him loved and revered him. Like most newcomers to these shores, he, too, had tasted what privation and want meant. Yet, in spite of this awareness, his desire to please his wife urged him to bring home lovely bouquets of flowers every weekend. When she protested that this was an extravagance, he merely embraced her and laughed. "Flowers are not an extravagance, they are a necessity. Where would we be if others did not indulge in these little luxuries? One can do without flowers and candies; they are not essential for living. Yet, if others did not feel just as I do, we candy merchants would be out of business." Henry Heide was the genial head of a fine family. No one loved his wife or children more than did he, who was warmly proud of his many sons and daughters. As he wanted them to have a memorial of their perfect family life, he ordered portraits of himself and his wife which could be treasured long after they themselves were gone.

Nicholas F. Brady, whom August had often met in the past, asked August to paint two portraits of the Papal Nuncio. One he wanted for his wife, the other to be hung in the Washington residence of the Nuncio himself. Archbishop Bonzano was a tall, handsome Italian with a brilliant mind, whose deep spirituality and humility made him loved and respected. August knew that this prelate had very little time for sittings so he requested that the *cappa magna* be left for him to photograph and sketch. This procedure gave the artist ample opportunity to decide which arrangement of the material would make the most attractive portrait. His children were away at boarding school and his wife was busy elsewhere. Making the best of a difficult situation, August put on the *cappa magna*, studied himself in the mirror, then snapped his own picture several times with varying arrangements, thus facilitating the future necessary sittings.

All during the war years, August continued to have more orders for portraits than he could manage. He was now at the height of his career; this was the time when he created his greatest masterpieces. In the larger-than-life painting of Mrs. Marjorie Merriweather Post and her children, he had embodied and combined the beauty and elegance of an outstanding personality. Had he never again touched paint or canvas, that portrait would have made him famous.

Though Marjorie Merriweather Post had inherited fame and fortune from her father, Charles William Post of Battle Creek, Michigan, it was the ethereal handsomeness of his sitter that captivated his fancy. He was intrigued because he had seldom met a woman who combined such loveliness with startling brilliance of mind. Her intuitive business sense startled him, and he saw in her all that was best in American womanhood. She had come from the pioneer stock that had founded the American nation. The Stephen Posts had settled and founded Hartford, Connecticut; the Merriweathers of Virginia were related to George Washington and Patrick Henry. Here was a person who would have been the envy of old Europe, but also one with all the charm and manners and enthusiasms of the New World.

Fearful of detracting from the exquisite flesh tints of mother and children, August concentrated on the pinkish complexion. In order not to dissipate this focal point, he harmonized varied shades of pink, thus enhancing with frail nuances the delicacy of his subjects.

He had taken pains to photograph the Skye terrier and the huge Labrador retriever included in the portrait. August selected from among many the dress to be worn by Mrs. Post. As a rule, he objected to the use of all dummies and insisted on photographs or the real model, but Mrs. Post was an exceptionally busy person; thus, in order to save her, he acquiesced and used a dress-form. Eleanor and Adelaide posed with their dogs, and the sketching began. The painting glowed.

Pink and white dominated the composition. When the tremendous canvas had been completed, the artist received his check for it. He then came to his youngest daughter, Marguerite, and with his thumb and forefinger touching, said to her, his eyes filled with pride and gratitude, "I never dreamt that with these two fingers I would one day get a check for $20,000 for one of my portraits."

Later August was asked to do a portrait of Mrs. Post alone. In creating it, he was just as daring as he had been with the first, using Natier blue instead of pink. The gray-blue tones blended perfectly with the soft pinkish complexion. This time, in order to bring about a greater contrast, he placed the warmth and vitality of his model against a cold, snowy background. The portrait made it easy to understand why, when the Prince of Wales once saw her in an elevator, he exclaimed "Where does this loveliest of all princesses come from? Never have I seen any beauty to equal hers!"

At this period, because World War I still raged, the Benzigers could no longer return to their summer estate in Switzerland. August was so engrossed in his work that he paid no attention to vacations. His wife protested; the children would never be able to endure the stifling city heat. She made up her mind that anything would do better than a New York City summer, and speedily made the rounds of the real estate agents. Site unseen, she rented a primitive cottage 12 miles from Portland, Maine.

None of the Benzigers had known what it meant to live a primitive out-of-door life. This cottage at Prince's Point thrilled the girls, even though the summer proved to be an extremely rainy one, and the shingle roof leaked. In order to keep dry, they had umbrellas suspended over their heads as they slept in their attic beds. August grumbled. He loved the comforts of life and loathed candlelight and fireplaces. The invasion of brown-tail moths gave him the itch. Whenever he and his wife were taken out by the chauffeur, they skidded into ruts or stuck in the mud. To make matters worse, there was a thief on the peninsula who stole his tires and the lobsters out of his lobster pots. He was humiliated beyond words when, after inviting six of his New York friends to a lobster dinner, the lobsters had mysteriously disappeared. Happily, his children had caught enough fish to prevent their father and his friends from being hungry.

That holiday was hardly a memorable one for the artist. The cottage was so dark that it was impossible to find the right light in which to paint, so he consoled himself by collecting the neighbors' cats as he loved these animals passionately. Having heard from the captain of a Holland American liner that the surest way to capture the affection of a kitten was to smear butter on its paws, August and his daughters tried the process on every cat in the vicinity. Those that had dropped in for a visit, came to stay; cats of all ages, sizes, colors. They could not be dragged away, fed as they were on fresh fish and plenty of cream! Gertrude was surfeited, and realized that her husband had not enough to keep him busy, and that a certain James Phinney Baxter from nearby Portland, Maine had written about the possibility of a portrait. They visited Baxter Island and, then and there, the portrait was begun. The sittings took place in a setting that reminded the artist of his Swiss estate. He had missed the mountains; he loathed the sight of the sea because it reminded him of the hundreds of times he had succumbed to *mal de mer*, so, with back to the ocean, he began to sketch, looking toward Maine woods. No one could have been kinder to him than his genial, scholarly client who was serving his 10th term as mayor of Portland.

From this time forward, invitations began to come from everywhere. Former Grand Hotel guests wanted to see the Benzigers. Soon August and Gertrude spent their free time between Bar Harbor, Bretton Woods, Poland Springs and Lake Placid. The summer that had threatened to be a fiasco turned out to be an enjoyable one in the end.

In nearby Vermont, another governor invited the entire family to come for a visit. James Hartness of Springfield welcomed them and took them in the evenings to an underground tunnel which connected his home with a new type of observatory. In this well-heated hideout, push buttons turned on the electricity and huge turrets revolved in every direction. Governor Hartness explained that during the coldest winter months, he could study the stars in their celestial setting. Not only was he a great astronomer, but a genius who had patented over a hundred inventions. In his free time, he managed his numerous factories. August was not to leave the Hartness estate until he promised to return with canvas and paints. Two portraits were ordered, one of the governor and the other of his wife.

When he did return, August became increasingly impressed by the man he was portraying. He claimed that in many ways Hartness was superior to Edison for his technical and astronomical inventions, only he was so shy and retiring that few ever really knew of his greatness. It was during the sittings that the press came out with a huge scandal. Headlines stated that the War Department had spent over a billion dollars for aircraft, but only 215 American-made planes reached the front. The governor, hearing this news, amazed August by his remarkable knowledge about a subject few understood. Hartness claimed that only when the United States had air-superiority would its people be safe.

August next went to Washington. He knew President Wilson but did not like him. In fact, being a man of very strong dislikes, he had flatly refused to paint his portrait. However, he had been asked by Wilson to be a guest of honor in the presidential reviewing stand during the Inaugural Parade; he accepted with some misgivings, but used the opportunity to tell the president that a great man was hidden in the Vermont mountains, one who could save the War Department from its dilemma. It was then that Wilson sent for Governor Hartness for an important conference. While there, he was named a member of the Aircraft Board. The president asked him to pick out the motors he felt best suited for army airplanes. Hartness insisted that the competing manufacturers place their engines on a roof of a building in Elizabeth, New Jersey. After running all of them for twenty-four hours, he personally inspected them and picked out an Ipana Suisse; it ran as smoothly as when it had first started. It was Hartness who had learned that 4,000 clumsy, dangerous DH-4 observation planes built for the War Department had been condemned for fighting purposes. The War Department had spent a fortune trying to fit a Liberty motor into a converted Bristol plane, then scrapped the machines as worthless.

At the Hartness home, August had one of the great joys of his artistic career. Little Constance Beardsley toddled into the room to visit her grandfather. She stopped before the portrait, waved her hands and said "Hello," then stood astonished that her grandfather had not paid any attention to her; he didn't even move!

In the neighboring state, Massachusetts, there was a very old friend to visit. Curtis Guild and August had met in Paris 20 years before, then later at the White House while the portrait of Teddy Roosevelt was being painted. Curtis Guild and President Wilson were close friends from their college days onward and August had enjoyed the candid opinions they exchanged when they were together.

In later years, Guild was named American Ambassador to Russia. In his comings and goings between that country and the

States, he invariably stopped at August's New York studio. He felt that the problems confronting the American and Russian people had to be dealt with firmly if order was to be brought out of the existing chaos. He explained that conferences between these people were punctuated by animated, even heated discussions leading nowhere. When things overheated, he would rise, excuse himself and suggest that someone else be named to replace him in his ambassadorial post. Only then was politeness reestablished and peace restored. He felt that the Russians were an extremely difficult people for us really to understand.

When Curtis Guild became governor of the State of Massachusetts, and asked to have his portrait painted, he insisted that he would only pose for one man; he wished his portrait to be executed by Benziger. There ensued a bitter political battle; certain politicians, being anti-Catholic and anti-foreign, claimed that he had no right to call in an outsider. Governor Guild wrote to August on May 4, 1914: "I am extremely sorry that there should have been any objections. They are, of course, very angry that I did not employ a Boston artist. Your portrait is an admirable likeness, better than I had ever expected to see."

During these years of World War I, food had become as essential as ammunition. The scarcity was so great that Congress debated a law which would place "a much-needed embargo" on all foods going to any country except an ally. On May 18, 1917, Louis Junod, the Swiss Consul General in New York, rushed to August's studio. He pleaded that something be done at once. Did he know what would happen if the embargo became law? Although there had been much talk about what would occur in that case, the Swiss government had done nothing to prevent the enactment. Now, at the eleventh hour, Bern had notified the Consul General that if the bill were passed, the people of Switzerland would die of starvation. Conditions inside neutral Switzerland were already desperate.

August realized how little time was left. With his customary promptness, he went to Washington and personally visited 20 senators and countless congressmen. On the day the bill was to be signed by President Wilson, he made one more desperate attempt to prevent an action that would lead to a catastrophe for the Swiss people, leaving Secretary of the Treasury John Burke no peace until he had arranged for a personal last-minute interview for him with the Secretary of State. Robert Lansing, on the very day the bill might have been signed, listened to him, and prevented the embargo from becoming law. Although all foreign shipments of food had been tied up, by the end of May a cargo of 100,000 tons of wheat and flour was *en route* to famished Switzerland. As a result of the Benziger protest, the president had vetoed the bill.

When the Armistice had been signed and the war ended, August hurried to finish the portraits he had already begun. From November to May he worked frantically, since he felt that it was essential that he leave as soon as possible to check what had gone on in Brunnen during his absence. Reports from those to whom he had entrusted his estates made him suspect that things had not been cared for as they should have been.

As on former occasions, it was again Gertrude, his extraordinary wife, who attended to the details of packing and transportation. August had, by this time, made up his mind that living in two countries was, for the future, out of the question. He would move back to Switzerland for good. This decision necessitated the crating and packing of 150 pieces of luggage. Everything of real value, as well as sketches, finished and unfinished portraits, were shipped to Brunnen.

August had very little sentimental feeling about the value of furniture, which he looked upon as merely necessary impedimenta. To whomever wanted them he gave furnishings, knickknacks, priceless china dishes and vases that his wife and children had prized.

On May 20, 1919, the steamer *Lorraine* was boarded. As the French liner sailed out of New York harbor, Gertrude and her children wept. They dreaded leaving America in exchange for Europe. To August, who had crossed the Atlantic nearly a hundred times, it meant returning to his cherished Swiss mountains, to the land of his birth, to his beautiful villa, his studio, his wonderful hotel. Little did any of them realize then that it would be the last time that all five of them would cross the ocean together. They were soon to be parted, each to go on his or her own way. The premonition that the womenfolk felt about this current going away from all they loved best would soon be translated into reality. Once again Gertrude, with heavy heart, turned from the Statue of Liberty and grimly faced Europe, now austere in its blood-drained, post-war days.

CHAPTER 16

End of the Era
(1919-1955)

When August planned to reopen his residence in Paris, he found his lovely home just as it had been left. Within a matter of weeks, he and his family would move back into the Rue Eugéne Flachat house. On all sides was grim evidence of the German occupation as war-torn France was slowly recuperating from the wounds left by the conflict. The celebrations held in honor of August's return were mostly quiet family affairs, yet everyone was most cordial, anxious to welcome their friend and his family. The flowering of his reputation had been made possible largely because of their efforts, which led to French recognition of his giftedness. The men who, 20 years before, had been his most intimate friends, had been top-ranking officials during the war years; some had even been generals. Still, he found that the scars of the conflict had changed them. Their attitudes and outlook on life were totally different from his.

Because of August's knowledge of the French language which he spoke as fluently as a native, it was difficult for the Parisians to consider him other than one of their own. This compliment often placed him in precarious positions, for over the dinner table confidences were exchanged which led to most embarrassing situations. The French had seen the Americans as conquering heroes out to achieve world domination. With bitterness and resentment, they criticized General Pershing and his staff, and they had but little sympathy for or understanding of the American doughboy who had fought their battles, and died on their soil to restore their freedom. August and his wife and daughters saw and heard much that they keenly resented. The head of the house had tried to explain tactfully to his former friends that a nation could not be judged by the errors of a few; heated discussions had then ensued with men who, it seemed, were no longer his dearest friends.

Late one night, the disillusioned artist had a heart-to-heart talk with his American wife. He had learned to love her profoundly, as well as the land that had adopted him. The United States and its generous people had opened their homes to him. He, who had come as a stranger, had acquired riches and fame in this land of opportunity. He had accepted its challenges and made good at a period when portraitists were scarce. But the French he had loved exceedingly as a student had changed. Never again could he feel at home in their hostile land where good, kind, honest people were defiantly jealous of what America had done for them. His friends had changed, but so had he. In the interim, he had become an American!

Dwellings in this much-devastated country were at a premium. Would Gertrude be willing to have him sell her house, the wedding gift her parents had given her when they had come to Paris as newlyweds? The day after this midnight conversation, without a word of explanation so as not to wound their Paris friends, they made arrangements to sell the house at 8 Rue Eugéne Flachat. With its sale went all their hopes of ever recapturing the glamorous pre-war days. That happy era had vanished for all time in the ruins of World War I.

Upon his return to Switzerland, the land of his birth, August found himself again ill-at-ease. Though everyone shook hands cordially, and seemed to welcome the Benzigers home, the cheerful spontaneity that once existed had gone. The same Benziger who had relentlessly clung to family tradition now suddenly found only hollowness in relationships. His Swiss villa, his studio, his beautiful hotel were still standing, yet heartache came from every side. The joys he had longed to recapture during his years of absence were also lost forever.

He did not realize then that he, the son of a Swiss industrialist and publisher, had also changed, had embraced the new opportunities offered by life and, in that acceptance, had outgrown an old-fashioned and outmoded Europe which, in 1919, still bitterly resented change. This artist who had acquired fame in both France and America, who had painted four Swiss presidents, now looked forward to exhibiting some of his latest works of art; yet he found himself *persona non grata*. He submitted portraits of renowned Americans; they were all returned to his studio without comment—

rejected. When he protested at this unjust attitude, he was bluntly told that he was far too old-fashioned for the modern art world. Finding himself thus ostracized wounded him to the quick. Nothing could have hurt more because, first and foremost, August had remained at heart an ardent Swiss patriot.

The Grand Hotel was a further source of disillusionment. It had been closed for five years when August, who had always boasted to all the world about impeccable Swiss honesty, returned to find that he had been robbed from all sides. He had sent a large amount of money each year to cover the running expenses during his absence. The money had never been used for the purpose intended; it had been squandered by the caretaker. The man had sold all the priceless walnut trees, over a century old, for gun butts, then built himself an apartment house in the village and retired. The very trunks containing his wife's trousseau had been pilfered. The same village folk who, 20 years before, had ridiculed his beautiful wife for her finery, now walked about the Brunnen and Schwyz streets in Paris creations! When the police finally tracked down the culprits, they retorted: "*Ach,* Benziger is rich enough; let him buy his wife new clothes." These were the dresses Gertrude had never been permitted to wear; by 1919 the unopened trunks with their lace finery were worth a fortune. But now, attention had to be turned to the hotel.

To Gertrude and her teen-aged daughters fell the sad lot of retrieving what was not irreparably damaged. For months on end, they opened windows and aired over 200 bedrooms. The caretaker had never used the money sent him for moth protection, nor had he cleaned the building. Now the especially-upholstered furniture, the pure white blankets, the oriental rugs were ruined. Moths had destroyed everything that had not been ravaged by mold or dampness. The marble corridors were aflutter with moths that billowed through the hotel; their work of destruction had been as thorough as would have been the flames of a fire.

Just three days before the outbreak of World War I, August had bought a huge farm in Ingenbohl, about four miles from his Brunnen estate. Far-sighted in all things, he had insisted that no hotel could succeed without a golf course; guests had to be entertained. In 1914 he had felt that he could make a drawing card out of his carefully-planned course which would entice Americans to sojourn in his hotel. As land was difficult to acquire, and as it was especially scarce in Canton Schwyz, August had spent a fortune to buy five contiguous farms. Now he had a huge white elephant on his hands!

Upon his return from America, he had stocked the farm land with a herd of pedigreed cows, hoping that the head of 40 Brown Swiss might bring in sufficient income to pay his exorbitant taxes. Barely had things been organized, and the farm put into working order, when word reached him that all the farmhands were on strike. The next morning, not a soul appeared to milk the lowing cows. August raced to the farm in his Lancia, then returned to his home in utter despair. He knew how to do a great many things but milking was not one of them. The vital new-mown hay lay in the sun waiting to be hauled away. August now had recourse to his daughters. Could they help him in his present dilemma?

In 1918 his two older girls had pleaded to be allowed to drive an ambulance. He protested that nice girls did not drive men about. If they wished to be patriotic, then they could serve in the Women's Land Army. That was when they had enrolled in the New York State School of Agriculture in Farmingdale, Long Island. It was there that they had taken a condensed and practical course on the working of farms. Marieli and Hélène needed little time to don their discarded khaki uniforms before they rushed to the rescue of the distressed cows. After milking and cleaning out stables, they salvaged the precious new-mown hay, got the cook and the maid employed in the villa to assist in stacking it on carts, then used the cows to haul the crops to the barns. Once it became evident that the farmers had no intentions of returning to their jobs, the girls took over the stables. They tossed out manure that had been rotting there for weeks. They whitewashed dirty walls, then scrubbed and cleaned until the two stables looked spick-and-span. Daily there was a plentiful supply of fresh milk to be churned, eggs, poultry and even vegetables. Never had any landowner been prouder of his daughters than was August.

After a hard day's work which started before dawn, the girls proudly carted home their staples. Once again the natives raised their eyebrows in scandalized horror. All Canton Schwyz was talking about these crazy Americans! How could nice folk permit their children to milk cows, clean out stables, pitch hay and dig vegetables! These Americans did not seem to realize that there were class distinctions. Peasant children did such things, not those from a fine old family. The Benziger girls were highly amused. That was all! They were really far too American at heart to care, having learned from their American mother the old adage, "All service ranks the same with God." They knew how their very much loved mother had been made to suffer during the early years of her married life; how this same insidious type of gossip had almost broken up the marriage. They were far too busy with farming chores to mind the new tongue-wagging and finger-pointing or the catcalls of *"verdammte Amerikaner!"* ("Damn Americans!")

Unexpectedly enough, everyone else suffered more than Benziger at this time. His American wife and his American daughters had helped tide him over a period that had paralyzed Swiss industry. Never had the industrious Swiss known anything to equal the wave of strikes that swept through the nation. Communists had sponsored and fermented the disruptions. They had attacked the people of Switzerland where they hurt most. A somewhat-educated peasantry had blindly accepted indoctrination, as the Communists had promised that their hard lot would be changed overnight. During the long winter evenings, the farmers had assimilated the propaganda; soon the dairy industry had been almost wrecked, and priceless, helpless cattle made to suffer. When the peasants eventually went back to work, the disgruntled, disillusioned strikers learned what a real mistake they had made. Nothing could have been more valuable than this experience; subversive literature which had flooded distant mountain hamlets was now banned. Swiss democracy won out in the battle with Communism.

By now the Benziger girls had acquired insight into age-old customs which fascinated them. They knew that on certain farms, cattle got better treatment than did the children. Children had to work all year round in many mountain hamlets, but the cows at least had holidays during the warm summer months! Cows were taken to the high Alps to pasture, where they fed only on the daintiest mountain flora. Annually, festivities were held when the cows returned to the farms for the winter season. Those that had produced the most milk were decorated with crowns, others wore bells worth a fortune.

Once peace was restored to Switzerland, August moved his family to Munich for the winter of 1921. His favorite daughter, Marguerite, had declared her intention of becoming a nun, but he insisted that, at 18, she was far too young to make such a decision. He had been a very strict father and never permitted his daughters to go out on dates, nor would he have thought of permitting them to go about unchaperoned. Now he had qualms of conscience about this sort of control. Perhaps he had been too strict. He was about to lose the one he loved the most!

Marguerite was musically inclined and had a lovely voice. As he had never done anything to encourage this talent, he would see that she had music lessons; the finest teachers would supervise her singing. In another area of the girls' lives, from this time on began a spree that lasted all winter. Papa and Mama took them on a round of pleasure; night after night there were Wagnerian operas, visits to student haunts where August had had much fun, and there were times spent in the wonderful beer gardens where the young women learned to distinguish the varied types of Munich brew.

Toward the end of October, a cable reached the hotel where the Benzigers were staying for the winter. Father John A. Zahm, who had been invited to join them, would meet them within a week. Great was the excitement this news aroused as all in the family revered the tiny priest with his large blue eyes, his sphinx-like reticence, his severely-polite manners. Father Zahm had been vice-president of Notre Dame University at 25 years of age. Later he had been sent to Rome as Procurator General. For years, in order to shield his identity, he had written under an assumed name, producing scholarly works of a high order. As an explorer and naturalist, he had won the admiration of many of August's friends, including Charles M. Schwab who kept a room in his Riverside Drive home where the priest could find seclusion and write his books. In Washington, while painting the portraits of President Roosevelt, August had seen the dapper little priest drop in to talk about scientific research. It had been largely due to his persistent pleas that Roosevelt had organized an expedition in which both Teddy Roosevelt and Father Zahm had explored the Amazon and Matto Grosso. Father Zahm felt that if a man like Roosevelt took the initial steps to penetrate the unknown jungles, other Americans might be influenced to devote more money to the exploring of further tracts of Latin America. August had been present when he had pleaded that the president finance the project in order to foster a good neighbor policy as quickly as possible.

Roosevelt had often told August that had it not been for the influence of this remarkable priest, he would never have had the courage to explore Hispanic America. It was while both men were there that they had met Japanese army and navy officials going about in disguise. They were waiting for an opening in Central

America to secure land, so that from this vulnerable spot the west coast of the United States could be attacked.

From the time that Father Zahm arrived in Munich, there was never a dull day. To a man possessing knowledge which encompassed many parts of the world, sightseeing might have proved boring, but he was really interested in everything. However, during the post-war reconstruction period, hotels and continental trains were unheated, and after a few days of intense activity he developed a persistent cough. Gertrude insisted that her husband take him to see a doctor. As nothing could induce the adamant priest to yield to such a plan, one day August went off on an important expedition; Father Zahm escorted him. They walked right into a doctor's office where there was no alternative but to obey. The verdict was far more serious than had been anticipated. The priest had pneumonia; he was to go straight to bed. The patient promised to carry out orders on condition that the girls be permitted to visit him.

Turns were taken beside the sickbed gladly, especially as the priest was not satisfied with giving snatches of information, but would spend hours talking to his visitors about world events. He had made a thorough study of the problems of black people and of the Caucasian avarice for wealth that had led to the extinction of the Indians of Cuba. He explained that, until 1807, when the English parliament had abolished slavery, six million blacks had been dragged from their native soil; that in one single year, 1768, 97,000 slaves had been imported, and then transported on British sailing vessels to Spain's new colonies. He was deeply concerned, as he felt it was high time that both the West Indies and the United States should take steps to remedy the appalling apathy with which the white race viewed the evil and the ever-increasing unrest which was the outcome of one of the most hideous crimes in history. Unless the white race remedied the existing evils of the North American Negro, serious troubles would arise, not only in the Southern states, but in the slums of large cities.

On another day, he spoke about the Hawaiian Islands where the "thermometer is always in an agreeable state of stable equilibrium." He called these islands "America's most prized tropical gardens." From his lips came strange warnings. He claimed that for over a century Japan, Germany, France and even England had fixed their covetous gaze on the peaceful islands. One day the Pacific would be turned into a vast battleground; then the ownership of the Hawaiian Islands would be highly appreciated, for it would establish control of the north Pacific. If the United States did not watch and keep armed, she would be attacked in this tropical paradise. When his listener looked amazed, he replied that although the war had ended, although there was a semblance of peace, that peace was only tentative and temporary; it could not, would not last.

The real purpose of Father Zahm's journey was to reach Baghdad; had he not been taken ill, he would already have arrived there. He saw it as a fairy city that had enthralled his youth and, when asked how it was that he had chosen Baghdad as his destination, he replied that he had written a book about it and now wished to further his research. He felt that this metropolis was doomed once again to become a center of world conflagration. Although Babylonian and Assyrian civilizations had made valuable contributions to the history of astronomy, science, art and literature, Baghdad, with its unusual gardens and its two million inhabitants, had been laid waste in the 9th century by Mongolian invaders. It had never really recuperated. All the same, it would eventually become the key to commercial supremacy, and would link the Far East with the European continent.

But the plans for a visit to his chosen city cherished by Father Zahm came to a speedy end after his health took a turn for the worse. August and his grieving family stayed by the deathbed of their friend. In their hour of sorrow, they rejoiced that at least he had been in their midst when the peaceful end came, and that nothing had been left undone to make his final moments happy ones, although he was very far away from his much-loved Notre Dame.

One of the memorable events of that winter in Munich had been another visit. August and his family had gone to call on the Papal Nuncio. The young Italian archbishop used to spend his vacations with the Holy Cross nuns at Rorschach in Switzerland, and August had met him there. Eugenio Pacelli had made quite a name for himself in Germany. He had been fearless in his denunciation of Communism, and had lived through the sacking of Munich when thousands of innocent citizens had been rounded up and slaughtered in cold blood. His was first-hand experience of these carefully planned raids when mass murder had been accompanied by photographic evidence. He himself told of how the German Communists had broken into his home. They had rushed up the main staircase and, on hearing the commotion, he had come to his door only to be confronted by arrogant Kommandos sent to kill him. These men were armed with pistols. Pointing to his heart, he told them, "You will gain absolutely nothing by killing me. I am here only to help you Germans, not to harm you!" Fortunately, the Papal Nuncio spoke fluent German. These men had been expecting to be confronted by a foreigner. They dropped their arms and retreated.

When asked if there was any grave danger at the moment, Pacelli replied that he felt that the worst was over; yet it would require great caution in order to avoid inciting a revolution. The Bavarians had been very concerned about his safety; they had kept him well-informed and well-protected. It was then that, turning to the Benziger girls, he said that if they cared to see from his study window what it meant to be a fugitive, he would show them. He led the way upstairs to his office; then, at the window, pointing in various directions, he explained that each night he slept in a different house. That had meant climbing over rooftops to reach security—once here, once there. Spellbound, Marieli, looking straight into those pensive dark eyes, asked: "Your Grace, were you never afraid that you would be caught and killed?" Those same eyes that a moment before had twinkled with amusement at some passing remark, now assumed a look of great seriousness:

> My child, why would I have been afraid? Afraid of what? Why fear when one is doing one's duty? I had been assigned to this post by obedience. The Holy Father wanted me here. To have run away, to have been afraid, would have been cowardly. When we do God's will we are safe, we cannot be safer; we are in God's hands.

The admiration the friendship aroused in 1921 was to last a lifetime. The Benzigers sensed in that young Nuncio the soul of a great and holy man. When they left his residence, they stopped to visit another fearless enemy of Communism. The Archbishop of Munich had risen from the ranks. As a simple army chaplain in the front trenches, he had endeared himself to the soldiers. In time, he had been called home to accept a vacant bishopric. None other than the King of Bavaria had given him the title of Prince Archbishop, but this Archbishop von Faulhaber always answered his own doorbell, and continued to be simplicity and hospitality personified.

The Benzigers were in Munich at a moment when Archbishop von Faulhaber proved what a truly fearless fighter he was. The

Communists were merely waiting for an excuse to reestablish their power, and their moment came sooner than expected in the death of King Ludwig III of Bavaria. As was customary in a Catholic country, the head of state was entitled to a state funeral. The interment ceremony was a public demonstration of national mourning. The Communists issued orders that there would be no such public demonstration for the King of Bavaria. The interment had to be a strictly private affair. No one outside of the immediate family could attend. Archbishop von Faulhaber immediately asserted his spiritual prerogative; he countermanded the orders and insisted that, since the King had been a Catholic subject and a Catholic sovereign, he was entitled to a solemn Catholic burial. Never before had the House of Wittelsbach had such a triumphant procession. The solemn funeral cortège took six hours to pass. All of the Bavarian Guilds in full costume, all the students wearing their colorful caps and uniforms, all the religious joined the mourners. This one act on the part of the archbishop endeared him to the people as a leader, and placed him in the category of ardent defenders of the Faith.

Later, when made a cardinal, he came to Brunnen, relaxing and talking about the troubled times ahead. He had foreseen the disaster that would sweep over Germany once Hitler ascended to power, and he was soon to fight bitterly against Naziism. In season and out, from his Munich cathedral he preached that no Catholic could take the Nazi oath. He insisted that the form of "Brown Bolshevism" then at work inside Germany, and Russia's "Red Communism" were twin sisters in their common purpose, the extermination of Christianity.

Fear of another war was already seeded so, during this postwar period, a large number of Swiss hotels faced bankruptcy. The American tourists who had flocked annually to Europe no longer came; most of them went to nearby beaches or resorts in the States. Furthermore, a bloodless revolution had struck the American continent. For the first time since Revolutionary days, Americans were confronted with burdensome taxation. This was the price to be paid for victory! No longer did the wealthy with retinues of servants cross the Atlantic. Instead, there was an invasion by teachers, students, secretaries and husband-hunters. Economy and thrift accompanied American spending. The "good old days" of minting money from American clientele had ended. The Swiss hotel industry was in agony. August, however, was among the fortunate during these years in being able to hold on to the Grand Hotel. It was finally reopened in 1922 with a capable manager in charge.

During this post-war period, August rarely painted. There were only a few close friends whom he saw frequently. One of these was the faithful village doctor of Schwyz, Dr. Paul Bommer, who had befriended him after his marriage and had come to assist at the delivery of his first-born. Another was Professor Zangger. Although August had a rule never, never to make a present of his paintings, he did make an exception for him. He left this noted criminologist no peace until he consented to pose for him. The hours these two men spent together in his studio were among his happiest memories. As he outlined with remarkable accuracy Professor Zangger's high forehead, his pensive deep-set eyes overshadowed by tufty eyebrows, the shaggy mustache which covered his mouth, August thought about the career of this unusual man.

Zangger had been a professor of pathology, toxicology, pharmacology and psychiatry. He had insisted that the University of Munich found a chair of Social Medicine. Once it was established, the university named him as its head.

His great aim had always been to better the standard of living of the working classes. He worked to protect their health by doing scientific research into the hazards encountered in factories and mines, by studying the causes of industrial accidents and diseases brought on by working in certain environments. He also studied the effects of the misuse of drugs. Far ahead of his time, he insisted that the importation of certain drugs should be carefully monitored, and their indiscriminate use stopped. He introduced the use of ultraviolet rays. When not occupied in this kind of study, he found a way to become one of Europe's leading criminologists. He became an international figure in his fields of expertise. France, Italy, Belgium, Austria, Russia and even Australia rewarded his extraordinary services with honors. His textbooks were sought by universities all over the world.

Unexpectedly, Professor Zangger sought August's help. He wanted his friend to contact prominent Americans who would curtail the sale of deadly lead, then used as a component in automobile fuel. He himself had been poisoned as a result of his research into this subject, and he felt strongly that gasoline strengthened by tetraethyl lead should be prohibited. For his part, he even wrote letters of protest to John D. Rockefeller, the Standard Oil Company and the Du Pont Corporation of Wilmington, Delaware. His warnings were heeded only many years later.

At this uneasy juncture, due to World War I, the Brunnen Grand Hotel had been closed for ten years. During this period of total inactivity and deterioration, it brought great financial losses upon August. Not only was he forced to pour money into back taxes, but the repairs needed in order to reopen the hotel were numerous. Forced to economize on all sides, he gave up having a chauffeur and learned how to drive a car himself when he was already in his 50s. When he got into the driver's seat, he soon forgot that he was not dashingly handling a horse but, rather, steering a high-powered Lancia, and he could never quite understand why he could not make his machine accomplish the acrobatic feats of his equestrian mount!

Willing passengers were few and foolhardy. August instilled such terror that even his own daughters dreaded accompanying him on wheels. Faithful Gertrude, whose wifely sense of duty obliged her to acquiesce, accompanied him with great trepidation. People stopped to gasp and stare at the white-bearded Herr Benziger as he came tearing through tiny hamlets and villages in a cloud of white dust. He was so well known for the risks he took, especially on dangerous curves, that the nickname given him by the peasants stuck; shaking their heads in amazement they would say, "There goes the devil on wheels." During those last 25 years of his life, his patron saint and his guardian angel had their hands full and their work cut out for them.

There was the day when his Lancia skidded over an icy embankment. The car hung in a perpendicular position, within inches of the Reuss River. Out crawled August, bidding his wife who had been badly bruised, to wait. Gertrude had no alternative for her slightest movement would have catapulted their car into the river bed! When help reached them and the car was righted, the rescue squad marveled that August could drive home as if nothing out of the ordinary had happened. In fact, on the way home, he announced to his wife that this was the wooded ravine where, 70 years before, as a five-year-old on skates, he had tied himself to his father's sled and come tearing down the mountainside from Einsiedeln!

On another excursion, he had not seen the railroad crossing signal. The great iron bars controlled from the distant station were being lowered. August's car was trapped on the tracks. The St.

Gotthard express train was thundering out of a tunnel a few hundred feet away! With unbelievable presence of mind, he stepped on the accelerator and steered his car so that it crashed through the lowered barrier in time to cheat death!

While driving through a 15 MPH zone in Schwyz, August became annoyed. Gertrude suggested that he slow down in the village. He did the contrary. Not seeing a woman coming down a narrow alley, he ran right into her baby carriage. Paralyzed with fear, Gertrude froze. She heard the infuriated shrieks, the curses of despair. This time she felt certain that her daredevil husband would land in jail. He must have killed the baby.

Angry peasants crowded around the car. Gertrude prayed for the necessary courage, then steeled herself to join her incorrigible mate. From her seat she studied what was left of the wrecked baby carriage. Still trembling, about to open the door, she realized that her ashen-faced husband was rejoining her. Quickly he took his place at the wheel. Then, in that ghastly silence, with a hundred pairs of eyes glued on them, he started the engine. The motor purred; the crowd parted. August was heading for the village of Brunnen. Not a soul had laid hands on him. He had not been arrested!

They were almost back home when August muttered, "For the love of God, Gerty, you ought to know better by now than to irk me with that backseat driving of yours. My fit of temper has cost me 100 francs!" Gertrude gulped hard: "100 francs? . . . Why, August! What has happened to the little baby?" August huffed, "*Ach*! That stupid ass! I've taught her a lesson. Perhaps the next time she will keep to her side of the road. The baby carriage is a total wreck, it's done for, she'll never use it again. In it she was only carrying kindling wood!"

Shortly before his 18th birthday, August drove home late one night. The road from Zug to Arth Goldau was pitch-black. As they were going around a winding curve, his companion shouted, "Uncle August, stop, stop! There is a cart of hay right in the middle of the road." Of course, it was then too late to stop or avert an accident. A terrifying crash and frightening groans brought driver and passenger to a halt, anxious to ascertain the damage. August rushed about in the darkness, shouting loudly, "Where is the horse? I cannot find it! Has it run away? Has it been hurt?" The wagon had been broken into splinters, the hay strewn over several hundred feet. A sobbing, limping boy of about 10 or 12 came dragging himself up to them. "There ain't no horse; I was hauling the hay home to our barn." "You? You hauling this monstrous load all alone?" asked August sympathetically. The boy nodded, "Yes! My dad will beat me black and blue . . . once I get home. I disobeyed him by going on the wrong side of the road. He warned me I would get hit; now I am in trouble. Because of the lateness of the hour, I was sure I'd have the road all to myself." August opened his wallet. Standing near the dim headlights, he pulled out a five-hundred franc note. "Here, my boy," he said, "Come dry your tears. Go home and tell him to buy you a new cart and a decent horse. If he does not, tell him from me that Benziger of Brunnen will beat him up for this outrageous cruelty to children!"

Not long after this incident, a telegram arrived from Cardinal Gasquet, dated the 25th of February. It was a request that August come to Rome immediately. He should be in the Eternal City by March 1 at the very latest. The cardinal was jubilant; his closest friend had been crowned pope! No sooner had August reached Rome than he headed for the residence of the English cardinal at 38 Piazza Santa Maria in Trastevere. At this ancient *Palazzo di San Callisto*, he was welcomed like a long-lost friend by Cardinal Gasquet. That evening while they chatted over their simple meal, the artist chuckled as he learned that even a cardinal could use intrigue to help a friend.

August had once commented that he had been discouraged by the thought that he had never been requested to arrange an official sitting inside the Vatican. Now he was being invited to be the first to sketch the new pontiff, Pope Pius XI, who had just been crowned on February 6. He heard from the Benedictine cardinal the first-hand story of what had transpired the evening before the major prelates had been walled up in the Vatican for the Conclave at which they would elect a new pope.

Cardinal Achille Ratti had worked side by side with the renowned English historian. Ratti had been Prefect of the Ambrosian Library of Milan as far back as 1907. In 1914, he had come to the Vatican Library where Cardinal Gasquet did much research. Both men had been in Rome during the war years—Gasquet in his headquarters at the *San Callisto Palazzo,* overseeing the translation of the Vulgate—Ratti assisting Benedict XV, who wanted him nearby to safeguard historical data in the Vatican Library.

Cardinal Ratti was the youngest of the cardinals. He had been wearing the red hat for barely six months when news reached him in Milan of the pope's demise. He left at once for that city and stayed with his friend, Cardinal Gasquet, during the days of mourning. There they awaited the opening of the Conclave. The evening before they were to be immured in the Vatican, Gasquet rose to drink a toast to the new pope, whoever he might be, and he remarked to Ratti without knowing why he said it, "I drink a toast to you, my friend, for you, Achille Ratti, will be named our next pope." Shocked at such a statement, the rather sedate Ratti protested:

> How could such a thought ever enter your head, my dear friend? God forbid that anything of the sort should ever happen to me. This is no joking matter. Fortunately, I happen to be one of the youngest cardinals. The College of Cardinals would never give me a single vote. Besides, I have held my present office for barely half a year.

Cardinal Gasquet, with his spirit of determination, shook his head. "Sorry, my friend, but this is going to be your very last dinner in the world. Enjoy it as best you can. Tomorrow we are going to lock you up in the Vatican forever." Achille Ratti, a great outdoorsman, seemed a bit annoyed at this levity. He pleaded, "Come, let us rather pray that God's will be done. The poor man on whom the burden of the papacy falls will need the grace and strength to carry his cross."

On the 6th of February, 1922, after the 14th ballot had been cast, Cardinal Achille Ratti of Milan was elected Pope. He chose the name of Pius XI, in memory of his saintly predecessor whom he had greatly revered. One of the first to pay homage to the new pope, and kiss his foot in *obéisance,* was the English cardinal. Then the two men embraced, clinging to each other with affection. The eyes of both were tear-filled. The Cardinal of Milan wept for grief, but he of England, for joy. At his first private audience with Pius XI, the Englishman, who never asked anything for himself, requested a great favor of the new pope: Would he permit a Swiss artist, one of his former Downside Abbey students, to paint his portrait? Pius XI gladly acquiesced. To whatever arrangements for sittings should be made, he would conform.

August was to encounter no difficulties. He was conducted to the Vatican by Gasquet. Immediate arrangements were made for the *Anticamera* audience at half-past twelve on the 5th of March. After that first audience, it would be advisable for August to wait about 10 days; then he could have as many sittings as he needed, but at present there were still too many cardinals in Rome clamoring for audiences to arrange a first sitting. A preliminary papal audience would be given for the artist to gain a general impression; after that, he would have every opportunity for a tête-á-tête, quite alone, with the Sovereign Pontiff. On March 22, the promised audience took place in the papal study. August prepared his camera. He had his sketchbook on hand and used it freely. As soon as the pope came into the room, after kneeling and kissing his ring, August asked the pontiff to be seated.

Intrigued by the detailed study, the pope asked questions about the preparations being made. August jotted down minute details: the coloring, the quality of the moiré silk of the cincture, the richness of the gold tassels. The rough pencil sketches were accentuated with red markings. Time was precious. He would not keep his sitter for one minute longer than was necessary. His eye and his camera's caught and stabilized each detail he needed to preserve.

After careful scrutiny, August remarked in German, for the pope spoke that language as fluently as he did his native Italian, "Holy Father, the pectoral cross you wear is too insignificant. I would really like one that has color; something to blend with your eyes." Obligingly, Pius XI pressed a button on his desk. He requested that his secretary notify Giuseppe. Giuseppe, who had been his faithful valet in Milan, came running, carrying an assortment of boxes. The pectoral crosses were carefully removed from their containers, then laid out on a desk. The dazzling brilliance of the jewels gave the artist intense satisfaction. With great care he held each in his hand and studied it. One in particular caught his eye. "Your Holiness, this is just what we need." The pope put it on and August, stepping back to survey its effect, seemed very gratified. Pius XI observed that nothing would give him greater pleasure than to wear it:

> This is a pectoral cross I bought in a Swiss antique shop. One day, coming back from a holiday of arduous mountain climbing—for there is not one of your prominent mountains that I have not studied or scaled, I saw this cross in the window of a small shop in St. Gall. Fascinated, I at once inquired about its price and history, and could not resist buying it. Strangely enough, now you, a Benziger, coming from Einsiedeln, should choose this one from among all the pectoral crosses that I have. You have singled out a cross made for a Benedictine Abbot of Reicheneau; Reicheneau, the

mother abbey from which your beloved Einsiedeln stemmed.
Little did I dream then that I would be wearing it as pope!

Everything possible had been done to facilitate August's painting, for even in so vast a palace it was extremely difficult to find a suitable place. Both artist and sitter had to have quiet, uninterrupted sessions. The Papal Chamberlain tried hard, until he finally found a room that suited the artist and had the correct lighting. To the 3rd-floor apartment were carried all the essentials required to begin the portrait. August had stretched the canvas at his hotel. He had even begun the preliminary sketches, and having drawn the general effect, laid in his foundations. As the painting was being taken to the upper story, people stopped to stare at the stark, grim outline in black and white.

The pope had been fascinated from the moment he looked at the canvas. As he sat in a chair carefully chosen by the artist, the kindly pontiff seemed captivated. The sittings rested the worn, tired-looking man. As August began to play with colors, and meticulously laid in one, then superimposed another, he noted that his model gradually relaxed.

August dreaded this ordeal. For him to paint a good likeness, he had to be keyed up, so as to catch the slightest reaction. The artist worked himself into a cold sweat in order to bring his client into the right mood. He had to pry open his heart, discuss what was most near and dear, otherwise he could never catch the expression in the eyes—that alert, yet relaxed expression that made his portraits outstanding.

After pondering all night, the artist had finally made a list of pertinent questions. Each heading pertained to topics of vital importance. He would thus, by tactful questioning, draw out his client. Once the sittings had begun, this was just what he did. In no time, the pope became quite natural and all self-consciousness vanished. August was delighted that the pope seemed comfortable, and even commented on the fact. The pope told him that it was a relief to be able to be himself; he enjoyed the informality of the sittings. Ever since he had ascended the papal throne, there had been many, many new things to learn and assimilate. After all, he had been pope barely six weeks.

From childhood days, August had lived in a home frequented by ecclesiastics. Rarely had a meal been eaten without a few guests, often bishops, cardinals or priests, so he was quite in his element. He spoke to the pope about those times when his mother felt that they should have opened a sort of ecclesiastical hostel.

For August, it was a great honor to paint within the confines of the Vatican. The pope, in turn, was happy to have someone treat him naturally. At long last he could catch his breath, once again be himself. There was no one around telling him what to do next. Popes, like monarchs, had to be instructed at the beginning of their reigns—primed at each step as to what was expected of them.

There were many traditions within the Vatican that had to be observed, strict protocol which had to be learned, taboos to be honored, besides the tremendous spiritual responsibilities that had to be embraced. While God gave the grace for these burdens, still this was a most pleasant interim during which the pope and the artist could meet as men and talk face-to-face.

Whenever August became intent on studying a pigment, squinting his eye to perceive a nuance, a shadow, he was lost within himself. Color was, to him, the most fascinating aspect of portraiture. He had the ability to catch what was needed at once. Spotless, immaculate, he never smeared paint on the canvas or on himself. With the tip of his brush he meticulously lifted a little red, blue, green, yellow, experimented with a fine stroke on his palette, perhaps thinned with turpentine, then applied the color to his canvas. He had been so intent on what he was doing this day that, when he suddenly looked up to compare the original with the canvas, he gasped, then looked around. The chair was vacant; the pope had gone.

Standing at his elbow, peering into his palette, the pope commented:

> Why, Herr Benziger, how do you do it? You fascinate me. Your brilliant array of colors seem bright and gaudy; yet once you take that pointed sable brush of yours, and daintily lift out one or another color and mix them together, you have acquired a combination of flesh tints that leaves me breathless. All my life I longed to be an artist. If I had met someone like you earlier, I am quite sure I would be painting now. The first, very first gift I asked for was a box of oil paints. I can never forget that feast of the Epiphany, our Italian Christmas. Nothing in later life equalled the joy that my parents gave me on yielding to my childish request.

August, being in a very solemn mood, nodded absent-mindedly:

Your Holiness, you will have to do me the favor of sitting in your chair and keeping your head very still. I will turn this mirror so that you can see what I am doing. Pretend you are having a photograph taken. I will be lenient, but this is tedious and takes time. You may talk all you wish, but you must not move your position. You must remember I have only a very few sittings allotted to me by your Papal Chamberlain, and I am human, so I cannot work miracles. To produce a good likeness takes time and detailed work.

There was a short silence, and then the pope responded:

Ah, Mr. Benziger, if you need more time, why not continue painting me during my retreat? Would you object to coming here during those seven days? They are days of prayer and recollection and quiet. I would be delighted to have you paint me at that time, for I would be able to give you far more sittings.

August stopped painting: "Do you really mean that, Your Holiness? Do you think they will permit me to come to you at such a moment?" But the pope had no worries about that point. "If I can help you, we will arrange it. Nothing would please me more. Besides, I realize now how essential it is for you to have at least one- or two-hour sittings."

August took back to his hotel his canvas, the white cassock, the moiré silk cincture with its gold fringes. These were the time-consuming, minute details on which he could work alone. He would leave the flesh tints, expression and eyes for the retreat sittings.

All Rome knew when the pope went into retreat. Twenty-four hours before, August sent his canvas back to the Vatican. On the appointed day, he reported at the Bronze Doors. This was the simplest way to enter the Vatican, but the entrance was partially blocked. A picket on duty confronted August. He saluted as he was accustomed to do, then addressed one of the Swiss Guards in his own native dialect. It gave him a cozy feeling in a strange city to be able to converse with his own countrymen. The soldier on duty marched up and down in total indifference. He acted as though he had not understood. August explained that he had an appointment with the pope. He was told curtly that there were no audiences; all appointments had been canceled. Did he not know that the pope was in retreat?

Then it dawned on August, who until then had had *carte blanche* to come and go as he pleased, that he had overlooked the fact that he might require an authorized credential permitting him to go to his work inside the Vatican, but he refused to budge. Not just one Swiss Guard stood near him now, but half a dozen congregated. They eyed him suspiciously. A Captain of the Guard arrived, but was as indifferent as all the rest. In no uncertain terms, he told August that absolutely no one, not even a cardinal, unless he were a member of the papal household, would be admitted during the period of the pope's retreat. He had better come back when the week was over.

When August explained that the pope himself had told him to return for a continuation of the sittings, they made fun of him. One of the French Swiss began to mutter that he must be out of his right mind. Who did he think he was, to get into the Vatican on such a pretext? Then August thought of a new approach: "Kindly phone the papal apartments. Giuseppe, the papal valet, is to be informed that I am waiting." The Swiss captain did as was requested. The message was relayed. August did not budge.

No one entered the Bronze Doors. The Captain of the Guard sat at his desk in the marble corridor that led to the *Scala Regia*. The colorful military guard marched up and down. Piercingly their heels clanked on the marble pavement. August waited—impatiently. Suddenly, out of nowhere, the papal valet rushed up to him, quite breathless. "His Holiness is waiting. He wonders what has happened." Then, taking the artist by the arm, he literally ran up the royal stairs, through secret corridors, until they reached the third floor. August turned toward the room where his easel and paints had been stored. "No, no, *Signor*, not this room. I have placed your belongings in a sunnier, quieter spot where the lighting is perfect. We have the entire Vatican to ourselves." August was still following the man when they reached the *Logge di Raffaello*. The artist was delighted. At the far end of the world-famous arcade stood his portrait of the pope. Giuseppe explained: "We hope you do not mind, but this Court of Damascus has far more light. For His Holiness, it is nearer to the Sistine Chapel where he makes his meditations and spends long hours in prayer."

The next seven days were spent in utter seclusion within the confines of the Vatican. The artist's only interruption came when Giuseppe arrived with a tray of food. While working, August was always an extremely light eater; he would gulp down a bowl of soup, a few soft-boiled eggs, then hurriedly resume his work. He arrived at the *Logge di Raffaello* as soon as it was light, remaining until it was too dark to see.

No one could have afforded the artist a more cordial welcome than did the pope. As August knelt to kiss his ring, he was immediately lifted to his feet. "Now I place myself entirely at your disposal. The hours not confided to prayer will be spent posing. I assure you, there will be no distractions of any kind." The sittings were started, but the pontiff found it extremely difficult to remain idle. It was then that he inquired, "Would you have any objections, Mr. Benziger, if I employed this period while you paint to dictate letters? I am anxious to catch up with my mail, and I would be more at ease if my mind were busy." August had no objection. "When I am at home," he said, "it is my wife who comes to my assistance. When I am busy studying my sitter, I find little time to talk, although I do find that conversation is the best means for bringing people out of themselves. When my clients are too self-conscious, then my wife reads them the daily newspaper." The pope reflected, "I have quite a few secretaries. I can have them come in one at a time to read my mail to me; then I can dictate my replies. This will relieve me of a great burden. Of course, should this interfere with you in any way, I would stop at once."

From that moment on, all stiffness on the part of the pope vanished. A steady stream of secretaries flowed into the room, each carrying a stack of letters which had been carefully annotated in advance. The salient facts were read, then the replies were dictated by the Holy Father. Sometimes his entire morning was set aside solely for German mail. That afternoon the correspondence might be in Italian; another secretary brought in the French or English mail. Meanwhile, first-hand reports poured in from all parts of the globe.

At this time, the revolution inside Russia was at its worst. The middle and upper classes were being systematically eradicated. Eyewitness accounts of mass murder were read; these were documented by photographs which had been smuggled out of Russia at the risk of life. The Soviet plan was to create its own master race, or a superman who would, in time, rule the whole world. To achieve this diabolical purpose, the men in power set aside a certain number of children. These were carefully selected from among those of noble lineage or from the intelligentsia, then mated with peasant stock. The leaders carried on experiments in breeding human beings as though the young people were merely cattle. Then, in order to prove that a well-ordered society was quite unnecessary, these children were left to run like wild animals, free to inhabit the forests and mountains. There was no supervision, no law, no order. These children, in turn, gave birth to babies in the most primitive surroundings. Driven by hunger and want, with their tiny offspring strapped to their backs, they finally turned on their elders, invaded villages, broke into homes like wild animals clamoring for food and shelter. When this was denied them, they fought back. They scratched, they bit all who opposed them; infected with venereal disease, they passed it on to the villagers. The Soviets then realized that these hordes of wild children were not forming a master race; just as they had put the plan into execution, now they planned to eradicate their mistake. Thousands of children were then enticed by hunger to a huge forest festival. Entire oxen were roasted; foods of all kinds were placed before the starving youths; then the order was given to shoot. Machine guns, carefully hidden in the underbrush, mowed them down. The dead were, finally, stacked like kindling wood and carted away.

These heartbreaking reports seemed endless. August studied the face of the man being portrayed; it was rigid with sorrow and pity. Only then did he realize the tremendous responsibility that fell on the shoulders of the pope, and sense what a truly humble and holy man this heroic pontiff was. For August, these moments were precious ones, giving him intimate contact with the inside affairs of the Catholic Church.

On one occasion, after a strenuous morning in which ghastly details of the persecution going on in Russia had been read, August heard what had been done to subjugate the people of the Ukraine, Latvia and Estonia. He mopped his brow, totally exhausted from painting and listening at the same time to the accounts of the terrifying events. When one of the secretaries left the pope, and the valet brought in a little refreshment, he said:

> Holy Father, how can you stand this daily, hourly *Via Dolorosa*? You hear appalling tales of woe concerning your spiritual children yet, in spite of all this, you remain calm. You never seem to hesitate in your replies. You have on your lips the right answer, the correct word, the needed phrase to instill courage and hope. Today we had atrocity stories from inside Russia; yesterday it was intrigue in Po-

land. What will happen if this diabolical force is not stopped?

The pope looked extremely sad, but replied, "God has permitted the crucifixion of the great Russian people. In his own good time, he himself will bring the needed relief. None of us can look into the future; perhaps it is best so." Palette in hand, August asked, "How can you endure this heavy responsibility? You seem to be carrying this crushing burden all alone." The pope looked up with a weary sigh, yet his kindly blue eyes were filled with light:

> God gives me the necessary graces to bear his burden. He has blessed me with a very remarkable constitution. Throughout life I have had the specific training of an athlete and sportsman. My health as a mountaineer has been of the best. I have never known what a day of illness means, nor have I ever had to call on a doctor. I can say the same about a dentist.

"Then, indeed, you have been most fortunate," August replied, "yet you have just started your career; this must be a very gruelling experience for an outdoorsman."
The Pope replied,

> To be truthful, I was at first totally bewildered. My work was so entirely different, the contrast so great. I had spent my life as a quiet librarian; study and prayer absorbed my life. Now, at last, God be praised, things are going much more smoothly. I have regulated my day; I need only five hours of sleep. The rest of the time is divided between prayer, work and study. One day a week, I cut out sleep entirely. I do not need it; there are too many pressing duties to absorb my time. Those 24 hours of steady work and prayer enable me to catch up with the arduous responsibilities of my sacred office.

In spite of the fact that no outsiders came to the Vatican during the papal retreat, Cardinal Gasquet had been invited by the pope to inspect the progress made. He admired the portrait greatly. Visibly pleased, he expressed delight at the realistic delineation of the Man in White. The pope regretted that the quiet, uninterrupted days had come to an end. As he rose to leave the *Logge di Rafaello*, he once again made a meticulous study of his portrait, observing that it was a very remarkable and exact likeness. The artist had hardly dared request two more sittings, although he felt that he did need to polish off details. When he made the request, Pope Pius XI agreed that he would set aside the required time. The artist was not to remove his belongings; he was to leave them just where they were.

On checking out of the Vatican that night, August spoke once again to Giuseppe, who informed him that arrangements had indeed been made by His Holiness, who never overlooked anything. He was assured that the painting paraphernalia was not to be touched; it would be perfectly safe there.

A week passed before August returned to the Vatican, requesting that a date be given him for another sitting. He was informed brusquely that his request was a bit premature; many diplomatic missions had priority; the pope was in arrears with his appointments; return later.

August fretted in Rome. The delay was irksome. Gertrude kept writing that he was needed at home; the Grand Hotel was being reopened after having been closed for years. There was a new manager who knew nothing; she was alone with 200 new domestics; she had the entire crew to break in. When the delay finally became too obvious—the requests for a conference with the papal valet were turned down on one pretext or another—August made a stiff protest. There were apologies; he would be given an appointment for the very next day. The pope would sit for half an hour. Arriving punctually, as was his wont, August was greeted coldly by an unknown monsignor who announced that he had been appointed by the Papal Chamberlain to escort the artist to the apartment. Instead of climbing the *Scala Reggia* as usual, they now remained on the ground floor. August exclaimed in surprise, "Monsignor, I believe this is a mistake. I have been here so often that I know my way. It is up these stairs that I always go." The ecclesiastic made no reply. He opened the door to a very dark room, with poor lighting. August strode forward, attempting to pull aside a dark green curtain so as to admit more light. He gasped in amazement, "Monsignor, this is where I am expected to have my final sitting?" The answer was direct and unadorned: "All the other places are occupied; this is the only room that is free. You can be content that we have put you up at all." August stalked over to his easel: his palette, *mahl-stick* and brushes had been tossed into an untidy pile, and the portrait had been stood against the wall. August, who was always so meticulous about his paintbox and tools, was now aghast. "I must have northern light. There are no adequate fixtures in this *sala* to give me even sufficient light to see what I am doing. It is imperative that I have the same northern light as in the *Logge di Raffaello*. These quarters are so dark that I could not even see to mix my colors. In all my life I have never been in such a dark, dismal spot." He went on to request that his easel and portrait be taken to the third floor, "Any tiny nook will do, but I must have northern light in order to complete the work."

The monsignor turned on August. In a haughty, disdainful manner he announced that the third floor was quite inaccessible; it had been closed to the public. Who did August think he was? From then on, no further exceptions could be made in his favor.

Then and there, the disdainful prelate, with all the arrogance for which certain Romans were renowned, slammed the door behind him, leaving August to his thoughts.

Cold sweat glistened on August's forehead. No one had ever been so insulting to him before; no one had ever spoken to him like that. What could have happened? He looked about with apprehension. Even the guards behaved differently. The ones who had formerly saluted him now acted as though they had never known him, and he knew that it would be absolutely impossible for him to continue the portrait in that dark setting.

He was never one to wait on ceremony. Always independent, he defiantly picked up his painting. Pope or no pope, he would never finish that portrait, nor would he give it to anyone. This was to be for all time the end of that episode. Carrying the unfinished painting, he strode from the *sala*.

One of the soldiers of the Swiss Guard had been present during this entire incident. He stepped forward. "Herr Benziger," he said in the dialect of Canton Schwyz, "do me the honor of letting me help you carry this wonderful painting." He went on:

> You must not let that rude monsignor hurt your feelings. He is blunt, curt and has no manners. He thinks that just because he is Roman, he is superior. We of the Swiss Guard cannot stand him. He has no right to be here. Someone in high office, with political aspirations, has just placed him in authority. They have even forbidden the pope's valet to see anyone but the pope. Restrictions have been clamped down on everyone. Let me tell you, the inside of the Vatican is buzzing. The pope knows nothing about what has taken place. A group of intriguers organized themselves during

the period of the pope's retreat; for the moment they are in full authority. Nothing gets through to the higher echelons.

August nodded, much too hurt to speak. Together they went through the Bronze Door. The Swiss Guards on duty clicked their heels, saluted—proud of their distinguished countryman. Once outside of the Vatican building, the portrait had been placed against one of Bernini's colonnades in St. Peter's Square. A few off-duty Swiss soldiers congregated around it. Their remarks expressed surprise, delight, but August, blinded by anger, infuriated by his treatment, never heard any of the compliments. He came to only when the cab, circling the fountain, came to a halt. Picking up his painting, he jumped in and, in Italian, gave the cabbie his address. A shout from the Swiss Guards stopped the coachman who, whip in hand, was ready to rattle across the square. The Guards had apparently been talking together. With perturbed faces, they expressed themselves in their own dialect:

> *Ach, Herr Kunstler*, you must not let these men upset you so. We see this same thing happening every day. When Merry del Val was Cardinal Secretary of State, he quickly put a stop to this sort of intrigue. Romans are Romans. There is now a new pope; they are going to make an all-out effort to control what goes on inside the Vatican. The outside world has no notion of what the pope really has to endure from those of his own household. Little by little he will sift and weed out. It may take months before he can surround himself with really trustworthy followers. In front of His Holiness there is always much bowing and scraping; behind his back a lot goes on. We are present; we cannot help but see and shudder. The Church must be divine to go on existing throughout the centuries, and still carry on. The pope must really be divinely inspired, for no human could endure what he puts up with. We want you to know that we are proud of you. There are great artists here in Italy, but you have created a wonderful likeness of the new pope.

Back in Brunnen, August was too bitter to discuss the incident. His wife wondered what had happened. He was so silent about his Roman experience that he gave cause for concern.

A full year later, Cardinal Gasquet came for a short rest at the Villa. Since 1900 he had been a steady visitor and was as much at home in Brunnen as he was in his own monastery. He had heard rumors about those sittings in the Vatican and wished to ascertain the truth. He then mentioned that ever since 1919, a number of the Roman cardinals had opposed him strenuously. As few of them understood the position of Belgium at the outbreak of the war, they insisted that that country had brought misfortune upon itself by refusing to permit the Germans to march through its terrain. Only the English-speaking cardinals had come to the defense of the Belgian people, and the Romans bitterly resented their carefully-reasoned arguments.

Although the Holy See was neutral, the Germans were well represented at the Vatican. Apart from Cardinal Gasquet, Great Britain had no one in Rome to express the British point of view; besides, the Irish were always antagonistic to anything English, so they would certainly never side with them on this matter.

Another sore point had been the sinking of the *Lusitania*. The Germans had moved heaven and earth to have Pope Benedict XV make a pronouncement against the countries that had furnished England with ammunition and arms. He was known as one of the Vatican's greatest fighters for truth. Benedict XV had Gasquet constantly at the Vatican where he was called in to advise, to inform, to assist in looking at a situation from an absolutely impartial point of view. Some of the cardinals even went so far as to suggest that the war had been created by French and English Freemasonry in order to embroil Italy, and eventually take over the Catholic Church! Certainly none of the Romans liked the idea that an Englishman of such prominence as Gasquet should be living in the Eternal City, nor that he should be a very, very frequent visitor to the Vatican.

Only when the war had ended was he looked upon as a hero by the nations that had won. He had had much to suffer, had endured much in silence, but he thanked God that he had been able to help steer the Ship of Peter along the right channels during the trying war years. Now he blamed himself for not having come to follow up on the sittings with Pope Pius XI. He had been snowed under by his work in *San Callisto*. He had been too busy even for an informal visit to the Vatican during these early post-war months.

August knew all of these things. He also knew that when Pope Benedict XV died, this Benedictine cardinal, whom his enemies liked to call the Black Cardinal in reference to his Benedictine robes and for other reasons, had been in charge of the funeral ceremonies. He was, in fact, a sort of *factotum* and Master of Ceremonies. With the elevation of his closest friend to the papacy, there was visible concern on the part of his enemies. Now a certain group of cardinals desired to demolish his influence with the incoming pontiff. Still, with a friend of his in power, they could merely hamper his actions. However, before long, they decided upon open intrigue. If they struck at August, it was not so much to hurt the Swiss artist as to prevent Aidan Gasquet from seeing the pope.

The attack had come so suddenly, so unexpectedly, that none of the Vatican prelates who were the pope's real friends could warn Gasquet at *San Callisto*. When he finally learned of the insults heaped on the artist, it was too late; August had fled from Rome. Naturally, it would have been unwise to write about anything so delicate as this. Gasquet's one regret was that August had not come to him at once but had, instead, gone directly to his hotel and then the train. If he had come, Gasquet would have gone with him to the Vatican and righted the wrong. The former Abbot of Downside shook his head sadly; in his older years, was not August just as impulsive as he had been when a pupil in his teens?

But now August was in Brunnen, where he and Gertrude were to suffer much from the long, cold, damp winter. Nothing could have been more cheerless or inhospitable. All trade stopped; hotels shut down. Brunnen became a dead village with the coming of autumn and remained so until spring. Used to the comforts of steam-heated apartments and homes, they finally felt that they had to flee, and went to a Paris hotel. There August busied himself with visiting friends or gambling on the stock market. He who had been remarkable in making huge sums of money painting portraits was hardly as successful in his stock market ventures, and his dealings with the New York Stock Exchange gave his wife many a heartache. He listened to the tips of his friends. When the market was bullish, he was in excellent humor, but was moody and depressed when there was a slump. He spent hours every night studying the financial pages of his paper; then, in the morning, posted his wife at the telephone and kept her busy contacting brokers.

August had some wild adventures with Wall Street sharks. He was too trusting of human nature, too much of a gentleman to see through the shrewd, hard-boiled bankers and brokers. One incident took place after the death of Mrs. Lytton. When Gertrude's mother died, she had left to her daughter a $4,000 pearl necklace. August, who belonged to the category of frugal Swiss, could not bear to see that much money wasted on jewels and left his wife absolutely no peace until she permitted him to sell that necklace, that heirloom. He would invest the profits in money; money was safe while pearls could be stolen!

A very devout Irish-Catholic friend was also a Wall Street broker. As head of a prominent firm, he assured August that he had just the right type of investment to bring in handsome returns. Late one afternoon, a jubilant husband came home carrying a new suitcase and promptly assembled the entire household before he opened the bag which was loaded with money. When Gertrude saw that her pearls had been transformed into Russian rubles, she was heartsick. She had a strong premonition that those stacks of paper might one day become worthless—then what? Time was to prove that she had been right. Later, August was to be caught exchanging good United States dollars for stacks of Mexican paper. The Irish-Catholic broker could never convince Gertrude that he was infallible; in fact, she felt that he was decidedly slippery, yet socially he was connected with some of the most reputable families in New York. August could never believe he was a cheat.

Later, back in Europe, August was plagued by the same type of experience. When prominent Swiss bank directors advised him to sell his American holdings, he talked the matter over with Gertrude. Hitler had come to power; these Zürich bank directors had long conferences and pointed out that the *Führer* would soon rule all of Europe. He had already conquered many countries by means of his surprise attacks; the handwriting was on the wall. America had no future, Germany was up and coming; America as a world power was done for. August argued in favor of America. He had lived there and seen what private enterprise and American initiative could do. Frightened at the ruthless efforts being made to divest him of his American holdings, he and Gertrude took a short trip back to the United States.

The first person he visited there was his friend, John J. Raskob who, with Pierre Du Pont and Al Smith, had managed to erect the Empire State Building which was then the tallest skyscraper in the world. Raskob had been a former Grand Hotel client and knew Europe well; he and August had been friends over a span of many years. In Raskob's office, August laid his cards on the table and humbly asked for help. He repeated what his advisors in Berne and Zürich had told him about the decline of America, and said that they were urging him to sell his American assets.

Should he do so? Personally, he had little faith in Germany's coming to world domination; he had made his fortune in America and all of his best friends were there. Yet, if America was going bankrupt, what should he do? Raskob shook his head and told August that he had been very ill-advised. He then gave him a bit of investigating to do: he was to visit a group of factories during the following week or ten days, all of them within a 200-mile radius of New York City. He was to ask certain questions while visiting and make notes of the replies.

August, who had never liked to walk, now pounded the pavement. He made his rounds and then returned to Mr. Raskob's office. As he stood at the window, Manhattan, below him, seemed like a tiny map. On all sides there was activity. It hardly looked like a dying city, a doomed country! Yet in Switzerland he had been made to feel that this was the beginning of the end for the United States. All the same, he had to admit that conditions were not what they used to be. Nowhere he went was there much to buy. The factory shelves were empty. The men to whom he had spoken were downhearted, even depressed. There was no work. Was the country really going to the dogs?

Mr. Raskob, who was small of stature, rose from his chair. For once August felt that he looked imposing, and his kindly face seemed fierce:

> Benziger, you are wrong! You are absolutely wrong! This pessimism is utter nonsense. Things could not look brighter. America is teeming with vitality. The possibilities are here—greater than ever before. You found nothing but empty shelves. Have you considered what that means? It means excellent business possibilities are right around the corner. Manufacturers have never had greater prospects! Our American factories will have to work night and day so as to stock those empty shelves. Consumer demands will rise. America is about to enter an era of prosperity unknown in the history of the world. Hold on to all you have. Do not think of selling. Talk to me of *buying*. This country is sound! Solid as the rock of Gibraltar!

When August left, he resolved then and there that he would include John J. Raskob permanently in his night prayers. He was honest; he was great. As he and Gertrude headed up Fifth Avenue to St. Patrick's Cathedral, he thanked God that he had come to America for guidance.

Once back in Europe, August was seized with fear. The Nazi regime had brought about a reign of terror. Nations tumbled like stacks of cards. Had he been able, he would have packed his belongings and moved to America for good. Unfortunately, his wife had become ill. As an invalid confined to her bed, she could not be moved. There would be no alternative; he would have to remain inside the heart of Europe until the war was over.

In Geneva, August had met a New York agent for a prominent American brokerage firm. For over 30 years, he had always kept some money in this Jewish man's establishment. The man now advised, as a security measure, that he form a Panamanian corporation; by doing so, he could avoid a Nazi confiscation of his goods. As the war years progressed, as anti-semitism grew, as Switzerland became surrounded by Nazi strongmen, August felt some security in the knowledge that at least part of his money was protected from confiscation.

In 1939, the Swiss radio blasted the news: Liechtenstein was about to be invaded. The Nazi troops had reached the Swiss border. With the invasion of Liechtenstein, would not Switzerland also fall? Just as at the beginning of World War I, now a World War II village *tocsin* sounded. August knew what to do. Every able-bodied man in Switzerland rushed to his assigned post; he formed part of a remarkable organization of free men bound under oath, and trained to defend the fatherland. The much-criticized Swiss military system now proved itself to be invaluable. August bade farewell to his wife. Being in his 70s, he might have found many excuses for not leaving home; yet, even to the end of his life, he was democratic in many of his ways. What others were expected to do, that would he do! The secret orders that had been given to him years before were now carried out. He was to report, in the event of war, to a specific place with his car.

He had spent a small fortune for his custom-built Buick, as cars had always been his chief extravagance. As he drove this high-powered American model, he noticed that the Axenstrasse and the road leading up the St. Gotthard Pass was jammed with one-way traffic. Apparently he was not the only man given orders to report there. Later he would learn that in the event of an invasion through Italy, the Swiss army would have blocked the mountain passes with abandoned cars. At that moment, it was just as well that August did not realize what might happen to his most prized possession!

Upon reaching the top of the St. Gotthard Pass, he received orders to wait at Andermatt. He stood at attention as his name was called. The commanding officer then told him that his car would be confiscated for the duration. He was well past military age, so they thanked him for his offer of service, but said that he would be free to return home.

Then, for the first time in his life, August really did feel sad and old. He, who until then had always ridden, was now obliged to walk, and he would have to walk for the duration. There were no taxicabs, there was no gasoline, so walk he did, without murmur or complaint.

Privations in war-bound Switzerland were few. Food was so well-rationed that scarcity of any kind was hardly noticeable. The only time August realized what privation meant occurred when his portion of breakfast cream was curtailed. Throughout the war time, then, he deprived himself and his wife of their daily portion of cream in favor of their six cats! This was a minor deprivation, but times grew increasingly worse.

The anti-Semitic campaign stirred up by Hitler in Austria and Germany brought added worries. Non-Aryans, even Jewish converts to Catholicism, suffered persecution. Now, all of a sudden, inside Switzerland the repercussions were felt. Even in the peaceful distant village of Brunnen, hostile attacks were begun. Villagers, on seeing Mrs. Benziger shopping, would whisper loud enough for her and her daughter to hear, "*Sau Judin*" ("Dirty Jew").

August's oldest daughter wrote in *America*, New York's Catholic weekly, of Nazi infiltration into neutral countries, and also of the plans afoot to invade Switzerland. Information for the article had been secured from persecuted German, Austrian and Polish journalists. August, in his Brunnen villa, was threatened as a result of this essay, and a prominent Zürich lawyer terrorized him and his wife. In Einsiedeln, the Benziger firm was informed that all German orders were canceled. In order to regain them, the managers would first have to refute these charges of planned invasion publicly, and then deny that Marieli Benziger was a relative. In Zürich, the Nazi mouthpiece, *Die Front,* carried headlines attacking "the half-American Jewess" and her malicious pen.

Nazi influence was gradually creeping closer and closer. August and Gertrude suffered many hardships, especially when the property adjoining his farm was purchased by a Nazi. This arrogant S.S. leader boasted openly that when Hitler invaded Switzerland, he would see to it that the Benzigers would be exterminated in the huge cement factories of Brunnen. Fortunately the war ended in favor of the Allies and, when it did, this Nazi and *Die Front*, along with thousands of other traitors, were properly dealt with by the real freedom-loving Swiss.

Like millions of Europeans, August and his wife sat for hours on end with their ears attuned to the British Broadcasting station. BBC brought them the only really reliable news available. Had the Nazis taken over, the death chambers would have been their fate. Never before had they been so isolated as during those terrible war years. Only two or three Swiss even dared to have anything to do with them. If Hitler won, Benziger would disappear, and few inside Switzerland felt that anyone could or would defeat Nazi Germany. For the Benzigers, the picture was a sad, grim one; their faith in God and in America saved their sanity. Gertrude was convinced right along that her country, which had fought tyranny in the past, would emerge victorious; but the road to their villa, unused for months, was overgrown with weeds. No one risked visiting them except three or four faithful villagers: kind old Dr. Bommer of Schwyz, Josef Hurlimann who brought them rice and Martin Zimmerman who saw to it what there was always cheese on hand. Otherwise August and Gertrude could have died of loneliness. No one came; no one cared!

Night after night, the great American bombers that destroyed northern Italy, that struck at Austria and the Lake of Constance, flew over the Brunnen estate as the people prayed to be delivered from the scourge of bombardment. August and Gertrude prayed that the daring American pilots would hit their targets so that peace would finally be restored to a war-torn Europe.

When peace finally did come, August told his wife that he was determined now that one day they would return to America. That was where he wished to end his days. They both had aged noticeably; the years of worry had left them broken and old.

In June 1945, their daughter, Marieli, came to Europe with her cousin, Rita. They were given the small cottage on the estate which was, for the time being, to become the headquarters of the "Pope's Children War Relief," founded by them to rehabilitate destitute European children. Many of these stayed in the cottage and the villa, awaiting the "quota" that would enable them and their parents, if these were still alive, to find a new home in America. More than 100 of these children at the same time were sent to

Catholic boarding schools, where all of their expenses were taken care of by the Relief. More than 700,000 pounds of food, medicine and clothing were sent to the cottage for redistribution in wartorn Austria and parts of France. Priests and nuns were also cared for, and one of the Benzigers' greatest joys was experienced when their youngest daughter, Marguerite, was sent by her superiors from Austria to have an operation, to recuperate and to be cared for in Brunnen. Her convent in Bregenz, where she was treasurer, had been closed down by the Nazis, like all other Catholic schools. Fortunately, this convent had been able to obtain a German military hospital on its premises, at first for 250 wounded soldiers, but in the last days of the war, it housed 750 wounded. The convent's having been taken over by the military had saved it from being confiscated by the Nazis and all the nuns being expelled.

Marguerite, who had Swiss citizenship and was the only foreigner in her community, knew what the nuns in her convent had suffered, most of them having been members of the Austrian or German nobility. On the one hand, they heard that their fathers, brothers, and other close relatives were being thrown into concentration camps for no other reason than their loyalty to their ancestral faith; on the other hand, all Europe was aflame.

Marguerite was unafraid. With her quick spirit of repartee, her quiet daring, she defended her convent against Nazi incursions. Her superior was later to say, "Had it not been for the heroic conduct of our treasurer, Riedenbourg would not have escaped confiscation or desecration. We owe this deliverance to Mother Marguerite Benziger." Later, Marguerite wrote a full account of her experiences in a book entitled *Austria Nazified,* a book which gives great insight into the hardships of her times and, incidentally, into her courage and faith.

August, who had saved his entire American fortune from Nazi seizure by having placed it in Panama, now, in 1946, found that he had to go to America. All of his assets were frozen. He induced his eldest daughter to go with him on this business venture and on his first transatlantic plane trip. In less than two weeks, they were to cover 13,000 miles. The old gentleman now regretted that he was not 40 years younger; he was fascinated by the comfort and speed of air transportation and felt that, instead of driving a car, he would now like to pilot a plane!

When he reached the Idlewild airport, the immigration inspector queried the Swiss national, "Where are you going?" "Officer, I plan to stop over in Chicago to visit my father-in-law; from there I fly to California with my daughter, who is an American citizen." The passport inspector looked doubtfully at the dignified old man with his shock of white hair. "Stop pulling my leg, old grandpa! Why, you are in your 80s." August grinned: "I am not lying, officer; my father-in-law will be 102 on his next birthday. *The Reader's Digest* recently carried an article on Henry C. Lytton, headed, 'Daddy Runs the Store at 100.' "

From his room at the Pierre Hotel in New York, August gleefully telephoned Switzerland. The connection was so perfect that it sounded as though his dear wife were in the next room. Everything about America thrilled him then, just as it had 50 years before. He kept reminding his daughter that he was deeply grateful for having lived in the 20th century, an era of revolution, of experiment, and of great inventions. He had known its greatest scientists, men like Alexander Graham Bell, Thomas Edison, George Eastman, Henry Ford, Dr. Alexis Carrel and Atlee Burpee. He had witnessed the revolution from horse and carriage days to the era of the automobile and plane.

Walking down Fifth Avenue, August, who usually lost little time in reminiscing, pointed to the traffic jams. He remembered when the same intersections were just as tangled up with horses and carriages as they were today with cars. He could remember that the fastest things were the Sixth and Seventh Avenue horsecars. Living was also cheaper: to board a Broadway horsecar cost a nickel. Those were the days when men earned a dollar-and-a-half for 12 long hours of work, when a ride home on a horsecar meant sacrificing a half-hour of that day's hard labor.

Though August considered the Fifth Avenue of 1946 no longer as beautiful as it had been with its great mansions and gardens, to him it was just fascinating. He regretted not being able to tilt his hat to many friends. Some of those he had once known were either dead or had moved to the suburbs. He was impressed by the great number of churchgoers and by the fact that the Catholics of America filled their churches to overflowing while, in Europe, most of the great cathedrals were empty on Sunday. He was also astonished by the fact that everyone seemed to own a car; he had had no notion that so many cars existed and could not believe that the average citizen could afford the luxury of an automobile.

Once back in Switzerland, August stressed the fact that he wished to return to New York. "I want to die there. I want to be laid to rest on Staten Island, facing the Statue of Liberty and the city of New York. It was here that I had *un succes fou!*" Then he continued:

> Artists, when I first went to America, were rare. Only very few commanded the prices I received. Life-sized portraits are on their way out. There is no space. The present-day home is so small, the apartments too crowded for huge paintings. Taxes are too high and the millionaires of the past are the ones who struggle to make ends meet. The new rich are only interested in the modernistic, which cannot live; it has no soul. America is going through a new era, one of change, of speed; the new American is trying to orient himself.

Gertrude found the idea of leaving her Swiss villa most distasteful. Was she again to break all ties? She was tired of change, of always moving, but her husband's wishes were her commands. Hélène was given the hotel, the family villa, the vast estate with its farms. Since Gertrude was too much of an invalid to walk, it was in a wheelchair that, in September of 1947, she was taken to the train for Holland. On reaching Rotterdam, great was her joy at being greeted by her favorite cousin, Tot. Dr. Herman Baruch, which was his real name, was now American Ambassador to the Netherlands. They had not seen each other since her wedding day in 1898.

Once aboard the *Nieu Amsterdam*, the aged couple took on a new lease of life. Gertrude who, because of a heart ailment, had been condemned to complete inactivity, now went to Mass daily, and accompanied her husband nightly to the lounge to see the latest movie.

They had been away from New York for 27 years. The same couple who, for these past years, had been sitting by their villa window with blankets over their knees, waiting for death, now went apartment-hunting. They found at 1 East Sixty-sixth Street just what they wanted. The rooms overlooked the scene of their former activities. There, in this haven of security and peace, with a lovely view of Central Park, they were determined to end their days.

Three years later, August, then aged 85, with his American wife at his side, became a citizen of the United States. For Gertrude, this 6th day of September of 1951 was one of the happiest of her life. Their apartment became a sort of meeting place for the old and young of every nationality. Few of their former friends were alive, yet their children or grandchildren dropped in to visit the elderly couple.

Those delft-blue eyes of the artist still twinkled as mischievously and merrily as before. There was nothing he enjoyed more than seeing a pretty woman. Though August was usually enveloped in a halo of smoke from the strong cigars he puffed from morning until far into the night, he still seemed to mesmerize the ladies. The fashions of half a century before might have changed, the sweater girl replacing the *tailleurs* of broadcloth and wasp-like waists, but there was no denying that August still charmed and was charmed by women.

Never was old age more gracefully accepted, never was death more hoped for. August, who had seldom known what it meant to sit quietly, now found that his tempo was at a standstill. Five years of illness confined him to his apartment yet, in his hour of great trial, the same deep-seated spirit of faith that had animated his parents now permeated his entire being. Hour after hour, as he sat in his armchair facing Central Park, he fumbled with his beads. Smoking away, he kept his eyes fixed on a painting he loved, his favorite "Madonna and Child" by Correggio, a painting which had once belonged to the Empress Marie Theresa. In old age, this man of action was perfectly resigned to contemplating his art treasure. Each Sunday, Mass was said in their apartment, where Gertrude prepared the altar. For both, there was no greater happiness than this unique privilege granted them by their old friend, the Papal Nuncio of Munich, now Pope Pius XII. All week August would look forward to that moment when the Mass would be offered by one of the many Indian priests whom his own brother, the missionary bishop, had ordained in Quilon.

Propped up with many pillows, looking daily more and more like the deathbed portrait he had made of his own father, August continued to slip the beads through his fingers. Those fingers were never idle; he recited in German all three Mysteries of the Rosary; then, during the long hours of the night when plagued with insomnia, he repeated his favorite short prayers, using the rosary given him by Pope Pius XI to guide him. August had his own set prayer formula which he never divulged to anyone.

Marieli had coaxed him to say his prayers aloud one evening when she was sitting by his side. Never one to confide the inner secrets of his spiritual life, he was hesitant; finally, he began to list, one by one, his relatives, his closest friends, then his benefactors. No one was forgotten. This man, whose exterior had seemed so cold, so forbidding, so austere, had a heart of gold. He had kept precious the memory of all who had crossed his path.

"Merciful Jesus, grant eternal rest to all the ladies I should pray for"; this was repeated 10 times. Then his fingers moved the beads as he repeated the next decade, "Merciful Jesus, grant eternal rest to all the men I should remember." Next came an act of contrition, a real cry of sorrow for all his sins. Night prayers terminated with the *Confiteor* which, in itself, was a meditation on the communion of saints. When too tired, after an exhausting night of pain, he used part of the next morning saying the omitted prayers.

On another occasion, his daughter, having made a mental note of the names she had heard him mention during his vocal prayer, asked, "Papa, why did you favor certain people like the Hachettes or the Didots?" He seemed incredulous, as though it were quite unnecessary to give any explanation:

> Why, they were the ones to whom I owe an undying debt of gratitude. How could I ever forget them? Even if after all these years they no longer need my prayers, they can pass them on to others . . .

Then, as if reminiscing aloud, he continued:

> Alfred Firmin Didot, and his daughter, Laure! How good they were to me when I first went to Paris! Laure prayed for me when I was in trouble . . .

> Dear old Papa Lorilleux, how could I ever forget all I owed to him! He gave me a home—my first orders—he made me what I became. His son Réné—he liked me so much that he wanted me to marry his only daughter.

> Louis Hachette, his dear mother, Madame Hachette!—old Madame Bonat!—they made the lonely art student feel so much at home—Good Doctor Bommer! The village doctor who had time for me and my family . . .

> Outstanding among my relatives—Catherine Gyr! . . . *Onkel von der Schwert* and his son, Franz Benziger! What fun we all had together in Einsiedeln! Franz was the boy who helped me with all my pranks!

Franz Aufdermauer, who was *Kantonsrat*—he advised me about my farm. He alone was honest when the rest of the men in Schwyz tried to cheat me because, they said, I had married an American!

Mrs. Edward Wren—what a great lady! The only one who ever offered to pay me for my time and services. I took her on a pilgrimage to Lourdes.

Henry Heide—that wonderful New York friend with a heart of gold.

Old Mrs. Lutcher, my greatest benefactress! She paid me my highest prices, never asking for discounts . . .

These were the names, and a long list of others, that August had engraved indelibly on his heart, just as indelibly as he would have had he painted their pictures.

During these agonizing moments of pain, he had asked that the crucifix be moved from the head of his bed in the hospital room; he wished to see it. "The picture of Christ suffering on the cross will help me bear my pain without murmuring."

August had always considered the 13th as his lucky day. Each month he celebrated some anniversary: on October 13, the day he had painted Pope Leo XIII; June 13, when Mrs. Lutcher placed an order for 14 life-sized portraits; 64 years before, on April 13, Papa Lorilleux had rescued him from his Paris attic. That day, his first order had been accepted at the Salon, winning him an award! That day had marked the turning point of his artistic career! He had become a portrait painter. Now, on that same date, April 13, 1955, in his 89th year, August gratefully turned his face toward his Maker and breathed his last.

August, who was to die of cancer, had suffered excruciating anguish. He had always been afraid of sickness and dreaded the thought of pain. When he slipped away after bearing his sufferings heroically, the doctors and nurses were not ashamed to weep. As they stood looking at him for the last time, they said he reminded them of St. Joseph, with his dignified mein. He looked so paternal, so at peace! Here was a great man who had been a model patient; he had never grumbled nor been difficult.

To those who knew him best, the words of his favorite author and friend came back to mind. Dr. Alexis Carrell had said:

. . . nearly always death is like the end of a sad, monotonous day. Sometimes it has the beauty of twilight in the mountains, or death resembles the sleep of a hero after the fight. But it can be, if we do desire, the immersion of the soul in the splendor of God.

In the case of August Benziger, the portrait painter and artist, who had tried with great fidelity to depict the souls of others on his canvas, this last moment was, indeed, that of the "immersion of his soul in the splendor of God."